W9-ARO-943

WORLD HISTORY
VOLUME I
Prehistory to 1500

Fourth Edition

Editor

David McComb
Colorado State University

David McComb received his Ph.D. from the University of Texas at Austin and is currently a professor of history at Colorado State University. Dr. McComb has written eight books, numerous articles and book reviews, and he teaches courses in the history of the United States, sports, and the world. He has traveled twice around the world as a Semester at Sea faculty member of the University of Pittsburgh, and he has spent additional time in India and Mexico.

A Library of Information from the Public Press

Cover illustration by Mike Eagle

Dushkin Publishing Group/
Brown & Benchmark Publishers
Sluice Dock, Guilford, Connecticut 06437

The Annual Editions Series

Annual Editions is a series of over 65 volumes designed to provide the reader with convenient, low-cost access to a wide range of current, carefully selected articles from some of the most important magazines, newspapers, and journals published today. Annual Editions are updated on an annual basis through a continuous monitoring of over 300 periodical sources. All Annual Editions have a number of features designed to make them particularly useful, including topic guides, annotated tables of contents, unit overviews, and indexes. For the teacher using Annual Editions in the classroom, an Instructor's Resource Guide with test questions is available for each volume.

VOLUMES AVAILABLE

Abnormal Psychology
Africa
Aging
American Foreign Policy
American Government
American History, Pre-Civil War
American History, Post-Civil War
American Public Policy
Anthropology
Archaeology
Biopsychology
Business Ethics
Child Growth and Development
China
Comparative Politics
Computers in Education
Computers in Society
Criminal Justice
Developing World
Deviant Behavior
Drugs, Society, and Behavior
Dying, Death, and Bereavement
Early Childhood Education
Economics
Educating Exceptional Children
Education
Educational Psychology
Environment
Geography
Global Issues
Health
Human Development
Human Resources
Human Sexuality
India and South Asia
International Business
Japan and the Pacific Rim
Latin America
Life Management
Macroeconomics
Management
Marketing
Marriage and Family
Mass Media
Microeconomics
Middle East and the Islamic World
Multicultural Education
Nutrition
Personal Growth and Behavior
Physical Anthropology
Psychology
Public Administration
Race and Ethnic Relations
Russia, the Eurasian Republics, and Central/Eastern Europe
Social Problems
Sociology
State and Local Government
Urban Society
Western Civilization, Pre-Reformation
Western Civilization, Post-Reformation
Western Europe
World History, Pre-Modern
World History, Modern
World Politics

Cataloging in Publication Data
Main entry under title: Annual editions: World history, vol. I: Prehistory to 1500.
1. World history—Periodicals. 2. Civilization, Modern—Periodicals. 3. Social problems—Periodicals. I. McComb, David, comp. II. Title: World history, vol. I: Prehistory to 1500.
905   ISBN 1-56134-434-6   90-656260

Fourth Edition

Printed in the United States of America

To the Reader

In publishing ANNUAL EDITIONS we recognize the enormous role played by the magazines, newspapers, and journals of the *public press* in providing current, first-rate educational information in a broad spectrum of interest areas. Within the articles, the best scientists, practitioners, researchers, and commentators draw issues into new perspective as accepted theories and viewpoints are called into account by new events, recent discoveries change old facts, and fresh debate breaks out over important controversies.

Many of the articles resulting from this enormous editorial effort are appropriate for students, researchers, and professionals seeking accurate, current material to help bridge the gap between principles and theories and the real world. These articles, however, become more useful for study when those of lasting value are carefully *collected, organized, indexed,* and *reproduced* in a *low-cost format,* which provides easy and permanent access when the material is needed.

That is the role played by *Annual Editions.* Under the direction of each volume's *Editor,* who is an expert in the subject area, and with the guidance of an *Advisory Board,* we seek each year to provide in each ANNUAL EDITION a current, well-balanced, carefully selected collection of the best of the public press for your study and enjoyment. We think you'll find this volume useful, and we hope you'll take a moment to let us know what you think.

In recognition of the importance of international events, world history courses, next to those about the United States, have become the most popular history courses of the secondary schools. World history, moreover, has spread through higher education in the past decade and a half, and the first generation of scholars trained in world history is just emerging. Increasingly, the U.S. government and its citizens are caught up in a daily vortex of current concerns such as exported terrorism, warfare in Bosnia, environmental degradation in Brazil, viral outbreaks in Africa, nuclear developments in North Korea, and illegal migrations from Cuba and Mexico. Responsible citizens must become informed about international matters in order to act and vote intelligently about these events for the welfare of individuals, the nation, and the world. Thus, educators and others have become sensitive to the need for instruction about global matters in the classroom.

The organizational problems in world history are the traditional difficulties of scope and relevance. What should be included and what may be left out? How can diverse material be arranged to make sense of the past? In all history courses, choices must be made, particularly in surveys of the United States or of Western civilization. The broader the survey, the greater the level of abstraction. No one learns all about each country of Europe, or of each state, county, and city of the United States, with the hope that the pieces add up to some sort of comprehensible story. Instead, there is an emphasis upon ideas, technology, turning points, significant people, movements, and chronology. An effort is made by historians and teachers to place events in perspective, to illustrate cause and effect, and to focus upon what is important.

World history is no exception, but the range of choices is greater. There are simply more people, places, and events in the history of the world. There is more material and thus world history courses demand the broadest level of abstraction from the teachers and students. World historians, consequently, focus upon civilizations, cultures, global systems, and international affairs. Often they attempt cross-cultural comparisons, but some historiographical problems remain unsettled.

Probably the most difficult question involves periodization—how to divide history into time spans. In Western civilization courses the division of ancient, medieval, and modern works nicely. In world history, however, this division does not fit so neatly because other civilizations have evolved at different times. The development of medieval Europe makes little sense for Asia, the Middle East, Africa, or the Americas. World historians, nevertheless, have reached some consensus about the following: the two most important events in human history are the invention of agriculture and the industrial revolution; the thousand years before Columbus are significant because of the rise of Islam, development of global trading routes, evolution of civilization in Mesoamerica, and the power of China; and 1500 is a reasonable dividing point for history classes because of the European explorations and their consequences.

In this volume, I use a periodization of early civilizations to 500 B.C.E., later civilizations to 500 C.E., and the world from 500 C.E. to 1500 C.E. This is fairly traditional, but there are additional units on natural history and culture that include the earliest developments of humankind, the great religions, and exploration. Within the broad units can be found information about women, technology, the family, historiography, urbanization, sports, and other subjects. The *topic guide* is a useful index for this information. The articles were selected for readability, accuracy, relevance, interest, and freshness. They are meant to supplement a course, to provide depth, and to add spice and spark. The articles do not cover everything; that is impossible, of course. Sometimes older articles have been included to provide balance. You may know of some other articles that would do a better job. Please return the prepaid article rating form at the back of the book with your suggestions.

David McComb

David McComb
Editor

Contents

Unit 1

Natural History: The Setting for Human History

Five articles discuss how the environment impacted on the shaping of early human society.

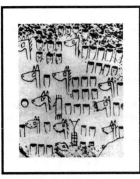

Unit 2

The Beginnings of Culture, Agriculture, and Urbanization

Six selections examine early milestones in the history of humankind: the origin of writing and numbers, the beginnings of agriculture, and urbanization.

The concepts in bold italics are developed in the article. For further expansion please refer to the Topic Guide and the Index.

Unit
3

The Early Civilizations to 500 B.C.E.

Seven articles consider the growing diversity of human life as civilization evolved in the ancient world.

The concepts in bold italics are developed in the article. For further expansion please refer to the Topic Guide and the Index.

Unit 4

The Later Civilizations to 500 C.E.

Seven articles discuss some of the dynamics of culture in
Peru, Greece, and Rome.

The concepts in bold italics are developed in the article. For further expansion please refer to the Topic Guide and the Index.

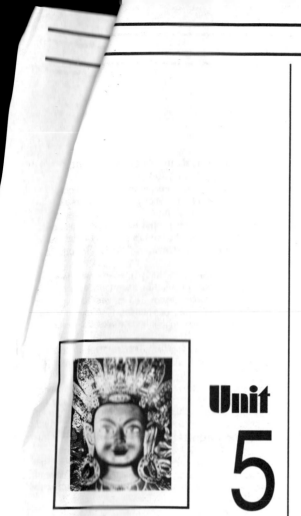

Unit 5

The Great Religions

Ten articles discuss the beginnings of the world's great religions, including Judaism, Christianity, Islam, Hinduism, and Buddhism.

The concepts in bold italics are developed in the article. For further expansion please refer to the Topic Guide and the Index.

Unit 6

The World of the Middle Ages, 500–1500

Seven selections examine the development of world cultures during this period: in the West, feudalism and the growth of the nation-state; in the East, the golden age of peak development.

The concepts in bold italics are developed in the article. For further expansion please refer to the Topic Guide and the Index.

Unit 7

1500: The Era of Discovery

Six articles examine the enormous global impact of the voyages of discovery.

The concepts in bold italics are developed in the article. For further expansion please refer to the Topic Guide and the Index.

Topic Guide

This topic guide suggests how the selections in this book relate to topics of traditional concern to world history students and professionals. It is useful for locating articles that relate to each other for reading and research. The guide is arranged alphabetically according to topic. Articles may, of course, treat topics that do not appear in the topic guide. In turn, entries in the topic guide do not necessarily constitute a comprehensive listing of all the contents of each selection.

TOPIC AREA	TREATED IN	TOPIC AREA	TREATED IN
Africa	7. Writing Right 14. Out of Africa 22. Dido Was Its Old Flame 43. Emperor's Giraffe	Economics	8. Origin of Numbers 9. Corn in the New World 12. Old Tablet from Turkish Site 13. Collapse of Earliest Known Empire 17. New Finds Suggest Even Earlier Trade on Fabled Silk Road
Agriculture	4. Frost and Found 9. Corn in the New World 10. Eloquent Bones of Abu Hureyra 11. How Man Invented Cities 13. Collapse of Earliest Known Empire	Egypt	14. Out of Africa 15. Marriage and Motherhood in Ancient Egypt 16. Tales from the Crypt 17. New Finds Suggest Even Earlier Trade on Fabled Silk Road
Americas	5. Ice-Age Mystery 9. Corn in the New World 19. Tales from a Peruvian Crypt 26. Mysterious Mexican Culture Yields Its Secrets 44. Columbus and His Four Fateful Voyages 46. Reconsidering Columbus	Environment	2. Evolution of Life on the Earth 3. Climate and the Rise of Man 4. Frost and Found 5. Ice-Age Mystery 9. Corn in the New World 11. How Man Invented Cities 13. Collapse of Earliest Known Empire 19. Tales from a Peruvian Crypt 46. Reconsidering Columbus
Ancient Civilizations	7. Writing Right 8. Origin of Numbers 11. How Man Invented Cities 12. Old Tablet from Turkish Site 13. Collapse of Earliest Known Empire 14. Out of Africa 15. Marriage and Motherhood in Ancient Egypt 19. Tales from a Peruvian Crypt 21. Women and Politics in Democratic Athens 22. Dido Was Its Old Flame 23. Ancient Roman Life 24. Murderous Games 25. Old Sports 26. Mysterious Mexican Culture Yields Its Secrets	Europe	4. Frost and Found 6. Neptune's Ice Age Gallery 20. In Classical Athens 21. Women and Politics in Democratic Athens 23. Ancient Roman Life 28. Women in Greek Myth 39. Women and the Early Church 40. Hazards on the Way to the Middle Ages 41. Making of Magna Carta 42. Clocks 44. Columbus and His Four Fateful Voyages 45. Sailors of Palos 46. Reconsidering Columbus 47. After Dire Straits, an Agonizing Haul across the Pacific 48. Europe of Columbus and Bayazid
Asia	5. Ice-Age Mystery 7. Writing Right 17. New Finds Suggest Even Earlier Trade on Fabled Silk Road 35. Confucius 38. All the Khan's Horses 43. Emperor's Giraffe	Evolution	1. Cosmic Calendar 2. Evolution of Life on the Earth 3. Climate and the Rise of Man
Buddhism	33. Charles Malamoud 34. Koran, Gita, and Tripitaka	Geography	3. Climate and the Rise of Man 5. Ice-Age Mystery 6. Neptune's Ice Age Gallery 9. Corn in the New World 11. How Man Invented Cities 12. Old Tablet from Turkish Site 13. Collapse of Earliest Known Empire 43. Emperor's Giraffe 44. Columbus and His Four Fateful Voyages 47. After Dire Straits, an Agonizing Haul across the Pacific
Christianity	29. Mysteries of the Bible 30. Who Was Jesus? 31. Christmas Covenant 32. World of Islam 39. Women and the Early Church 40. Hazards on the Way to the Middle Ages		

TOPIC AREA	TREATED IN	TOPIC AREA	TREATED IN
Greeks	18. Herodotus 20. In Classical Athens 21. Women and Politics in Democratic Athens 28. Women in Greek Myth	**Religion**	16. Tales from the Crypt 26. Mysterious Mexican Culture Yields Its Secrets 27. Death Cults of Prehistoric Malta 28. Women in Greek Myth 29. Mysteries of the Bible 30. Who Was Jesus? 31. Christmas Covenant 32. World of Islam 33. Charles Malamoud 34. Koran, Gita, and Tripitaka 35. Confucius 39. Women and the Early Church 40. Hazards on the Way to the Middle Ages
Hinduism	33. Charles Malamoud 34. Koran, Gita, and Tripitaka		
Historiography	18. Herodotus 37. Master-Chronologers of Islam 40. Hazards on the Way to the Middle Ages		
India	8. Origin of Numbers 33. Charles Malamoud 36. Lilavati 43. Emperor's Giraffe	**Romans**	22. Dido Was Its Old Flame 23. Ancient Roman Life 24. Murderous Games
Islam	32. World of Islam 34. Koran, Gita, and Tripitaka	**Sports**	24. Murderous Games 25. Old Sports
Judaism	29. Mysteries of the Bible 30. Who Was Jesus?	**Technology**	4. Frost and Found 7. Writing Right 8. Origin of Numbers 9. Corn in the New World 10. Eloquent Bones of Abu Hureyra 36. Lilavati 42. Clocks 45. Sailors of Palos
Middle Ages.	39. Women and the Early Church 40. Hazards on the Way to the Middle Ages 48. Europe of Columbus and Bayazid		
Middle East	7. Writing Right 10. Eloquent Bones of Abu Hureyra 12. Old Tablet from Turkish Site 13. Collapse of Earliest Known Empire 29. Mysteries of the Bible 30. Who Was Jesus? 32. World of Islam 36. Lilavati 37. Master-Chronologers of Islam 48. Europe of Columbus and Bayazid	**Trade**	8. Origin of Numbers 12. Old Tablet from Turkish Site 17. New Finds Suggest Even Earlier Trade on Fabled Silk Road 43. Emperor's Giraffe 44. Columbus and His Four Fateful Voyages 48. Europe of Columbus and Bayazid
Politics	20. In Classical Athens 21. Women and Politics in Democratic Athens 41. Making of Magna Carta 48. Europe of Columbus and Bayazid	**Urbanization**	7. Writing Right 8. Origin of Numbers 10. Eloquent Bones of Abu Hureyra 11. How Man Invented Cities 12. Old Tablet from Turkish Site 20. In Classical Athens 22. Dido Was Its Old Flame 23. Ancient Roman Life 24. Murderous Games 26. Mysterious Mexican Culture Yields Its Secrets
Population	5. Ice-Age Mystery 11. How Man Invented Cities 12. Old Tablet from Turkish Site 46. Reconsidering Columbus		
Prehistoric Culture	4. Frost and Found 6. Neptune's Ice Age Gallery 9. Corn in the New World 10. Eloquent Bones of Abu Hureyra 11. How Man Invented Cities 19. Tales from a Peruvian Crypt 26. Mysterious Mexican Culture Yields Its Secrets 27. Death Cults of Prehistoric Malta	**Warfare**	22. Dido Was Its Old Flame 24. Murderous Games 38. All the Khan's Horses 41. Making of Magna Carta
		Women	15. Marriage and Motherhood in Ancient Egypt 21. Women and Politics in Democratic Athens 23. Ancient Roman Life 27. Death Cults of Prehistoric Malta 39. Women and the Early Church

Natural History: The Setting for Human History

The stage for human history has been planet Earth and the environment it provided for life. Human beings have been shaped by this environment and have used the resources of their surroundings for survival and comfort. It was not until recently, however, and then without planning, that humankind began to influence the environment on a global scale. Coincidentally, and perhaps fortunately, space exploration made us recognize the potential danger of disrupting the life-sustaining atmosphere that wraps our planet like the thin skin of an apple. Buckminster Fuller's concept of "spaceship Earth" captured both the wonder—how did we get here on this blue planet orbiting in black space?—and the warning—we have no other home, we had better take care of it.

Carl Sagan's book *The Dragons of Eden* (1979) imagined all time pressed into a calendar year. In such a circumstance the first humans appeared at 10:30 p.m. on December 31 and agriculture was invented at 40 seconds before midnight. In comparison to geologic time, human history amounts to less than a minute on the time scale of one year. That humbling fact is enlarged by Stephen Jay Gould, the most important naturalist currently writing for the public. Without fortuitous circumstances, human beings might not be here at all, according to Gould. If it had to be done over again, events are so unpredictable the chances are we would not make it a second time.

Among the important circumstances of human evolution are changes in climate, a fact that causes concern today with regard to the warming of the atmosphere. "Climate and the Rise of Man" reports that climatic changes have been instrumental at the major turning points in evolution and suggests that this will probably continue to be the case. We are still living in the interstice between ice ages, and our human civilizations have flourished in this brief period. Migrations have populated the planet from the New World to the tip of South America during this time. Evan Hadingham offers a further confirmation of the hypothesis of Asiatic movement across the Bering Strait. Dental patterns seem to prove the point. There is still debate, however, about the time of crossing. Although there is strong archaeological evidence to indicate a passage during the past ice age of 12,000 years ago, it could have been much earlier.

The most dramatic reminder of our recent ascent as a species came in 1991 when the body of a tattooed Bronze Age man emerged from the ice of a glacier in the Alps between Austria and Italy. The man who may have been a shepherd had been preserved frozen for 5,000 years. His clothing, weapons, and even some coarse grain had been preserved by the glacier that was now retreating as a result of global warming. Discoveries such as the Iceman, as he came to be called, demonstrate how closely humankind has been linked to the environment for survival. Current circumstances with neighborhood supermarkets and shopping malls tend to insulate us from this reality. This short unit on natural history serves as a reminder of our humble beginnings and our comparatively brief sojourn on spaceship Earth.

Looking Ahead: Challenge Questions

How did the universe, Earth, and life begin? Discuss other theories that should be considered.

What has been the influence of climate on human life? What might happen when the climate shifts again?

How did human beings get to the New World? What is the evidence for this? Did humans evolve in the New World? Why or why not?

What are the scientific tools that provide information about the distant past?

Of what use is the Iceman? Is it important for human beings to know how the species evolved? Why?

The Cosmic Calendar

How a Pulitzer Prize-winning scientist-author visualizes cosmic history—from the Big Bang creation of the universe up to present-day time on Earth. His "calendar" may stagger your imagination.

Carl Sagan

The world is very old, and human beings are very young. Significant events in our personal lives are measured in years or less; our lifetimes, in decades; our family genealogies, in centuries; and all of recorded history, in millennia. But we have been preceded by an awesome vista of time, extending for prodigious periods into the past, about which we know little—both because there are no written records and because we have real difficulty in grasping the immensity of the intervals involved.

Yet we are able to date events in the remote past. Geological stratification and radioactive dating provide information on archaeological, paleontological, and geological events; and astrophysical theory provides data on the ages of planetary surfaces, stars, and the Milky Way galaxy, as well as an estimate of the time that has elapsed since that extraordinary event called the Big Bang—an explosion that involved all of the matter and energy in the present universe. The Big Bang may be the beginning of the universe, or it may be a discontinuity in which information about the earlier history of the universe was destroyed. But it is certainly the earliest event about which we have any record.

	PRE-DECEMBER DATES
January 1	Big Bang
May 1	Origin of the Milky Way galaxy
September 9	Origin of the solar system
September 14	Formation of the Earth
September 25	Origin of life on Earth
October 2	Formation of the oldest rocks known on Earth
October 9	Date of oldest fossils (bacteria and blue-green algae)
November 1	Invention of sex (by microorganisms)
November 12	Oldest fossil photosynthetic plants
November 15	Eucaryptes (first cells with nuclei) flourish

The most instructive way I know to express this cosmic chronology is to imagine the 15-billion-year lifetime of the universe (or at least its present incarnation since the Big Bang) compressed into the span of a single year. Then every billion years of Earth history would correspond to about 24 days of our cosmic year, and 1 second of that year to 475 real revolutions of the Earth about the sun. I present the cosmic chronology in three forms: a list of some representative pre-December dates; a calendar for the month of December; and a closer look at the late evening of New Year's Eve. On this scale, the events of our history books—even books that make significant efforts to deprovincialize the present—are so compressed that it is necessary to give a second-by-second recounting of the last seconds of the cosmic year. Even then, we find events listed as contemporary that we have been taught to consider as widely separated in time. In the history of life, an equally rich tapestry must have been woven in other periods—for example, between 10:02 and 10:03 on the morning of April 6th or September 16th. But we have detailed records only for the very end of the cosmic year.

DECEMBER

SUNDAY	MONDAY	TUESDAY	WEDNESDAY	THURSDAY	FRIDAY	SATURDAY
	1 Significant oxygen atmosphere begins to develop on Earth.	**2**	**3**	**4**	**5** Extensive vulcanism and channel formation on Mars.	**6**
7	**8**	**9**	**10**	**11**	**12**	**13**
14	**15**	**16** First worms.	**17** Precambrian ends. Paleozoic era and Cambrian period begin. Invertebrates flourish.	**18** First oceanic plankton. Trilobites flourish.	**19** Ordovician period. First fish, first vertebrates.	**20** Silurian period. First vascular plants. Plants begin colonization of land.
21 Devonian period begins. First insects. Animals begin colonization of land.	**22** First amphibians. First winged insects.	**23** Carboniferous period. First trees. First reptiles.	**24** Permian period begins. First dinosaurs.	**25** Paleozoic era ends. Mesozoic era begins.	**26** Triassic period. First mammals.	**27** Jurassic period. First birds.
28 Cretaceous period. First flowers. Dinosaurs become extinct.	**29** Mesozoic era ends. Cenozoic era and Tertiary period begin. First cetaceans. First primates.	**30** Early evolution of frontal lobes in the brains of primates. First hominids. Giant mammals flourish.	**31** End of the Pliocene period. Quaternary (Pleistocene and Holocene) period. First humans.			

The chronology corresponds to the best evidence now available. But some of it is rather shaky. No one would be astounded if, for example, it turns out that plants colonized the land in the Ordovician rather than the Silurian period; or that segmented worms appeared earlier in the Precambrian period than indicated. Also, in the chronology of the last 10 seconds of the cosmic year, it was obviously impossible for me to include all significant events; I hope I may be excused for not having explicitly mentioned advances in art, music, and literature, or the historically significant American, French, Russian, and Chinese revolutions.

The construction of such tables and calendars is inevitably humbling. It is disconcerting to find that in such a cosmic year the Earth does not condense out of interstellar matter until early September; dinosaurs emerge on Christmas Eve; flowers arise on December 28th; and men and women originate at 10:30 p.m. on New Year's Eve. All of recorded history occupies the last 10 seconds of December 31; and the time from the waning of the Middle Ages to the present occupies little more than 1 second. But because I have arranged it that way, the first cosmic year has just ended. And despite the insignificance of the instant we have so far occupied in cosmic time, it is clear that what happens on and near Earth at the beginning of the second cosmic year will depend very much on the scientific wisdom and the distinctly human sensitivity of mankind.

DECEMBER 31

1:30 p.m.	Origin of *Proconsul* and *Ramapithecus*, probable ancestors of apes and men
10:30 p.m.	First humans
11.00 p.m.	Widespread use of stone tools
11:46 p.m.	Domestication of fire by Peking man
11:56 p.m.	Beginning of most recent glacial period
11:58 p.m.	Seafarers settle Australia
11:59 p.m.	Extensive cave painting in Europe
11:59:20 p.m.	Invention of agriculture
11:59:35 p.m.	Neolithic civilization; first cities
11:59:50 p.m.	First dynasties in Sumer, Ebla, and Egypt; development of astronomy
11:59:51 p.m.	Invention of the alphabet; Akkadian Empire
11:59:52 p.m.	Hammurabic legal codes in Babylon; Middle Kingdom in Egypt
11:59:53 p.m.	Bronze metallurgy; Mycenaean culture; Trojan War; Olmec culture; invention of the compass
11:59:54 p.m.	Iron metallurgy; First Assyrian Empire; Kingdom of Israel; founding of Carthage by Phoenicia
11:59:55 p.m.	Asokan India; Ch'in Dynasty China; Periclean Athens; birth of Buddha
11:59:56 p.m.	Euclidean geometry; Archimedean physics; Ptolemaic astronomy; Roman Empire; birth of Christ
11:59:57 p.m.	Zero and decimals invented in Indian arithmetic; Rome falls; Moslem conquests
11:59:58 p.m.	Mayan civilization; Sung Dynasty China; Byzantine empire; Mongol invasion; Crusades
11:59:59 p.m.	Renaissance in Europe; voyages of discovery from Europe and from Ming Dynasty China; emergence of the experimental method in science
Now: The first second of New Year's Day	Widespread development of science and technology; emergence of a global culture; acquisition of the means for self-destruction of the human species; first steps in spacecraft planetary exploration and the search for extraterrestrial intelligence

The Evolution of Life on the Earth

*The history of life is not necessarily progressive;
it is certainly not predictable. The earth's creatures have evolved
through a series of contingent and fortuitous events*

Stephen Jay Gould

STEPHEN JAY GOULD teaches biology, geology and the history of science at Harvard University, where he has been on the faculty since 1967. He received an A.B. from Antioch College and a Ph.D. in paleontology from Columbia University. Well known for his popular scientific writings, in particular his monthly column in *Natural History* magazine, he is the author of 13 books.

Some creators announce their inventions with grand éclat. God proclaimed, "Fiat lux," and then flooded his new universe with brightness. Others bring forth great discoveries in a modest guise, as did Charles Darwin in defining his new mechanism of evolutionary causality in 1859: "I have called this principle, by which each slight variation, if useful, is preserved, by the term Natural Selection."

Natural selection is an immensely powerful yet beautifully simple theory that has held up remarkably well, under intense and unrelenting scrutiny and testing, for 135 years. In essence, natural selection locates the mechanism of evolutionary change in a "struggle" among organisms for reproductive success, leading to improved fit of populations to changing environments. (Struggle is often a metaphorical description and need not be viewed as overt combat, guns blazing. Tactics for reproductive success include a variety of nonmartial activities such as earlier and more frequent mating or better cooperation with partners in raising offspring.) Natural selection is therefore a principle of local adaptation, not of general advance or progress.

Yet powerful though the principle may be, natural selection is not the only cause of evolutionary change (and may, in many cases, be overshadowed by other forces). This point needs emphasis because the standard misapplication of evolutionary theory assumes that biological explanation may be equated with devising accounts, often speculative and conjectural in practice, about the adaptive value of any given feature in its original environment (human aggression as good for hunting, music and religion as good for tribal cohesion, for example). Darwin himself strongly emphasized the multifactorial nature of evolutionary change and warned against too exclusive a reliance on natural selection, by placing the following statement in a maximally conspicuous place at the very end of his introduction: "I am convinced that Natural Selection has been the most important, but not the exclusive, means of modification."

Natural selection is not fully sufficient to explain evolutionary change for two major reasons. First, many other causes are powerful, particularly at levels of biological organization both above and below the traditional Darwinian focus on organisms and their struggles for reproductive success. At the lowest level of substitution in individual base pairs of DNA, change is often effectively neutral and therefore random. At higher levels, involving entire species or faunas, punctuated equilibrium can produce evolutionary trends by selection of species based on their rates of origin and extirpation, whereas mass extinctions wipe out substantial parts of biotas for reasons unrelated to adaptive struggles of constituent species in "normal" times between such events.

Second, and the focus of this article, no matter how adequate our general theory of evolutionary change, we also yearn to document and understand the actual pathway of life's history. Theory, of course, is relevant to explaining the pathway (nothing about the pathway can be inconsistent with good theory, and theory can predict certain general aspects of life's geologic pattern). But the actual pathway is strongly *underdetermined* by our general theory of life's evolution. This point needs some belaboring as a central yet widely misunderstood aspect of the world's complexity. Webs and chains of historical events are so intricate, so imbued with random and chaotic elements, so unrepeatable in encompassing such a multitude of unique (and uniquely interacting) objects, that standard models of simple prediction and replication do not apply.

History can be explained, with satisfying rigor if evidence be adequate, after a sequence of events unfolds, but it cannot be predicted with any precision beforehand. Pierre-Simon Laplace, echoing the growing and confident determinism of the late 18th century, once said that he could specify all future states if he could know the position and motion of all particles in the cosmos at any moment, but the nature of universal complexity shatters this chimerical dream. History includes too much chaos, or extremely sensitive dependence on minute and unmeasurable differences in initial conditions, leading to massively divergent outcomes based on tiny and unknowable disparities in starting points. And history includes too much contingency, or shaping of present results by long chains of unpredictable antecedent states, rather than immediate determination by timeless laws of nature.

Homo sapiens did not appear on the earth, just a geologic second ago, be-

1. NATURAL HISTORY: THE SETTING FOR HUMAN HISTORY

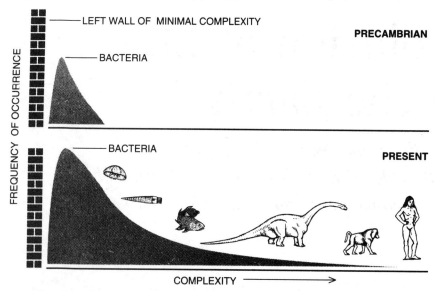

PROGRESS DOES NOT RULE (and is not even a primary thrust of) the evolutionary process. For reasons of chemistry and physics, life arises next to the "left wall" of its simplest conceivable and preservable complexity. This style of life (bacterial) has remained most common and most successful. A few creatures occasionally move to the right, thus extending the right tail in the distribution of complexity. Many always move to the left, but they are absorbed within space already occupied. Note that the bacterial mode has never changed in position, but just grown higher.

cause evolutionary theory predicts such an outcome based on themes of progress and increasing neural complexity. Humans arose, rather, as a fortuitous and contingent outcome of thousands of linked events, any one of which could have occurred differently and sent history on an alternative pathway that would not have led to consciousness. To cite just four among a multitude: (1) If our inconspicuous and fragile lineage had not been among the few survivors of the initial radiation of multicellular animal life in the Cambrian explosion 530 million years ago, then no vertebrates would have inhabited the earth at all. (Only one member of our chordate phylum, the genus *Pikaia*, has been found among these earliest fossils. This small and simple swimming creature, showing its allegiance to us by possessing a notochord, or dorsal stiffening rod, is among the rarest fossils of the Burgess Shale, our best preserved Cambrian fauna.) (2) If a small and unpromising group of lobe-finned fishes had not evolved fin bones with a strong central axis capable of bearing weight on land, then vertebrates might never have become terrestrial. (3) If a large extraterrestrial body had not struck the earth 65 million years ago, then dinosaurs would still be dominant and mammals insignificant (the situation that had prevailed for 100 million years previously). (4) If a small lineage of primates had not evolved upright posture on the drying African savannas just two to four

million years ago, then our ancestry might have ended in a line of apes that, like the chimpanzee and gorilla today, would have become ecologically marginal and probably doomed to extinction despite their remarkable behavioral complexity.

Therefore, to understand the events and generalities of life's pathway, we must go beyond principles of evolutionary theory to a paleontological examination of the contingent pattern of life's history on our planet—the single actualized version among millions of plausible alternatives that happened not to occur. Such a view of life's history is highly contrary both to conventional deterministic models of Western science and to the deepest social traditions and psychological hopes of Western culture for a history culminating in humans as life's highest expression and intended planetary steward.

Science can, and does, strive to grasp nature's factuality, but all science is socially embedded, and all scientists record prevailing "certainties," however hard they may be aiming for pure objectivity. Darwin himself, in the closing lines of *The Origin of Species*, expressed Victorian social preference more than nature's record in writing: "As natural selection works solely by and for the good of each being, all corporeal and mental endowments will tend to progress towards perfection."

Life's pathway certainly includes many features predictable from laws of na-

ture, but these aspects are too broad and general to provide the "rightness" that we seek for validating evolution's particular results—roses, mushrooms, people and so forth. Organisms adapt to, and are constrained by, physical principles. It is, for example, scarcely surprising, given laws of gravity, that the largest vertebrates in the sea (whales) exceed the heaviest animals on land (elephants today, dinosaurs in the past), which, in turn, are far bulkier than the largest vertebrate that ever flew (extinct pterosaurs of the Mesozoic era).

Predictable ecological rules govern the structuring of communities by principles of energy flow and thermodynamics (more biomass in prey than in predators, for example). Evolutionary trends, once started, may have local predictability ("arms races," in which both predators and prey hone their defenses and weapons, for example—a pattern that Geerat J. Vermeij of the University of California at Davis has called "escalation" and documented in increasing strength of both crab claws and shells of their gastropod prey through time). But laws of nature do not tell us why we have crabs and snails at all, why insects rule the multicellular world and why vertebrates rather than persistent algal mats exist as the most complex forms of life on the earth.

Relative to the conventional view of life's history as an at least broadly predictable process of gradually advancing complexity through time, three features of the paleontological record stand out in opposition and shall therefore serve as organizing themes for the rest of this article: the constancy of modal complexity throughout life's history; the concentration of major events in short bursts interspersed with long periods of relative stability; and the role of external impositions, primarily mass extinctions, in disrupting patterns of "normal" times. These three features, combined with more general themes of chaos and contingency, require a new framework for conceptualizing and drawing life's history, and this article therefore closes with suggestions for a different iconography of evolution.

The primary paleontological fact about life's beginnings points to predictability for the onset and very little for the particular pathways thereafter. The earth is 4.6 billion years old, but the oldest rocks date to about 3.9 billion years because the earth's surface became molten early in its history, a result of bombardment by large amounts of cosmic debris during the solar system's coalescence, and of heat generated by radioactive decay of short-lived isotopes. These oldest rocks are too metamorphosed by subsequent heat and pressure to preserve fossils (though some scientists interpret the proportions of carbon isotopes in these rocks as signs of organic production). The oldest rocks sufficiently unaltered to retain cellular fossils—African and Australian sediments dated to 3.5 billion years old—do preserve prokaryotic cells (bacteria and cyanophytes) and stromatolites (mats of sediment trapped and bound by these cells in shallow marine waters). Thus, life on the earth evolved quickly and is as old as it could be. This fact alone seems to indicate an inevitability, or at least a predictability, for life's origin from the original chemical constituents of atmosphere and ocean.

No one can doubt that more complex creatures arose sequentially after this prokaryotic beginning—first eukaryotic cells, perhaps about two billion years ago, then multicellular animals about 600 million years ago, with a relay of highest complexity among animals passing from invertebrates, to marine vertebrates and, finally (if we wish, albeit parochially, to honor neural architecture as a primary criterion), to reptiles, mammals and humans. This is the conventional sequence represented in the old charts and texts as an "age of invertebrates," followed by an "age of fishes," "age of reptiles," "age of mammals," and "age of man" (to add the old gender bias to all the other prejudices implied by this sequence).

I do not deny the facts of the preceding paragraph but wish to argue that our conventional desire to view history as progressive, and to see humans as predictably dominant, has grossly distorted our interpretation of life's pathway by falsely placing in the center of things a relatively minor phenomenon that arises only as a side consequence of a physically constrained starting point. The most salient feature of life has been the stability of its bacterial mode from the beginning of the fossil record until today and, with little doubt, into all future time so long as the earth endures. This is truly the "age of bacteria"—as it was in the beginning, is now and ever shall be.

For reasons related to the chemistry of life's origin and the physics of self-organization, the first living things arose at the lower limit of life's conceivable, preservable complexity. Call this lower limit the "left wall" for an architecture of complexity. Since so little space exists between the left wall and life's initial bacterial mode in the fossil record, only one direction for future increment

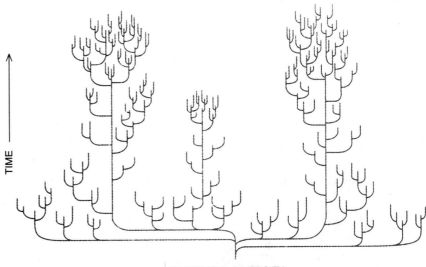

NEW ICONOGRAPHY OF LIFE'S TREE shows that maximal diversity in anatomical forms (not in number of species) is reached very early in life's multicellular history. Later times feature extinction of most of these initial experiments and enormous success within surviving lines. This success is measured in the proliferation of species but not in the development of new anatomies. Today we have more species than ever before, although they are restricted to fewer basic anatomies.

exists—toward greater complexity at the right. Thus, every once in a while, a more complex creature evolves and extends the range of life's diversity in the only available direction. In technical terms, the distribution of complexity becomes more strongly right skewed through these occasional additions.

But the additions are rare and episodic. They do not even constitute an evolutionary series but form a motley sequence of distantly related taxa, usually depicted as eukaryotic cell, jellyfish, trilobite, nautiloid, eurypterid (a large relative of horseshoe crabs), fish, an amphibian such as *Eryops,* a dinosaur, a mammal and a human being. This sequence cannot be construed as the major thrust or trend of life's history. Think rather of an occasional creature tumbling into the empty right region of complexity's space. Throughout this entire time, the bacterial mode has grown in height and remained constant in position. Bacteria represent the great success story of life's pathway. They occupy a wider domain of environments and span a broader range of biochemistries than any other group. They are adaptable, indestructible and astoundingly diverse. We cannot even imagine how anthropogenic intervention might threaten their extinction, although we worry about our impact on nearly every other form of life. The number of *Escherichia coli* cells in the gut of each human being exceeds the number of humans that has ever lived on this planet.

One might grant that complexifica-

tion for life as a whole represents a pseudotrend based on constraint at the left wall but still hold that evolution within particular groups differentially favors complexity when the founding lineage begins far enough from the left wall to permit movement in both directions. Empirical tests of this interesting hypothesis are just beginning (as concern for the subject mounts among paleontologists), and we do not yet have enough cases to advance a generality. But the first two studies—by Daniel W. McShea of the University of Michigan on mammalian vertebrae and by George F. Boyajian of the University of Pennsylvania on ammonite suture lines—show no evolutionary tendencies to favor increased complexity.

Moreover, when we consider that for each mode of life involving greater complexity, there probably exists an equally advantageous style based on greater simplicity of form (as often found in parasites, for example), then preferential evolution toward complexity seems unlikely a priori. Our impression that life evolves toward greater complexity is probably only a bias inspired by parochial focus on ourselves, and consequent overattention to complexifying creatures, while we ignore just as many lineages adapting equally well by becoming simpler in form. The morphologically degenerate parasite, safe within its host, has just as much prospect for evolutionary success as its gorgeously elaborate relative coping with the slings and arrows of outrageous fortune in a tough external world.

Even if complexity is only a drift away from a constraining left wall, we might view trends in this direction as more predictable and characteristic of life's pathway as a whole if increments of complexity accrued in a persistent and gradually accumulating manner through time. But nothing about life's history is more peculiar with respect to this common (and false) expectation than the actual pattern of extended stability and rapid episodic movement, as revealed by the fossil record.

Life remained almost exclusively unicellular for the first five sixths of its history—from the first recorded fossils at 3.5 billion years to the first well-documented multicellular animals less than 600 million years ago. (Some simple multicellular algae evolved more than a billion years ago, but these organisms belong to the plant kingdom and have no genealogical connection with animals.) This long period of unicellular life does include, to be sure, the vitally important transition from simple prokaryotic cells without organelles to eukaryotic cells with nuclei, mitochondria and other complexities of intracellular architecture—but no recorded attainment of multicellular animal organization for a full three billion years. If complexity is such a good thing, and multicellularity represents its initial phase in our usual view, then life certainly took its time in making this crucial step. Such delays speak strongly against general progress as the major theme of life's history, even if they can be plausibly explained by lack of sufficient atmospheric oxygen for most of Precambrian time or by failure of unicellular life to achieve some structural threshold acting as a prerequisite to multicellularity.

More curiously, all major stages in organizing animal life's multicellular architecture then occurred in a short period beginning less than 600 million years ago and ending by about 530 million years ago—and the steps within this sequence are also discontinuous and episodic, not gradually accumulative. The first fauna, called Ediacaran

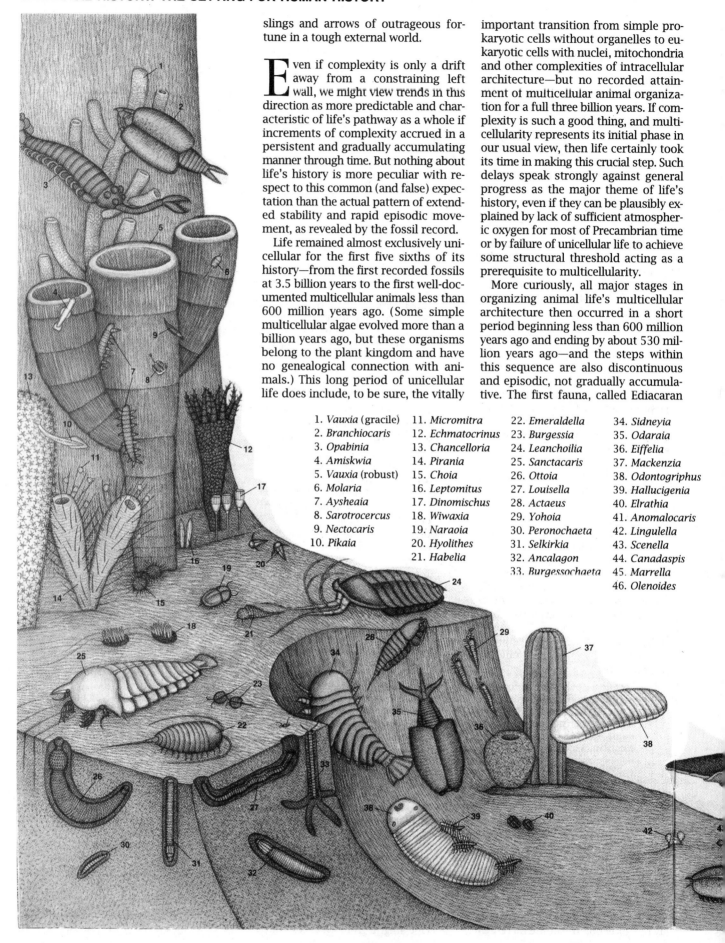

1. Vauxia (gracile)
2. Branchiocaris
3. Opabinia
4. Amiskwia
5. Vauxia (robust)
6. Molaria
7. Aysheaia
8. Sarotrocercus
9. Nectocaris
10. Pikaia
11. Micromitra
12. Echmatocrinus
13. Chancelloria
14. Pirania
15. Choia
16. Leptomitus
17. Dinomischus
18. Wiwaxia
19. Naraoia
20. Hyolithes
21. Habelia
22. Emeraldella
23. Burgessia
24. Leanchoilia
25. Sanctacaris
26. Ottoia
27. Louisella
28. Actaeus
29. Yohoia
30. Peronochaeta
31. Selkirkia
32. Ancalagon
33. Burgessochaeta
34. Sidneyia
35. Odaraia
36. Eiffelia
37. Mackenzia
38. Odontogriphus
39. Hallucigenia
40. Elrathia
41. Anomalocaris
42. Lingulella
43. Scenella
44. Canadaspis
45. Marrella
46. Olenoides

to honor the Australian locality of its initial discovery but now known from rocks on all continents, consists of highly flattened fronds, sheets and circlets composed of numerous slender segments quilted together. The nature of the Ediacaran fauna is now a subject of intense discussion. These creatures do not seem to be simple precursors of later forms. They may constitute a separate and failed experiment in animal life, or they may represent a full range of diploblastic (two-layered) organization, of which the modern phylum Cnidaria (corals, jellyfishes and their allies) remains as a small and much altered remnant.

In any case, they apparently died out well before the Cambrian biota evolved. The Cambrian then began with an assemblage of bits and pieces, frustratingly difficult to interpret, called the "small shelly fauna." The subsequent main pulse, starting about 530 million years ago, constitutes the famous Cambrian explosion, during which all but one modern phylum of animal life made a first appearance in the fossil record. (Geologists had previously allowed up to 40 million years for this event, but an elegant study, published in 1993, clearly restricts this period of phyletic flowering to a mere five million years.) The Bryozoa, a group of sessile and colonial marine organisms, do not arise until the beginning of the subsequent, Ordovician period, but this apparent

GREAT DIVERSITY quickly evolved at the dawn of multicellular animal life during the Cambrian period (530 million years ago). The creatures shown here are all found in the Middle Cambrian Burgess Shale fauna of Canada. They include some familiar forms (sponges, brachiopods) that have survived. But many creatures (such as the giant *Anomalocaris*, at the lower right, largest of all the Cambrian animals) did not live for long and are so anatomically peculiar (relative to survivors) that we cannot classify them among known phyla.

delay may be an artifact of failure to discover Cambrian representatives.

Although interesting and portentous events have occurred since, from the flowering of dinosaurs to the origin of human consciousness, we do not exaggerate greatly in stating that the subsequent history of animal life amounts to little more than variations on anatomical themes established during the Cambrian explosion within five million years. Three billion years of unicellularity, followed by five million years of intense creativity and then capped by more than 500 million years of variation on set anatomical themes can scarcely be read as a predictable, inexorable or continuous trend toward progress or increasing complexity.

We do not know why the Cambrian explosion could establish all major anatomical designs so quickly. An "external" explanation based on ecology seems attractive: the Cambrian explosion represents an initial filling of the "ecological barrel" of niches for multicellular organisms, and any experiment found a space. The barrel has never emptied since; even the great mass extinctions left a few species in each principal role, and their occupation of ecological space forecloses opportunity for fundamental novelties. But an "internal" explanation based on genetics and development also seems necessary as a complement: the earliest multicellular animals may have maintained a flexibility for genetic change and embryological transformation that became greatly reduced as organisms "locked in" to a set of stable and successful designs.

In any case, this initial period of both internal and external flexibility yielded a range of invertebrate anatomies that may have exceeded (in just a few million years of production) the full scope of animal form in all the earth's environments today (after more than 500 million years of additional time for further expansion). Scientists are divided on this question. Some claim that the anatomical range of this initial explosion exceeded that of modern life, as

many early experiments died out and no new phyla have ever arisen. But scientists most strongly opposed to this view allow that Cambrian diversity at least equaled the modern range—so even the most cautious opinion holds that 500 million subsequent years of opportunity have not expanded the Cambrian range, achieved in just five million years. The Cambrian explosion was the most remarkable and puzzling event in the history of life.

Moreover, we do not know why most of the early experiments died, while a few survived to become our modern phyla. It is tempting to say that the victors won by virtue of greater anatomical complexity, better ecological fit or some other predictable feature of conventional Darwinian struggle. But no recognized traits unite the victors, and the radical alternative must be entertained that each early experiment received little more than the equivalent of a ticket in the largest lottery ever played out on our planet—and that each surviving lineage, including our own phylum of vertebrates, inhabits the earth today more by the luck of the draw than by any predictable struggle for existence. The history of multicellular animal life may be more a story of great reduction in initial possibilities, with stabilization of lucky survivors, than a conventional tale of steady ecological expansion and morphological progress in complexity.

Finally, this pattern of long stasis, with change concentrated in rapid episodes that establish new equilibria, may be quite general at several scales of time and magnitude, forming a kind of fractal pattern in self-similarity. According to the punctuated equilibrium model of speciation, trends within lineages occur by accumulated episodes of geologically instantaneous speciation, rather than by gradual change within continuous populations (like climbing a staircase rather than rolling a ball up an inclined plane).

Even if evolutionary theory implied a potential internal direction for life's pathway (although previous facts and arguments in this article cast doubt on such a claim), the occasional imposition of a rapid and substantial, perhaps even truly catastrophic, change in environment would have intervened to stymie the pattern. These environmental changes trigger mass extinction of a high percentage of the earth's species and may so derail any internal direction and so reset the pathway that the net pattern of life's history looks

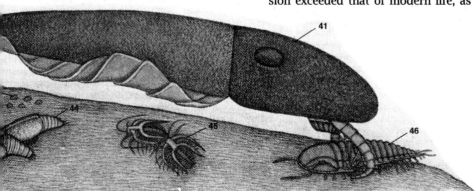

more capricious and concentrated in episodes than steady and directional. Mass extinctions have been recognized since the dawn of paleontology; the major divisions of the geologic time scale were established at boundaries marked by such events. But until the revival of interest that began in the late 1970s, most paleontologists treated mass extinctions only as intensifications of ordinary events, leading (at most) to a speeding up of tendencies that pervaded normal times. In this gradualistic theory of mass extinction, these events really took a few million years to unfold (with the appearance of suddenness interpreted as an artifact of an imperfect fossil record), and they only made the ordinary occur faster (more intense Darwinian competition in tough times, for example, leading to even more efficient replacement of less adapted by superior forms).

The reinterpretation of mass extinctions as central to life's pathway and radically different in effect began with the presentation of data by Luis and Walter Alvarez in 1979, indicating that the impact of a large extraterrestrial object (they suggested an asteroid seven to 10 kilometers in diameter) set off the last great extinction at the Cretaceous-Tertiary boundary 65 million years ago. Although the Alvarez hypothesis initially received very skeptical treatment from scientists (a proper approach to highly unconventional explanations), the case now seems virtually proved by discovery of the "smoking gun," a crater of appropriate size and age located off the Yucatán peninsula in Mexico.

This reawakening of interest also inspired paleontologists to tabulate the data of mass extinction more rigorously. Work by David M. Raup, J. J. Sepkoski, Jr., and David Jablonski of the University of Chicago has established that multicellular animal life experienced five major (end of Ordovician, late Devonian, end of Permian, end of Triassic and end of Cretaceous) and many minor mass extinctions during its 530-million-year history. We have no clear evidence that any but the last of these events was triggered by catastrophic impact, but such careful study leads to the general conclusion that mass extinctions were more frequent, more rapid, more extensive in magnitude and more different in effect than paleontologists had previously realized. These four properties encompass the radical implications of mass extinction for understanding life's pathway as more contingent and chancy than predictable and directional.

Mass extinctions are not random in their impact on life. Some lineages succumb and others survive as sensible outcomes based on presence or absence of evolved features. But especially if the triggering cause of extinction be sudden and catastrophic, the reasons for life or death may be random with respect to the original value of key features when first evolved in Darwinian struggles of normal times. This "different rules" model of mass extinction imparts a quirky and unpredictable character to life's pathway based on the evident claim that lineages cannot anticipate future contingencies of such magnitude and different operation.

To cite two examples from the impact-triggered Cretaceous-Tertiary extinction 65 million years ago: First, an important study published in 1986 noted that diatoms survived the extinction far better than other single-celled plankton (primarily coccoliths and radiolaria). This study found that many diatoms had evolved a strategy of dormancy by encystment, perhaps to survive through seasonal periods of unfavorable conditions (months of darkness in polar species as otherwise fatal to these photosynthesizing cells; sporadic availability of silica needed to construct their skeletons). Other planktonic cells had not evolved any mechanisms for dormancy. If the terminal Cretaceous impact produced a dust cloud that blocked light for several months or longer (one popular idea for a "killing scenario" in the extinction), then diatoms may have survived as a fortuitous result of dormancy mechanisms evolved for the entirely different function of weathering seasonal droughts in ordinary times. Diatoms are not superior to radiolaria or other plankton that succumbed in far greater numbers; they were simply fortunate to possess a favorable feature, evolved for other reasons, that fostered passage through the impact and its sequelae.

Second, we all know that dinosaurs perished in the end Cretaceous event and that mammals therefore rule the vertebrate world today. Most people assume that mammals prevailed in these tough times for some reason of general superiority over dinosaurs. But such a conclusion seems most unlikely. Mammals and dinosaurs had coexisted for 100 million years, and mammals had remained rat-sized or smaller, making no evolutionary "move" to oust dinosaurs. No good argument for mammalian prevalence by general superiority has ever been advanced, and fortuity seems far more likely. As one plausible argument, mammals may have survived partly as a result of their small size (with much larger, and therefore extinction-resistant, populations as a consequence, and less ecological specialization with more places to hide, so to speak). Small size may not have been a positive mammalian adaptation at all, but more a sign of inability ever to penetrate the dominant domain of dinosaurs. Yet this "negative" feature of normal times may be the key reason for mammalian survival and a prerequisite to my writing and your reading this article today.

Sigmund Freud often remarked that great revolutions in the history of science have but one common, and ironic, feature: they knock human arrogance off one pedestal after another of our previous conviction about our own self-importance. In Freud's three examples, Copernicus moved our home from center to periphery; Darwin then relegated us to "descent from an animal world"; and, finally (in one of the least modest statements of intellectual history), Freud himself discovered the unconscious and exploded the myth of a fully rational mind.

In this wise and crucial sense, the Darwinian revolution remains woefully incomplete because, even though thinking humanity accepts the fact of evolution, most of us are still unwilling to abandon the comforting view that evolution means (or at least embodies a central principle of) progress defined to render the appearance of something like human consciousness either virtually inevitable or at least predictable. The pedestal is not smashed until we abandon progress or complexification as a central principle and come to entertain the strong possibility that *H. sapiens* is but a tiny, late-arising twig on life's enormously arborescent bush—a small bud that would almost surely not appear a second time if we could replant the bush from seed and let it grow again.

Primates are visual animals, and the pictures we draw betray our deepest convictions and display our current conceptual limitations. Artists have always painted the history of fossil life as a sequence from invertebrates, to fishes, to early terrestrial amphibians and reptiles, to dinosaurs, to mammals and, finally, to humans. There are no exceptions; all sequences painted since the inception of this genre in the 1850s follow the convention.

Yet we never stop to recognize the almost absurd biases coded into this universal mode. No scene ever shows another invertebrate after fishes evolved, but invertebrates did not go away or stop evolving! After terrestrial reptiles emerge, no subsequent scene ever shows a fish (later oceanic tableaux depict only such returning reptiles as ichthyosaurs and plesiosaurs). But fishes did not stop evolving after one small lineage managed to invade the land. In fact, the major event in the evolution of fishes, the origin and rise to dominance of the teleosts, or modern bony fishes, occurred during the time of the dinosaurs and is therefore never shown at all in any of these sequences—even though teleosts include more than half of all species of vertebrates. Why should humans appear at the end of all sequences? Our order of primates is ancient among mammals, and many other successful lineages arose later than we did.

We will not smash Freud's pedestal and complete Darwin's revolution until we find, grasp and accept another way of drawing life's history. J.B.S. Haldane proclaimed nature "queerer than we can suppose," but these limits may only be socially imposed conceptual locks rather then inherent restrictions of our neurology. New icons might break the locks. Trees—or rather copiously and luxuriantly branching bushes—rather than ladders and sequences hold the key to this conceptual transition.

We must learn to depict the full range of variation, not just our parochial perception of the tiny right tail of most complex creatures. We must recognize that this tree may have contained a maximal number of branches near the beginning of multicellular life and that subsequent history is for the most part a process of elimination and lucky survivorship of a few, rather than continuous flowering, progress and expansion of a growing multitude. We must understand that little twigs are contingent nubbins, not predictable goals of the massive bush beneath. We must remember the greatest of all Biblical statements about wisdom: "She is a tree of life to them that lay hold upon her; and happy is every one that retaineth her."

FURTHER READING

THE BURGESS SHALE. Henry B. Whittington. Yale University Press, 1985.
EXTINCTION: A SCIENTIFIC AMERICAN BOOK. Steven M. Stanley. W. H. Freeman and Company, 1987.
WONDERFUL LIFE: THE BURGESS SHALE AND THE NATURE OF HISTORY. S. J. Gould. W. W. Norton, 1989.
THE BOOK OF LIFE. Edited by Stephen Jay Gould. W. W. Norton, 1993.

CLIMATE AND THE RISE OF MAN

The history of human evolution holds sobering lessons for those gathering at the Earth Summit

When global warming finally came, it stuck with a vengeance. In some regions, temperatures rose several degrees in less than a century. Sea levels shot up nearly 400 feet, flooding coastal settlements and forcing people to migrate inland. Deserts spread throughout the world as vegetation shifted drastically in North America, Europe and Asia. After driving many of the animals around them to near extinction, people were forced to abandon their old way of life for a radically new survival strategy that resulted in widespread starvation and disease. The adaptation was farming: the global-warming crisis that gave rise to it happened more than 10,000 years ago.

As environmentalists convene in Rio de Janeiro this week to ponder the global climate of the future, earth scientists are in the midst of a revolution in understanding how climate has changed in the past—and how those changes have transformed human existence. Researchers have begun to piece together an illuminating picture of the powerful geological and astronomical forces that have conspired to change the planet's environment from hot to cold, wet to dry and back again over a time period stretching back hundreds of millions of years.

Most important, scientists are beginning to realize that the gyrations of this climatic dance have had a major impact on the evolution of the human species. New research now suggests that climate shifts have played a key role in nearly every significant turning point in human evolution: from the dawn of primates some 65 million years ago to human ancestors rising up to walk on two legs, from the prodigious expansion of the human brain to the rise of agriculture. Indeed, the human saga has not been merely touched by global climate change, some scientists argue, it has in some instances been *driven* by it.

The new research has profound implications for the environmental summit in Rio. Among other things, the findings demonstrate that dramatic climate change is nothing new for planet Earth. The benign global environment that has existed over the past 10,000 years—during which agriculture, writing, cities and most other features of civilization appeared—is a mere blip in a much larger pattern of widely varying climate over the eons. In fact, the pattern of climate change in the past reveals that Earth's climate will almost certainly go through dramatic changes in the future—even without the influence of human activity.

At the same time, the research provides little comfort for those who would like to believe the Earth is a self-regulating machine that can unfailingly absorb the impact of any human activity. Over Earth's history, tiny alterations in the positions of the continents, the flow of air currents and other influences on the world's weather have sometimes cascaded into huge changes in global climate. If the study of prehistory is any guide, a large shift in climate is likely to bring a fundamental change in the nature of human life.

If not for a dramatic climate shift some 65 million years ago, most of the animals on Earth today—including humans—would probably not even be here. Scientists have long suspected that a giant meteor collided with the Earth at that point in time, sending huge clouds of climate-altering dust into the atmosphere. The recent discovery in the Caribbean of tiny nuggets of glass whose chemical makeup suggests that they were formed in the heat of such a cosmic collision lends new support to the theory.

Breadfruit in Greenland. Scientists find evidence that in the heyday of the dinosaurs, 100 million years ago, the world was 10 to 14 degrees warmer than it is today. Breadfruit trees grew in what is now Greenland and dinosaurs wandered an ice-free Antarctica. In the wake of the meteor's impact, dinosaurs vanished in massive numbers, leaving the world wide open for colonization by mammals, including a small, shrewlike creature that was the ancient ancestor of humans.

Most shifts in Earth's climate have not been so sudden or dramatic. But even slowly changing environments have had an enormous influence on the evolution of the human species. After the demise of the dinosaurs, for instance, the Earth continued to grow cooler for tens of millions of years. The cooling resulted from the slow absorption into the Earth of atmospheric carbon dioxide through the weathering of rock, suggests Yale University's Robert Berner, who recently used computer modeling to show how carbon dioxide levels in the atmosphere have changed over the past 600 million years. Because carbon dioxide traps heat to create the so-called greenhouse effect, over time the reduction in CO_2 in the Earth's atmosphere made the global temperature drop several degrees.

This gradual cooling helped set the stage for a crucial phase of human evolution: the beginning of upright walking. Ever since Darwin, anthropologists have speculated that our ancestors rose onto two legs in order to free their hands for some uniquely human activity, such as making tools. But Peter Rodman and Henry McHenry of the University of California at Davis argue instead that the first bipeds were trying to maintain their apelike lifestyle amid environmental change.

New evidence indicates that the Earth's cooling climate caused the dense forests that blanketed Africa to break up into clumps of trees separated by open patches of grassy savanna. Geochemist Thure Cerling of the University of Utah has pioneered a technique that measures tiny amounts of carbon left behind in the soil as plants died. Grasses leave a different chemical "signature" in the soil than do trees. By analyzing the composition of ancient soils, Cerling has discovered that grasses began to appear and spread in Africa about 7 million years ago.

The African environment's gradual shift to a patchwork of forests and plains made walking on two legs an ideal way for human ancestors to move about, Rodman and McHenry contend. Analyzing how much energy various animals use as they walk, the researchers calculated that walking upright is a more efficient way to travel long distances than is walking on the feet and knuckles in the manner of chimps and gorillas. They conclude that our ancestors rose up on two legs not in order to make tools—which do not appear in the archaeological record until more than a million years later—but because walking was simply an easier way for the tree-loving creatures to travel from one clump of forest to another.

One of Earth's most dramatic climatic shifts coincided almost exactly with the most important turn in human evolution: the emergence of the first large-brained primate. An analysis of the

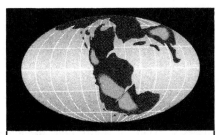

200 MILLION YEARS AGO

AVERAGE TEMPERATURE: 70°F
TURNING POINT: The appearance of the first mammals

All the land masses that now form the continents were once part of a single supercontinent that scientists call Pangea. Thrown together by massive geological forces, the colliding land masses pushed up enormous mountain ranges, remnants of which exist today as the Appalachians in the United States and the Urals in Russia. Pangean environments ranged from lush tropics to torrid deserts, and in some areas the temperature varied as much as 130 degrees. Across this land roamed huge reptiles, the ancestors of the dinosaurs, and a tiny, badgerlike creature that is the distant ancestor of nearly all mammals—including humans.

chemical makeup of seashells taken from the deep sea floor suggests that about 2.5 million years ago, Earth's temperature dipped suddenly and dramatically. The rapid cooling appears to have been global in scope: For the first time in Earth's history, an icecap formed at the North Pole, and the continents became drier and dustier.

Himalayan highs. One cause of the cold snap may have been the skyward thrusting of the Himalaya Mountains, which began rising when the Indian subcontinent collided with Asia some 40 million years before. Using a computer simulation of the flow of air currents around the world, William Ruddiman of Columbia University's Lamont-Doherty Geological Observatory and John Kutzbach of the University of Wisconsin found that by 2.5 million years ago, the Himalayas' peaks towered high enough to alter the flow of major air currents in the Northern Hemisphere, significantly shifting weather patterns.

The drying of Africa opened the way for new kinds of life to emerge. Yale University paleontologist Elisabeth

Vrba points out that African fossils from several species of animals indicate a dramatic change at precisely the same time as the climate shift. Many kinds of antelopes that made their home in woody environments, for example, suddenly disappeared about 2.5 million years ago and were replaced by new types of antelopes that lived in more open, grassy landscapes. Similarly, various rodent species that thrived in wet environments became extinct and were replaced by new kinds of rodents that thrived in drier climates.

Vrba argues that this "pulse" of climate change 2.5 million years ago also created conditions that caused ancient human forebears to undergo a burst of biological innovation. "Our ancestors behaved like perfect mammals," says Vrba. The fossil record shows that at about that time, the species of human ancestor that had existed for more than a million years disappeared, and three or possibly four new upright primates emerged. One of these, a creature that chipped stones to make tools, is the first to be called homo.

With the onset of cooler tempera-

65 MILLION YEARS AGO

AVERAGE TEMPERATURE: 73°F
TURNING POINT: Dinosaurs become extinct; first primates appear.

Ripped apart by upwelling lava, Pagea broke up into land masses roughly the shape of the modern continents, which continued to wander toward the positions they now occupy. For 100 million years, the world was dominated by dinosaurs. A host of evidence suggest that about 65 million years ago, the Earth was rammed by a huge meteor. The collision sent clouds of dust into the atmosphere and triggered a drastic climate change. The dinosaurs quickly became extinct, leaving the world wide open for mammals to thrive in. One of those mammals was the first primate, the ancestor to all modern monkeys, apes, and humans.

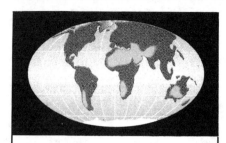

5 MILLION
YEARS AGO

AVERAGE TEMPERATURE: 60°F
TURNING POINT: Chimpanzee and human lineages split from their common ancestor; human ancestors begin to walk on two legs.

As the continents continued to settle into their present positions, a geologic shift cut the Mediterranean Sea off from the Atlantic. Over a period of a thousand years the sea evaporated, leaving barren flats of salt. When sea levels rose again, water flowed back into the Mediterranean basin with a force hundreds of times greater than Niagara Falls. The cycle repeated itself again and again. Meanwhile, the Himalayas pushed higher, changing the flow of atmospheric winds and weather. The world cooled, and the great forests of Africa were broken up by patches of grassy plain. At about this time the family of primates split, one branch leading to modern apes and the other to humans. Fossilized footprints show that by 3.75 million years ago, these ancestors were walking upright.

far into Europe, Asia and North America, sea levels falling dramatically and the land masses near the equator becoming cooler and drier. In the warmer, "interglacial" periods — the Earth is in one today — the glaciers retreat and the climate becomes more temperate. Earth has undergone at least 15 such cycles since about 1.6 million years ago, and if this climate pattern holds, another chilly plunge into glaciation is due to arrive within 2,000 years or so.

Some scientists suggest that these rapid shifts between warm and cold were the driving force behind the human species' ballooning brain. The peri-

2.5 MILLION
YEARS AGO

AVERAGE TEMPERATURE: 55°F
TURNING POINT: Appearance of the first humans

The Himalaya Mountains pushed even higher, disturbing the flow of the atmospheric currents in the Northern Hemisphere. For the first time in Earth's history, a northern polar icecap appeared. As the Earth grew cooler, the vast tracks of dense woods disappeared from many parts of Africa; fossil evidence from the period shows that many species of forest-dwelling antelopes vanished, and many new species of antelopes that made their home in patchier, more open environments suddenly appeared. The line of upright primates splintered into several new species, including Homo habilis, a toolmaking creature whose brain was larger than that of any previous primate. It marked the beginning of the human lineage. At this point, Earth's climate shifted into a new pattern of cyclical change that has continued to the present: Tiny, periodic fluctuations in the Earth's tilt and the path of its orbit around the sun cause repeating cycles of long, cold periods—lasting 50,000 to 80,000 years—and episodes of warmth lasting about 10,000 years. The Earth today is near the end of one of these brief warm spells.

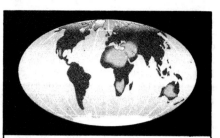

125,000
YEARS AGO

AVERAGE TEMPERATURE: 59°F
TURNING POINT: Anatomically modern humans appear.

The last time Earth's climate was as warm as it is today was 125,000 years ago, when the glaciers that had waxed and waned more than a dozen times receded once again. By this time, the human ancestor Homo habilis had given way to another species of early human known as Homo erectus. These creatures were the first human ancestors to leave Africa, migrating out from the continent about 1 million years ago and spreading throughout much of the Old World. When the warm spell ended about 115,000 years ago, the Earth's climate plunged into another intense bout of cold and glaciation. Intriguingly, it is around the time of this last climate shift that the first modern-looking humans—Homo sapiens—began to appear in Africa and the Near East. Over the next 80,000 years, modern humans would migrate throughout the Earth, from the frozen tundra of the Artic to the tip of South America.

tures some 2.5 million years ago, Earth suddenly entered a whole new pattern of cyclical climate change that acted as an "evolutionary pump," causing the brains of ancient humans to grow larger and larger. Before that landmark, large shifts in Earth's climate typically were the result of geologic processes that took place over millions of years. After 2.5 million years ago, however, the global climate pattern suddenly became much more sensitive to minor perturbations in Earth's orbit and in the tilt of Earth's axis as it circled the sun.

Glacial cycles. These astronomical cycles have caused Earth's climate to fluctuate rapidly between long periods of cold lasting 50,000 to 80,000 years and shorter periods of warmth lasting, on average, about 10,000 years. During the colder periods, the Earth has been locked in ice, with glaciers extending

ods of warm, wet climate caused a population boom among our ancestors, argues neuroscientist William Calvin of the University of Washington. Then a new bout of cold weather would arrive, bringing harsh conditions that would winnow out all but the most intelligent creatures. When the "boom times" came again, these brainier human ancestors would grow in number, increasing their percentage in the overall population. The last time the Earth was as warm as it is today began about 125,000 years ago — a period that lasted roughly 10,000 years before another cold snap set in. Intriguingly, the first fossils of Homo sapiens — anatomically modern humans — come from about this time.

Even after modern humans had established themselves throughout much of the world some 30,000 years ago, the waxing and waning of Earth's glaciers continued to have a major impact on how they conducted their lives. As the world was plunged into a harsher climate, human societies appear to have responded with increasing complexity. Some researchers believe that the magnificent artwork that graces the cave walls of Europe, for instance, was part of a spiritual or religious reaction to the difficult conditions caused when the huge glaciers reached their southernmost point 18,000 years ago.

Though the rise of agriculture is sometimes depicted as an "invention" that was a pivotal step forward in human progress, it was more likely a last-ditch effort for survival in a rapidly deteriorating environment caused when the glaciers began to recede again 15,000 years ago, argues anthropologist Ofer Bar-Yosef of Harvard University. It was then that the human race got its first real taste of global warming. Sea levels rose nearly 400 feet in some areas, cutting off Alaska from Siberia and New Guinea from Australia. The tundra that had covered much of Europe,

18,000
YEARS AGO

AVERAGE TEMPERATURE: 50°F
TURNING POINT: Humans live through the coldest climate in Earth's history.

At the peak of Earth's last period of intense glaciation, mile-thick glaciers reached down to what is now Chicago and covered most of New England. Glaciers also blanketed much of Europe, and those areas that were not locked in ice were covered with frozen tundra. The Cro-Magnon humans of Europe were well into the explosion of culture that would yield thousands of art objects—including the magnificent paintings that grace the walls of caves in southern France and Spain. Bone needles from the time suggest that humans were making warm, close-fitting clothing. Bows and arrows from soon after indicate that they had intensified their hunting-and-gathering way of life.

11,000
YEARS AGO

AVERAGE TEMPERATURE: 59°F
TURNING POINT: Humans begin to depend on agriculture.

The glaciers receded as an intense bout of "global warming" began. The lush, nearly Eden-like conditions that had existed in the Middle East suddenly shifted northward, leaving arid land behind. A group of people known as the Natufians became concentrated in a small, fertile area bounded by mountains, sea and desert, and they ceased their nomadic ways. A sudden climate shift led to a cold spell that lasted for 1,000 years, forcing the Natufians to turn to farming to survival. When the climate finally warmed up again, a population explosion among the Natufians further locked them and their descendants into an agricultural life.

Asia and North America was replaced by forest and grass, leaving the climate much like today's.

The changes wrought by global warming were acutely felt in the Levant, an area in the Middle East now occupied by Israel, Syria, Lebanon and Jordan. Some 15,000 years ago, the Levant was a lush hill country filled with a bounty of plants and animals, making it easy for humans to hunt and gather the food they needed to thrive. But as the world became warmer, the region experienced repeated droughts, and vegetation shifted northward. One group of hunter-gatherers who lived in the Levant, the Natufians, became increasingly hemmed in by the mountains to the north and spreading deserts to the south and east. According to Bar-Yosef, the Natufians responded to their ever diminishing range by abandoning their wandering ways and settling down, though they continued to hunt and gather food.

Bar-Yosef's theory is buttressed by new research by Daniel Lieberman of Harvard University, who examined the patterns of growth in the fossilized teeth of gazelles at sites in the Levant.

Lieberman found that sites made by the Natufians' immediate predecessors contain the remains of gazelles that were killed in only a single season, such as the spring or fall. At Natufian sites, however, the gazelle remains are from animals that were killed year-round, indicating that the Natufians were living at a permanent camp. It is at about this time also that fossils of the "house" mouse began to appear at Natufian sites.

A time to sow. Just as the Natufians were adjusting to a new sedentary life in their drier environment, however, they suddenly were hit by another bout of climate change, this time to much cooler temperatures. Scientists are still unsure why, but about 11,000 years ago the Earth's climate returned to a glacial climate for nearly 1,000 years. The environment in the Levant quickly grew cooler, changing the plant and animal life, and the Natufians found themselves with a tough choice, says Bar-Yosef: They had to either begin moving again or find a new source of food. The Natufians started cultivating grains to survive.

The Natufians' shift to agriculture required no grand technological breakthroughs, argues Bar-Yosef. Despite their hunting-and-gathering lifestyle, the ancient people of the Levant appear to have been familiar for millenniums with cereals and grains: Scientists recently unearthed grains of wild barley at a newly discovered archaeological site in Israel that dates back 19,000 years.

The rapid swings of climate that occurred between 13,000 and 10,000 years ago—and the shift to agriculture that resulted from them—must have created a wrenching change in how people lived. After all, people had been hunting and gathering for as long as modern humans had walked the Earth. Research by Mark Cohen, an anthropologist at the State University of New York at Plattsburgh, suggests that the first farmers suffered malnutrition, vitamin deficiencies and a host of new diseases that arose because of their sedentary ways. Social life changed, too, since people could no longer simply walk away from disputes and so had to devise new social strategies for resolving conflicts. The increasing reliance on stored goods meant that for the first time people had possessions that could be stolen, creating the need for defensive walls and militia.

Out of Eden. One of the epic "origin" tales to come out of the region—the biblical book of Genesis—speaks of humans being expelled from a garden of plenty and being punished by having to "eat the herb of the field" and "in the sweat of thy face . . . eat bread." Yet for all of the troubles that farming at first caused the Natufians and their descendants, they had no choice but to adopt it, says Bar-Yosef. And once they did, there was no turning back: Farming produces more food per acre than hunting and gathering, and the sedentary life led to a population boom that could then be supported only by tilling the earth. As the world began to warm again about 10,000 years ago, the Natufian sites suddenly ballooned to nearly 25 times their previous size.

A yearning to return to an Eden-like existence seems to be an unspoken theme among some environmentalists, who see modern human civilization as a blight on Earth's landscape. But as the new findings on climate and human evolution demonstrate, there was no point in time when humans and Mother Nature lived in perfect harmony. From walking on two legs to making the first stone tools, from harnessing fire to settling down in farming villages, humans have always had to change their ways to cope with changing climate.

While there may be comfort in the fact that the human species has survived large climatic shifts in the past, the ultimate lesson for the conferees gathering in Rio this week is far more complex. Whether the Earth's climate will shift dramatically in the near future as a result of human activities remains uncertain. But if the new research on climate and human evolution reveals anything, it is that if Earth's climate does radically change, the way humans live is likely to change in radical ways, too.

WILLIAM F. ALLMAN
WITH BETSY WAGNER

Frost and Found

The melting of an Alpine glacier brings scientists face to face with the Stone Age

Torstein Sjøvold

Sjøvold received his doctorate from the University of Stockholm, Sweden, where he now heads the Osteological Research Laboratory.

Recovering human remains from glaciers is almost routine in the Alps because mountain-climbing casualties occur all too often. In some cases the victims are not readily retrieved, but disappear in a glacier or are covered by snow. Several such bodies turn up nearly every year. From the information given to the police, nothing indicated that this case was to be any different.

Thursday, September 19, 1991, came at the end of a sunny spell in the Otztal Alps, between Austria and Italy. Erika and Helmut Simon, a German couple who had extended their climbing holiday an extra day, had climbed the area's second highest peak and were headed down toward a mountain lodge. At 10,500 feet, they spotted the upper part of a body protruding from the ice. It was face down in a small depression and apparently naked.

Everyone's assumption was that this was the body of a climber who had suffered an accident, perhaps some decades ago. The police in both South Tyrol in Italy and Tyrol in Austria were called from the lodge. After the Italian police decided that the find lay outside their territory, the recovery was organized from Austria. Two attempts were made to free the body from the ice, the first on Friday (the day after the discovery) and the second on Sunday. During this time, not only the recovery teams but also several curious tourists visited the site. Whatever objects had lain about the body disappeared over the weekend.

At the nearby University of Innsbruck, Rainer Henn, the head of the forensics department, received a court order to bring the body down for identification. He traveled by helicopter to the site on Monday, September 23. In the meantime, unknown to the authorities, rumors had begun to circulate that the body could be several hundred years old. An Austrian television crew was already on the spot when Henn arrived.

Henn had been told that the body had been freed from the ice and was ready to be collected and transported. But during the previous night, the water in which it was lying had refrozen, and

Henn had to free the body using the equipment at hand, which happened to be an ice ax and a ski pole. The operation took place in front of the television cameras.

Henn immediately realized that the body was not typical of those usually retrieved from glaciers; moisture had not turned the tissues into the fatty, waxy substance known as adipocere, or "grave wax." This body was dehydrated. But there were no obvious signs that it might be very old. Just before the body was loaded aboard the helicopter, however, someone at the site discovered a small flint knife with a wooden handle. People who had found other artifacts at the site soon brought them forth; these included an ax, whose head later proved to be of copper. The next day, Henn and archeologist Konrad Spindler held a press conference: based on inspection of the artifacts, the world was told that the body belonged to a man who had perished 4,000 years ago. Several carbon-14 dates that have since been obtained prove that the Iceman, as he is now commonly called, is 5,200 to 5,300 years old, a relic of the late Stone Age.

The find is unusually important because, first, this was not a grave site but something far more rare—the body of a man who died on the spot. The equipment found with him was what he thought he needed for his venture in the high mountains, whereas articles found in a grave may be what those burying the body believed the dead would need in the afterlife. Second, the artifacts, including things made from perishable organic materials, such as wood, fur, and grass, are extremely well preserved, although most of the Iceman's clothing is rather torn. Third, several of the artifacts are unprecedented finds, such as the wooden handle of the stone knife and the handle of the copper ax-head.

Political complications arose because the body was discovered exactly on the border between the Schnals Valley in Italy and the Otz Valley in Austria. The confusion was directly related to the melting of the glacial ice that revealed the Iceman. Generally, the border follows the watershed. The Iceman lay to the north of the watershed and therefore appeared to be on Austrian soil. But when South Tyrol was incorporated into Italy in 1919, the mountain passage where the Iceman was found was covered by a glacier, and so the border was defined by a series of border posts. When Austrian surveyors reexamined the posts a few weeks after the discovery, they realized that the site was about 100 yards into the Italian side.

By then, the body had been moved to Innsbruck and stored under conditions approximating those in the glacier (21° F and a relative humidity of 98 percent). Any attempt to move it risked causing deterioration because the body was a "cold mummy," not completely dried out. Negotiations were therefore carried out between the University of Innsbruck and the autonomous province of South Tyrol, both of which agreed that the find had to be examined on a broad, international basis. An agreement was signed stipulating that the research on the body and artifacts would be organized by the University of Innsbruck, at least for a period of three years, with the artifacts to be conserved at the Central Museum of Roman and Germanic Antiquities in Mainz, Germany. Some one hundred scientists are working on this project, under the supervision of a new department headed by the university president. Two lines of research are being pursued: the one in which I am participating is directed by anatomist Werner Platzer and emphasizes the study of the body, while the second, directed by Konrad Spindler, concerns the artifacts and their cultural context. Eventually, the archeological finds are likely to be put on exhibit. But the Iceman himself may be kept in cold storage indefinitely to allow medical or scientific research on a Stone Age man to continue many years hence.

The body itself is well preserved, except for the left hip and thigh, which were damaged during the early recovery attempts. Although dried up, the eyes, brain, and intestines are present. The head hair and body hair have been lost because of the long period in the ice, but strands of wavy brown or black head hair have been found among the equipment; they are about 3.5 inches long, indicating that the hair had been cut. On the back and on the legs are patterns of short, dark lines resembling tattoos.

The Iceman's teeth are very worn, and a broad gap separates the two upper middle incisors. The upper lip has receded and the soft part of the nose has been pressed flat. In addition, the shell of the left ear is bent, leading scientists to speculate that the Iceman fell asleep, probably out of exhaustion at the high altitude, while lying on his left side, and froze to death in this position. Later, the body probably rotated to lie on the stomach. The Iceman's age at death has so far been conservatively estimated at between twenty-five to forty years.

A fortuitous combination of circumstances permitted the Iceman to reach us. He lived in a fairly warm time period, when the permanent snowcaps lay several hundred feet above the discovery site. By chance, he must have died just the year the climate changed, with the Alpine glaciers starting to grow and the snowcaps reaching farther down the mountains. Even though the climate varied during the thousands of years to follow, the Iceman did not emerge from the ice until the warm summer of 1991 (if he had, he would not have been so well preserved).

Indications are that the Iceman died in late summer or in autumn, just before the first snowfall. He was probably covered for a while under a thin layer of snow, permitting the tissues to become almost completely dehydrated by the wind. As the snows of the first winter gradually changed into ice, the glacier grew above him, covering him for more than 5,000 years.

Because the weight of the ice and the accumulation of new snow each year forces the Alpine glaciers to move gradually down into the valleys, where they melt, glaciologists had assumed that the region's ice was no more than 1,000 years old. But the Iceman was lying in a little depression, between two transverse ridges of rock. Apparently the glacial ice passed over the depression, leaving what was lying on the bottom undisturbed. During the past seventy years, however, the thick ice has gradually melted away. As a final impetus, a dust storm in the Sahara Desert in March 1991 sent large amounts of dust up into the atmosphere, depositing it in the Alps and elsewhere. The dust darkened the white snow, combining with the warm and sunny summer of 1991 to speed up the melting process. The Iceman probably emerged at most three days before he was discovered. Even before he was removed, the season's first snowfall covered the site.

The Iceman's equipment, in addition to the flint knife and copper ax, includes an unfinished, seventy-one-inch longbow (eight inches longer than the Iceman himself); a quiver of leather or fur with two arrows—complete with three steering feathers and flint arrowheads—and twelve shafts for making more arrows; a leather pouch; and a frame to some kind of rucksack. The remains of his clothing consist of patches of fur from red deer, goat, or chamois that were sewn together, as well as shoes. This past summer, archeologists revisited the site to complete their excavation and discovered a fur cap behind the rock on which the Iceman had been lying. The cap is well preserved, with the hairs of the fur still attached.

The Iceman's shoes had been lined with grass. In addition he carried several threads and ropes made from grass and some kind of plaited shoulder cape of grass, perhaps used as a raincoat. Suitable kinds of wood were used in making the equipment: yew for the bow and ax handle, viburnum for the arrow shafts, ash for the knife handle, hazel for the frame of the rucksack and for stiffening the side of the quiver, and larch for crossboards of the rucksack. Why the Iceman carried an unfinished bow—it had never been strung—remains a mystery.

Two lumps of tree fungus joined by a composite leather strap were first thought to belong to a species commonly used for tinder, but they turned out to be a different species, most likely chosen for its antibiotic properties. Some of the contents of the leather pouch, on the other hand, seem to be remains of the kind of fungus used as tinder. Two grains of a primitive kind of wheat were found among the remnants of the clothing, showing that the Iceman was connected with communities practicing agriculture.

The farmers who now live in the adjacent Schnals Valley in South Tyrol are familiar with the mountain passage where the Iceman was found: they used to drive their sheep to pastures north of the watershed, where they possessed grazing rights even after South Tyrol was incorporated into Italy. According to the most accepted current theory, the Iceman himself could have been a shepherd. The copper ax—something of a luxury item—reinforces this theory, for in certain societies shepherds enjoyed a high social status. Although domesticated animals were common at the time the Iceman lived, they probably were considered valuable, and the task of guarding them could have been an important responsibility.

We still do not know for sure why the Iceman died, but exhaustion seems likely. In order to understand what the Iceman may have experienced, in late August of last year I climbed to the site from the nearest villages in the adjacent valleys. From both the north and the south, marked foot paths lead to the mountain lodge, which lies at 9,900 feet. From there one can continue for about 45 minutes along the side of a mountain ridge to the site. This approach is safer than directly crossing the mountain passage where the Iceman was found, where there is a risk of rockslides.

My first ascent was from the north, from about 4,600 feet below the site. I was dressed for normal high Alpine hiking, with solid boots, an anorak for protection from the wind, sun cap and sun block to combat the strong sunlight, and sunglasses because of reflection from the snow at high elevations. After I had walked two or three hours through the valley, the path became steeper. The sunshine felt warm, and the temperature may have been about 45° F. After hiking for another two or three hours through a rocky landscape and crossing a tongue of glacier at the upper end of the valley, I reached the lodge. I felt quite exhausted, in part owing to the thin air at that altitude. Because of a sudden thunderstorm, I waited until the next day and then continued on to the site.

The hike from the south was quicker, but the path was steeper. The 4,900-foot climb took about three hours and was extremely tiring. The last third of the way was along a serpentine path to the lodge. During my ascent, I observed some clouds lying fairly low in the mountains. When I was almost at the top, the clouds suddenly rose from the valley and I was enveloped in a white fog; the temperature dropped markedly, to below freezing. I rested in the fog for a while and proceeded to the lodge when the visibility improved. I considered it too risky to continue to the site in the fog, so I returned to the village instead. That very night it rained heavily in the valley, and the season's first heavy snowfall fell in the mountains.

I imagine the Iceman may have encountered a similar situation 5,300 years ago. If he had just climbed to the top of the mountain passage, he would have been quite tired. He might then have been caught in a fog, lain down, and fallen asleep while waiting for the fog to dissipate. If later on it started to snow, he could have been chilled and, remaining unconscious, fallen into his eternal sleep.

TRACKING THE FIRST AMERICANS

AN ICE-AGE MYSTERY

From Chile to northern Canada, striking archaeological finds are changing our concept of the earliest humans to inhabit the New World—who they were, when they arrived, how they lived.

Evan Hadingham

Evan Hadingham is the author of several popular books on archaeology and is science editor of the PBS series "NOVA." His most recent book is "Lines to the Mountain Gods: Nazca and the Mysteries of Peru."

AROUND 12,000 YEARS AGO, ACCORDing to long-held theory, A handful of fur-clad hunters crossed a now-submerged land bridge between Asia and Alaska and became the first humans to enter the New World. Ahead lay forbidding terrain: a frigid, treeless corridor through present-day Yukon and Alberta, bounded by huge glaciers on either side.

Archaeologists have long believed that the hunters pioneered this bleak corridor in pursuit of bison, mammoth, musk ox, and caribou. Eventually they emerged on the Great Plains, grasslands teeming with an astounding variety of prey for the hunters. A human population explosion resulted, and in a matter of decades the hunters helped drive species such as mastodons, mammoths, and native camels and tapirs into extinction.

This dramatic "big game" theory of American origins has been stoutly defended by archaeologists for half a century.

But is it correct?

Today, thanks to a wave of discoveries outside North America, nearly every aspect of the migration theory is under intense scrutiny. Fresh insights on the peopling of China, Japan, and Siberia are redrawing the lines of debate on a much broader canvas, framed by the entire Pacific Rim. And a rash of controversial early dates from South America—a few even hinting at settlement prior to 30,000 years ago—challenges many of the assumptions of the old theory.

The timing question stirs passionate debate among archaeologists. More than an academic quibble, the date of human entry into the New World has a crucial impact on our understanding of how it happened. Each timing possibility involves entirely different episodes of Ice Age climate, ways of life, and human skills. Even if the migration happened a mere 2,000 or 3,000 years before the traditional 12,000-year

benchmark, it would dictate a drastic new vision of the peopling of the Americas. Instead of "big game" hunters migrating down from the north as they tracked woolly mammoths and bison and dispatched them with skillfully hewn spearheads, the earlier dates indicate less advanced tribes feeding off smaller game and sea life. Those with marine skills would, in fact, have migrated down a coastal strip now submerged by rising ocean.

DISCOVERY IN CHILE

One of the most phenomenal of the South American discoveries is the site of Monte Verde, located in a remote, swampy flood plain, 30 miles from the Pacific, in southern Chile. Here, beside a creek, 13,000 years ago, a hunting and gathering band lived year-round in a dozen or so log-framed huts roofed with hides. Archaeologist Tom Dillehay of the University of Kentucky has uncovered the ancient living surface, complete with wood, plant, and even food remains. Such evidence is nearly always destroyed at conventional cave sites, but at Monte Verde a layer of waterlogged peat sealed the living floor almost as if it were a prehistoric Pompeii.

Astonishingly, a human footprint, a chunk of uneaten mastodon meat, even traces of herbal medicine (indicated by a concentration of 27 different plants still used by traditional healers in the Andes) were preserved under the peat. Monte Verde's inhabitants were skilled carpenters, to judge from numerous worked wood fragments carefully scorched and scraped into shape.

Dillehay's dig has won attention not only because of its uniquely preserved finds but also because of the meticulous nature of the study, involving more than 70 specialists from different fields. Monte Verde has helped convince many researchers that humans must have entered the New World as early as 15,000 to 13,000 years ago.

Meanwhile, similar claims from other sites have mounted. Among the more convincing are hearths and stone tools unearthed from remote, spectacular sandstone gorges at Pedra Furada, Brazil, dated back to at least 12,000 years ago; a spearpoint lodged in the bones of a young mastodon at

Taima-Taima, Venezuela, around 13,000; and a deeply layered rock-shelter deposit at Meadowcroft, Pennsylvania, studied over many years by James Adovasio of the University of Pittsburgh. Adovasio's latest estimates for his earliest levels cluster around 14,000 to 12,000 years ago. Surveying the new dating and environmental clues, George Frison of the University of Wyoming says we are in for "one of the most exciting times in the history of early man research in the Americas."

Why the excitement? An entry time of 15,000 to 13,000 years ago presents a profound challenge to the traditional picture of the peopling of the Americas much later.

'IT'S A MYTH!'

For more than 50 years that traditional picture has revolved around a North American big-game hunting culture that is known as Clovis because it was discovered at Clovis, New Mexico, in 1932. Clovis culture is famed for its stone spearpoints skillfully flaked on both sides to give a leaf-shaped, fluted appearance—soon viewed as the technology of the first Americans. Experiments on elephant carcasses have confirmed how effectively the spearpoints could have dispatched large Ice Age game such as mastodon and bison.

Recent Clovis digs show that some hunters also dined on less glamorous fare such as frogs and snails. But, on the basis of the earlier findings, the "big game" theory took hold. It was easy to picture how the earliest Americans—armed with such efficient hunting gear—could have wandered into Alaska, following the great herds as they migrated along the grassy plain now covered by the Bering Strait. And then eventually following other game southward until they reached what is now New Mexico.

"The trouble with the 'big game' origins theory," declares its leading critic, Alan Bryan of the University of Alberta, "is, quite simply, it's a myth!"

Not that Bryan denies the big-game connections of the Clovis spearpoints. Indeed, Clovis obviously does represent a highly successful response to the almost unlimited big-game hunting opportunities on the Great Plains.

The problem is that it was clearly a short-lived episode. All of the radiocarbon dates cluster tightly around 11,500 to 11,000 years ago. If we accept the conventional view that Clovis people really were the first Americans, it cannot explain how humans could have reached South America around 15,000 (or even 13,000) years ago. Nor does it explain why evidence for Clovis-like sites in Alaska and Siberia remains so meager.

The obvious alternative—the humans came over earlier, bringing with them a different and less specialized pre-Clovis culture—now tantalizes prehistoric archaeologists throughout the Americas.

In a sparsely populated region of northeast Brazil known as São Raimundo Nonato, a thorn-covered volcanic plain meets a 120-mile wall of flame-covered sandstone cliffs up to 800 feet high. At the foot of these crags, erosion has hollowed out steep gorges and deep overhangs. Many of the rock surfaces are covered with ancient paintings, executed in vivid red, yellow, black, and white pigments. They depict deer, armadillos, lizards, and jaguars, as well as people. There are scenes suggesting hunting, sexual relations, or childbirth.

When French archaeologist Nième Guidon was alerted to this rock art in 1973, she selected one particularly impressive decorated overhang known as Pedra Furada and excavated in the soil below. Reporting on her preliminary paper published in 1986, The New York Times ran a banner headline, "New Finds Challenge Ideas on First Americans." Guidon claimed that hunters had lit fires and painted at Pedra Furada at least 30,000 years ago. Not only did such dates defy the conventional picture of New World settlement, but they also implied that the Brazilian rock art was even earlier than the celebrated painted caves of Western Europe such as Lascaux and Altamira.

BACK TO 45,000 YEARS AGO

Then, in May of last year, Guidon startled archaeologists further by announcing at a conference at the University of Maine that her team had pushed back the dates for human occupation at the rock-shelter even further, to 45,000 years ago.

Could this claim be true?

Doubts were raised by several leading experts at the conference, including Dillehay. To begin with, Guidon herself has now revised earlier claims about the rock art, indicating that painting at the site probably began no earlier than 12,000 years ago. While extensive burned layers have indeed been dated right back to 45,000, no animal bones are present in the charcoal. Nor are the alleged "tools" in these early layers obviously distinguishable from natural quartz flakes, which are present in the local rock and could well have fallen from the cliffs overhead.

Although the skeptics may be right about Pedra Furada, others suggest that the possibility of an entry long before 13,000 years ago should be taken seriously. Dillehay, for example, is cautiously studying evidence from the lowest layers at Monte Verde, which includes three apparent clay-lined hearths dating to around 33,000 years ago.

If humans arrived that early in South America, how did they get there? Could they have traveled across the Pacific? No evidence of boats or rafts has survived, but some Ice Age people were surprisingly adventurous sailors. We know that anatomically modern humans reached Australia prior to 40,000 years ago, a feat that could have been achieved only by crossing a 55-mile stretch of shark-infested open sea.

Even so, the vast expanses of the Pacific would have presented a formidable obstacle for a boat migration eastward to South America. Thor Heyerdahl's celebrated Kon-Tiki adventure, sailing a balsa-log craft across the Pacific from Peru in 1947, showed that drift voyages in the reverse direction were possible. But a far greater challenge faced the earliest Pacific colonists, who we know originated in Indonesia. That was lack of a reliable long-distance sailing craft.

In fact, archaeologists are confident that the islands of Polynesia were deserted until about 3,500 years ago. That was when the outrigger canoe was invented, making a gradual west-to-east colonization of the islands feasible. Scholars agree that the idea of a much earlier drift voyage to the Americas is highly improbable.

A more serious suggestion by Ruth Gruhn of the University of Alberta supports the traditional Asia-Alaska route but challenges the traditional emphasis on big-game hunting. In her view, Asian coastal hunters could have taken advantage of a relatively warm interlude around 50,000 years ago, when temperatures in Alaska might actually have been milder than at present. Gruhn imagines that her coast dwellers worked their way around the northern coasts, fishing, hunting sea mammals, and snaring migrating wildfowl. Their adaptation to the coast meant they had little interest in the inland game herds exploited much later by Clovis hunters. Instead, their communities would have multiplied rapidly along the coastal strip of North America until they reached Panama. Here, Gruhn supposes, the pioneers scattered to many different regions, including Chile and Brazil.

Attractive though her scenario is, the vital evidence that would confirm or disprove it now lies under the Pacific Ocean. As the climate slowly warmed toward the end of the Ice Age, huge volumes of water locked up in northern glaciers melted, refilling the ocean basins. Sea levels have risen by at least 300 feet over the past 15,000 years—a process that has continued in recent decades and is expected to proceed during the next century owing to the human-influenced warming trend known as the greenhouse effect.

The rising seas inundated not only the Bering land bridge but also most of the original Ice Age coastline of the Americas. So it is nearly impossible to establish exactly when the first coastal communities sprang up along the Pacific Rim.

The only option for archaeologists is to study the inland sites—where ancient lifestyles would certainly have been very different from those on the now-submerged coast—in the hope of establishing a broad picture of when and how humans spread through Asia and Alaska.

The migration to the Americas marks the final act of a worldwide drama of human origins. Recent discoveries of fossil skulls and clues from the study of modern genetics both point to a similar conclusion: Humans physically identical to ourselves were present in Africa and the Near East at least 90,000 years ago. From there, they spread out across the face of Europe and Asia in slowly advancing waves, reaching China and Japan around 30,000 years ago. In some areas the hunters replaced, and in others interbred with, less advanced humans such as the ruggedly built Neanderthals.

The time span involved was so vast that the migrants were most likely quite unaware of their inexorable spread across the Ice Age landscape. All it took was for each new generation to claim fresh hunting grounds a few miles on from the last. Even at a pace of a few miles per year, the cumulative impact was considerable. (For example, a handful of coastal hunters and their descendants could easily have spread down the entire coastal strip of the Americas in less than 1,000 years.)

As for the fate of premodern humans in Asia, we still lack clear evidence. Some Chinese scholars, notably Wu Xinzhi of the Beijing Academy, are convinced there was a gradual transition to modern man, not an abrupt replacement. In any case, few sites of premodern humans are known anywhere in Europe or Asia north of latitude 50 degrees, which runs through northern China. Many archaeologists believe that only fully modern man possessed the skills and tools necessary to push farther north, into the arid grasslands of Siberia. But when did this happen?

WITH THE AID OF GLASNOST

Intact early-man sites in the far north are a rarity, partly because of extreme natural processes of erosion and disruption of geological layers. Thanks to the Soviet Union's glasnost, we know of a half dozen sites in northeast Siberia that undoubtedly represent the presence of modern man as far back as 18,000 years ago. This date corresponds with the most frigid final phase of the Ice Age, when the Bering land bridge was not so much a bridge as a vast arid landmass 1,000 mile wide. There was no physical obstacle, apart from extreme cold, preventing the hunters from walking into Alaska.

Surprisingly, no site in Alaska has yet been dated earlier than the Clovis era, around 11,500 years ago. Skeptics argue that this gap in the evidence casts doubt on the whole pre-Clovis theory.

However, a recent discovery across the Canadian border in the Yukon suggests that traces of earlier hunters may yet be found farther west. In the remote limestone foothills of the Keele Range, a well-preserved site known as Bluefish Caves has provided clear evidence of stone tools dating back at least 14,000 years. Even more remarkable is a chunk of mammoth bone, with flakes alongside it obviously detached by a human craftsman, dating to around 25,000 years ago.

BURYING THE GREAT LAKES

This evidence persuades one of the excavators, Jacques Cinq-Mars of the Canadian Museum of Civilization, that "people occupied eastern Beringia north of the ice sheets throughout the last glacial cycle." These people, he says, "were in a position to spread into areas south of the ice sheets." The question is, when and how did they do it?

The ice sheets in question were two giant systems of glaciers, one straddling the mountain ranges near the Pacific, the other burying much of eastern Canada and the Great Lakes. Throughout the final surge of cold climate from 25,000 to 15,000 years ago, these sheets must have presented a formidable barrier. Their immediate neighborhood was one of constant dust storms and howling winds, brutal temperatures, and minimal vegetation.

Even the coast route would have been arduous. Thomas Hamilton, an Alaskan geologist with the US Geological Survey, says the mighty glaciers of the coastal ranges would have reached down to the ocean in many places. Farther north, the remnant of the Bering Sea bordering the land bridge would likely have been covered with treacherous pack ice for much of the year, severely limiting hunters' access to sea mammals and other resources.

In theory, at least, there was an inland alternative: a narrow north-south corridor some 1,200 miles long, dividing the two great ice sheets. Here was the gateway to the Americas, yet opinions have swung to and fro on how practical a route it would have offered the hunters.

"Recently," Hamilton explains, "scientists in Alberta and Montana discovered errors in the dating of several sites which had supported the idea of the corridor remaining open during the last glacial phase. It now seems more likely that the corridor was closed by ice-dammed lakes or glaciers. In any case, it would have been a most forbidding environment. My own view is that the corridor wasn't really accessible until the climate began to warm and the glaciers retreat—say, around 15,000 or 14,000 years ago." While some researchers are more optimistic about the corridor, most agree that any hunters brave enough to explore it before 15,000 years ago were few and far between.

TEETH AND TIMING

Confirmation of this timing comes from a surprising source: human teeth. For 25 years anthropologist Christy Turner has pored over dental roots and crowns at his Arizona State University lab, building up an intricate picture of the similarities and differences between Old and New World teeth. Since the shapes of teeth change so slowly and constantly over thousands of years, the dental record offers Turner a powerful tool for probing relationships between ancient peoples.

In fact, by documenting how the tooth shapes change from one region or time period to another, Turner has arrived at stunning proof of the Asian heritage of all Native Americans: More than two dozen detailed similarities—specific features of roots or crowns—all link the dental record of northern Asia with that of the Americas. Turner's data support his estimate that the common ancestors of all New World peoples emerged in northern China around 20,000 years ago. He places the crossing to Alaska around 16,000 years ago. In addition, his findings suggest that the first wave of Asian hunters was eventually followed by two further major influxes, all three giving rise to the present-day native peoples of North and South America.

THE NEW PICTURE

Today the study of the first Americans involves a multitude of disciplines and nationalities, engaging experts on a least three continents. While scholars are still far from a consensus, the broad strokes of a new picture of American origins have begun to emerge.

No solid evidence exists to suggest that humans made it to the New World before 40,000 years ago. Gruhn's theory of an earlier coastal migration is an intriguing conjecture, yet evidence from Asia implies that humans do not penetrate the far northern latitudes till much later. In fact, the windy plains of Beringia were most likely not crossed until the cold cycle of 25,000 to 15,000 years ago, when dry land linked the two continents for the last time.

All through this era, the great ice sheets farther south probably held the colonists in check. But once the great thaw began around 15,000 years ago, the hunters spread rapidly, establishing footholds in settings as diverse as the Meadowcroft rock-shelter in Pennsylvania and the skin-covered huts of Monte Verde. There in southern Chile the journey of modern humanity ended, an odyssey that had begun in Africa at least three thousand generations before.

The Beginnings of Culture, Agriculture, and Urbanization

Although the points are debatable, the characteristics of civilization include urbanization; literacy; complex economic, political, and social patterns; and an advanced technology. Civilization, it would seem, represents the highest level of human organization and accomplishment, but the definition can ignite arguments. If, for example, a people or tribe cannot write, are they uncivilized? Since historians embrace written records as the main source of information for the writing of history, moreover, are illiterate peoples prehistoric? This is obviously a problem since the definition implies a value or worth. World historians, nevertheless, often use civilization and its characteristics as an organizing principle.

In the development of humankind the tool of writing has been useful as a means to keep permanent, accurate records. It may be that the start of writing came from pictures and symbols painted on cave walls such as those in the cave sealed by Mediterranean waters until 1985. Jean Clottes and Jean Courtin describe a treasure trove of Paleolithic art discovered by divers probing an underwater cave. The divers surfaced from the submerged entrance to find a sealed cave with pictures of bison, horses, and sea animals as well as handprints 27,000 years old. This type of art, a form of communication, may well have been the start of literacy.

Jared Diamond, in "Writing Right," is more analytical about the development of writing and finds that there are three main strategies. People have used alphabets, symbols for entire words, or symbols for parts of words. Alphabets are the most flexible strategy and have undergone 4,000 years of changes. Phonetic qualities are also important so that the written word and the spoken word can be matched. It makes communication easier than having to memorize independent symbols, as in the Chinese written language. Although English has become the current *lingua franca*, Diamond argues that it is not nearly as easy as others. That raises a question, incidentally, about why English is so widely studied and used. Is it because of politics or technology? It is also interesting that number systems evolved at the same time as literacy and that counting, at first, seemed to be as important as writing. They certainly went hand in hand and were important bureaucratic tools of empire and business where it was necessary to keep track of transactions and taxes.

Literacy developed in settled agricultural civilizations—hence the linkage with urbanization—but the agricultural revolution had occurred centuries earlier. Bread wheat developed about 8,000 B.C.E. in the Middle East, followed by rice in Southeast Asia and corn in the Western Hemisphere. John Noble Wilford summarizes the latest research about the development of corn, a hybrid plant, which occured about 5,000 years after wheat in the Middle East. What remains unknown is who developed it and how it spread in the New World.

Agriculture, of course, gave greater assurance of food supply and dictated a settled life. Men ceased to be hunters and tended the fields; women helped in the fields, took over household tasks, and looked after children. An analysis of female skeletons from an early agricultural village reveal bone malformations from long hours spent kneeling over flat stones to grind the grain. Successful settlements of this kind, according to John Pfeiffer, occurred in Asia, Mesoamerica, and the Middle East. They grew because of the need to feed larger populations. That was how civilization began.

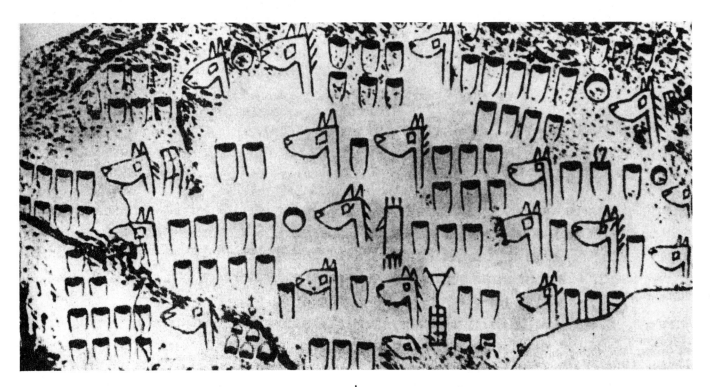

Looking Ahead: Challenge Questions

How did writing and counting start? Why was this done, and what is its significance?

What is known about the invention of corn?

Which came first—settlement or agriculture?

What was the advantage and disadvantage of living in cities?

What was the role of agriculture in the growth of civilization?

What is the importance of writing in the development of civilization? Can there be civilization without literacy?

Does the history of agriculture support local origins theory (people invent the same things at different places) or diffusionist theory (inventions spread from a single source)?

Neptune's Ice Age Gallery

A Mediterranean sea cave preserves artwork painted 27,000 years ago

Jean Clottes and Jean Courtin

Jean Clottes, who earned his Ph.D. at the University of Toulouse, served for twenty-one years as director of prehistoric antiquities for the central Pyrenees region. His research focuses on the dating of cave art and its archeological context.

Born in St. Tropez, France, Jean Courtin is a director at the National Center for Scientific Research, as well as director of prehistoric antiquities of Provence—Côte d'Azur.

In 1985, Henri Cosquer, a professional deep-sea diver, discovered a narrow, underwater opening, barely nine feet by three, beneath the base of a cliff rising from the Mediterranean Sea. Located in the Calanque area between Marseille and Cassis, the cave was 110 feet below sea level. Cosquer dived down several times and cautiously explored his way along a 450-foot-long sloping gallery. Eventually he emerged in a huge, air-filled chamber with many stalactites and stalagmites. However, it was not until a return dive, in July 1991, that he happened to notice the silhouette of a handprint on the cave wall—a common feature of Paleolithic art, made by blowing or spraying pigment around the artist's hand. After photographing it, he noticed two more handprints. Sometime later he returned to the cave with friends to search for additional artworks. This time the explorers began to discern many paintings and engravings of animals on the rock walls.

News of Cosquer's discovery of apparently prehistoric cave paintings circulated among the diving community, and on September 1, three divers from another region went into the cave on their own, could not find their way out, and died there. Hoping to prevent further accidents, Cosquer belatedly reported his discovery to French government officials and submitted photographs that reached us through the Ministry of Culture.

Judging from the pictures he had taken, the paintings and engravings seemed genuine. Many were partly obscured by bright, white calcite deposits, and most of the engravings seemed to be covered by a patina, formed by a natural process that requires long periods of time. However, we could not authenticate the art unless we could examine it directly.

An expedition would require investigators who were both specialists in prehistoric rock art and experienced divers, an uncommon combination. Our exploration of the painted chamber was organized in late September 1991 by R. Lequément, director of the Department of Submarine Archaeological Research (DRASM) and included Cosquer, archeologists from DRASM, several divers from the French navy, and coauthor Courtin.

Even after only a preliminary inspection, Courtin became convinced that the art was genuine. All the figures were weathered, so that when they were examined under a magnifying glass, numerous minute bare spots were visible where the ancient pigment no longer adhered to the cave walls. Many drawings were coated not only with calcite but also with small stalactites that had grown on top of the coating. A patina, often the same as that of the surrounding walls, partly filled in engraved lines of the petroglyphs. Microcrystals had formed on them as well. On the walls were dozens of animal figures, a number of stenciled hands, and thousands of tracings made by human fingers in the once-soft surface coating. A hoax was out of the question. This was a major find.

A close examination of its contents showed that the cave had not been lived in. Two fires had been made but they were quite small, about a foot in diameter, and no bones or flint flakes could be seen around them. Unlike hearths found in Paleolithic cave dwellings, usually surrounded by a large amount of refuse from human activities, these fires were used for light, not cooking. Hundreds of pieces of charcoal littered the hard calcite floor, probably the remnants of torches used by the Paleolithic artists.

Stéphanie Thiébault, of the National Center for Scientific Research, examined a number of charcoal samples from the site and determined that they belonged to two varieties of pine (*Pinus silvestris* and *P. nigra*) that no longer grow in the Calanque area; nowadays the Alep pine grows there, but this species was not found among the charcoal we analyzed. A preliminary pollen analysis by Thiébault's colleague Michel Girard also revealed that the ancient cave painters had inhabited a bleak landscape with only a few species of trees, among

 Reprinted with permission from *Natural History*, April 1993, pp. 64-70. © 1993 by the American Museum of Natural History.

them *P. silvestris* and birch. Radiocarbon dating methods applied to the charcoal samples indicated that they were 18,440 years old.

These analyses confirmed what Courtin's on-site observations and the photographic studies had already indicated: the art was genuine, and it belonged to a pre-Lascaux period. However, after the discovery was announced in late October 1991, a few specialists publicly expressed doubts about its authenticity. Despite the fact that our evidence had been made public, the controversy went on for months, petering out only after we published a comprehensive technical analysis of the cave in July 1992.

One of the main reasons for this lingering skepticism was that a really important discovery does not always fit into familiar patterns of expectation. Sometimes experts find it painful to have to change long-held assumptions. Therefore, whenever a new painted or engraved cave is discovered, its authenticity can be more convincingly established through physical studies and analyses than by comparing the art with what is known elsewhere. To evaluate newly discovered artworks by the comparative method alone would imply that our knowledge of the 20,000 years of Upper Paleolithic cave art is so complete that it cannot admit of any significant modifications.

The evidence tells us that ancient people went into the Cosquer cave during at least two different periods. During Paleolithic times, the sea level was about 360 feet lower than it is now, and the coast was several miles away from the cliff. When the sea rose dramatically at the end of the Würm Glaciation (about 12,000 years ago) and even later—it is still slowly rising today—more than half the cave was flooded. The whole entrance passageway and the lower part of the main chamber remain underwater, but their huge stalagmites and stalactites could not have formed unless these areas had been free of water for a very long time. Some digital tracings in the soft wall surface are covered with calcite and are still preserved underwater, but only for the first two feet. Below that, the walls have been eroded by water and scoured by tiny mollusks. We can thus safely assume that what remains above water is just part of the art in what must have been one of the greatest decorated caves in Europe.

The first period of activity at the Cosquer cave produced the forty-five stenciled handprints and thousands of finger tracings discovered so far. The two forms must be contemporaneous because although handprints are usually on top of finger tracings, occasionally it is the other way around. This period can also be differentiated from the one that followed because animal paintings and engravings are always superimposed on either digital tracings or handprints and were therefore made later. What we have called Phase 1 is now well dated at about 27,000 years ago by four radiocarbon analyses performed in the laboratory at Gif-sur-Yvette, France. In addition, one piece of charcoal found on the ground was dated at approximately 27,870 years ago and another at 26,360 years. The late Abbé Breuil, France's premier prehistorian, always attributed hand stencils and finger tracings to the beginnings of cave art; radiocarbon results for the handprints confirm his idea of a very early date. In fact, our date of 27,000 years ago is the oldest-known direct date not just for hand stencils but for any painting anywhere in the world.

The hand stencils in Cosquer cave can be compared with those of Gargas, a well-known cave 250 miles away in the Pyrenees. In both caves, the prints were produced by applying hands to the walls and by blowing red or black paint on top of and around them, so that they left a stenciled outline. As in other prehistoric caves, a majority of the hands seem to have incomplete fingers. Early twentieth-century researchers explained the missing finger joints as examples of ritual mutilation, a gruesome hypothesis that has long since been abandoned. Some later specialists argued that severe frostbite or diseases such as ainhum or Raynaud's syndrome could have caused the loss of fingertips, while others thought they were more likely a sort of sign language such as hunters use. Experiments have demonstrated, however, that the Gargas "mutilations" could be duplicated with normal hands. The Cosquer discovery may put an end to the debate since it seems unlikely that the same disease would have struck different human groups such a long distance apart and, even if it had, that both groups would then have recorded their mutilations on cave walls.

Sixteen of the stenciled hands in the Cosquer cave have been tampered with in one way or another. Some have been crisscrossed with deep engravings and are now hardly visible; sections of the calcite on which other handprints had been painted have been deliberately broken off; red dots or lines have been applied to a few more. Compared with other painted caves, this is most unusual. There is no way to tell exactly when this defacing was done. It may well have happened shortly after the hands were stenciled—perhaps they had served their purpose, whatever it was, and were no longer useful. (However, although ours is an untested hypothesis, we believe much more time passed before the tampering took place. When the people of Phase 2 went into the cave, they could not have missed seeing the handprints that bore testimony to long-forgotten magical practices. They may have wanted to eradicate any power the handprints retained, either by destroying them outright or by putting their own signs on top of them.)

Finger tracings in Cosquer cave have no discernible pattern, and this technique is not used to draw animals as it is in other caves. However, hardly any soft area was left untouched; in some cases digital tracings can be as high up as twelve or even fifteen feet, so getting there may have involved the use of a climbing device. Some wall panels are entirely covered with such tracings, perhaps reflecting a desire to demonstrate possession of the whole cave. The stenciled handprints may also have been a symbol of power and possession, so the conjunction of the two during the same period is probably significant.

Following Phase 1, the cave was abandoned for about 8,000 years, unless people used it without leaving any evidence of their presence. We will never know whether this abandonment was deliberate, perhaps because the cave had a reputation for being sacred or maleficent—many such cases are known to ethnographers—or whether it was deserted because the entrance was blocked by rock falls or bushes. Whatever the case, it was probably not abandoned because it was flooded, since so far as we know water entered the chamber only after the end of the last glaciation, thousands of years later.

We believe it was during Phase 2 that all the animal paintings and other engravings were made. This period is well dated at about 18,500 to 19,000 years ago by radiocarbon analyses of the charcoal in some of the paintings, as well as by some charcoal lumps found on the floor. Shortly after the cave's discovery, one of these lumps was dated at 18,400 years old. Another was unfortunately mixed with calcite and sediment and thus gave a less reliable date of between 15,570 and 20,370 years ago. However, three paintings of animals made with charcoal were directly dated (two of them twice) by the recently developed accelerator mass spectrometer. This apparatus requires much less material—about half a milligram of charcoal—than the usual radiocarbon dating technique, and it can therefore be applied to minute charcoal samples from Paleolithic paintings or drawings. Using this technique, the Gif-sur-Yvette laboratory dated the image of a feline head at about 19,000 years old and a horse drawing at 18,500 years.

Animal paintings and engravings seem to have been placed where they are because of the smoothness and the availability of particular surfaces. Sometimes they appear on a wall and at other times on a ceiling. In one case, several large animals—one red deer, two horses, and one ibex—were painted in black on a very low roof, barely one and a half feet from the floor, perhaps by a supine artist.

We have now documented about one hundred images of animals. Horses are the most numerous, making up nearly one-third of the total. In some drawings they are represented by a single head; in others, by the whole animal. Such minute details as the difference in coat color between belly and flank are discernible on one painting. On the same panel are three black horses with an ibex engraved over one of them. Horses are the animals most often depicted in other Upper Paleolithic caves, so their dominant presence in the Cosquer cave is not unusual.

The next most commonly depicted animals are ibexes and chamois, animals that favored the rocky environments that existed during Paleolithic times. All but one of the black ibexes are engraved. Their bodies are accurately proportioned, except for the horns, which in some cases are disproportionately large. Male ibex horns grow longer as the animal ages, so representing an ibex with huge horns may have been a way of emphasizing the animal's maleness and possibly its age.

Also represented are several European bison—some engraved, others painted black. Bison are pictured very frequently in Paleolithic art, but some of the Cosquer cave renditions are unusual. In one example, the bison's body is in profile, the horns are seen frontally, and the head is in three-quarter profile. In another engraving the animal's head is lowered as though in readiness to attack. Among the other images found on the cave walls are deer: one buck is painted and two others engraved, as are several hinds. In addition, two strange animals, one painted and one engraved, each with the same massive body and huge hump, seem to be giant deer, rather like Irish "elk." A feline's head painted in black is also present.

One of the most delightful surprises of the Cosquer cave was its depiction of sea animals. A few paintings and engravings of saltwater fish are known in Upper Paleolithic cave art, but drawings that look like seals had so far only been recorded in two caves, at La Pileta and at Nerja in Andalusia. In the Cosquer cave we found three painted auks, eight seals, three strange engraved figures that might be fish, and seven painted sea creatures that resemble either jellyfish or squid. All this is highly unusual and can only be explained by the cave's seaside location. The seals may have had a special symbolic significance, because unlike the other sea animals depicted in the caves, all of them are represented with spearlike signs on top of them.

The unvarying conventions used in the drawing of the land animals lend unity to Phase 2 and tell us that the period did not last long. Bodies are well proportioned but stiff and lacking anatomical detail. Horns and antlers—and at times ears and legs—are seen from the front, in twisted perspective. An ibex's horns bracket a skull that is not drawn in. Legs are always sketchy and spindly, without hoofs, drawn quickly in the form of a Y. These distinctive artistic conventions indicate an early phase of Paleolithic art, well before Lascaux; and in fact the great age of the paintings was obvious on first examination. The radiocarbon datings of Phase 2 came more as a confirmation than as a surprise. The best comparisons can be made with Ebbou, a cave in the lower valley of the Ardèche, about 100 miles west of the Cosquer cave, where similar animal representations have long been known. In Upper Paleolithic times, people traveled, met other groups, and shared their knowledge as well as their goods. Therefore, we find an overall unity in most Paleolithic art, with "styles" confined to definite periods. Recognizable conventions may have been common to contemporary peoples living hundreds of miles apart, while at the same time unique local features arose in various cave paintings. From this point of view, the Cosquer cave does not depart from the norm.

The discovery of the Cosquer cave is an important event in the history of European Paleolithic art—probably the most important discovery since Lascaux in 1940. There are enough animals represented to allow a detailed analysis of the species chosen and their relative importance, of specific artistic conventions, and of the paintings' relationships to one another and to accompanying symbols. Both phases occurred before Lascaux, adding important new data to our knowledge of that period. Even more important, the solidity of the new dating provides a baseline for understanding the chronology of less well defined sites. Not all departures from the expected norm reflect profound changes in symbolism or culture. Use of sea-animal themes shows the importance of local environment in influencing the choice of images—a lesson that can also be applied elsewhere.

The Cosquer cave will never be open to the public. That cave art should have survived under such conditions is a sort of miracle, due only to the gallery's being sloped up and the cave's not being flooded in its entirety. Changing the natural conditions that prevail now could have disastrous consequences for the paintings, an unacceptable risk. In the next few years, the climate of the cave will be thoroughly studied by means of sensors that will transmit information from the main chamber to an outside laboratory. Meanwhile, the cave will remain sealed, although our photographs enable us to share these remarkable paintings with the world.

WRITING RIGHT

Some written languages are a precise reflection of a people's speech, while others, like English, are a complete mess. Is this alphabetical evolution? Or the unequal application of logic to literacy?

Jared Diamond

Jared Diamond is a contributing editor of DISCOVER, a professor of physiology at the UCLA School of Medicine, a recipient of a MacArthur genius award, and a research associate in ornithology at the American Museum of Natural History. Expanded versions of many of his DISCOVER articles appear in his book The Third Chimpanzee: The Evolution and Future of the Human Animal.

Do you know how to read and write English? You answer, "Of course, Jared Diamond, you dope. How else would I be reading this magazine?" In that case have you ever tried to *explain* the rules behind written English to someone? The logic, say, of spelling the word *seed* as we do instead of *cede, ceed, or sied*? Or why the sound *sh* can be written as *ce* (as in *ocean*), *ti* (as in *nation*), or *ss* (as in *issue*), to name just a few possibilities?

Innumerable examples like these illustrate the notorious difficulties of written English, even for educated adults. As I am now rediscovering through my twin sons in the first grade, English spelling is so inconsistent that children who have learned the basic rules (insofar as there are any) still can't pronounce many written words or spell words spoken to them. Danish writing is also difficult, Chinese and South Korean harder, and Japanese hardest of all. But it didn't have to be that way. French children can at least pronounce almost any written word, though they often cannot spell spoken words. In Finland and North Korea the fit between spoken sounds and written signs is so nearly perfect that the question "How do you spell it?" is virtually unknown.

"Civilized" people have always considered literacy as the divide between themselves and barbarians. Surely, if we civilized English speakers sat down to devise a writing system, we could do as well as Finns or North Koreans. Why, then, is there such variation in the preci-sion of writing systems? With thousands of years of literacy now behind us, are today's writing systems—even imperfect ones like our own—at least more precise than ancient ones, such as Eyptian hieroglyphics? Why do we, or any other people, cling to systems that are demonstrably lousy at doing what they're supposed to do?

Before exploring these questions, we need to remind ourselves of the three basic strategies that underlie writing systems. The strategies differ in the size of the speech unit denoted by one written sign: either a single basic sound, or a whole syllable, or a whole word.

The most widespread strategy in the modern world is the alphabet, which ideally would provide a unique sign—a letter—for every basic sound, or phoneme, of the language. Another widespread strategy employs logograms, written signs that stand for whole words. Before the spread of alphabetic writing, systems heavily dependent on logograms were common and included Egyptian hieroglyphs, Mayan glyphs, and Sumerian cuneiform. Logograms continue to be used today, notably in Chinese and in kanji, the predominant writing system employed by the Japanese.

The third strategy uses a sign for each syllable. For instance, there could be separate signs for the syllables *fa*, *mi*, and *ly*, which could be strung together to write the word *family*. Such syllabaries were common in ancient times, as exemplified by the Linear B writing of Mycenaean Greece. Some persist today, of which the most important is the kana syllabary, used by the Japanese for telegrams, among other things.

I've intentionally termed these three approaches strategies rather than writing systems because no actual writing system employs one strategy exclusively. Like all "alphabetic" writing systems, English uses many logograms, such as numerals and various arbitrary signs—+, $, %, for example—that are not made up of phonetic elements. "Logographic" Egyptian hieroglyphs included many syllabic signs plus a virtual alphabet of individual letters for each consonant.

Writing systems are still coming into existence, consciously designed by trained linguists. Missionaries, for example, are translating the Bible into native languages of New Guinea, and Chinese government linguists are producing writing materials for their tribal peoples. Most such tailor-made systems modify existing alphabets, although some instead invent syllabaries. But those conscious creations are developed by professional linguists, and linguistics itself is barely a few centuries old. How did writing systems arise before that—also through purposeful design, or by slow evolution? Is there any way we can figure out whether Egyptian hieroglyphs, for example, were a conscious creation?

One way of approaching that question is to look at historical examples of systems that we know were consciously designed by nonprofessionals. A prime example is Korea's remarkable hangul alphabet. By the fifteenth century, when this alphabet was invented, Koreans had been struggling for more than 1,000 years with cumbersome adaptations of already cumbersome Chinese writing—a "gift" from their larger, influential neighbor. The unhappy results were described in 1446 by Korea's King Sejong:

"The sounds of our country's language differ from those of the Middle Kingdom [China] and are not confluent with the sounds of our characters. Therefore, among the ignorant people there have been many who, having something they want to put into words, have in the end been unable to express their feelings. I have been distressed because of this, and have newly designed 28 letters, which I wish to have everyone practice at their ease and make convenient for their daily use."

The King's 28 letters have been described by scholars as "the world's best alphabet" and "the most scientific system of writing." They are an ultrarational system devised from scratch to incorporate three unique features.

First, hangul vowels can be distinguished at a glance from hangul consonants: the vowels are written as long vertical or horizontal lines with small attached marks; consonants, meanwhile, are all compact geometric signs. Related vowels or consonants are further grouped by related shapes. For example, the signs for the round vowels *u* and *o* are similar, as are the signs for the velar consonants *g*, *k*, and *kh*.

Even more remarkable, the shape of each consonant depicts the position in which the lips, mouth, or tongue is held to pronounce that letter. For instance, the signs for *n* and *d* depict the tip of the tongue raised to touch the front of the palate; *k* depicts the outline of the root of the tongue blocking the throat. Twentieth-century scholars were incredulous that those resemblances could really be intentional until 1940, when they discovered the original

draft of King Sejong's 1446 proclamation and found the logic explicitly spelled out.

Finally, hangul letters are grouped vertically and horizontally into square blocks corresponding to syllables, separated by spaces greater than those between letters but less than those between words. That's as if the Declaration of Independence were to contain the sentence:

```
A  me  a  cr  a  te  e  qua
ll     n  re  e      d     l
```

As a result, the Korean hangul alphabet combines the advantages of a syllabary with those of an alphabet: there are only 28 signs to remember, but the grouping of signs into larger sound bites facilitates rapid scanning and comprehension.

The Korean alphabet provides an excellent example of the cultural phenomenon of "idea diffusion." That phenomenon contrasts with the detailed copying often involved in the spread of technology: we infer that wheels, for example, began to diffuse across Europe around 3500 B.C. because all those early wheels conformed to the same detailed design. However, the Korean alphabet conformed to no existing design; instead it was the *idea* of writing that diffused to Korea. So too did the idea of square blocks, suggested by the block format of Chinese characters; and so did the idea of an alphabet, probably borrowed from Mongol, Tibetan, or Indian Buddhist writing. But the details were invented from the first principles.

There are many other writing systems that we know were deliberately designed by historical individuals. In addition, there are some ancient scripts that are so regularly organized that we can safely infer purposeful design from them as well, even though nothing has come down to us about their origins.

For example, we have documents dating from the fourteenth century B.C., from the ancient Syrian coastal town of Ugarit, that are written in a doubly remarkable 30-letter alphabet. The letters were formed by a technique then widespread in the Near East called cuneiform writing, in which a reed stylus was pressed into a clay tablet. Depending on the stylus's orientation, a sign could be a wedge-tipped vertical line, a wedge-tipped horizontal line, or a broad wedge.

The Ugaritic alphabet's most striking feature is its regularity. The letterforms include one, two, or three parallel or sequential vertical or horizontal lines; one, two, or three horizontal lines crossed by the same number of vertical lines; and so on. Each of the 30 letters requires, on average, barely three strokes to be drawn, yet each is easily distinguished from the others. The overall result is an economy of strokes and consequently, we assume, a speed of writing and ease of reading. The other remarkable feature of the Ugaritic alphabet is that the letters requiring the fewest strokes may have represented the most frequently heard sounds of the Semitic language then spoken at Ugarit. Again, this would make it easier to write fast.

Those two laborsaving devices could hardly have arisen by chance. They imply that some Ugarit genius sat down and used his or her brain to design the Ugaritic alphabet purposefully. As we shall see, by 1400 B.C. the idea of an alphabet was already hundreds of years old in the Near East. And cuneiform writing was by then nearly 2,000 years old. However, as with King Sejong's 28 letters, the Ugarit genius received only those basic ideas by diffusion, then designed the letterforms and the remaining principles independently.

There were other ancient writing systems with such regular organization and for which we can similarly infer tailor-made creation. Furthermore, evidence suggests that even some highly irregular systems were consciously designed. The clearest example of these is the most famous of all ancient writing systems: Egyptian hieroglyphics, a complex mixture of logograms, syllabic signs, unpronounced signs, and a 24-letter consonantal alphabet. Desite this system's complexity, two facts suggest that the underlying principles were quickly designed and did not evolve through a lengthy process of trial and error. The first is that Egyptian hieroglyphic writing appears suddenly around 3050 B.C. in nearly full-blown form, as annotations to scenes carved on ceremonial objects. Even though Egypt's dry climate would have been favorable for preserving any earlier experiments in developing those signs, no such evidence of gradual development has come down to us.

The other fact arguing for the deliberate creation of Egyptian hieroglyphic writing is that it appears suspiciously soon after the appearance of Sumerian cuneiform a couple of centuries earlier, at a time of intense contact and trade linking Egypt and Sumer. It would be incredible if, after millions of years of human illiteracy, two societies in contact happened independently to develop writing systems within a few hundred years of each other. The most likely explanation, again, is idea diffusion. The Egyptians probably learned the idea and some principles of writing from the Sumerians. The other principles and all the specific forms of the letters were then quickly designed by some Egyptian who was clever, but not quite as clever as Korea's King Sejong.

So far, I've been discussing writing systems created by conscious design. In contrast, other systems evolved by a lengthy process of trial and error, with new features added and old features modified or discarded at different stages. Sumerian cuneiform, the oldest known writing system in the world, is one prime example of such an evolved writing system.

Sumerian cuneiform may have begun around 8000 B.C. in the farming villages of the prehistoric Near East, when clay tokens of various simple shapes were developed for accounting purposes, such as recording numbers of sheep. In the last centuries before 3000 B.C., changes in accounting technology and the use of signs rapidly transformed the tokens into the first system of writing. This included a number of innovations, such as the organization of writing into horizontal lines. The most important, however, was the introduction of phonetic representation. The Sumerians figured out how to depict an abstract noun, one that could not be readily drawn as a picture, with another sign that was depictable and that had the same phonetic pronunciation. For instance, it's hard to draw a recognizable picture of *life*, say, but easy to draw a recognizable picture of *arrow*. In Sumerian, both these words are pronounced *ti*. The resulting ambiguity was resolved by adding a silent sign called a determinative to indicate the category of noun the intended object belonged to. Later the Sumerians expanded this phonetic practice, employing it to write syllables or letters constituting grammatical endings.

While revolutionary, the phonetic signs in Sumerian writing nonetheless fell far short of a complete syllabary or alphabet. Some symbols lacked any written sign, while the same sign could be written in different ways or be read as a word, syllable, or letter. The result was a clumsy mess. Eventually, as with the subsequent users of cuneiform writing and along with the 3,000 years of Egyptian hieroglyphics, all passed into oblivion, vanquished by the advantages of more precise alphabetic writing.

Most areas of the modern world write by means of alphabets because they offer the potential advantage of combining precision with simplicity. Alphabets apparently arose only once in history: among speakers of Semitic languages, roughly in the area from modern Syria to the Sinai, during the second millennium B.C. All the hundreds of ancient and modern alphabets were ultimately derived from that ancestral alphabet, either by idea diffusion or by actually copying and modifying letterforms.

There are two likely reasons that alphabets evolved first among Semites. First, Semitic word roots were specified uniquely by their consonants; vowels merely provided grammatical variations on that consonantal root. (An analogy is the English consonantal root *s-ng*, where vowel variations merely distinguish verb tenses—*sing, sang,* and *sung*—from one another and from the corresponding noun *song*.) As a result, writing Semitic languages with consonants alone still yields much of the meaning. Consequently, the first Semitic alphabet makers did not yet have to confront the added complication of vowels.

The second reason was the Semites' familiarity with the hieroglyphics used by nearby Egypt. As in Semitic languages, Egyptian word roots also depended mainly on consonants. As I've mentioned, Egyptian hieroglyphics actually included a complete set of 24 signs for the 24 Egyptian consonants. The Egyptians never took what would seem (to us) to be the logical next step of using just their alphabet and discarding all their other beautiful but messy signs. Indeed, probably no one would have noticed that the Egyptians even had a consonantal alphabet lost within their messy writing system had it not been for the rise of a true alphabet. Starting around 1700 B.C., though, the Semites did begin experimenting with that logical step.

Restricting signs to those for single consonants was only one crucial innovation that distinguished alphabets from other writing systems. Another helped users memorize the alphabet by placing the letters in a fixed sequence and giving them easy-to-remember names. Our English names are otherwise-meaningless monosyllables ("a," "bee," "cee," "dee," and so forth). The Greek names are equally meaningless polysyllables ("alpha," "beta," "gamma," "delta"). Those Greek names arose, in turn, as slight modifications, for Greek ears, of the Semitic letter names "aleph," "beth," "gimel," "daleth," and so on. But those Semitic names did possess meaning to Semites: they are the words for familiar objects (aleph = ox, beth = house, gimel = camel, daleth = door). Those Semitic words are related "acrophonically" to the Semitic consonants to which they refer—that is, the first letter of the object is also the letter that is named for the object. In addition, the earliest forms of the Semitic letters appear in many cases to be pictures of those same objects.

A third innovation laying the foundations for modern alphabets was the provision for vowels. While Semitic writing could be figured out even without vowel signs, the inclusion of vowels makes it more comprehensible since vowels carry the grammatical information. For Greek and most other non-Semitic languages, however, reading is scarcely possible without vowel signs. (Try reading the example "ll mn r crtd ql," used earlier in the Korean hangul format.)

The Semites began experimenting in the early days of their alphabet by adding small extra letters to indicate selected vowels (modern Arabic and Hebrew indicate vowels by dots or lines sprinkled above or below the consonantal letters). The Greeks improved on this idea in the eighth century B.C., becoming the first people to indicate all vowels systematically by the same types of letters used for consonants. The Greeks derived the forms of five vowel letters by co-opting letters used in the Phoenician Semitic alphabet for consonantal sounds lacking in Greek.

From those earliest Semitic alphabets, lines of evolutionary modifications lead to the modern Ethiopian, Arabic, Hebrew, Indian, and Southeast Asian alphabets. But the line most familiar to us was the one that led from the Phoenicians to the Greeks, on to the Etruscans, and finally to the Romans, whose alphabet with slight modifications is the one used to print this magazine.

As a group, alphabets have undergone nearly 4,000 years of evolution. Hundreds of alphabets have been adapted for individual languages, and some of those alphabets have now had long separate evolutionary histories. The result is that they differ greatly in how precisely they match signs to sounds, with English,

linguists agree, being the worst of all. Even Danish, the second worst, doesn't come close to us in atrocity.

How did English spelling get to be so imprecise? (As a reminder of how bad it is, recall seven fascinating ways we can pronounce the letter *o*: try *horse, on, one, oven, so, to,* and *woman.*) Part of the reason is simply that it has had a long time to deteriorate—the English language has been written since about A.D. 600. Even if a freshly created writing system at first represents a spoken language precisely, pronunciation changes with time, and the writing system must therefore become increasingly imprecise if it is not periodically revised. But German has been written for nearly as long as has English, so that's not the sole answer. Another twist is spelling reforms. As anyone familiar with English and German books printed in the nineteenth century knows, nineteenth-century spelling is essentially identical to modern spelling for English, but not for German. That's the result of a major German spelling reform toward the end of the nineteenth century.

The tragicomic history of English spelling adds to the horror. Those Irish missionaries who adapted the Latin alphabet to Old English did a good job of fitting signs to sounds. But disaster struck with the Norman conquest of England in 1066. Today only about half of English words are of Old English origin; the rest are mostly derived from French and Latin. English words were borrowed from the French using French spellings, according to rules very different from English spelling rules. That was bad enough, but as English borrowings from French continued, French pronunciation itself was changing without much change in French spelling. The result? The French words borrowed by English were spelled according to a whole spectrum of French spelling rules.

English pronunciation itself changed even more radically with time; for example, all written vowels came to sound the same in unstressed syllables. (That is, when pronounced in normal speech, the *a* in *elegant, e* in *omen, i* in *raisin, o* in *kingdom,* and *u* in *walrus* all sound much the same.) As new words were borrowed from different languages, they were spelled according to the whim of the individual writer or printer. But many English printers were trained in Germany or the Netherlands and brought back still other foreign spelling conventions besides French ones. Not until Samuel Johnson's dictionary of 1755 did English spelling start to become standardized.

While English may have the worst writing system in Europe, it is not the worst in the world. Chinese is even more difficult because of the large number of signs that must be independently memorized. As I said earlier, probably the most gratuitously difficult modern writing system is Japan's kanji. It originated from Chinese writing signs and now has the added difficulty that signs can variously be given Japanese pronunciations or modifications of various past Chinese pronunciations. An attempted remedy that compounds the confusion for Japanese readers is the insertion of spellings in yet another writing system, the kana syllabary, for hard-to-read kanji. As George

Sansom, a leading authority on Japanese, put it, back in the 1920s: "One hesitates for an epithet to describe a writing system which is so complex that it needs the aid of another system to explain it."

Do sub-ideal writing systems really make it harder for adults to read, or for children to learn to read? Many observations make clear that the answer is yes. In 1928 Turkey switched to the Latin alphabet from the Arabic alphabet, which has the twin disadvantages of a complex vowel notation and of changing the forms of letters depending on where they stand within a word. As a result of the switch, Turkish children learned to read in half the time formerly required. Chinese children take at least ten times longer to learn to read traditional Chinese characters than pinyin, a Chinese adaptation of the Latin alphabet. British children similarly learned to read faster and better with a simplified English spelling termed the Initial Teaching Alphabet than with our conventional spelling. Naturally, the educational problems caused by inconsistent spelling can be overcome by increased educational effort. For example, Japan, with the modern world's most difficult spelling system, paradoxically has one of the world's highest literacy rates—thanks to intensive schooling. Nevertheless, for a given educational effort, a simpler spelling system results in more literate adults.

Hebrew provides interesting proof that not only spelling but also letter shapes make a difference. Hebrew writing has several sets of extremely similar letters: only one letter is distinctively tall, and only one letter stands out by dipping below the line (ignoring the special forms of Hebrew letters at the ends of words). As a result, a study suggests that, on the average, readers of Hebrew have to stare at print for longer than do readers of Latin alphabets in order to distinguish those indistinctive letter shapes. That is, distinctive letter shapes permit faster reading.

Since details of writing systems do affect us, why do so many countries refuse to reform their writing systems? There appear to be several reasons for this seeming perverseness: aesthetics, prestige, and just plain conservatism. Chinese writing and Arabic writing are widely acknowledged to be beautiful and are treasured for that reason by their societies; so were ancient Egyptian hieroglyphics. In Japan and Korea, as in China, mastery of Chinese characters implies education and refinement and carries prestige. It's especially striking that Japan and South Korea stick to their fiendishly difficult Chinese-based characters when each country already has available its own superb simple script: kana for the Japanese, and the hangul alphabet for Korea.

Unlike some of these writing systems, our awful English spelling is not considered beautiful or prestigious, yet all efforts to reform it have failed. Our only excuse is conservatism and laziness. If we wanted, we could easily improve our writing to the level of Finland's, so that computer spell-check programs would be unneeded and no child beyond fourth grade would make spelling errors. For example, we should match English spelling consistently to English sounds, as does the Finnish alphabet. We should junk our superfluous letter *c* (always replaceable by either *k* or *s*), and we should coin new letters for sounds now spelled with arbitrary letter combinations (such as *sh* and *th*). Granted, spelling is part of our cultural heritage, and English spelling reform could thus be viewed as a cultural loss. But crazy spelling is a part of our culture whose loss would go as unmourned as the loss of our characteristic English medieval torture instruments.

But before you get too excited about those glorious prospects for reform, reflect on what happened to Korea's hangul alphabet. Although it was personally designed by King Sejong, not even a king could persuade his conservative Sinophilic countrymen to abandon their Chinese-derived script. South Korea persists with the resulting mess even today. Only North Korea under Premier Kim Il Sung, a dictator far more powerful than King Sejong ever was, has adopted the wonderful hangul alphabet as the writing norm. Lacking a president with Kim Il Sung's power to ram unwanted blessings down our throats, we Americans shall continue to suffer under spelling rules that become more and more archaic as our pronunciation keeps changing.

The origin of numbers

The story of a great intellectual adventure

Tony Lévy

TONY LÉVY,
of France, is a research associate at his country's National Centre for Scientific Research (CNRS) and teaches the history of science at the University of Paris VIII-Saint Denis. His main centre of academic interest is the Hebraic mathematical tradition in the Middle Ages and its relationship to the Arab and Latin traditions. He is the author of a study on the history of the idea of infinity entitled *Figures de l'infini. Les mathématiques au miroir des cultures,* published by Editions du Seuil, Paris, 1987.

IT is generally accepted that some animal species are capable of perceiving quantitative differences, such as a chick missing from the brood or a more or less abundant food supply. The human infant also shows a kind of quantitative perception in relation to familiar objects long before it is able to speak. The development of language and the use of words widen and refine this quantitative perception, so that some cultures have invented names for vast multiplicities such as the stars in the sky or the sand on the seashore, and have even attempted to quantify infinity.

■ Counting and recounting

Of all the powers conferred by speech, that of naming numbers certainly seems to be among the oldest. After all, "numbering" means organizing and putting in order the real world and our ideas about it. This is apparent in the idiom of different languages.

In some European languages, for example, there is a strong similarity or even an overlapping between words meaning "count" and words meaning "tell": *compter/raconter* in French, *contare/raccontare* in Italian, *contar/contar* in Spanish and Portuguese, and *zählen/erzählen* in German. In modern English the word *tale* denotes a story, but the word *teller* can be used to designate a bank cashier as well as someone who tells a story. So it is not surprising that this similarity is found in older Indo-European languages. Etymologically, the Sanskrit term for number, *sankhya,* denotes a way of saying things. The Greek word *logos,* denoting both reckoning and also word or speech, derives these different meanings from the old sense of the verb *lego,* to collect, choose, gather, and hence to reckon, count, enumerate, and then to recount or say. Similarly the Greek word *arithmos* means both number in the arithmetical sense and also adjustment or disposition. This ambivalence later shifted to the Latin *numerus* and its derivatives. The adjective *numerosus* means both numerous and harmonious.

Moving away from the Indo-European languages, we find a similar situation in two Semitic languages, Arabic and Hebrew. In Arabic the word for account is *hisab,* from the triliteral root h.s.b. The verb "to count" is *hasaba,* which with one vowel change becomes *hasiba,* to imagine, believe. Likewise with Hebrew, which from one root, s.p.r., constructs the words for book, *sepher;* number, *mispar;* and story, *sippur.*

■ Words and numbers

Whatever numerical facility a given language may have developed, the names it uses for num-

 Reprinted with permission from *The UNESCO Courier,* November 1993, pp. 9-13.

bers seem to go back to a very early period in the history of that language and have, moreover, remained amazingly stable through the ages. They are reminders of human strivings since time immemorial to bestow names on the diversity of the real world, and occasionally they provide us with a glimpse of the process that preceded and underlay the naming of the various orders of quantity.

One example, that of the number 9, illustrates the interest—as well as the difficulty—of historical analysis. In many Indo-European languages the word for this number is strikingly close to the adjective conveying the idea of newness: Latin *novem/novus*, French *neuf/neuf*, English nine/new, German *neun/neu*, Sanskrit *nava/navas*. Combining the disciplines of the linguist and the historian, one is tempted to explain the phenomenon as follows: at the dawn of counting, the number 9 was perceived as a "new" level after 8. The word for 8 (*octo, huit, eight, acht, ashta* in the five languages cited above) could be derived in its turn from a grammatical dual of the word for 4 (*quattuor, quatre, four, vier, tchatvara*). In the light of many other linguistic and cultural phenomena it turns out that the number 4 really does represent a new stage in our perception of numbers. We can easily discern one, two, three or four objects without needing to count them, but from five onwards we have to count them before we can say how many there are.

This is an attractive hypothesis, although in such a field it is impossible to be dogmatic. If we pursue our linguistic investigations a little further, we can even find new arguments to support it. Most Semitic languages use phonetically related terms to denote the number 9: Akkadian uses *tishu*, Hebrew *tesha'*, Syriac *tscha'*, Arabic *tis'un*, and Ethiopian *tes'u*. Arabic grammar indicates that the word *tis'un* is derived from the verbal root *wasa'a*, "to be or become wide". Thus it is possible that the notion of "newness" observed in the Indo-European languages recurs in the Semitic ones.

■ Ordering, combining and counting

Any number system, however elementary, presupposes the adoption of a small number of symbols—words, pictograms or graphic signs—structured according to two principles. A principle of order or arrangement distinguishes the first symbol (one) from the second (two) and if necessary from the third (three) etc., and a principle of grouping or combining interrupts the series of distinct individual symbols by introducing a symbol of a higher order of magnitude which is then combined with the previous symbol to continue the system. Thus "one, two, three…, **ten**, ten-one, ten-two…, ten-ten or a **hundred,** a hundred and one, a hundred and two…" is called a base-10 system or decimal system.

But other bases have been or still are used: base two (the binary system), five (quinary), twenty (vigesimal) and sixty (sexagesimal). It seems likely that the bases 5, 10 and 20 were

English	eighteen	8-10
French	dix-huit	10-8
German	acht-zehn	8-10
Ancient Greek	okto-kai-deka	8 and 10
Modern Greek	deka-okto	10-8
Latin	decem et octo	10 and 8
Latin	duo-de-viginti	2 from 20
Lithuanian	ashtuno-lika	8 left over (from 10)
Breton	tri-ouch	3-6
Welsh	deu-naw	2-9
Mexican	caxtulli-om-mey	15 and 3
Finnish	kah-deksan-toista	2 (from) 10 (in the) second (ten)

(from K. Menninger, *Number Words and Number Symbols*)

Different ways of forming the number 18.

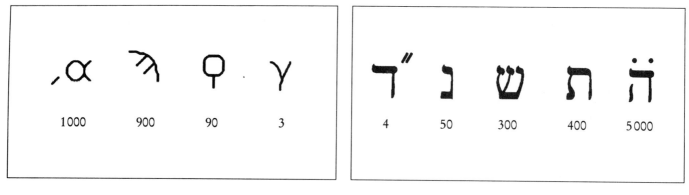

Figure I. Alphabetical number systems
1993 in Greek alphabetical numeration (left) 5754 in Hebrew alphabetical numeration (right)

originally chosen because of their relationship to characteristics of the human body, and traces of this remain in some oral counting systems. In Api, the spoken language of the New Hebrides, the word *luna* denotes a hand, and also the number 5; the number 2 is *lua,* and 10 is of course *lualuna*—literally, two hands.

The variety of the rules governing the formation of the names of numbers is a striking instance of human cultural and linguistic diversity. The table on the opposite page illustrates how the number eighteen is formed in various languages.

We must recognize, however, that little is known about the methods of reckoning used in very ancient times. Certainly the numbers for which words already existed had to be represented symbolically. In addition to verbal numeration manual gestures were used (counting on the fingers) or physical devices such as an abacus, a counting frame, a sandtable or a knotted cord. To the historian, this representational numeration seems in some cases to foreshadow certain forms of written numeration.

■ Counting systems, writing systems and alphabets

The advent of writing resulted in a fantastic growth in numerical capacity. Written counting systems or numerations may be divided into two main types: additive numeration, in which a number is produced by directly adding together the numerical value of its component symbols, as in Ancient Egyptian hieroglyphic numeration and in Roman numerals, and positional or place-value numeration, in which the value of a symbol (units, tens, hundreds, etc.) is determined by the position it occupies. Thus 1034 (written from the left to the right, "one-zero-three-four") represents one (thousand) plus zero (hundreds) plus three (tens) plus four (units). This system, which requires the use of a zero (a blank space or a graphic sign) appeared historically only in four civilizations with written languages: in Mesopotamia, in China, in ancient India and in the Maya civilization of central America.

Though writing first appeared in Sumer during the fourth millennium B.C., alphabetical scripts were doubtless invented in the middle of the second. The best-known and most influential script was that developed by a trading and seafaring people, the Phoenicians, who spoke a Semitic language. It was adopted or adapted by other languages in the same group (Hebrew, Aramaic and later Arabic), as well as by other languages less closely related to Phoenician. The Phoenician alphabet only transcribed consonants, of which there were 22. The Greeks later added vowels to it. The Latin alphabets, descended directly from the Greek, retain the order of the Phoenician alphabet almost unchanged.

Mastery of this extraordinary tool led to the development of a number of counting systems including the ancient Hebrew system, the so-called "learned" Greek counting system, and the Arabic counting system known as *hisab al-jummal* or *hisab abjadi.* These were alphabetical additive numerations, whose principle is extremely simple provided the user knows the order and numerical value of the letters of the alphabet. The first nine letters correspond to

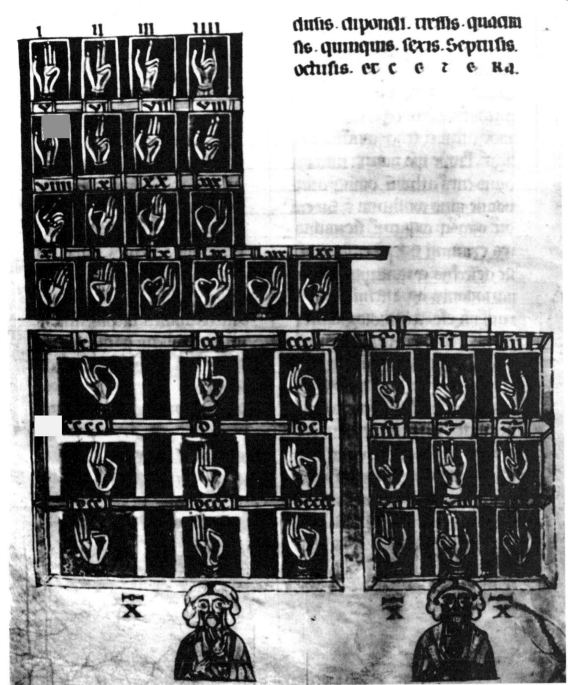

A system for counting on the fingers is shown in this illustration from a 13th-century Spanish manuscript.

the nine digits (1, 2 , 3, . . ., 9), and the next nine to the nine tens (10, 20, 30 . . . 90). The remaining letters are used to denote the hundreds. Thus alphabetical numbers are written in descending order of numerical value of their constituent letters, in the direction of the script (**figure 1**).

Since the alphabet comprises only a small number of different signs (22 in Hebrew, 28 in Arabic and 27 in Greek), this counting system initially only allowed the representation of numbers below 10,000. Various expedients were available for going further, but it became difficult to handle large numbers. Consequently scholars, particularly astronomers, had to adopt the far more efficient Babylonian sexagesimal positional number system and adapt it to their script. In principle this numeration requires 59 different symbols plus a sign for zero. These "sexagesimal digits" would often be expressed in alphabetical numeration, thus combining the power of positional notation with the convenience of alphabetical notation.

■ A legacy from India

The decimal positional numeration system with a zero, as developed in India, gradually came to

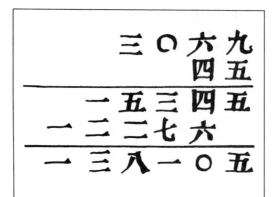

Figure 2. Use of the zero in ancient China **Multiplication of 3069 by 45 (from a 14th-century Chinese mathematical treatise).**

supersede other written systems and is now in virtually universal use. It spread slowly, however, and in a complex fashion.

China, for instance, acquired a decimal positional system of its own quite early on, independently of the Indian one, but one which did not use a zero. It may even be supposed that the Chinese could have designed a system like the Indian positional system on their own. But the introduction of the zero into the Chinese positional notation seems to have been of Indian origin (**figure 2**).

Nowadays schoolchildren in the West learn to count with "Arabic numbers": but what exactly are they? We owe our knowledge of the principles of Indian arithmetic to Arab scholars of the eighth century. In about 774 A.D. an Indian scholar passing through Baghdad made known a Sanskrit book on astronomy which adopted the principles of "Indian arithmetic" (*hisab al-hind*), and al-Fazzari's Arabic translation of this book represented the first stage in the history of "Indian arithmetic" in the Muslim-Arab empire. The Arabic word *sifr*, "emptiness", is a translation of the Sanskrit *sunya*. It

was chosen in the ninth century to represent zero. *Sifr* gave rise to the Latin *cifra* in the thirteenth century, the French *chiffre* in the fourteenth century and the German *Ziffer* in the fifteenth century. It is also the forebear of the English *cipher*. By a parallel development *sifr* gave rise to the Latin *zefirum* in the thirteenth century, the Italian *zefiro/zevero* in the fifteenth, and finally the word *zero*. Western terminology is unquestionably Hindu-Arabic.

We must, however, distinguish between the spread of knowledge about the principles of Indian numeration and the development of the graphic signs used for its notation. The relationship between the written forms recorded from India and those that appeared in the Arab world from the ninth century onwards is not clear. Moreover there is a difference between eastern and western Arabic numerals. While the principles of Indian numeration spread in Latin in the medieval West in the twelfth century, the figures we call "Hindu-Arabic" spread through intermediaries that have not all been identified, sometimes borrowing from earlier Roman or Visigothic forms in Spain.

Corn in the New World: A Relative Latecomer

John Noble Wilford

A new technique for dating ancient organic matter has upset thinking about the origins of agriculture in the Americas. The earliest known cultivation of corn, it now seems, occurred much more recently than had been thought—4,700 years ago, not 7,000—and scientists are perplexed as they ponder the implications.

The new date means that people in the New World, in the Tehuacán valley of the central Mexican state of Puebla in particular, probably did not begin growing their most important crop until as much as 4,000 or 5,000 years after the beginning of agriculture in the Old World. Hunter-gatherers who settled along the Jordan River valley managed to domesticate wild progenitors of wheat and barley as early as 9,000 to 10,000 years ago, and thus became, as far as anyone knows, the first farmers anywhere. Perhaps such a lengthened time gap could suggest clues to the circumstances favoring the transition to agriculture, one of the foremost innovations in human culture.

Settlement in the Americas preceded cultivation.

The new evidence, said Dr. Gayle J. Fritz, a paleobotanist at Washington University in St. Louis, "makes it necessary to begin building new models for agricultural evolution in the New World."

But reliable as they may be, are the new ages definitive? Because all the ancient corn specimens examined so far were fully domesticated, scientists suspect they have yet to find the intermediate and earliest examples of cultivated corn. They may have been looking in the wrong places.

Dr. Lawrence Kaplan, a botanist at the University of Massachusetts in Boston and a specialist in dating ancient plants, cautioned that it was premature to revise the chronology of New World agriculture. "We ought to reserve judgment on whether the maize for Tehuacán is really as old as it's going to get in Mexico," he said. "Somewhere else, there may be older stuff."

Botanists are urging archeologists to widen their search for evidence of early agriculture in Mexico, the only country where the nearest wild relatives of maize are native. Look in places where the wild teosinte grows, botanists recommend.

In many parts of Mexico, teosinte, an annual plant that shows the greatest biochemical similarity to domesticated corn, is still called Madre de maiz, "mother of maize." The plant thrives in the verdant Balsas River basin, 150 miles west of the Tehuacán valley, but the area has never been systematically surveyed. Rivers and lakes, moreover, are just the places where animals go to drink and are easy prey, where fish can supplement the diet and the soil is moist for planting, all conditions encouraging early settlements and farming.

"The whole issue of origins of agriculture in the Americas is still out there for people to try and figure out," said Dr. Bruce D. Smith, an archeologist at the National Museum of Natural History of the Smithsonian Institution and the author of "The Emergence of Agriculture," a book published last fall by Scientific American Library.

For several decades, archeological research in this field had been somewhat dormant. Archeologists may have been discouraged by the paucity of artifacts among the remains of corncobs in the Tehuacán caves; nothing much to reconstruct the lives of the people who were the corn farmers. Besides, expeditions could count on more fruitful hunting in the ruins of the Olmecs, Maya and Aztecs, whose civilizations afforded more flamboyant discoveries.

Planting in the Old World dates from 5,000 years earlier.

So it was that the timing and pattern of early farming in the New World seemed fixed beyond serious questioning. Corn, or maize, known scientifically as Zea mays, had been established as the first American crop. It was the dietary staple in Mexico and eventually became the

2. THE BEGINNINGS OF CULTURE, AGRICULTURE, AND URBANIZATION

New Theory Of New World

A revised and much later date for the earliest known domesticated corn, based on new dating methods, is making scientists rethink the chronology of Western Hemisphere civilization.

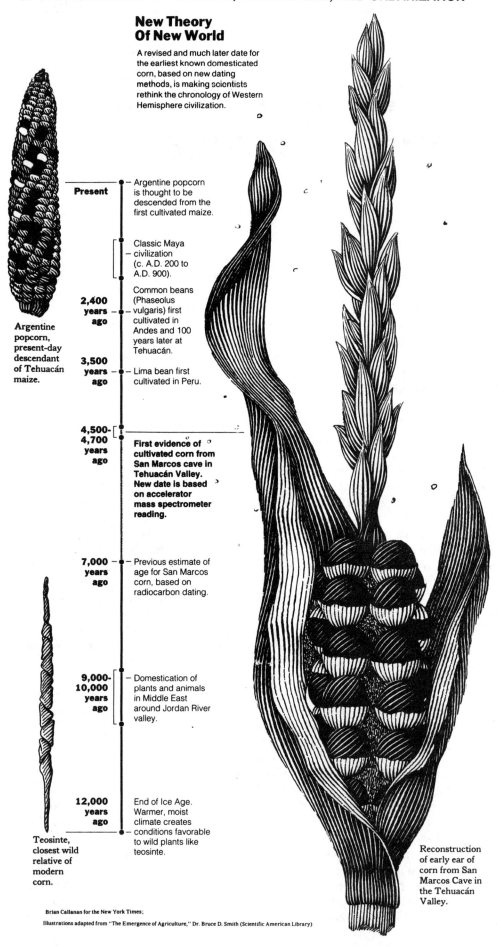

Argentine popcorn, present-day descendant of Tehuacán maize.

Present	Argentine popcorn is thought to be descended from the first cultivated maize.
	Classic Maya civilization (c. A.D. 200 to A.D. 900).
2,400 years ago	Common beans (Phaseolus vulgaris) first cultivated in Andes and 100 years later at Tehuacán.
3,500 years ago	Lima bean first cultivated in Peru.
4,500-4,700 years ago	**First evidence of cultivated corn from San Marcos cave in Tehuacán Valley. New date is based on accelerator mass spectrometer reading.**
7,000 years ago	Previous estimate of age for San Marcos corn, based on radiocarbon dating.
9,000-10,000 years ago	Domestication of plants and animals in Middle East around Jordan River valley.
12,000 years ago	End of Ice Age. Warmer, moist climate creates conditions favorable to wild plants like teosinte.

Teosinte, closest wild relative of modern corn.

Reconstruction of early ear of corn from San Marcos Cave in the Tehuacán Valley.

Brian Callanan for the New York Times;

Illustrations adapted from "The Emergence of Agriculture," Dr. Bruce D. Smith (Scientific American Library)

same throughout most of the two continents.

This decisive cultural step, planting and harvesting, was confidently dated at 7,000 years ago, based on standard radiocarbon analysis of material found in the Tehuacán caves in the 1960's by Dr. Richard S. Mac-Neish of the Andover Foundation for Archeological Research in Andover, Mass. Buried in the dry sediments were two-inch-long ears of corn, each with eight rows of six to nine tiny popcorn-like kernels—a poor foretaste of sweet corn on the cob.

But one thing kept puzzling some scholars. These early New World farmers appeared to be seasonally mobile hunter-gatherers who visited the Tehuacán valley just long enough to plant and harvest a crop, then moved on to where the hunting might be better. Indeed, it has long been a tenet of pre-Columbian anthropology that it was the domestication of corn, providing a steady source of food and thus increasing populations and encouraging a more sedentary life, that cleared the way for complex societies.

In the Old World, though, the sequence was reversed: sedentary life first, then agriculture. People there typically settled into communities near where wild animals and plants were abundant and then over time learned to increase and regularize their food supply through domestication of certain animals and plants, thus making the transition from hunting and gathering to agriculture. The more recent corn date, Dr.

Search for Ancient Agriculture
Archeologists suggest looking for evidence of early farming in places where corn's wild ancestor is still found.

The New York Times

Fritz thinks, could have given the hunter-gatherers more time to experiment with possible sedentary living before taking up agriculture.

"I would not be at all surprised to find sedentary life before agriculture, probably in river and lake areas," she said. "But we don't have any evidence for it. We haven't really been looking."

In her own research in northeastern Louisiana, Dr. Fritz has already found evidence of other early American societies of hunter-gatherers leading sedentary village life. This way of life was practiced in many places in eastern North America in the centuries before Columbus. The search for evidence of this in Mesoamerica also stands high on the agenda of research into early American farming.

"The problem in Mexico is, the information we have on early sedentary villages is not very good," said Dr. T. Douglas Price, a University of Wisconsin archeologist who specializes in the study of early agriculture. "We've been trying to encourage more people to investigate the archeology of the early farmers."

Many of the old assumptions about New World agriculture are being reexamined in light of the new age estimates for early corn, reported in 1989 by Dr. Austin Long and colleagues at the University of Arizona in Tucson. The scientists applied the new technology of accelerator mass spectrometry, which overcomes a serious limitation of conventional radiocarbon dating: the sample-size barrier.

In the standard method, developed in the 1940's, scientists could determine the age of once-living material, a piece of wood, cloth or corncob, by detecting and counting the decay rate of the radioactive isotope carbon-14 in the material. But this meant destroying a large sample to get the five grams of carbon necessary for the test. In the case of the early Mexican corn, the specimens were too small and too few to part with.

So archeologists had done the next best thing. For the destructive radiocarbon tests, they used large samples of other organic material, usually charcoal found in the same sediments with the corncobs and kernels and thus assumed to be contemporary. It was an indirect measure and not very reliable, as they have found out. Seeds and other small objects have a way of being displaced in sediments, shifting up or down by the actions of burrowing animals, moisture and other disturbances.

With accelerator mass spectrometry, scientists can determine the age

Reproduced by permission of Robert S. Peabody Museum of Archaeology, Phillips Academy, Andover, Mass.
Newly redated maize cobs from San Marcos Cave in Tehuacán Valley. Structures that enclosed kernels are still visible.

of samples as small as one-thousandth the size of those required for the conventional method. Just a pinch of a cob or husk will do; not the whole thing. Rather than counting decay events, the particle accelerator separates and counts directly the carbon-14 atoms. This gives the time elapsed since the material was alive.

In addition to the corn dating, the technique has been used by archeologists to date the skulls of horses found with chariot remains in burial mounds in Kazakhstan, leading them to conclude that the earliest known chariots came from this region 4,000 years ago. This is earlier than Russian scientists had estimated, and

several centuries before the best evidence for chariots in the Middle East. Also, French and Spanish scientists recently used the technique to show that painted bison on the ceiling of the Altamira Cave in northern Spain were painted not at the same time but centuries apart.

The earliest Mexican corn samples proved to be 4,700 years old; others were as recent as 1,600 years old. Dr. Kaplan has used the same technology to test the ages of primitive beans in Mexico and South America, once placed at 6,000 to 8,000 years ago. Like corn, domesticated beans, Phaseolus vulgaris, also turn out to be younger than thought—about 2,300 years at Tehuacán and 2,400 years in the Andes. Lima beans from Peru were dated at 3,500 years.

Which came first: sedentary life or agriculture?

As the new findings undermined the record for a much earlier New World agriculture, Dr. Fritz grew impatient with textbooks and some professors who persisted in using the old corn dates and with researchers doing little to incorporate the new dates in their interpretations of early agriculture.

Writing in the Journal Current Anthropology last June, she urged colleagues to "forge ahead with drastic revisions for New World agricultural beginnings based on the earliest good dates available" rather than to cling to chronologies unsupported by solid evidence.

Several scientists, notably Dr. Do-lores Piperno of the Smithsonian Institution Tropical Research Institute in Panama, insist that they have pollen and other evidence for domesticated corn and other plants in South America 7,000 years ago. But Dr. Fritz said she remained unconvinced by claims that corn farming had spread into Central America and northern South America before 5,500 years ago. Other botanists familiar with the work tended to side with Dr. Fritz.

Acknowledging that Dr. Fritz was correct to wake up scientists to the new data, Dr. Kaplan of the University of Massachusetts cautioned that the new dates for corn and beans "in no way represent the ultimate answer" concerning the fateful time at which early Americans turned to farming and cultivated a wild plant that became corn. After it was discovered by the rest of the world, corn became the third largest crop, after wheat and rice.

The Eloquent Bones
of Abu Hureyra

*The daily grind in an early Near Eastern
agricultural community left revealing marks
on the skeletons of the inhabitants*

Theya Molleson

*Theya Molleson works in the paleontology
department of the Natural History Museum in London, where she does research
on the effects of the environment on the
human skeleton, both in life and after
burial. She also lectures on human osteol-
ogy at Birkbeck College of the University of
London. Molleson studied geology at the
University of London and social anthropology at the University of Edinburgh.*

Reconstructing how people lived in ancient times is like detective work: clues are scarce. Inferences must be made from spotty evidence such as bones, durable artifacts and the ruins of habitations. In my work as a paleontologist at the Natural History Museum in London, I knew that a collection of early Neolithic human bones had been brought to England from ex-cavations at Abu Hureyra, in what is now northern Syria. The archaeological work was done in 1972 and 1973—shortly before the site was due to be flooded by the reservoir behind the new Tabqa dam—by Andrew M. T. Moore, then at the University of Oxford [see "A Pre-Neolithic Farmers' Village on the Euphrates," by Andrew M. T. Moore; SCIENTIFIC AMERICAN, August 1979]. The

skeletal remains of about 162 individuals—75 children and 87 adults, of whom 44 were female, 27 male and 16 of undetermined sex—have been identified from seven trenches dug at Abu Hureyra. The deposits span about 3,000 years.

It seemed to me and my colleagues that the bones might reveal details of the daily life of the Abu Hureyra people and therefore that of other Neolithic groups whose members had made the transition from hunting and gathering to an agricultural economy. The marks of life experience—some wrought by disease, some by work—can be imprinted on the bones and teeth of the skeleton. Close study has indeed yielded a fund of information that might not otherwise have been discovered, particularly about the women of the community.

Abu Hureyra was inhabited in two different times. The first one was from roughly 11,500 to 10,000 years ago, just preceding the development of agriculture. The pre-Neolithic people of this settlement gathered a wide range of wild seeds, including lentils, einkorn, rye, barley, hackberries and pistachios. They also hunted the gazelles that migrated toward the Euphrates in the spring. The second settlement followed an unexplained hiatus of 200 years. The early Neolithic people of the later settlement cultivated a range of domestic cereals: emmer, einkorn, oats, barley, chickpeas and lentils. All these plants required preparation before they could be eaten. The preparation took much labor and time.

The record of this effort can be read in the bones of the people of Abu Hureyra. One of the first skeletal traits we noticed were signs of extra and sometimes excessive strains caused by the carrying of loads, most likely game,

grain and building materials. The evidence was most conspicuous among the young. If adolescents are required to labor in this way, one can expect changes in the shape of the upper vertebrae. That is what we found. It is also probable that the loads were carried on the head: the hook-shaped parts of the vertebrae in the neck are enlarged, indicating that the bones developed a buttressing support. Otherwise, the neck might have wobbled under the weight of a heavy burden. In some individuals, we found degenerative changes in the neck vertebrae that may have arisen from injuries sustained by bearing weight.

These cases were not common. In fact, the general health of the people appears to have been good, except for bone deformities that turned up repeatedly: collapsed vertebrae (always the last dorsal one) and grossly arthritic big toes. These malformations were associated with evidence of muscular arms and legs. Clearly, the bones bespoke a demanding physical activity that was also injurious.

For a time, we actually entertained the idea that the people of Abu Hureyra had engaged in some sport or athletics, but crippled ballerinas seemed unlikely to have appeared during the Neolithic. We remained mystified until a colleague who was vacationing in Egypt noticed that the kneeling suppliants depicted on temple walls always had their toes curled forward. This observation suggested that some activity that involved kneeling had produced the pathology that we observed among the residents of Abu Hureyra.

During the excavations, Moore had found saddle querns in the rooms of the houses, abandoned after they had

last been used. (A quern is a primitive stone mill for grinding grain by hand; a saddle quern is so named because it resembles a saddle in shape.) I was convinced that the kneeling action consisted of long hours spent grinding cereal grains on the saddle quern. Gordon Hillman of the University of London, who had worked on the plant remains from the site, was not so sure. He pointed out that removing the outer husk of the seeds by pounding them with a pestle in a mortar—another chore done while kneeling—would have been an essential step in preparing the grains. Probably both tasks were involved in creating the vertebral deformities, but it is unlikely that mortar-and-pestle work caused the toe deformities: the laborer could have changed positions while pounding but not while grinding.

So it was the preparation of grain for eating that was the most demanding and labor-intensive activity of the settlement, as it still is in many places. The grain had to be pounded every day because the seeds would not keep once they were dehusked. The dehusking with mortar and pestle and the subsequent grinding in a saddle quern would have taken many hours. What we had found on the bones, then, were the telltale signs of long hours spent at such labor. Also evident were marks of injuries, perhaps caused by using the saddle quern with too much enthusiasm or haste.

Querns and rubbing stones found at Abu Hureyra suggest how such wear and tear came about. The querns were set directly on the ground rather than mounted on a plinth or other raised structure, a practice followed in later times (debris surrounding the querns

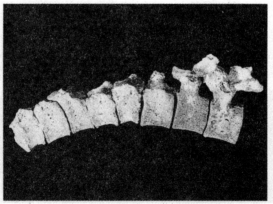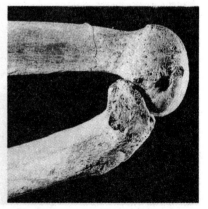

GRINDING GRAIN on a saddle quern, a daily task for Abu Hureyra females, put strain on several of the joints. On her knees, the woman repeatedly pushed the rubbing stone forward and then pulled back to her starting position. The activity, taking up several hours a day, affected particularly the bones shown above: the big toe, the spine and the leg. The toe is hyperflexed and damaged; the spine shows bony growths of the vertebrae; the leg, pictured with the femur (thigh bone) at the top and the tibia (shin bone) below it, has a buttress along the shaft of the femur and bony growths at the knee.

supports the conclusion that each was found where it had been used). Thus, the individual using the quern would have had to kneel.

Picture the operation. The grinder puts the grain on the quern and holds the rubbing stone with both hands. On her knees (yes, it was women's work, as we shall see), with toes bent forward, she pushes the stone toward the far end of the quern, ending the stroke with her upper body almost parallel to the ground so her arms are at or near the level of her head. On reaching the far end of the quern, she jerks back to her starting position. I call this part of the grinding action the recoil. The movement that raises the arms as the grinder pushes forward employs the deltoid muscles of the shoulder. During this stroke, the arms also turn inward, a motion accomplished by the biceps muscles.

It is precisely the places where the deltoid muscles attach to the humerus (the long bone of the upper arm) and the biceps muscles to the radius (one of the two forearm bones) that are markedly developed in these individuals. The overdevelopment of the muscles was symmetrical, affecting both arms equally. On the forearm of these individuals,

the radial tuberosity—the bulged area of the radius where the biceps muscle attaches—is particularly noticeable.

Kneeling for many hours strains the toes and knees, whereas grinding puts additional pressure on the hips and, especially, the lower back. The characteristic injuries we found on the last dorsal vertebra were disk damage and crushing. Such injuries could occur if the grinder overshot the far end of the saddle quern during the forward push or recoiled to the starting position too quickly or vigorously.

During grinding, the body pivots alternately around the knee and hip joints. The movement subjects the femurs (thigh bones) to considerable bending stresses. These bones thus develop a distinct buttress along the back to counteract the bending moments imposed from the hip and the knee as the weight of the body swings back and forth across the saddle quern. The knee also takes a lot of pressure because it serves as the pivot for the movement. Thus, the joint surfaces enlarge. All these effects appear on a set of bones we studied. The femurs were curved and buttressed. The knees show bony extensions on their articular surfaces.

The feet are also subjected to heavy

pressure as one grinds grain on a quern. The toes are curled forward to provide leverage, which is supplied in large part by the big toes. In the remains from Abu Hureyra, the first metatarsal joints of the toes are enlarged and often injured. There are also signs of cartilage damage: smooth, polished surfaces at the metatarsal joint indicate that bone had rubbed on bone. In some individuals, a gross osteoarthritis had developed. In one case, the right big toe is much more severely affected than the left. Although an infective origin for this condition cannot be ruled out, perhaps the grinder was in the habit of resting one foot on the other to relieve the pain. Just such a position is shown in a model, illustrated in J. H. Breasted's *Egyptian Servant Statues,* of an Egyptian woman using a quern.

The changes to the arm, thigh and toe bones that we observed affected the overall bone morphology. This result would come about only if the stresses had been applied to the bones for long hours daily while the individual was still growing. Travelers have observed such activity quite recently. Michael Aster writes in *A Desert Dies:* "Life in the [Saharan] oasis seemed to grind on at its own pace. For the women this was literally true, for they spent much of their time grinding grain on their hand mills.... I often watched Hawa as she placed a few grains at a time on the stone-base and let them trickle down as she ground them, sweeping the flour into a bowl every few minutes. After an hour or so her little daughter, aged about nine, would take over and begin grinding furiously. It might take several hours to produce enough flour for one meal."

We wanted to know whether members of both sexes ground grain at Abu Hureyra. Finding the answer proved difficult. The skeletons were so fragmented that we had to devise a way of determining the sex of an individual from the specific bones that showed the changes we believed resulted from using a saddle quern. Measurements of the first metatarsal bone of the foot demonstrated that it was generally larger in males, and by this means we could see that most of the bones showing the saddle-quern effects were from females.

EATING

WEAVING

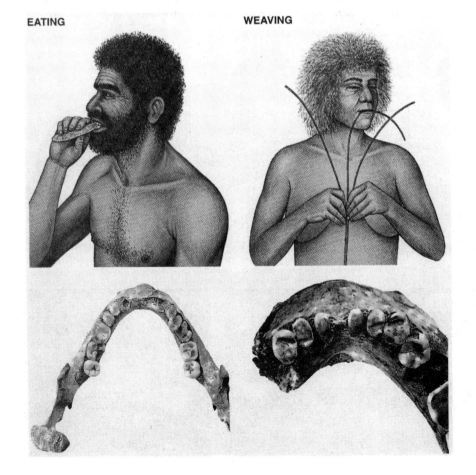

TOOTH WEAR was severe among the early Neolithic people of Abu Hureyra. The coarse flour produced by grinding on a quern abraded teeth. Pulling canes through the teeth while making baskets resulted in deep grooves.

2. THE BEGINNINGS OF CULTURE, AGRICULTURE, AND URBANIZATION

We concluded that the grain was usually prepared by the women and girls in the household. A rather loose division of roles thus appears among these early Neolithic people. The inhabitants of Abu Hureyra must soon have discovered that the most efficient way to operate was to divide up the work of supplying food. We can assume that the men hunted and, with the advent of agriculture, cultivated food plants. The women of the household took on the job of grain preparation—a laborious task, or rather a series of tasks, that occupied many hours a day and could lead to back, knee and toe injuries. These are the repetitive stress injuries of the Neolithic. There is no need to assume that this division of roles implies any inequality between the sexes or between roles—that comes later.

The women were not the only ones to suffer. The coarsely ground grain had an appalling effect on everyone's teeth. One precaution necessary with all grain products except sifted flour is careful sorting to remove hard kernels and small stones. The number of fractured teeth among the early Neolithic people of Abu Hureyra bears witness to a failure to do this sorting effectively—and probably to an absence of sieves. For the same reason, awns or glumes from the outer covering of the grains remained in the flour and occasionally became lodged between the teeth, causing gum infection. On the other hand, caries (tooth decay) was rare. Apparently the flour was not sufficiently refined or cooked (if it was cooked) to provide the right environment for the bacteria that cause cavities.

Fracturing was only one problem. The grains, even after being pounded and ground, yielded a hard meal that was exceedingly abrasive. Apart from the damage caused by rock powder from the grindstone, the flour itself rapidly wore down the teeth. Many people lost teeth at an early age. Moreover, scanning electron micrographs of teeth from Abu Hureyra show pits comparable in size to those that date stones and other hard objects make on the teeth of nonhuman primates.

Something had to be done about the horrendous wear on the teeth. The archaeologists at Abu Hureyra had occasionally noticed the imprints of woven mats in plaster from later levels of the settlement. This finding was evidence that the people had by then mastered the skills of weaving. The invention of the sieve—an application of the principles of weaving—would have meant that grain could be sifted from grit and coarse chaff. Women in the Near East today can operate a sieve so deftly that they produce three piles on it: stones, chaff and grains. They then flip the stones into the palm of the hand. The result is fewer fractured teeth. We have no direct evidence of sieves at Abu Hureyra, but tooth wear is notably less severe in the later times.

Some way also had to be found to contain the harvested grain in order to bring it in from the fields. Baskets may have been the solution. We noted strange grooves on the front teeth of individuals from the later levels at Abu Hureyra. In making a basket, three canes have to be maneuvered at once. Because the hands are occupied hold-

LOAD BEARING

BONE ABNORMALITIES appeared among the people of Abu Hureyra as a result of the activities depicted here. Carrying loads on the head deformed the bones of the upper spine; the pitting on the vertebra indicates disk damage. Pounding grain in a mortar and pestle and operating a quern strongly developed the arm muscles, as reflected by the bulging in the two humerus (upper arm) bones (*top of photograph*),

USING MORTAR AND PESTLE

SQUATTING AT REST

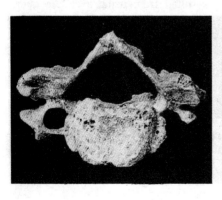

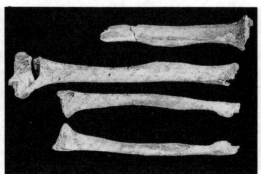

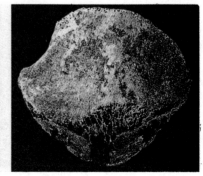

ing the first staves of the basket, the teeth are used to control the working canes. Clark S. Larsen of the University of North Carolina at Chapel Hill has illustrated how a modern Paiute Indian woman holds the canes between her teeth. The habit of weaving in this way forms grooves on the surface of the front teeth. The grooves are almost identical to those we have observed on the teeth from Abu Hureyra.

The skeletal evidence for weaving and basket making is rare among the bones we studied, presumably because the skills for those crafts were confined to a few people. Those individuals are all from one part of the settlement, which suggests a craft area. Such specialization would be a natural outcome of any division of roles. Role specialization allows the development of expertise, speed and improved technology. If an expert is relieved of the need to produce her own food, she can manufacture more than enough sieves or baskets to supply the community. Any surplus can be used in trade.

From a different part of the settlement came evidence for another group of craftswomen. We noticed that several jaws found there have enormously enlarged joint surfaces, together with extremely uneven wear on the teeth. To display this pattern of wear, the teeth must have been subjected to immense crushing forces that abraded the lower teeth on the outside and the upper teeth on the inside. In some cases, the wear extends right down to the root.

Tetsuya Kamegai of Iwate Medical University in Japan has found similar changes among Maori people who chew plant stems to make fiber string. Some years ago J. D. Jennings of the University of Utah described the marks on quids chewed by worn teeth. The quids, made by people of the same epoch as the Abu Hureyra community, are found by the thousands at Danger Cave in Utah. The cave yielded pieces of cord made of chewed bulrush stems and mats bound with the cord. I believe mats were being made in a similar way at Abu Hureyra, a view also supported by the impressions of matting found during the excavation.

Some 7,300 years ago the new technology of pottery making brought great changes to the community. Pottery vessels provided a container in which grains could be soaked and cooked. That made the cereals so much softer that wear on the teeth was significantly reduced, as can be seen in scanning electron micrographs.

Cooked cereal is also tastier and easier to digest. Cooking releases the carbohydrates from the grain and makes them easy for the digestive system to absorb. One result was porridge, which soon had a dramatic effect on the community's population structure. A single consequence is evident in the unmended fracture of a woman's jaw; it is unlikely that she could have survived if a nutritious gruel or porridge were not available. Much more significant is that once porridge was available, women could give it to infants in place of breast milk. The mothers, too, consumed a diet quite rich in carbohydrates. The result of early weaning and better nourishment was to increase fertility substantially by reducing the interval between births.

This effect can be seen in the much larger proportion of infant skeletons recovered from the pottery levels compared with their percentage in the earlier strata. The proportion is so high as to suggest that infants were at increased risk of dying from disease, presumably because the rising population density gave more opportunity for pathogens to spread from one person to another. Some of the children have a thickening and pitting of the eye sockets, known as cribra orbitalia, that probably was the result of anemia following long-term infection by parasites.

It is from the pottery levels that we find evidence of dental caries. The change in food preparation, with greater emphasis on cooked cereals made into bread and porridge, created sticky foods that adhere to the teeth and provide a medium for the growth of the bacteria that cause caries.

where the deltoid muscles attach, and in the two radius (forearm) bones (*bottom*), where the biceps muscles attach. Squatting to rest put strain on the knee, resulting in this notched patella (kneecap). Using a quern damaged the last dorsal vertebra; wedging and pitting indicate crushing and disk damage. Also affected were the bones of the big toe; here there is wear near the right end of the upper toe bone and severe osteoarthritis near the right end of the lower bone.

USING QUERN

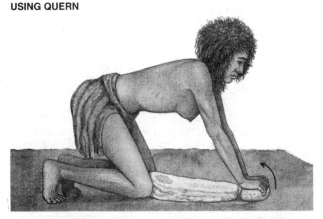

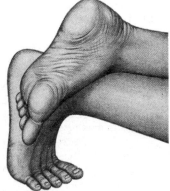

Abu Hureyra was abandoned about 7,000 years ago, as were many other Neolithic sites in the Near East. One cannot say why; disease, famine and climatic change are all possibilities. Abu Hureyra, although it was a structured society, remained egalitarian to the end—at least in terms of burial practices. But during the Neolithic, roles probably became more defined and more circumscribed.

The incorporation of role in the so-

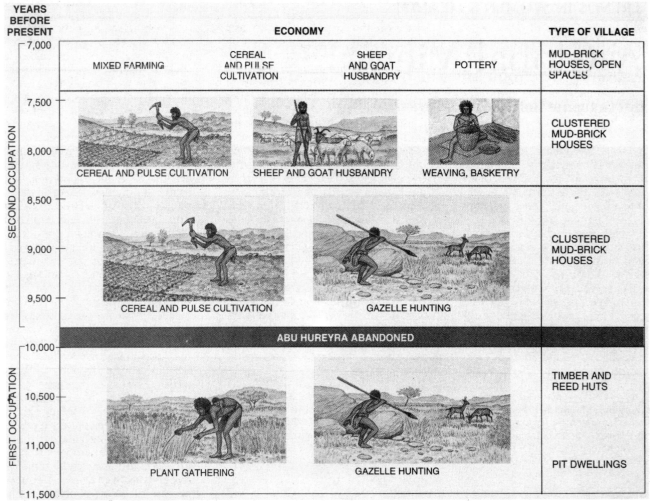

	ECONOMY				TYPE OF VILLAGE
	MIXED FARMING	CEREAL AND PULSE CULTIVATION	SHEEP AND GOAT HUSBANDRY	POTTERY	MUD-BRICK HOUSES, OPEN SPACES

ABU HUREYRA'S CHRONOLOGY extended through two different occupations of the site over some 4,500 years. The first occupants were pre-Neolithic people who lived primitively and did not farm. Early Neolithic people of the second occupation gradually came to the cultivation of crops, the domestication of animals and such crafts as pottery and basket making.

cial fabric is reflected in the burial practices. The dead were buried under the floors of the houses or in pits in the yards outside. Many more women than men are buried in the rooms. This was their domain, where they had lived and worked. The women, it seems, had specific parts of space bounded by the limits of the house; their territory was a frame for their activities. John Gold of Oxford Brookes University sees this territoriality as a fundamental expression of social organization. The role boundaries established in life were maintained after death. The skeletal changes indicating how women spent their days—grinding, spinning, making baskets and mats—reflect a commitment in terms of time and economics that constitutes role specialization.

The very division of roles may have encouraged people not immediately immersed in preparing food to develop crafts. Crop cultivation, in fact, created its own challenges. Water had to be conveyed to seedlings for irrigation; ani-mals had to be kept from destroying the crops; and harvested grain had to be transported. These problems provoked the exploration of technologies to solve them. Vessels, fences and baskets were devised, and certain people became expert in making them.

At Abu Hureyra, we see a progression of changes that can be understood in the light of such innovations. The improvements brought problems that called for further innovations. There was a constant progress toward a better life—a striving that continues to this day. Abu Hureyra represents the first step on the path toward civilization. But signs of wealth, class, elite institutions and scholarship have not been found in this settlement. We must look for them elsewhere.

FURTHER READING

THE EXCAVATION OF TELL ABU HUREYRA IN SYRIA: A PRELIMINARY REPORT. A.M.T. Moore in *Proceedings of the Prehistoric Society*, Vol. 41, pages 50–77; December 1975.

DENTAL MODIFICATIONS AND TOOL USE IN THE WESTERN GREAT BASIN. Clark Spencer Larsen in *American Journal of Physical Anthropology*, Vol. 67, No. 4, pages 393–402; August 1985.

SEED PREPARATION IN THE MESOLITHIC: THE OSTEOLOGICAL EVIDENCE. T. Molleson in *Antiquity*, Vol. 63, No. 239, pages 356–362; June 1989.

DENTAL EVIDENCE FOR DIETARY CHANGE AT ABU HUREYRA. Theya Molleson and Karen Jones in *Journal of Archaeological Science*, Vol. 18, No. 5, pages 525–539; September 1991.

DIETARY CHANGE AND THE EFFECTS OF FOOD PREPARATION ON MICROWEAR PATTERNS IN THE LATE NEOLITHIC OF ABU HUREYRA, NORTHERN SYRIA. T. Molleson, K. Jones and S. Jones in *Journal of Human Evolution*, Vol. 24, No. 6, pages 455–468; June 1993.

How Man Invented Cities

John Pfeiffer

The most striking mark of man's genius as a species, as the most adaptable of animals, has been his ability to live in cities. From the perspective of all we know about human evolution, nothing could be more unnatural. For over fifteen million years, from the period when members of the family of man first appeared on earth until relatively recent times, our ancestors were nomadic, small-group, wide-open-spaces creatures. They lived on the move among other moving animals in isolated little bands of a few families, roaming across wildernesses that extended like oceans to the horizon and beyond.

Considering that heritage, the wonder is not that man has trouble getting along in cities but that he can do it at all—that he can learn to live in the same place year round, enclosed in sharp-cornered and brightly-lit rectangular spaces, among noises, most of which are made by machines, within shouting distance of hundreds of other people, most of them strangers. Furthermore, such conditions arose so swiftly, practically overnight on the evolutionary time scale, that he has hardly had a chance to get used to them. The transition from a world without cities to our present situation took a mere five or six millenniums.

It is precisely because we are so close to our origins that what happened in prehistory bears directly on current problems. In fact, the expectation is that new studies of pre-cities and early cities will contribute as significantly to an understanding of today's urban complexes as studies of infancy and early childhood have to an understanding of adolescence. Cities are signs, symptoms if you will, of an accelerating and intensive phase of human evolution, a process that we are only beginning to investigate scientifically.

The first stages of the process may be traced back some fifteen thousand years to a rather less hectic era. Homo sapiens, that new breed of restless and intelligent primate, had reached a high point in his career as a hunter-gatherer subsisting predominantly on wild plants and animals. He had developed special tools, special tactics and strategies, for dealing with a wide variety of environments, from savannas and semideserts to tundras and tropical rain forests and mountain regions. Having learned to exploit practically every type of environment, he seemed at last to have found his natural place in the scheme of things—as a hunter living in balance with other species, and with all the world as his hunting ground.

But forces were already at work that would bring an end to this state of equilibrium and ultimately give rise to cities and the state of continuing instability that we are trying to cope with today. New theories, a harder look at the old theories, and an even harder look at our own tendencies to think small have radically changed our ideas about what happened and why.

We used to believe, in effect, that people abandoned hunting and gathering as soon as a reasonable alternative became available to them. It was hardly a safe or reliable way of life. Our ancestors faced sudden death and injury from predators and from prey that fought back, disease from exposure to the elements and from always being on the move, and hunger because the chances were excellent of coming back empty-handed from the hunt. Survival was a full-time struggle. Leisure came only after the invention of agriculture, which brought food surpluses, rising populations, and cities. Such was the accepted picture.

The fact of the matter, supported by studies of living hunter-gatherers as well as by the archaeological record, is that the traditional view is largely melodrama and science fiction. Our preagricultural ancestors were quite healthy, quite safe, and regularly obtained all the food they needed. And they did it with time to burn. As a rule, the job of collecting food, animal and vegetable, required no more than a three-hour day, or a twenty-one-hour week. During that time, collectors brought in enough food for the entire group, which included an appreciable proportion (perhaps 30 per cent or more) of dependents, old persons and children who did little or no work. Leisure is basically a phenomenon of hunting-gathering times, and people have been trying to recover it ever since.

Another assumption ripe for discarding is that civilization first arose in the valleys of the Tigris, Euphrates, and Nile rivers and spread from there to the rest of the world. Accumulating evidence fails to support this notion that civilization is an exclusive product of these regions. To be sure, agriculture and cities may have appeared first in the Near East, but there are powerful arguments for completely independent origins in at least two other widely separated regions, Mesoamerica and Southeast Asia.

In all cases, circumstances forced hunter-gatherers to evolve new ways of surviving. With the decline of the ancient life style, nomadism, problems began piling up. If only people had kept on moving about like sane and respectable primates, life would be a great deal simpler. Instead, they settled down in increasing numbers over wider areas, and society started changing with a vengeance. Although the causes of this settling down remain a mystery, the fact of independent origins calls for an explanation based on worldwide developments.

An important factor, emphasized recently by Lewis Binford of the University of New Mexico, may have been the melting of mile-high glaciers, which was well under way fifteen thousand years ago, and which released enough water to raise the world's oceans 250 to 500 feet, to flood previously exposed coastal plains, and to create shallow bays and estuaries and marshlands. Vast numbers of fish and wild fowl made use of the new environments, and the extra resources permitted people to obtain food without migrating seasonally. In other words, people expended less energy, and life became that much easier, in the beginning anyway.

Yet this sensible and seemingly innocent change was to get mankind into all sorts of difficulties. According to a recent theory, it triggered a chain of events that made cities possible if not inevitable. Apparently, keeping on the move had always served as a natural birth-control mechanism, in part, perhaps, by causing a relatively high incidence of miscarriages. But the population brakes were off as soon as people began settling down.

One clue to what may have happened is provided by contemporary studies of a number of primitive tribes, such as the Bushmen of Africa's Kalahari Desert. Women living in nomadic bands, bands that pick up and move half a dozen or more times a year, have an average of one baby every four years or so, as compared with one baby every two and a half years for Bushman women living in settled communities—an increase of five to eight babies per mother during a twenty-year reproductive period.

The archaeological record suggests that in some places at least, a comparable phenomenon accompanied the melting of glaciers during the last ice age. People settled down and multiplied in the Les Eyzies region of southern France, one of the richest and most-studied centers of prehistory. Great limestone cliffs dominate the countryside, and at the foot of the cliffs are natural shelters, caves and rocky overhangs where people built fires, made tools out of flint and bone and ivory, and planned the next day's hunt. On special occasions artists equipped with torches went deep into certain caves like Lascaux and covered the walls with magnificent images of the animals they hunted.

In some places the cliffs and the shelters extend for hundreds of yards; in other places there are good living sites close to one another on the opposite slopes of river valleys. People in the Les Eyzies region were living not in isolated bands but in full-fledged communities, and populations seem to have been on the rise. During the period from seven thou-

sand to twelve thousand years ago, the total number of sites doubled, and an appreciable proportion of them probably represent year-round settlements located in small river valleys. An analysis of excavated animal remains reveals an increasing dietary reliance on migratory birds and fish (chiefly salmon).

People were also settling down at about the same time in the Near East—for example, not far from the Mediterranean shoreline of Israel and on the border between the coastal plain and the hills to the east. Ofer Bar-Yosef, of the Institute of Archaeology of Hebrew University in Jerusalem, points out that since they were able to exploit both these areas, they did not have to wander widely in search of food. There were herds of deer and gazelle, wild boar, fish and wild fowl, wild cereals and other plants, and limestone caves and shelters like those in the Les Eyzies region. Somewhat later, however, a new land-use pattern emerged. Coastal villages continued to flourish, but in addition to them, new sites began appearing further inland—and in areas that were drier and less abundant.

Only under special pressure will men abandon a good thing, and in this case it was very likely the pressure of rising populations. The evidence suggests that the best coastal lands were supporting about all the hunter-gatherers they could support; and as living space decreased there was a "budding off," an overflow of surplus population into the second-best back country where game was scarcer. These people depended more and more on plants, particularly on wild cereals, as indicated by the larger numbers of flint sickle blades, mortars and pestles, and storage pits found at their sites (and also by an increased wear and pitting of teeth, presumably caused by chewing more coarse and gritty plant foods).

Another sign of the times was the appearance of stone buildings, often with impressively high and massive walls. The structures served a number of purposes. For one thing, they included storage bins where surplus grain could be kept in reserve for bad times, when there was a shortage of game and wild plants. They also imply danger abroad in the countryside, new kinds of violence, and a mounting need for defenses to protect stored goods from the raids of people who had not settled down.

Above all, the walls convey a feeling of increasing permanence, an increasing commitment to places. Although man was still mainly a hunter-gatherer living on wild species, some of the old options no longer existed for him. In the beginning, settling down may have involved a measure of choices, but now man was no longer quite so free to change locales when the land became less fruitful. Even in those days frontiers were vanishing. Man's problem was to develop new options, new ways of working the land more intensively so that it would provide the food that migration had always provided in more mobile times.

The all-important transition to agriculture came in small steps, establishing itself almost before anyone realized what was going on. Settlers in marginal lands took early measures to get more food out of less abundant environments—roughing up the soil a bit with scraping or digging sticks, sowing wheat and barley seeds, weeding, and generally doing their best to promote growth. To start with at least, it was simply a matter of supplementing regular diets of wild foods with some domesticated species, animals as well as plants, and people probably regarded themselves as hunter-gatherers working hard to maintain their way of life rather than as the revolutionaries they were. They were trying to preserve the old self-sufficiency, but it was a losing effort.

The wilderness way of life became more and more remote, more and more nearly irretrievable. Practically every advance in the technology of agriculture committed people to an increasing dependence on domesticated species and on the activities of other people living nearby. Kent Flannery of the University of Michigan emphasizes this point in a study of one part of Greater Mesopotamia, prehistoric Iran, during the period between twelve thousand and six thousand years ago. For the hunter-gatherer, an estimated one-third of the country's total land area was good territory, consisting of grassy plains and high mountain valleys where wild species were abundant; the rest of the land was desert and semidesert.

The coming of agriculture meant that people used a smaller proportion of the countryside. Early farming took advantage of naturally distributed water; the best terrain for that, namely terrain with a high water table and marshy areas, amounted to about a tenth of the land area. But only a tenth of that tenth was suitable for the next major development, irrigation. Meanwhile, food yields were soaring spectacularly, and so was the population of Iran, which increased more than fiftyfold; in other words, fifty times the original population was being supported by food produced on one-hundredth of the land.

A detailed picture of the steps involved in this massing of people is coming from studies of one part of southwest Iran, an 880-square-mile region between the Zagros Mountains and the Iraqi border. The Susiana Plain is mostly flat, sandy semidesert, the only notable features being manmade mounds that loom on the horizon like islands, places where people built in successively high levels on the ruins of their ancestors. During the past decade or so, hundreds of mounds have been mapped and dated (mainly through pottery styles) by Robert Adams of the University of Chicago, Jean Perrot of the French Archaeological Mission in Iran, and Henry Wright and Gregory Johnson of the University of Michigan. Their work provides a general idea of when the mounds were occupied, how they varied in size at different periods and how a city may be born.

Imagine a time-lapse motion picture of the early settling of the Susiana Plain, starting about 6500 B.C, each minute of film representing a century. At first the plain is empty, as it has been since the beginning of time. Then the pioneers arrive; half a dozen families move in and build a cluster of mud-brick homes near a river. Soon another cluster appears and another, until, after about five minutes (it is now 6000 B.C.), there are ten settlements, each covering an area of 1 to 3 hectares (1 hectare = 2.47 acres). Five minutes more (5500 B.C) and we see the start of irrigation, on a small scale, as people dig little ditches to carry water from rivers and tributaries to lands along the banks. Crop yields increase and so do populations, and there are now thirty settlements, all about the same size as the original ten.

This is but a prelude to the main event. Things become really complicated during the next fifteen minutes or so (5500 to 4000 B.C.). Irrigation systems, constructed and maintained by family groups of varying sizes, become more complex. The number of settlements shows a modest increase, from thirty to

forty, but a more significant change takes place—the appearance of a hierarchy. Instead of settlements all about the same size, there are now levels of settlements and a kind of ranking: one town (7 hectares), ten large villages (3 to 4 hectares), and twenty-nine smaller villages of less than 3 hectares. During this period large residential and ceremonial structures appear at Susa, a town on the western edge of the Susiana Plain.

Strange happenings can be observed not long after the middle of this period (about 4600 B.C.). For reasons unknown, the number of settlements decreases rapidly. It is not known whether the population of the area decreased simultaneously. Time passes, and the number of settlements increases to about the same level as before, but great changes have occurred. Three cities have appeared with monumental public buildings, elaborate residential architecture, large workshops, major storage and market facilities, and certainly with administrators and bureaucrats. The settlement hierarchy is more complex, and settlements are no longer located to take advantage solely of good agricultural opportunities. Their location is also influenced by the cities and the services and opportunities available there. By the end of our hypothetical time-lapse film, by the early part of the third millennium B.C., the largest settlement of all is the city of Susa, which covers some thirty hectares and will cover up to a square kilometer (100 hectares) of territory before it collapses in historical times.

All Mesopotamia underwent major transformations during this period. Another city was taking shape 150 miles northwest of Susa in the heartland of Sumer. Within a millennium the site of Uruk near the Euphrates River grew from village dimensions to a city enclosing within its defense walls more than thirty thousand people, four hundred hectares, and at the center a temple built on top of a huge brick platform. Archaeological surveys reveal that this period also saw a massive immigration into the region from places and for reasons as yet undetermined, resulting in a tenfold increase in settlements and in the formation of several new cities.

Similar surveys, requiring months and thousands of miles of walking, are completed or under way in many parts of the world. Little more than a millennium after the establishment of Uruk and Susa, cities began making an independent ap-

pearance in northern China not far from the conflux of the Wei and Yellow rivers, in an area that also saw the beginnings of agriculture. Still later, and also independently as far as we can tell, intensive settlement and land use developed in the New World.

The valley of Oaxaca in Mexico, where Flannery and his associates are working currently, provides another example of a city in the process of being formed. Around 500 B.C., or perhaps a bit earlier, buildings were erected for the first time on the tops of hills. Some of the hills were small, no more than twenty-five or thirty feet high, and the buildings were correspondingly small; they overlooked a few terraces and a river and probably a hamlet or two. Larger structures appeared on higher hills overlooking many villages. About 400 B.C. the most elaborate settlement began to appear on the highest land, 1,500-foot Monte Albán, with a panoramic view of the valley's three arms; and within two centuries it had developed into an urban center including hundreds of terraces, an irrigation system, a great plaza, ceremonial buildings and residences, and an astronomical observatory.

At about the same time, the New World's largest city, Teotihuacán, was evolving some 225 miles to the northwest in the central highlands of Mexico. Starting as a scattering of villages and hamlets, it covered nearly eight square miles at its height (around A.D. 100 to 200) and probably contained some 125,000 people. Archaeologists are now reconstructing the life and times of this great urban center. William Sanders of Pennsylvania State University is concentrating on an analysis of settlement patterns in the area, while Rene Millon of the University of Rochester and his associates have prepared detailed section-by-section maps of the city as a step toward further extensive excavations. Set in a narrow valley among mountains and with its own man-made mountains, the Pyramid of the Sun and the Pyramid of the Moon, the city flourished on a grand scale. It housed local dignitaries and priests, delegations from other parts of Mesoamerica, and workshop neighborhoods where specialists in the manufacture of textiles, pottery, obsidian blades, and other products lived together in early-style apartments.

The biggest center in what is now the United States probably reached its peak about a millennium after Teotihuacán.

But it has not been reconstructed, and archaeologists are just beginning to appreciate the scale of what happened there. Known as Cahokia and located east of the Mississippi near St. Louis, it consists of a cluster of some 125 mounds (including a central mound 100 feet high and covering 15 acres) as well as a line of mounds extending six miles to the west.

So surveys and excavations continue, furnishing the sort of data needed to disprove or prove our theories. Emerging patterns involving the specific locations of different kinds of communities and of buildings and other artifacts within communities can yield information about the forces that shaped and are still shaping cities and the behavior of people in cities. But one trend stands out above all others: the world was becoming more and more stratified. Every development seemed to favor social distinctions, social classes and elites, and to work against the old hunter-gatherer ways.

Among hunter-gatherers all people are equal. Individuals are recognized as exceptional hunters, healers, or storytellers, and they all have the chance to shine upon appropriate occasions. But it would be unthinkable for one of them, for any one man, to take over as full-time leader. That ethic passed when the nomadic life passed. In fact, a literal explosion of differences accompanied the coming of communities where people lived close together in permanent dwellings and under conditions where moving away was not easy.

The change is reflected clearly in observed changes of settlement patterns. Hierarchies of settlements imply hierarchies of people. Emerging social levels are indicated by the appearance of villages and towns and cities where only villages had existed before, by different levels of complexity culminating in such centers as Susa and Monte Albán and Cahokia. Circumstances practically drove people to establish class societies. In Mesopotamia, for instance, increasingly sophisticated agricultural systems and intensive concentrations of populations brought about enormous and irreversible changes within a short period. People were clamped in a demographic vise, more and more of them living and depending on less and less land—an ideal setting for the rapid rise of status differences.

Large-scale irrigation was a highly effective centralizing force, calling for new duties and new regularities and new levels of discipline. People still depended on the seasons; but in addition, canals had to be dug and maintained, and periodic cleaning was required to prevent the artificial waterways from filling up with silt and assorted litter. Workers had to be brought together, assigned tasks, and fed, which meant schedules and storehouses and rationing stations and mass-produced pottery to serve as food containers. It took time to organize such activities efficiently. There were undoubtedly many false starts, many attempts by local people to work things out among themselves and their neighbors at a community or village level. Many small centers, budding institutions, were undoubtedly formed and many collapsed, and we may yet detect traces of them in future excavations and analyses of settlement patterns.

The ultimate outcome was inevitable. Survival demanded organization on a regional rather than a local basis. It also demanded high-level administrators and managers, and most of them had to be educated people, mainly because of the need to prepare detailed records of supplies and transactions. Record-keeping has a long prehistory, perhaps dating back to certain abstract designs engraved on cave walls and bone twenty-five thousand or more years ago. But in Mesopotamia after 4000 B.C. there was a spurt in the art of inventing and utilizing special marks and symbols.

The trend is shown in the stamp and cylinder seals used by officials to place their "signatures" on clay tags and tablets, man's first documents. At first the designs on the stamp seals were uncomplicated, consisting for the most part of single animals or simple geometric motifs. Later, however, there were bigger stamp seals with more elaborate scenes depicting several objects or people or animals. Finally the cylinder seals appeared, which could be rolled to repeat a complex design. These seals indicate the existence of more and more different signatures and more and more officials and record keepers. Similar trends are evident in potters' marks and other symbols. All these developments precede pictographic writing, which appears around 3200 B.C..

Wherever record keepers and populations were on the rise, in the Near East or Mexico or China, we can be reasonably sure that the need for a police force or the prehistoric equivalent thereof was on the increase, too. Conflict, including everything from fisticuffs to homicide, increases sharply with group size, and people have known this for a long time. The Bushmen have a strong feeling about avoiding crowds: "We like to get together, but we fear fights." They are most comfortable in bands of about twenty-five persons and when they have to assemble in larger groups—which happens for a total of only a few months a year, mainly to conduct initiations, arrange marriages, and be near the few permanent water holes during dry seasons—they form separate small groups of about twenty-five, as if they were still living on their own.

Incidentally, twenty-five has been called a "magic number," because it hints at what may be a universal law of group behavior. There have been many counts of hunter-gatherer bands, not only in the Kalahari Desert, but also in such diverse places as the forests of Thailand, the Canadian Northwest, and northern India. Although individual bands may vary from fifteen to seventy-five members, the tendency is to cluster around twenty-five, and in all cases a major reason for keeping groups small is the desire to avoid violence. In other words, the association between large groups and conflict has deep roots and very likely presented law-and-order problems during the early days of cities and pre-cities, as it has ever since.

Along with managers and record keepers and keepers of the peace, there were also specialists in trade. A number of factors besides population growth and intensive land use were involved in the origin of cities, and local and long-distance trade was among the most important. Prehistoric centers in the process of becoming urban were almost always trade centers. They typically occupied favored places, strategic points in developing trade networks, along major waterways and caravan routes or close to supplies of critical raw materials.

Archaeologists are making a renewed attempt to learn more about such developments. Wright's current work in southwest Iran, for example, includes preliminary studies to detect and measure changes in the flow of trade. One site about sixty-five miles from Susa lies close to tar pits, which in prehistoric times served as a source of natural asphalt for fastening stone blades to handles and waterproofing baskets and roofs. By saving all the waste bits of this important raw material preserved in different excavated levels, Wright was able to estimate fluctuations in its production over a period of time. In one level, for example, he found that the amounts of asphalt produced increased far beyond local requirements; in fact, a quantitative analysis indicates that asphalt exports doubled at this time. The material was probably being traded for such things as high-quality flint obtained from quarries more than one hundred miles away, since counts of material recovered at the site indicate that imports of the flint doubled during the same period.

In other words, the site was taking its place in an expanding trade network, and similar evidence from other sites can be used to indicate the extent and structure of that network. Then the problem will be to find out what other things were happening at the same time, such as significant changes in cylinder-seal designs and in agricultural and religious practices. This is the sort of evidence that may be expected to spell out just how the evolution of trade was related to the evolution of cities.

Another central problem is gaining a fresh understanding of the role of religion. Something connected with enormous concentrations of people, with population pressures and tensions of many kinds that started building up five thousand or more years ago, transformed religion from a matter of simple rituals carried out at village shrines to the great systems of temples and priesthoods invariably associated with early cities. Sacred as well as profane institutions arose to keep society from splitting apart.

Strong divisive tendencies had to be counteracted, and the reason may involve yet another magic number, another intriguing regularity that has been observed in hunter-gatherer societies in different parts of the world. The average size of a tribe, defined as a group of bands all speaking the same dialect, turns out to be about five hundred persons, a figure that depends to some extent on the limits of human memory. A tribe is a community of people who can identify closely with one another and engage in repeated face-to-face encounters and recognitions; and it happens that five hundred may represent about the number of persons a hunter-gatherer can remember well enough to approach on what would amount to a first-name basis in our society. Beyond that number the level of familiarity declines, and there is an increasing tendency to regard individuals as "they" rather than "we," which is when trouble usually starts. (Architects recommend that an elementary school should not exceed five hundred pupils if the principal is to maintain personal contact with all of them, and the headmaster of one prominent prep school recently used this argument to keep his student body at or below the five-hundred mark.)

Religion of the sort that evolved with the first cities may have helped to "beat" the magic number five hundred. Certainly there was an urgent need to establish feelings of solidarity among many thousands of persons rather than a few hundred. Creating allegiances wider than those provided by direct kinship and person-to-person ties became a most important problem, a task for full-time professionals. In this connection Paul Wheatley of the University of Chicago suggests that "specialized priests were among the first persons to be released from the daily round of subsistence labor." Their role was partly to exhort other workers concerned with the building of monuments and temples, workers who probably exerted greater efforts in the belief that they were doing it not for mere men but for the glory of individuals highborn and close to the gods.

The city evolved to meet the needs of societies under pressure. People were being swept up in a process that had been set in motion by their own activities and that they could never have predicted, for the simple reason that they had no insight into what they were doing in the first place. For example, they did not know, and had no way of knowing, that settling down could lead to population explosions.

There is nothing strange about this state of affairs, to be sure. It is the essence of the human condition and involves us just as intensely today. Then as now, people responded by the sheer instinct of survival to forces that they understood vaguely at best—and worked together as well as they could to organize themselves, to preserve order in the face of accelerating change and complexity and the threat of chaos. They could never know that they were creating what we, its beneficiaries and its victims, call civilization.

The Early Civilizations to 500 B.C.E

Agriculture and urbanization became human destiny. The cycle of more food and more people and more cities has continued to the present. Add to this the Industrial Revolution when agriculture and cities both received a boost, and the situation is like that of the current United States where less than two percent of the population supplies the food for the rest of the people, who live either in or near cities. From archaeological finds it is apparent that a robust Sumerian urban life spread quickly through Turkey, as John Noble Wilford notes in the unit's first essay. This made possible the first great empire, but prolonged drought brought its downfall along with abandoned cities and fields.

Other empires based upon agriculture developed, and one of the lesser known is that of Nubia. South of Egypt in the upper Nile River area, land that is now barren, this empire flourished in competition with Egypt. The two nations often were at war with each other, and most of our information about Nubians comes from their enemies. Nubian writing has not been deciphered; thus, historians are at a loss for information. History, therefore, may have been distorted. There is a current argument that the inspiration for Greek culture came from Nubia through Egypt. Most world historians are waiting for additional proof of that assertion, but David Roberts, in "Out of Africa: The Superb Artwork of Ancient Nubia," praises the quality of Nubian artwork, the main artifacts through which this mysterious civilization is known.

Much more is known about Egypt because of the connection with the Mediterranean Sea and with the civilizations of Greece and Rome. Scholars of Western civilization have long probed this linkage, and an extended archaeological interest has uncovered much about Egyptian heritage. The successful tour of King Tutankhamen's treasure a decade and a half ago also renewed interest in the history of this riverine civilization. The Valley of the Kings, where Tut's tomb was located in the 1920s, has long been a tourist destination. It was to the surprise of many, including the Egyptian government, when an American Egyptologist uncovered a large compound tomb area under a tourist parking lot. Although long since looted, the rubble and wall inscriptions indicate that it was to be the burial site for the 50 male children of Ramses II.

Another intriguing find in Egypt was a simple strand of silk in the hair of a mummy from 1000 B.C.E. as discussed by John Noble Wilford. This hints that the fabled silk road, the trade route across Asia, may have been open 800 years sooner than supposed. It pushes back in time the operation of one of the great early trade systems, the beginnings of a global market. Trading is significant because ideas, culture, disease, and business goods travel the routes of the caravans. These interchanges, according to historian William McNeill, the father of world history, help to bring about innovations in societies.

Egyptian society is interesting beyond this, however. The pyramids apparently were constructed without the use of slave labor or wheels, for example. Herodotus, one of the first great historians of the West, traveled to Egypt to report on the pyramids. His methods of inquiry became a hallmark of historiography. In addition, Joyce Tyldesley points out that in Egyptian society women and men both desired many children, divorce was easy, and women inherited one-third of his property at her husband's death. This attitude toward women seems much more liberal than elsewhere in the ancient world.

Looking Ahead: Challenge Questions

Explain the role of climate in the success and failure of early civilizations.

Why has Nubia been ignored by historians?

Why was the silk road significant? Where did it go and for what purpose?

What was the role of women in Egyptian society?

Why are the tombs of Egypt of interest today? What sort of society can build such places, and for what reason?

Who was Herodotus, and what did he contribute to the study of history?

Why do historians emphasize the importance of writing?

Old Tablet From Turkish Site Shows Early Spread of Culture

John Noble Wilford

New discoveries in Turkey and northern Syria, two buried cities and intriguing clay tablets with cuneiform writing, are expanding the known horizons of early urban civilization and literacy well beyond the Sumerian city-states of southern Mesopotamia.

Archeologists say the discoveries are among the most exciting in Mesopotamian studies in recent decades. They are confident that further excavations at the sites will provide answers to one of the most important questions in archeology: how and when did the phenomena of urban living and the first writing spread from their place of origin more than 5,000 years ago in the lower valley of the Tigris and Euphrates rivers far into adjacent regions?

Working in the Balikh River valley of southern Turkey, near the Syrian border, a team of American and Turkish archeologists found traces of a large city that apparently flourished in 2600 B.C. A single tablet with cuneiform inscriptions, the earliest known writing system, was found lying on the surface, prompting hopeful speculation that other, more revealing tablets would eventually be uncovered.

Dr. Patricia Wattenmaker, an archeologist at the University of Virginia and director of the excavations, said the discovery should overturn conventional thinking that confined the development of large urban centers of the period to southern Mesopotamia and dismissed the cultures to the north and west as mere backwaters. Further research, she said, could extend the known range of early literacy.

Preliminary excavations indicate that the site, known as Kazane Hoyuk, holds the remains of a city that spread over at least 250 acres, large for its time and place. One tentative hypothesis is that these are the ruins of Urshu, a northern city mentioned in some Sumerian texts.

"Kazane's a huge place," said Dr. Glenn Schwartz, an archeologist at Johns Hopkins University who is familiar with the discovery, "and has to have been one of the most important political and economic centers of its region."

The other discovery that has excited archeologists is the buried ruins of a smaller city of the third millennium B.C. at Tell Beidar in northern Syria. There European and Syrian archeologists have found a well-preserved temple, administrative buildings and a collection of as many as 70 clay tablets with Sumerian writing and Semitic names, as well as many other tablet fragments. And they have only begun to dig.

"It's the most spectacular find this year in Syria," said Dr. Marc Lebeau, the leader of the discovery team, who is president of the European Center for Upper Mesopotamian Studies in Brussels.

Dating of Tablets

Preliminary analysis places the time of the tablets and other artifacts at about 2400 B.C., during the Sumerian ascendancy in southern Mesopotamia and just before the rise of the Akkadian empire under Sargon the Great. The tablets that have been deciphered appear to be bureaucratic records of a robust economy, including lists of donkeys, oxen and sheep and the names of towns and villages.

Archeologists find traces of Sumerians far north of Mesopotamia.

Dr. Harvey Weiss, a Yale University archeologist, recently visited Tell Beidar and said that it and Kazane Hoyuk "prove everything we've been saying about northern Mesopotamia for many years," namely that the cuneiform archive discovered in 1974 at Ebla, also in Syria, was not an anomaly but strong evidence of the widespread expansion of Sumerian urban civilization, beginning as early as 2600 B.C.

If Ebla, near the city of Aleppo, revealed the civilization's western progression, excavations by Dr. Weiss at Tell Leilan, begun in 1979, produced the first strong evidence of its northern reach. Tell Leilan, identified as the ancient walled city of Shubat Enlil that experienced sudden growth in 2500, lies on the fertile plains of Syria near the borders of Turkey and Iraq. Nearby is the European dig site of Tell Beidar. Farther north is Kazane Hoyuk, at least twice as large as Tell Beidar and the same size as Tell Leilan or larger.

Other scholars had previously failed to recognize this expansion phenomenon mainly because the most thorough excavations had until recently been confined to the Sumerian heartland in the lower Tigris and Euphrates valley.

New View of Mesopotamia

"People used to think of ancient Mesopotamia as small and restricted, but not any longer," said Dr. Elizabeth Stone, an archeologist at the State University of New York at Stony Brook.

The two discoveries were made over the last two summers, but the results have only now become known by word of mouth (and computer mail) to many other archeologists. The details and their implications were discussed in interviews last week.

Dr. Wattenmaker was driving on the road south of the modern Turkish city of Urfa when she saw a prominent mound in the fields near an irrigation canal. In her initial survey last year, pottery shards were found scattered over the ground. Some were as much as 7,000 years old. Others were at least 4,500 years old and in the Sumerian style.

This and other evidence gathered this year indicated that the site had been occupied almost continuously since 5000 B.C., and so should provide evidence of the transition from a simple farming society to an urban culture. It grew to be a large city about 2600 B.C. and was abandoned for an unknown reason around 1800 B.C.

A worker found the baked clay tablet lying on the surface. It is 22 inches by 22, and encrusted in dirt. Cleaning away some of the dirt, archeologists saw the wedge-shaped cuneiform inscriptions typical of early writing, which was first developed by Mesopotamians about 5,000 years ago.

Scholars are especially cautious in their assessment of the tablet because it was a "stray find." It was picked up on the ground, out of context with archeological ruins and in an area that had been disturbed by construction of the canal. Still, they said it appeared to be genuine and from the third millennium B.C.

"It's a tease," said Dr. Piotr Michalowski, a specialist in Sumerian and Babylonian languages at the University of Michigan, who is examining photographs of the tablet inscriptions. "It doesn't tell you much. It is not a connected narrative of any sort, just signs and not very good ones. Somebody might have been practicing writing, and wasn't good at it."

Speculation of Literacy

Since early writing was associated with official record-keeping related to the collection and distribution of grain and goods and since Kazane Hoyuk was a city on known trade routes, Dr. Michalowski said: "I will stick my neck out and say it had to be a literate society. Other tablets may be found there. I've always thought Ebla was only a symptom of a much more widespread literacy in this period."

Although archeologists said they could not yet determine the ancient name of this city, Dr. Michalowski said there was a "good degree of probability" that it was Urshu, which Sumerian inscriptions of 2100 B.C. refer to as a city in the highlands of Ebla; that would put it at some distance to the northwest. The site of Urshu has never been identified. But confirmation of this surmise will have to await the discovery of more and better tablets.

Dr. Wattenmaker plans more excavations, looking for tablets and other evidence regarding the nature of economic and social forces that contributed to the rise of centralized government and urban society. Her research team included archeologists from the Universities of Chicago and Virginia, Istanbul University and the Urfa Museum.

Preliminary study of the tablets at Tell Beidar, Dr. Lebeau said, showed that they are approximately the same age as the Ebla archive, probably a century or two later than the Kazane Hoyuk fluorescence, and that they provide a clear link between this ancient city, Ebla in the west and southern Mesopotamia.

These are the first tablets of this period to be found in northern Syria, and archeologists expect to find more as they dig deeper at the site. The discovery team included archeologists from Belgium, France, Germany, the Netherlands, Spain and Syria.

The new discoveries, Dr. Weiss said, were further evidence for the sudden rise beginning around 2600 B.C. of cities in nearly all directions beyond the bounds of southern Mesopotamia and may help account for this expansion. Was this the consequence of trade among independent people or incipient colonialism and imperialism? If these burning questions in Mesopotamian archeology can be answered, scholars will still be left to ponder the bigger question of how state societies and urban civilization happened to begin then and there in the first place.

Collapse of Earliest Known Empire Is Linked to Long, Harsh Drought

John Noble Wilford

Under the renowned Sargon and his successors, the Akkadians of Mesopotamia forged the world's first empire more than 4,300 years ago. They seized control of cities along the Euphrates River and on the fruitful plains to the north, all in what is now Iraq, Syria and parts of southern Turkey. Then, after only a century of prosperity, the Akkadian empire collapsed abruptly, for reasons that have been lost to history.

The traditional explanation is one of divine retribution. Angered by the hubris of Naram-Sin, Sargon's grandson and most dynamic successor, the gods supposedly unleashed the barbaric Gutians to descend out of the highlands and overwhelm Akkadian towns. More recent and conventional explanations have put the blame on overpopulation, provincial revolt, nomadic incursions or managerial incompetence, though many scholars despaired of ever identifying the root cause of the collapse.

A team of archeologists, geologists and soil scientists has now found evidence that seems to solve the mystery. The Akkadian empire, they suggest, was beset by a 300-year drought and literally dried up. A microscopic analysis of soil moisture at the ruins of Akkadian cities in the northern farmlands disclosed that the onset of the drought was swift and the consequences severe, beginning about 2200 B.C.

"This is the first time an abrupt climate change has been directly linked to the collapse of a thriving civilization," said Dr. Harvey Weiss, a Yale University archeologist and leader of the American-French research team.

Such a devastating drought would explain the abandonment at that time of Akkadian cities across the northern plain, a puzzling phenomenon observed in archeological excavations. It would also account for the sudden migrations of people to the south, as recorded in texts on clay tablets. These migrations doubled the populations of southern cities, overtaxed food and water supplies, and led to fighting and the fall of the Sargon dynasty.

The new findings thus call attention to the role of chance—call it fate, an act of God or simply an unpredictable natural disaster—in the development of human cultures and the rise and fall of civilizations.

Among the drought's refugees were a herding people known as Amorites, characterized by scribes in the city of Ur as "a ravaging people with the instincts of a beast, a people who know not grain"—the ultimate putdown in an economy based on grain agriculture. An 110-mile wall, called the "Repeller of the Amorites," was erected to hold them off. But when the drought finally ended in about 1900 B.C., leadership in the region had passed from Akkad to Ur and then to the Amorites, whose power was centered at the rising city of Babylon. Hammurabi, the great ruler of Babylon in 1800 B.C., was a descendant of Amorites.

The correlation between drastic climate change and the Akkadian downfall also appears to complete the picture of widespread environmental crisis disrupting societies throughout the Middle East in the same centuries. Earlier studies had noted the effects of severe drought, including abandoned towns, migrations and nomad incursions, in Greece, Egypt, Palestine and the Indus Valley. Until now, the connection between chronic drought and unstable social conditions had not been extended to Mesopotamia, the land between the two rivers, the Euphrates and the Tigris, often called "the cradle of civilization."

As to what caused such a persistent dry spell, the scientists said they had no clear ideas, though they suggested that changing wind patterns and ocean currents could have been factors. A tremendous volcanic eruption that occurred in Turkey near the beginning of the drought, the scientists said, almost certainly could not have triggered such a long climate change.

Archeology's Sophistication

"This is a research frontier for climatologists," Dr. Weiss said in an interview.

Dr. Weiss proposed the new theory for the Akkadian collapse at a recent meeting of the Society of American Archeology in St. Louis and then in a report in the current issue of the journal Science. His principal collaborators in the research were Dr. Marie-Agnès Courty, an archeologist and soil scientist at the National Center for Scientific Research in Paris, and Dr. François Guichard, a geologist at the same institution.

Other archeologists said the theory was plausible and appeared to provide the first logical explanation for the Akkadian downfall. Although he had not studied the report, Dr. Robert Biggs, a specialist in Mesopotamian archeology at the University of Chicago, said this was a good example of "archeology's growing sophistication in seeking reasons for serious political changes in the past."

In an article accompanying the report in Science, Dr. Robert McC. Adams, secretary of the Smithsonian Institution and an anthropologist specializing in Mesopotamia, cautioned that Dr. Weiss and his colleagues had not thoroughly established the link between climate and the empire's fall. He questioned whether such widespread and persistent drought could be inferred from local soil conditions at a few sites.

"It will demand of other people in the field to either refute it or replicate it with their own work," Dr. Adams said of the theory. "And the only way to get people to pick up that challenge is for Weiss to stick his neck out. I applaud it."

Dr. Weiss said the conclusions were based on tests of soils mainly at the sites of three Akkadian cities within a 30-mile radius, places now known as Tell Leilan, Tell Mozan and Tell Brak in present-day Syria. Evidence of similar climate change was found in adjacent regions, and the archeologist said further tests of the theory would be conducted with the resumption of field work this week.

Land of Rainy Winters

The most revealing evidence has come from Tell Leilan, where Dr. Weiss has been excavating for 14 years and finding successive layers of ruins going back some 8,000 years. For several millennia, this was a small village established by some of the world's first farmers. Around 2600 B.C., it suddenly expanded sixfold to become the city of Shekhna, with 10,000 to 20,000 inhabitants. They lived in the middle of a land of rainy winters, dry summers and a long growing season for wheat and barley, much as it is today.

All the more reason the kings of Akkad, or Agade, a city-state whose location has never been exactly determined but is assumed to have been near ancient Kish and Babylon, reached out and conquered places like Tell Leilan about 2300 B.C. The region became the breadbasket for the Akkadian empire, which stretched 800 miles from the Persian Gulf to the headwaters of the Euphrates in Turkey.

Ceramics and other artifacts established the Akkadian presence there in Tell Leilan and other northern towns. And for years archeologists puzzled over the 300-year gap in human occupation of Tell Leilan and neighboring towns, beginning in 2200 B.C. It occurred to Dr. Weiss that since no irrigation works had been uncovered there, the region must have relied on rain-fed agriculture, as is the case there today, in contrast to the irrigated farming in southern Mesopotamia. A severe drought, therefore, could be disastrous to life in the north.

This idea was tested by Dr. Courty, using microscopic techniques she pioneered in a scientific specialty, soil micromorphology. By examining in detail the arrangement and nature of sediments at archeological sites, it is possible to reconstruct ancient environmental conditions and human activity.

One of the first discoveries was a half-inch layer of volcanic ash covering the rooftops of buildings at Tell Leilan in 2200 B.C. All ash falls leave distinctive chemical signatures. An analysis by Dr. Guichard traced the likely source of this potassium-rich ash to volcanoes a few hundred miles away in present-day Turkey.

Migration from North

Since the abandonment of Tell Leilan occurred at the same time and the climate suddenly became more arid, volcanic fallout was first suspected as the culprit. Ash and gases from volcanic eruptions can remain suspended in the atmosphere for years, creating sun-blocking hazes and reducing temperatures. But from their knowledge of recent volcanoes, scientists doubted that the eruptions could have perturbed the climate over such a large area for 300 years.

And there seemed no doubt about the drought lasting that long, Dr. Courty said. In the surrounding countryside at Tell Leilan and elsewhere, she examined a layer of soil nearly two feet thick and lying just above the volcanic ash. This layer contained large amounts of fine windblown sand and dust, in contrast to the richer soil in earlier periods. Another telltale sign was the absence of earthworm holes and insect tracks, which are usually present in soils from moister environments.

This was strong evidence, the researchers reported, of a "marked aridity induced by intensification of wind circulation and an apparent increase" of dust storms in the northern plains of Mesopotamia.

It was during the 300-year desertification that archives of the southern cities reported the migration of barbarians from the north and a sharp decline in agricultural production, and showed an increasing number of names of people from the northern tribes, mainly the Amorites.

According to the evidence of the sediments, rain in more abundance returned to northern Mesopotamia in 1900 B.C. and with it the tracks of earthworms and the rebuilding of the deserted cities. Over the ruins of Shekhna, buried in the sands of the drought, rose a new city named Shubat Enlil, which means "dwelling place of Enlil," the paramount Mesopotamian god. The builders were Amorites.

In earlier excavations at Tell Leilan, Dr. Weiss discovered an archive of clay tablets showing that this was the lost capital of a northern Amorite

Akkadians to Babylon

• Sometime before the third millennium B.C.: A tribe of Semitic-speaking herding nomads, perhaps originally from Arabia, gradually settles down in northern Mesopotamia, which comes to be called Akkad.

• Middle of the third millennium B.C.: Akkadian names first appear in Sumerian documents.

• Around 2500 B.C.: Inscriptions written in Akkadian appear.

• 2340–2316 B.C.: Reign of Lugal-zagesi, last of a line of Sumerian kings. It is a time of struggles among city-states for regional supremacy.

• Around 2300 B.C.: Rise of Sargon of Agade or Akkad, a Semitic-speaking ruler; he defeats Lugal-zagesi and reigns for 56 years. The exact location of his city has never been found.

• 2278–2270 B.C.: Reign of his son Rimush, killed in a palace revolt.

• 2270–2254 B.C.: Reign of Rimush's brother Manishtushu, also killed in a palace revolt.

• 2254–2218 B.C.: Reign of Manishtushu's son Naram-Sin, thought to be the first to claim kingship as a divine right. His downfall was traditionally ascribed to divine retribution in the form of invading hordes from the east, called the Gutians. However, new research suggests complex internal problems and the beginning of a 300-year drought as the culprits.

• 2217–2193: Reign of his son Shar-kali-sharri, followed by a period of anarchy.

• 2200 B.C.: Volcanic eruption in Anatolia, after which many Akkadian settlements are abandoned.

• Around 2220–2120: A Gutian dynasty is recorded, among others.

• 2123–2113: Rise of Utu-hegal, who appoints Ur-Nammu as military governor at Ur. Ur-Nammu overthrows his protector, assumes the title of King of Ur and founds a well-organized dynasty. The ziggurat, or stepped tower, prototype of the Tower of Babel, is first recorded in his reign. Ur falls gradually, besieged by invaders like the Amorites and Elamites.

• 2028–2004: Reign of Ibbi-Sin ends with loss of empire. Some years later, a former underling, Ishbi-Erra, expels the Elamites.

• 1984–1975: His son, Shu-ilishu, using the title King of Ur, continues a dynasty noted for peace and prosperity. Amorite influence remains strong and the desert sheiks who lead them are respected. An Amorite dynasty is founded at Larsa. Amorites are gradually assimilated into the Babylonian population.

• 1932–1906 B.C.: An Amorite king, Gungunum, claims titles of King of Sumer and Akkad and of Ur.

• Around 1894 B.C.: Emergence of an Amorite dynasty at Babylon. A city called Shubat-Enlil is built on the ruins of Skekhna, abandoned in the drought.

• 1813–1781: Reign of Shamshi-Adad, a powerful Amorite king.

• 1792–1750 B.C.: Reign of Hammurabi, famous king and lawgiver; toward the end of his reign, Babylon becomes a great military power and the seat of kingship.

• 1595 B.C.: Sack of Babylon by the Hittites, an Indo-European-speaking people from Asia Minor.

---

kingdom often mentioned in the cuneiform writing of the period. This was the archive of Shamshi-Adad, the Amorite king who reigned from 1813 to 1781 B.C., containing the king's correspondence with neighboring rulers who concluded the ransoming of spies.

By then, the Akkadian kingdom of Sargon and Naram-Sin—the world's first empire—was long lost in the dust, apparently also the first empire to collapse as a result of catastrophic climate change.

"Since this is probably the first abrupt climate change in recorded history that caused major social upheaval," Dr. Weiss said, "it raises some interesting questions about how volatile climate conditions can be and how well civilizations can adapt to abrupt crop failures."

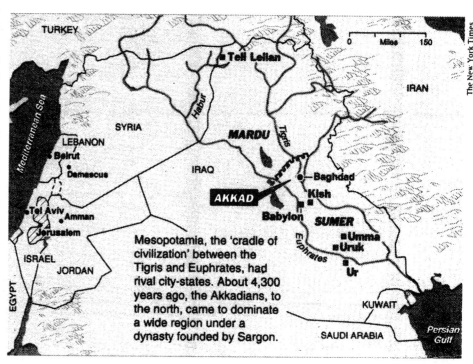

Mesopotamia, the 'cradle of civilization' between the Tigris and Euphrates, had rival city-states. About 4,300 years ago, the Akkadians, to the north, came to dominate a wide region under a dynasty founded by Sargon.

Out of Africa: the superb artwork of ancient Nubia

The rich heritage and tradition of this venerable, long-neglected civilization beside the Nile is now celebrated in four great Western museums

David Roberts

David Roberts' latest book, Once They Moved Like the Wind: Cochise, Geronimo and the Apache Wars, *is published by Simon & Schuster.*

To the ancient Greeks and Romans, Nubia was one of the foremost civilizations of the world. Because its domain lay on the edge of the unknown–south of Egypt, along the tortured cataracts of the upper Nile, where few Greek or Roman travelers had ventured–Nubia shimmered with legend. But there was no mistaking the area's might or wealth.

For centuries, exotic goods had flowed north in an inexhaustible stream from this African font: gold, frankincense, ebony, ivory, panther skins, giraffe tails and hippopotamus teeth. Brave mercenary soldiers, virtuosos of the bow and arrow, also traveled north out of the storied land. Herodotus described Nubians as the "tallest and handsomest" people in the world, adding that they reputedly lived to an age of 120, thanks to a diet of boiled meat and milk. Roman chroniclers reported that the southern empire was ruled by queens. From their own artwork, we know that the Nubian ideal of female beauty put a premium on fatness. Indeed, the sardonic Juvenal claimed that the breasts of Nubian women were bigger than their chubbiest babies. Writing in the third century A.D., a romantic biographer of Alexander the Great insisted that in Nubia there were whole temples carved from a single stone, and houses with translucent walls; the queen traveled in a mobile palace on wheels drawn by 20 elephants.

Although these accounts veered into the fabulous, Nubia was no mere phantasm of the poets, no El Dorado. Within Nubia, stretching along the Nile from present-day Aswan in Egypt to Khartoum in the Sudan, at least six distinct, supremely accomplished cultures evolved between 3800 B.C. and A.D. 600. Nubian civilizations lasted far longer than either classical Greece or Rome. Always a rival to the kingdom to its north, Nubia conquered Egypt around 730 B.C. and ruled it for the following 60 years.

Ta-Seti or Yam or Wawat

Why is it, then, that most of us today have barely heard of Nubia?

One reason is semantic. Over millennia, Nubia was known under many different names. To the early Egyptians, it was Ta-Seti or Yam or Wawat. Later it appears as Meroe. The Greeks and Romans called it Aethiopia (today's Ethiopia being Abyssinia to them). In the Bible it appears as Kush.

Another reason has to do with prejudice. Nubia has always been exceedingly remote and difficult of access. From its Christianization in the 6th century A.D. all the way down to the 19th, the kingdom vanished from the European record: only the glowing reports of the classical authors kept its memory alive. This neglect had everything to do with race–for Nubia had been an African empire, and a black African one at that. Even the Greeks perpetrated the prejudice. An early biographer of Alexander the Great records the queen of Nubia responding to an inquisitive letter from the youthful conqueror in the following words: "Do not despise us for the color of our skin. In our souls we are brighter than the whitest of your people."

The first archaeologists to document the glory that was Nubia succumbed to a kindred bias. Even as he dug the remarkable royal cemeteries of El Kurru below the Fourth Cataract, George A. Reisner, working for Harvard University and the Boston Museum of Fine Arts, concluded that the rulers whose tombs he unearthed must have been an offshoot of a dynasty of Libyan (thus, white-skinned) pharaohs. For decades, everything Nubian was regarded as derived from the Egyptian, hence "decadent" and "peripheral."

Only now, perhaps, is the Western world beginning to acknowledge the achievements of ancient Nubia, as signaled by four dazzling new exhibitions at major North American museums. At the Boston Museum of Fine Arts (MFA)–which, thanks to Reisner and his colleagues, owns one of the finest collections of Nubian treasures in the world–a permanent display opened in 1992. Another permanent installation was unveiled the year before at the Royal Ontario Museum in Toronto. Through September 1993, the Oriental Institute Museum in Chicago will host "Vanished Kingdoms of the Nile: The Rediscovery of Ancient Nubia." And at the University of Pennsylvania's Museum of Archaeology and Anthropology, "Ancient Nubia: Egypt's Rival in Africa" recently opened. After closing in Philadelphia in October 1993, the exhibition will travel to seven other museums around the country, through 1996.

The exhibitions have had strong attendance, particularly among African-Americans, many of them in school groups. And there's evidence that awareness of Nubia is seeping into the popular culture. A new comic-book character called "Heru: Son of Ausar," which was created by cartoonist Roger Barnes, is a Nubian hero. A rap band out of New York City calls itself Brand Nubian.

The surge of interest in Nubia did not arise in a vacuum. For the past 30 years, scholars in Europe and the United States have been piecing together a vivid but tan-

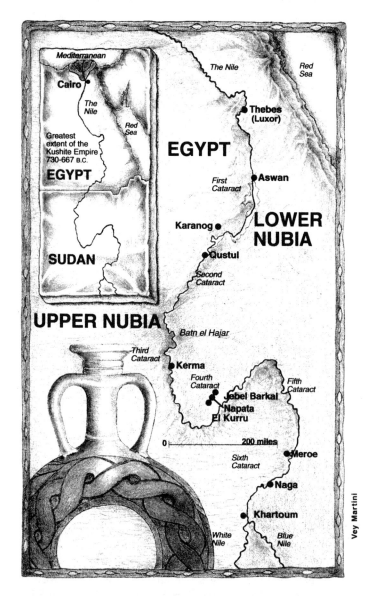

Map of Lower and Upper Nubia displays image of a ring flask from a Meroitic grave, c. 1st/2d century B.C.

talizing picture of the neglected civilization. Yet it took the building of a dam to stimulate this new appraisal of ancient Nubia.

Reisner, the pioneer of Nubian archaeology, was an Egyptologist working on the lower Nile in 1906 when the Egyptian government decided to raise the dam at Aswan by 16.5 feet. Before the resultant flooding could drown forever many unexcavated sites, Reisner was invited to survey and dig upriver. Thus was launched what one scholar calls the "earliest program of extensive salvage archaeology" in the world.

Close on Reisner's heels came two British archaeologists working for the University of Pennsylvania, David Randall-MacIver and Leonard Woolley. The rich collections existing today in Boston and Philadelphia derive from the seminal fieldwork of these scholars. Yet so strong was the lingering condescension toward Nubia as a kind of second-rate Egypt, that as late as 1960 only one American scholar–Dows Dunham, Reisner's protégé and successor at the MFA–was working in Nubian studies.

In 1959 Egypt announced plans to build a huge new dam at Aswan. The waters of the Nile would create Lake Nasser, stretching 300 miles south to the Second Cataract, just across the border in the Sudan. UNESCO launched an all-out appeal to the archaeologists of the world, who responded with scores of energetic expeditions, sowing the seeds of our current understanding of ancient Nubia.

The disruption wrought by the dam was tragic. Nubians whose ancestors had lived along the middle Nile for as long as the oldest tales could testify gathered their belongings and made their exodus north to the planned villages that would replace their own. They kissed the graves of their ancestors; many filled their pockets with sand, their only keepsake of the lost homeland.

Losing one's way could mean losing one's life

On the face of it, Nubia seems an unlikely place for a major civilization to sprout. It lies in the middle of the hottest and driest area on Earth's surface; in much of Nubia, rain never falls. Farther north, in classical Egypt, the Nile creates a generous floodplain up to 15 miles wide, but in Nubia the fertile land bordering the river comes only in intermittent patches rarely exceeding 1,600 yards in width. The cataracts–canyons seamed with big rapids–as well as long, tormented passages such as Batn el Hajar, the "Belly of Rocks"–make continuous navigation up and down the Nile impossible. In the Sudan, where the river makes two great loops in the shape of an *S*, the ancient trade routes struck off on bold shortcuts across the empty desert. To lose one's way often meant to lose one's life. Even today, travel here remains as difficult and as dangerous as anywhere in Africa.

As Reisner plunged into this archaeologically pristine wilderness, where he worked tirelessly from 1907 to 1932, he slapped provisional names on the various cultures he began to identify. Unfortunately, these temporary labels have stuck. Thus we still allude to some Nubian cultures–each as complex and impressive as, say, that of the Hittites or the Etruscans–as the A-Group, the C-Group and the X-Group.

With the emergence of the A-Group around 3800 B.C., Nubia takes its place on the prehistoric stage. We still know relatively little about this early civilization, which became a serious rival to Pre-Dynastic Egypt. The A-Group's most distinctive artifact is a handsome "eggshell" pottery, named for its thin walls. Crisscross hatches and geometric patterns in red and cream seem to conjure up weaving; it is as if the potters were celebrating the discovery of the vessel that worked better than basketry.

Toward the end of its thousand-year sway, the A-Group emerges also in the written record, as the Egyptians invented their hieroglyphic script. The domain of the blacks in Lower Nubia was known in Egypt as Ta-Seti–the "Land of the Bow." Eventually the pharaohs waged war with Ta-Seti. A great victory around 2600 B.C. was won by the pharaoh Sneferu, who bragged that he took 7,000 Nubians and 200,000 domestic animals captive.

Bruce Williams of Chicago's Oriental Institute believes that the earliest definite evidence anywhere in the world of the institution of kingship may be among the A-Group of Nubia. Williams' argument hinges upon a handful of extraordinary objects found in royal A-Group graves. During my own visit to the Oriental Institute, Williams showed me a beautiful stone incense burner found at Qustul (just north of the Sudanese border), dated to around 3300 B.C. The cylindrical burner is encircled by a frieze of incised figures.

Peering through the display glass, I followed Williams' pointing finger. "The falcon means a god," he said. "That's definitely a representation of a king, and he's wearing a crown. The bound prisoner is going to be bashed in the head in front of the god. The burner is definitely a typical Nubian, not an Egyptian, object."

Other scholars, however, reject Williams' theory. Says David O'Connor of the University of Pennsylvania, "I think there may well have been an elite group in Nubia at the time, in charge of a complex chiefdom. But the objects Williams' argument depends on are almost certainly Egyptian, not Nubian–traded to Nubia in early pharaonic times. The kings he sees were Egyptian kings."

One of the most formidable obstacles to an appreciation of ancient Nubia is that, in terms of the written record, we learn about the civilization almost entirely in the words of its enemies–Egyptians above all, but also Hebrews, Assyrians, Persians and Romans. Thus, for the Egyptians, Nubia is always "vile," "miserable," "wretched." The pharaohs had images of Nubians carved on their footstools and on the bottoms of their sandals so that they could trample on their enemies daily.

The aggression of Egypt throughout the third millen-

nium B.C. seems to have driven A-Group survivors south into the little-known lands above the Second Cataract. Around 2300 B.C., a pair of new cultures springs into view. One, appearing in Lower Nubia, was called by Reisner the C-Group. Elaborate tombs suggest these people were skilled pastoralists, raising huge herds of livestock and perhaps worshiping their gods through a cattle cult.

The C-Group kept peace with the kingdom to the north for centuries, during which time trade flourished and ideas flowed both ways. Then, in the 19th century B.C., the pharaohs turned belligerent again. Their motive may have been to control the gold mines that were being opened in the eastern desert. Thrusting above the Second Cataract, Egyptian armies built a series of colossal fortresses along the tortuous Belly of Rocks. These fortresses were placed so that line-of-sight signals could be flashed from one to the next.

Meanwhile, 170 miles beyond the southernmost Egyptian fortress, the most powerful empire Nubia had yet seen was flourishing. Named the Kerma culture by Reisner, who in 1913 excavated tombs close to the modern town of that name, it was known to the Egyptians as the Kingdom of Kush. An ancillary motive for erecting the Egyptian fortresses, with their intensely defensive character, was no doubt fear of Kush.

A flamboyant and grandiose glory

After 1700 B.C., racked by internal struggles, Egypt retreated from Nubia, abandoning its fortresses along the Belly of Rocks. In the void, Kerma grew magnificently. Nothing declares the flamboyant, even grandiose glory of Kerma more forcefully than its royal tombs. The king was buried under a huge tumulus–a circular mound–with the diameter nearly the length of a football field. He was laid on a gold-covered bed, and the finest objects wrought of gold, bronze, ivory and faience were placed beside him. Into the tomb's central corridor crowded a host of followers and concubines (400 of them in one king's tomb), who, dressed in their best clothes, came willingly to be buried alive in honor of their master.

All through Nubia, from Reisner until the present day, burial sites have monopolized archaeologists' attention. This has been true in part because the remains of habitation sites are so hard to find; houses were made of perishable stuff, but tombs were built to last. Only two large villages from the C-Group, for instance, have ever been excavated. Consequently we know much more about the rulers of Nubia than about the commoners.

At Kerma, however, for the past 28 years an international team under Charles Bonnet, of the University of Geneva, has carried out one of the most ambitious digs in Africa. In the process, they have revealed not only the palaces and cemeteries but the main town of Kerma. When I visited Bonnet in Geneva last fall, he showed me the plan of the settlement. Tapping an outlying area with his pencil, he said, "Just last year we found a whole new section of houses here. It goes on and on!" Bonnet's work documents the oldest city that has ever been found in Africa outside Egypt.

Many of the houses Bonnet's team excavated were rectangles of mud bricks, but the most characteristic domicile was a circular hut made of wood (always a rare substance along the Nile), topped with a thatched roof. Each hut was ingeniously designed to allow the prevailing north wind to blow through it during the desperate heat of summer; in winter, a temporary wall blocked the same breeze. Small neighborhoods of huts were bordered by fields and gardens where crops (chiefly wheat and barley) were raised, and cattle and goats pastured. No general plan governed the shape of the sprawling city, but a defensive palisade surrounded it.

Once more the tides of empire shifted. Around 1550 B.C., a newly invigorated Egypt invaded Nubia. The struggle against Kerma lasted 100 years, but at last the pharaohs conquered all but the southernmost reaches of Nubia. Their sway lasted another 350 years, during which the Nubian upper class became thoroughly Egyptianized, decorating their tombs with images of workers on date palm plantations and with performing dancers and musicians.

But the tides shifted again. At the end of the New Kingdom, about 1080 B.C., Egypt was torn by conflict between the pharaohs and the priesthood. The country began to fragment into city states, among them several in Nubia that became all but autonomous. What happened after 1080 remains a great mystery.

According to Timothy Kendall of the MFA, "the greatest gap in our knowledge of ancient Nubia is the period from 1000 to 850 B.C. We know almost nothing about it. Only one or two sites in Nubia can be dated to this period, and then, only to the latter part of it. Some experts believe Nubia was growing stronger and politically independent; others think that Egyptian enclaves and temple estates persisted. But these are theories spun out of thin air. Nobody really has a clue, except that a series of elaborate tombs began to be built in 850 B.C."

When Nubia emerged from this historical void in the eighth century B.C., it did so dramatically, achieving the greatest triumph in all its long history. By this time the center of power lay at Napata, which was just below the Fourth Cataract. Here a holy mountain called Jebel Barkal was believed to be the home of the ram-headed god Amun, who spoke oracles through statues and even selected the country's rulers.

Whatever their motive, after 750 B.C. the Napatan kings pushed boldly north. Around 730, a great army under a king named Piye conquered all of Egypt. He and his successors became the pharaohs of the 25th Dynasty, the later kings moving from Napata to Memphis to govern. The Nubian empire now stretched all the way from the junction of the Blue and White Niles to the delta (present-day Alexandria)–1,200 miles as the crow flies.

Although the inscribed victory stela Piye erected to proclaim his triumph alludes to him in Egyptian hieroglyphs as "raging like a panther" and bursting upon his enemies "like a cloudburst," the Nubian pharaohs of the 25th Dynasty ruled with an enlightened benevolence. They were Medicis, rather than Caesars, who awoke Egypt to the artistic and cultural splendor of its own past as they patronized artists, revived lost learning and rebuilt derelict temples.

Piye was also a great lover of horses, the first of four successive pharaohs to have whole chariot teams buried near his grave. The horses, interred in a standing position, were decked with bead nets and brilliant jewelry. When Piye conquered Hermopolis, the defeated King Nemlot opened his harem. But Piye averted his eyes from the women and demanded to see the king's horses instead. These he found nearly starved to death. "That my horses were made to hunger," he thundered at Nemlot (as recorded on Piye's stela), "pains me more than any other crime you committed in your recklessness. Do you not know God's shadow is above me?"

The brilliance of the Napatan empire speaks in many of the objects now on display in Boston, Philadelphia, Chicago and Toronto. In the MFA, I gazed at haunting rows of *shawabtis*, part of a cache of 1,070 found in the tomb of King Taharqo, Piye's son. Figurines carved out of alabaster and gray or black granite, ranging from seven inches to two feet in height, these sober-looking humans with arms crossed were "answerers" who would perform for the deceased king the work the gods commanded of him. (Here, I thought, was a humane alternative to the retainers buried alive at Kerma!)

One of the most exquisite objects ever recovered from Nubia is also on display in Boston. It is a small pendant from the tomb of one of Piye's wives, a gold head of Hathor, goddess of beauty, mounted on a ball of rock crystal, thought to have magical properties.

The Napatan supremacy was short-lived. By 667 B.C. the Nubian pharaohs had abandoned Egypt to another raging panther, King Esarhaddon of Assyria. Once again, we learn of a profoundly pivotal moment in Nubian history only in the contemptuous boasts of its enemies: "I tore up the root of Kush," crowed Esarhaddon, "and not one therein escaped to submit to me."

Gradually through the next four centuries, the Nubian political and cultural center shifted south beyond the Fourth Cataract. In isolation and relative obscurity, the last Nubian empire evolved. Its center was the town of Meroe, halfway between the Fifth Cataract and the junction with the Blue Nile.

Meroe, which flourished from about 270 B.C. to A.D. 350, is in many respects the most intriguing of all the incarnations of Nubian greatness. Cambyses of the Persians, as well as Petronius among the Romans, sent out armies to conquer the distant country, without success. Even Nero contemplated the possibility of an attack. Despite all this contact, the veil of mystery that clung to the legendary southern land never really lifted.

One reason was linguistic. In their isolation from Egypt, the Meroites lost the use of Egyptian hieroglyphs. By 170 B.C. they had developed their own written language, a quasi-cursive script now called Meroitic. Stelae and plaques covered with this writing abound. By 1909 scholars had proved that it was an alphabetic script (unlike the hieroglyphs, which are part ideographic, part phonetic and part alphabetic). Thanks to a few parallel inscriptions, they had learned the sound values for each of the 23 Meroitic letters. Yet more than eight decades later, the language remains undeciphered.

At first, scholars were confident that Meroitic would turn out to be a cognate of the Nubian tongues spoken today along the Nile. That hope faded, and all that the experts can now assert is that Meroitic seems to be related to no other known language. Decipherment must await the discovery of a Nubian Rosetta Stone—a stela with lengthy parallel texts in Meroitic and Egyptian or Meroitic and Greek.

A royal offering to Amun

In the MFA, I walked around and around a five-foot-tall stela found at Jebel Barkal; covered on all sides with writing, the stone bears the longest known inscription in Meroitic. We know the text has something to do with an offering by King Tanyidamani to the god Amun, and we can see places where lines have been deliberately erased. The rest is enigma.

Timothy Kendall tantalized me further by describing the second-longest Meroitic inscription known, found on a stela now in the British Museum. "If we could read it," he sighed, "we'd have the Meroitic version of the war against Petronius and the Romans in 24 B.C."

In its drift away from Egyptian culture over the centuries, Meroitic art developed its own idiosyncratic genius. At the Oriental Institute, Emily Teeter explained to me its quirks. "It becomes a very spontaneous art, full of free-flowing improvisation," she said, pausing before a Meroitic pot. "You see that?" She pointed to a curling snake painted on the vessel, holding in its mouth a drooping flower. "The flower is obviously an *ankh*."

I gasped in sudden recognition. I had seen many an *ankh* on Egyptian objects: a cross-shaped symbol topped with an oval, which is the hieroglyph for the verb "to live." In Egyptian art, the *ankh* appears alone or in rows of declarative rigidity. On the Meroitic pot, the snake stings the world to life with a flower. "The Egyptians are too staid for this," Teeter said. "They don't like loopy things."

At the University of Pennsylvania museum, David O'Connor guided me through several hundred Meroitic objects from the provincial capital of Karanog, excavated by MacIver and Woolley in 1907-08. The same freedom—a set of wild variations on Egyptian themes—graced these priceless objects. In Egypt, O'Connor explained, the *ba* statue, which represents a dead person's spirit, is a formal-looking bird with a human head; in Meroe, the *ba* becomes a human with wings. The pots dance with two-legged crocodiles, with giraffes ranging from the lordly to the comic, with deer darting through shadows. There are abstract designs made of endless waves of draped festoons and floral curlicues.

The sheer exuberance of Meroitic art proclaims a civilization that believed in pleasure and playfulness. The pots were largely used for wine drinking. At certain Meroitic sites, whole barrooms have been excavated.

At the end of the fourth century A.D., Meroe declined. The distinctive script fell out of use, and no new temples were built. It has long been the fashion to regard the 250-year interim before Christianity, whose culture Reisner called the X-Group, as a Nubian Dark Age; but recent scholars point to the continued excellence of pottery and jewelry, to a flowering of brilliant work in bronze and iron, as well as to the magnificent royal tombs at Ballana and Qustul, as signs of a healthy culture, original in its own right.

Although the Meroitic language seems to have been lost forever, scholars who travel in the Sudan have been struck by the remarkable survival in living cultures of traits and belongings they know also from archaeology. The wood-and-palm-fiber bed a Sudanese sleeps on today looks very much like ones found in royal tombs in Kerma. The throwstick, a proto-boomerang still used for hunting today, is identical to ones retrieved by Reisner from a Kerma tomb. Even current Sudanese fashions in hairstyle and facial scarification find their counterparts in ancient paintings of Nubians.

Thus the discipline of ethnoarchaeology, still in its infancy, may yield new insights into Nubia, as scholars ask living informants to comment on ancient relics. Emily Teeter told me of a pair of small revelations. Shortly after the Oriental Institute's exhibition opened, she met Awad Abdel Gadir, a Sudanese teaching in Texas. He took her aside, pointed to a stone object and said politely, "That's not an incense burner. We have those in our village. It's a receptacle for a liquid offering." Teeter changed the label. He paused before a "thorn-removal kit" from the X-Group—a kind of Swiss Army Knife of iron tools on a chain, including tweezers, picks and scrapers. "I remember," said Abdel Gadir, "my grandmother used to wear a set like that on her belt."

Meanwhile, the archaeological surface of ancient Nubia has barely been scratched. The sites that lie in lower Nubia, north of the Egypt-Sudan border, are gone forever, swallowed by Lake Nasser. In the Sudan, the 1989 coup that brought Islamic fundamentalists to power, as well as the civil war that continues to rage in the country's south, have made it harder than ever for Western archaeologists to work there.

Yet, in the Sudan, a French survey has counted one million ancient mounds, only a fraction of which have been excavated. There are more royal pyramids in the Sudan than in all of Egypt. I asked Timothy Kendall, who has done breakthrough work at Jebel Barkal, where he would dig if he had carte blanche to choose among the Sudan's best Nubian sites.

He leaned back in his chair, put his hands behind his head and smiled. "I'd go to Naga," he said, "although it's just a pipe dream, because the Sudanese Antiquities Service is saving it for themselves."

I knew Naga as a Meroitic site that, uncharacteristically, lay inland in the Butana Desert, some 25 miles south of the Nile. "Why Naga?"

"It's a complete Meroitic city founded about the first century A.D., with important temples, a settlement and a cemetery," Kendall answered. "The residents built an artificial reservoir of water. Not a single spadeful of earth has ever been turned there.

"Of course," he added, gazing off into space at the eternal dilemma that bedevils archaeologists, "you'd need a lot of money, a big team, a lot of cooperation, extreme physical endurance." He paused. "And a very, very long life."

Additional reading

Nubia: Corridor to Africa by William Y. Adams, Princeton University press, 1977

Meroe by Peter L. Shinnie, Praeger (New York), 1967

Nubia Under the Pharaohs by Bruce G. Trigger, Westview Press (Boulder, Colorado), 1983

The African Origin of Civilization: Myth or Reality by Cheikh Anta Diop, Lawrence Hill, 1974

MARRIAGE AND MOTHERHOOD IN ANCIENT EGYPT

We may all know about Nefertiti, but what was life like
for the less-famous women of Ancient Egypt?

Joyce Tyldesley

Joyce Tyldesley *is Honorary Research
Fellow at the School of Archaeology,
Classics and Oriental Studies, Liverpool University. This article has been
adapted from her book* Daughters of
Isis: The Women of Ancient Egypt *Published by Viking 1994, priced £18.*

Found your household and love your
wife at home as is fitting. Fill her stomach with food and provide clothes for
her back … Make her heart glad, as
long as you live.
(Old Kingdom wisdom text)

Those of a cynical disposition
may take the view that marriage
is merely a contract intended to
create an efficient working unit,
strengthen alliances and legitimise
children. For women in particular the
wedding ceremony may also mark the
transition from child to adult and the
start of a new role in society. All these
generalisations are true of marriage
in ancient Egypt, where the formation
of a tight-knit family unit provided
much-welcomed protection against
the harsh outside world. And yet the

Egyptians, through their paintings,
their statues and their lyric love
songs, have passed on to us their satisfied contentment with the romance
of marriage. To marry and beget children may have been the duty of every
right-thinking Egyptian, but it was a
duty which was very much welcomed:
the Egyptians were a very uxorious
race.

The state was remarkably relaxed
in its attitude to marriage, placing no
restriction on unions with either foreigners or slaves, and permitting both
multiple marriages and the marriage
of close relations. However,
polygamy and incest were never rife
in ancient Egypt. With the exception
of the royal family who inter-married
to safeguard the dynastic succession
and emphasise their divine status,
there is no evidence for widespread
brother-sister unions until the Roman
period, while parent-child incest is
virtually unrecorded. The use of the
affectionate term 'sister' to encompass a wide group of loved women,
including wife, mistress, niece and
aunt, has contributed to our misunderstanding of the prevalence of sibling incest. The often-quoted evidence for polygamous marriages is a
papyrus in which the lady Mutemheb
states that she is the fourth wife of

Ramose, adding that two of his other
wives are dead while one is still living. Although the precise circumstances of this marriage are not spelt
out, there is nothing further to suggest a polygamous alliance, and it
may well be that Ramose had
divorced his third wife before marrying his fourth.

There was no legal age of consent,
although it is generally assumed that
a girl would not have been considered eligible before the onset of menstruation at about the age of fourteen. A 26th Dynasty document
recording a father's refusal to agree
to his daughter's wedding because
'her time has not yet come' supports
this view. However, evidence from
Rome, where female puberty was
legally fixed at twelve, indicates that
ten or eleven-year-old brides were
not uncommon, and we have no reason to doubt that equally young girls
were married in Egypt. Indeed, it is
only within the past fifty years that in
modern rural Egypt marriage for girls
as young as eleven has been prohibited by law. There is evidence from the
Graeco-Roman period for Egyptian
girls marrying as young as eight or
nine, and we have a mummy label,
written in demotic, which identified
the body of an eleven-year-old wife.

Vain hopes: appearing attractive to each other (left, a New Kingdom lady with elaborate coiffure, and right, a bronze hand mirror) was a high priority for both sexes in a society which relished the romantic frissons of courtship.

when the marriage ended. One Ptolemaic text gives us a very clear picture of the legal equality of women when it records the business deal of an astute wife who lent her spendthrift husband three *deben* of silver to be paid back within three years at a hefty annual interest rate of 30 per cent.

* * *

I shall not leave him even if they beat me and I have to spend all day in the swamp. Not even if they chase me to Syria with clubs, or to Nubia with palm ribs, or even into the desert with sticks or to the coast with reeds.
(*New Kingdom love song*)

The marriage ended either in death or divorce. Death loomed as an ever present threat to happiness; young girls married to older men frequently became teenage widows, while the dangers associated with childbirth contributed to the many motherless families. Fortunately the woman's right to inherit one third of her husband's property meant that a widow was not forced to rely on the charity of her children or to return to her father's house. Tomb scenes indicate that loving couples torn apart by death confidently expected to be re-

* * *

I see my sister coming. My heart exults and my arms open to embrace her … Oh night, be mine forever, now that my lover has come.
(*New Kingdom lover's song*)

The Egyptians regarded marriage as a personal matter of no concern to the state. Consequently it required no religious or legal ceremony. There was no Egyptian word meaning wedding, no special bridal clothing, no symbolic exchange of rings and no change of name to indicate the bride's new status. The cohabitation of the happy couple served as the only outward sign that the marriage negotiations had been successfully concluded, and it was by physically leaving the protection of her father's

house and entering her new home that a daughter became universally acknowledged as a wife. The nuptial procession, where the young bride was escorted through the streets by a happy crowd of friends and relations, was an occasion for great family rejoicing, with wedding celebrations lasting well into the night.

The new husband assumed the father's former role of protecting and caring for his bride, although he in no way became her legal guardian. The wife retained her independence, and was able to continue administering her own assets. Although the husband usually controlled any joint property acquired during the marriage it was acknowledged that a share of this belonged to the wife; she was able to collect her portion united in the afterlife. In the meantime re-marriage after widowhood was very common, and funerary stelae indicate that some individuals married three or even four times.

Just as marriage was not seen as a matter for state intervention, so divorce was an equally private affair. Almost any excuse could be cited to end an alliance, and in effect any marriage could be terminated at will. Those who had had the foresight to draw up a marriage contract were bound to honour its terms, while those who became involved in acrimonious disputes over the division of joint property could invest in a legal deed to resolve their differences. Legal cases were, however, unusual, and most of marriages ended with the couple separating. The wife left the matrimonial home and returned to her family, setting both parties free to marry again.

* * *

Man is more anxious to copulate than a donkey. What restrains him is his purse.
(*Scribal advice aimed at young men*)

The more intimate aspects of married life were very important to the Egyptians who held the continuing cycle of birth, death and rebirth as a central and often repeated theme in their theology. Intercourse naturally formed an integral part of this cycle, and the Egyptians displayed no false prudery when dealing with the subject of sex. Unlike modern views of heaven, which tend to concentrate on spiritual rather than physical gratification, potency and fertility were regarded as necessary attributes for a full enjoyment of the afterlife, and consequently false penises were moulded onto the mummified bodies of dead men, while their wives were equipped with artificial nipples designed to become fully functional in the afterlife.

The Egyptians were not coy about sexual matters. However, as most of the evidence which they have left us comes from religious or funerary contexts where explicit references to intimate subjects would have been inappropriate, we do not have much opportunity for archaeological voyeurism. Love songs, myths and stories all make veiled references to intercourse, while crude graffiti, dirty

(Above) Middle Kingdom model of a female dwarf and baby.

(Below) Fertility dolls such as these were frequently placed in graves to ensure the deceased against impotence in the next life.

jokes and explicit drawings scribbled on potsherds are far more basic.

One of the world's earliest examples of pornography, the so-called Turin erotic papyrus, contains a series of cartoons depicting several athletic couples cavorting rather self-consciously in a wide variety of imaginative and uncomfortable-looking poses. Unfortunately, we do not know whether the papyrus was a true record of observed events or, as seems more likely, simply represented the draftsman's more extravagant fantasies. Certainly, basing our understanding of conjugal relations on the Turin papyrus would be similar to believing all that is suggested by blue movies to be typical of modern Western life. More down-to-earth evidence compiled from texts and ostraca confirms that 'face-to-face' positions and intercourse from behind were the preferred sexual postures for most couples.

* * *

Then Seth said to Horus: 'Come, let us have a party at my house'. And Horus said to him: 'I will'. When evening had come a bed was prepared for them, and they lay down together. During the night Seth let his penis become stiff, and he inserted it between the thighs of Horus. And Horus placed his hand between his thighs and caught the semen of Seth.
(*New Kingdom tale*)

We must assume that alternative sexual tastes did exist, but the Egyptians themselves maintained a discreet silence in these matters. Homosexual activity, which was by no

means frowned upon in the ancient world, seems to have played little part in Egyptian daily life, while lesbianism is completely unrecorded. *The Book of the Dead* lists abstinence from homosexual acts amongst the virtues but gives us no indication of how common such acts might have been, while the homosexual episode in the New Kingdom tale of Horus and Seth, quoted above, has been variously interpreted as either a symbol of Seth's general unfitness to rule or as a sign of Seth's physical dominance over his nephew.

Rumours of more fantastic sexual behaviour were recorded by the Greek historian, Herodotos, who seems to have been particularly fascinated by the seamier side of Egyptian life: 'In my lifetime a monstrous thing happened in this province, a woman having open intercourse with a he-goat'. Even if this was true it was clearly not a common occurrence. Necrophilia involving the abuse of freshly dead female bodies in the embalming houses, also hinted at by Herodotos, is again totally unrecorded by the Egyptians themselves.

Adultery, 'the great sin which is found in women', was the most serious marital crime which a wife could commit. Men in turn were expected to respect another man's sole right of access to his wife, and indulging in sexual relations with a married woman was frowned upon. Relationships between two unmarried and consenting lovers appear to have been acceptable, but a liaison between an unmarried woman and a married man could be fraught with danger; one letter tells us how a group of Deir el-Medina villagers ganged together to confront a woman known to be conducting a clandestine affair with the husband of a neighbour. The wronged wife had attracted the sympathy of her community, and her husband was ordered to regularise his affairs at once. The adulterous woman was clearly seen as a temptress, and indeed Egyptian myths and wisdom texts are full of warnings to stay clear of wives who would deliberately snare men into sexual relationships.

A wife caught in adultery was open to the harshest of physical punishments. In theory she could be put to death; the New Kingdom Westcar Papyrus tells how an unfaithful wife was burned and her ashes scattered on the River Nile, while in the tale of the Two Brothers Anubis eventually kills his guilty wife and throws her body to the dogs. In practice divorce and social disgrace seem to have been the accepted penalty, and an adulterous wife was roundly condemned by everyone.

* * *

Double the food which your mother gave you and support her as she supported you. You were a heavy burden to her but she did not abandon you. When you were born after your months she was still tied to you as her breast was in your mouth for three years. As you grew larger and your excrement was disgusting she was not disgusted. (*New Kingdom scribal instruction*)

In the days following her wedding the bride would have eagerly looked for signs that a baby was on the way. It would be very difficult for us to over-emphasise the importance of her fertility to the Egyptian woman. A fertile woman was a successful woman. She was the envy of her less fortunate sisters and, as the mother of many children, she gained the approval of both society and her husband. Every man needed to prove his masculinity by fathering as many children as possible, and to do this he needed a fruitful wife. The wife, for her part, needed many children to ensure her security within the marriage. To produce a large brood of children was every Egyptian's dream, and babies were regarded as a cause for legitimate boasting; we must assume, however, that the 11th Dynasty army captain claiming to have fathered 'seventy children, the issue of one wife' was exaggerating to emphasise his virility.

Although the mechanism of menstruation was not fully understood the significance of missing periods was clear, and most Egyptian women were able to diagnose their own pregnancies. Those who were in doubt could consult a doctor who would conduct a detailed examination of the skin, eyes and breasts. As an additional test, a urine sample was poured over sprouting vegetables or cereals, with subsequent strong growth confirming pregnancy. Following a positive test it was possible to anticipate the sex of the unborn child by sprinkling more urine over sprouting wheat and barley: a rapid growth of barley would indicate a boy; wheat a girl.

Doctors developed a number of tests to determine whether a childless woman was ever likely to conceive. A physical inspection could prove helpful as, 'if you find one of her eyes similar to that of an Asiatic, and the other like that of a southerner, she will not conceive'. However, even the most experienced of physicians could offer no hope to those faced with the tragedy of a childless marriage. Infertility was invariably blamed on the wife, and consequently barren marriages were often 'cured' by divorce, with the husband simply taking a different and hopefully more fertile partner. This harsh treatment was generally frowned upon, and a Late Period scribe advised 'do not divorce a woman of your household if she does not conceive and does not give birth'. A more socially acceptable means of ending sterility was adoption. The short life expectancy and high birth rate meant that there was always a supply of orphaned children, and infertile couples frequently adopted the child of a poorer relation.

Childbirth was not considered a matter for male interference, and the medical texts offered little practical advice to the midwives who customarily assisted at the delivery. Indeed, the whole process of birth developed into a secretive female-controlled rite. This means that our understanding of the single most important event in the Egyptian woman's life has to be pieced together from fragments of surviving stories and myths combined with the illustrations of divine births carved on certain temple walls. This type of evidence is strong on ritual and symbolic content but rather weak on practical details.

The Westcar Papyrus gives our most detailed account of childbirth when telling the story of the birth of triplets to the lady Reddjedet. Reddjedet was assisted by four goddesses who arrived at her house disguised as itinerant midwives. Isis stood in front of the mother-to-be and delivered the babies, Nephthys stood behind her, and Heket used an unspecified technique to 'hasten' the births. Meskhenet then told the fortunes of the new-born babies while the god Khnum gave them life. All three infants were washed, their umbilical cords were cut, and they were placed on a cushion on bricks. Reddjedet then presented the midwives with a payment of corn, and 'cleansed herself in a purification of fourteen days'.

Although ostraca recovered from Deir el-Medina suggest that women in labour may have entered a 'birth bower', a tent-like structure with walls hung with garlands, these representations probably have more symbolic than literal meaning, with most births occurring within the family home. For her delivery the naked mother-to-be either knelt or squatted on two low piles of bricks or sat on a birthing-stool, a seat with a hole large enough for the baby to pass through. Gravity was used to assist the birth, and the midwife who squatted on the floor was able to help the mother by easing the baby out. For more difficult cases there were several approved procedures intended to 'cause a woman to be delivered'; these included bandaging the lower abdomen and the use of vaginal suppositories. The only surgical implement used by the midwife was the obsidian knife used to cut the umbilical cord after the delivery of the afterbirth.

Tragedies associated with childbirth were all too common. Pelvic abnormalities sufficient to make delivery difficult if not impossible have been recognised in several mummies; one of the worst examples is the 12th Dynasty mummy of the lady Henhenet which shows a dreadful tear running from the bladder to the vagina, almost certainly caused when a large baby was dragged through the mother's abnormally narrow pelvis. The royal family was not exempt from these tragedies, and the body of Mutnodjmet, wife of King Horemheb, was recovered with the body of a foetus or new-born child, suggesting that the queen had died attempting to provide an heir to the throne.

Few infant burials have been recovered, and it seems that a baby who was stillborn or who died soon after birth was not accorded full funerary rites; the recovery of small corpses buried under villages houses implies that the dead baby itself may have

had some religious or superstitious value. This suggestion is reinforced by the discovery of two miniature coffins of gilded wood within the tomb of Tutankhamun. Each contained an inner coffin and a tiny mummified foetus. These could be two premature children born to the young king and his queen, but the inclusion of the small bodies within the tomb may have had a more complex symbolic meaning as yet unexplained.

* * *

I made live the names of my fathers which I found obliterated on the doorways ... Behold, he is a good son who perpetuates the names of his ancestors.
(*Middle Kingdom tomb inscription*)

The mother named her baby immediately after the birth, thereby ensuring that the child had a name even if he or she died. Names were very important to the Egyptians, who felt that knowledge of a name conferred power over the named person or object. One of their greatest fears was that a personal name might be forgotten after death. Dying a 'second death', the complete obliteration of all earthly memory of the deceased including the name, was too awful to contemplate, and specific spells 'for not perishing in the land of the dead' were routinely painted on coffins.

Most non-royal Egyptians were given only one name. We know of many examples of personal names being favoured repeatedly within one family; a good example is the family of the New Kingdom Third Prophet of Amun, where sons were named in alternate generations Pediamunnebnesttawy ('Gift of Amun who is Lord of the Thrones of the Two Lands') and Hor ('Horus'). Family names were also given to girls, and it was not considered confusing that both a mother and one or more of her daughters should share the same name. The Egyptians did not baulk at very long names; Hekamaatreemperkhons son of Hekhemmut would not have felt particularly hard done by, although it is not surprising that nick-names were widely used. Naming children in honour of members of the royal family was popular, and attractive animals or flowers made nice names; Susan, 'a lily', was a favourite for Egyptian girls.

* * *

My son, O King, take thee to my breast and suck it ... He has come to these his two mothers, they of the long hair and pendulous breasts ... They draw their breasts to his mouth and evermore do they wean him.
(*Old Kingdom pyramid text*)

It was customary to breast-feed infants for up to three years, way beyond the point where the child would happily eat solid foods. Not only did breast milk provide the most nutritious, convenient and sterile form of nourishment for babies, it also had a contraceptive effect, reducing the chances of the new mother becoming pregnant too soon after giving birth. The image of a woman squatting to suckle a child at her left breast became symbolic of successfully fertile womanhood, frequently depicted in both secular and religious Egyptian art. Medical papyri suggested that the quality of the milk should be tested; 'to recognise milk which is bad, you shall perceive that its smell is like the stench of fish'. To ensure a copious supply of milk the same texts advise rubbing the mother's back with a special mixture, or feeding her with sour barley bread.

Mothers of high birth frequently left the feeding of their baby to a wetnurse who would undertake to feed the child for a fixed period of time at an agreed salary. Late Period contracts usually included a clause stating that the nurse would not indulge in sexual intercourse for the duration of her employment as this may have resulted in pregnancy and the end of lactation. Throughout the dynastic period the position of royal wet-nurse was one of the most important and influential positions that a non-royal woman could hold. However, by the Roman period wet-nurses had become less valued, and we have a number of contracts which make it clear that nurses were being paid to rear foundlings. These orphan children were later sold by their owners, a practice which made sound economic sense at a time of high slave-prices.

As they grew up, children played with a range of carved animals, miniature boats, wooden balls and spinning tops which would delight any modern child. For those who could not afford such luxuries there were the open fields to run in and the river and canals to swim in, while the thick Nile mud made a satisfying modelling clay. However, childhood was a relatively short-lived experience, and as the children grew older they were gradually introduced to the work which they would be doing for the rest of their lives. Young children supervised their tiny brothers and sisters or cared for animals, girls helped their mothers around the house and older boys were sent to school or started to learn their trade.

After a mere thirteen or fourteen years the wheel had turned full circle. Parents could start to consider eligible marriage partners for their teenage girl, working hard to arrange a suitable marriage which would strengthen the family unit and re-enforce alliances whilst giving protection to both their child and future grandchildren. The age, wealth and social connections of prospective bridegrooms would all be subjected to detailed scrutiny. The daughter herself would already be eagerly anticipating the day when she would meet her intended husband and embark upon the most important female role in Egyptian society – that of wife and mother.

FOR FURTHER READING:
R.M. Janssen & J.J. Janssen, *Growing up in Ancient Egypt*, (The Rubicon Press, 1990); M. Lichtheim, *Ancient Egyptian Literature I, II & III*, (University of California Press, 1973-80); L. Manniche, *Sexual Life in Ancient Egypt*, (Kegan Paul International, 1987); P.W. Pestman, *Marriage and Matrimonial Property in Ancient Egypt*, (E.J. Brill, 1961); G. Robins, *Women in Ancient Egypt*, (British Museum Publications, 1993); B. Watterson, *Women in Ancient Egypt*, (Alan Sutton, 1991).

TALES

FROM   THE

CRYPT

*The secrets of a pharaoh's sons could lie in the
tomb that sheltered them for three millenniums*

For years, the ground rumbled and shook mysteriously in one area where tourist buses parked in Egypt's Valley of the Kings. But few paid attention to ground noises in the region of the pharaohs' tombs, except a plucky Egyptologist named Kent Weeks, who was transfixed. Could the reason be that the limestone bedrock, the color of mist, hid unknown caves? Out of the question, experts scoffed. Two centuries of exploration had unearthed everything useful from the era between 1550 B.C. and 1070 B.C., including the phenomenal, gold-strewn burial site of Tutankhamen. All the pharaohs had been accounted for.

But 53-year-old Weeks, an archaeologist from the American University in Cairo, had clues that *something* was there. From 1986 on, he had been mapping the Valley of the Kings and the adjacent ancient capital of Thebes, now known as Luxor. In his research he found a report from 1820 by an Englishman, James Burton, who had explored an entranceway 100 feet from the tomb of Ramses II but stopped after partially digging up three seemingly unpromising

chambers. Moreover, an ancient papyrus recorded the arrest, torture and execution of a thief who in 1150 B.C. robbed not only the tomb of Ramses II but another tomb "across the path."

Weeks played his hunch when he heard in 1987 that the Egyptian government planned to expand a road and parking lot to accommodate the ever increasing tourist traffic to Ramses's crypt. Hold the bulldozers, he suggested. "Nobody would want a cave-in," he argued.

After seven summers of digging, the estimable Weeks was proved right. He discovered this February that the site contains the largest, most elaborate and most unusual tomb in the Valley of the Kings and perhaps the remains of 50 of the 52 sons of Ramses II. (The daughters, numbering as many as 50, are nowhere to be found.) Archaeologists are calling it one of the most significant discoveries in Egyptology this century—because it sheds new light on the 66-year reign of a great pharaoh, conqueror and builder who also might have suffered humiliation at the hands of his Hebrew slaves. In the Old Testament, the final blow that

prompted the pharaoh, believed to be Ramses II, to free the Israelites was the death of all firstborn Egyptian sons. And inscriptions in the newly discovered tomb suggest that one of those buried there is Amen-hir-khopshef, the firstborn son of Ramses. The expansionist era of Ramses is enormously important in Egyptian history, and the hieroglyphics, artifacts and information from mummified remains in the tomb could reveal rich insights into his reign from 1279 B.C. to 1213 B.C. "This is a multiple burial of many royal children, a tomb of unique plan and size," says Weeks.

A long haul. Weeks knew fairly soon after he began digging in 1988 that the site was important. He began at the bottom of the slope in an area 30 feet by 100 feet, where test tunnels called sondages were dug. On the sixth or seventh try, the team hit solid, smooth bedrock about 5 feet down, unmistakably chiseled with flintstone tools. More excavation with picks and trowels yielded an entrance cut into the bedrock. It was nearly 7 feet tall and more than 4 feet wide, and Weeks knew it had to be the entrance Burton had seen. After unblocking the entrance, Weeks crawled behind it, but, to his disappointment, his electric light exposed no decoration on the walls. This lack of ornamentation was what had deterred Burton in 1820. Weeks pressed on.

For the rest of the season—a mere six weeks, Weeks's summer break—the diggers removed more rubble from the cave, much of it carried in by the torrential flash floods that rip through the desert once in a century. The outlines of four symmetrical chambers, two to the right and two to the left, began to appear. To protect the site from intruders, the laborers installed a door of hefty steel bars in the entranceway, padlocked it and departed.

A year later, the team returned, and its digging yielded evidence that the traffic and a leaking sewer line were causing cracks in the tomb's ceiling. Weeks persuaded the authorities to reroute traffic above the dig and to lay the sewer pipes elsewhere. As the rubble was removed, the emerging walls revealed more and more hieroglyphics. The inscriptions brought the stunning revelation that the first two chambers, to the right of the entranceway, referred to two children of Ramses II: the eldest, Amen-hir-khopshef, who, the text says, served in the Army, and the son born next, also named Ramses.

As the rubble kept offering fragments of mummies, undoubtedly hacked apart by robbers looking for amulets and jewelry, Weeks theorized that he might have found the burial site of Ramses's sons. He figured that the robbers must have brought the mummies from rooms still unexplored.

Into the cave. Resuming work the following summer, in 1990, he had more rubble removed and put up wooden supports to block loose rocks from falling from the ceiling. Crawling deeper into the cave through the narrow corridor from which the first four chambers open, Weeks found himself in a large hall 50 feet square and 12 feet high. He knew the magnitude of his find had grown when he counted 16 pillars cut out of the bedrock. "The room," he says, "is larger than all others in the Valley of the Kings, exceeded only by the burial chamber of Ramses II."

For the next four summers, the team continued to sift the rubble, finding hundreds of fragments. "There is nothing intact in the tomb," says Weeks. "The robbers have been through everything." The shattered finds include the finest goods of Ramses's Egypt: faience jewelry, inlaid wooden furniture, alabaster sarcophagi and stone and terra-cotta pots.

The dig speeded up this winter when Weeks went on a sabbatical and did not have to wait until the summer to start the season. The next breakthrough came in

February when workmen removed from the back of the pillared hall a large rock that had fallen centuries ago and blocked a doorway leading to yet another corridor—the end of which branched, T-shaped, into two more corridors. Identical small chambers lined the corridors on either side. It is a baffling design, unlike any other in the valley. Weeks hopes eventually to understand the significance of the special design of the crypt and its contents in his quest to probe Ramses's life and times.

At the end of the first corridor came another surprise: a 5-foot-high statue of Osiris, the god of the dead, cut from

THE FORGOTTEN TOMB

This February, after seven years of exploration, a team led by Kent Weeks uncovered a doorway leading to an enormous tomb that might contain the remains of 50 of the 52 sons of Ramses II, one of Egypt's greatest pharaohs. The site may be the largest and most complex ever discovered in Egypt's Valley of the Kings. Silt and debris brought down by flash floods and recent tour-bus traffic left only crawl space below the ceiling. Archaeologists hope to find another floor below the first when they return to the site in July.

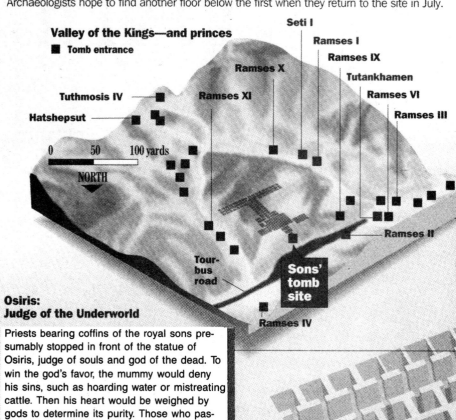

Valley of the Kings—and princes
■ Tomb entrance

Tuthmosis IV
Hatshepsut
Ramses XI
Ramses X
Seti I
Ramses I
Ramses IX
Tutankhamen
Ramses VI
Ramses III
Ramses II
Tour-bus road
Sons' tomb site
Ramses IV

0   50   100 yards
NORTH

Osiris: Judge of the Underworld

Priests bearing coffins of the royal sons presumably stopped in front of the statue of Osiris, judge of souls and god of the dead. To win the god's favor, the mummy would deny his sins, such as hoarding water or mistreating cattle. Then his heart would be weighed by gods to determine its purity. Those who passed the test would be transformed into happy beings in the afterlife. Elaborate preparations were made for death and burial. Objects laid in tombs—chairs, chariots, boats, living-room furniture—were placed so the pharaohs, who had successfully navigated the netherworld, would have a more comfortable afterlife.

Stairway
Midway through each corridor, ceilings slope dramatically, suggesting a stairway beneath the rubble.

Outer rooms
Archaeologists worked for seven summers in the outer rooms before discovering a wooden door here that led to the inner area. The fact that the door is off center from the tomb entrance suggests that there may be other corridors or stairways leading out of the room.

Names of Ramses sons 1, 2, 7 and 15 found in two outer rooms and entranceway

DAVID S. MERRILL, ROBERT KEMP AND ROD LITTLE—*USN&WR*

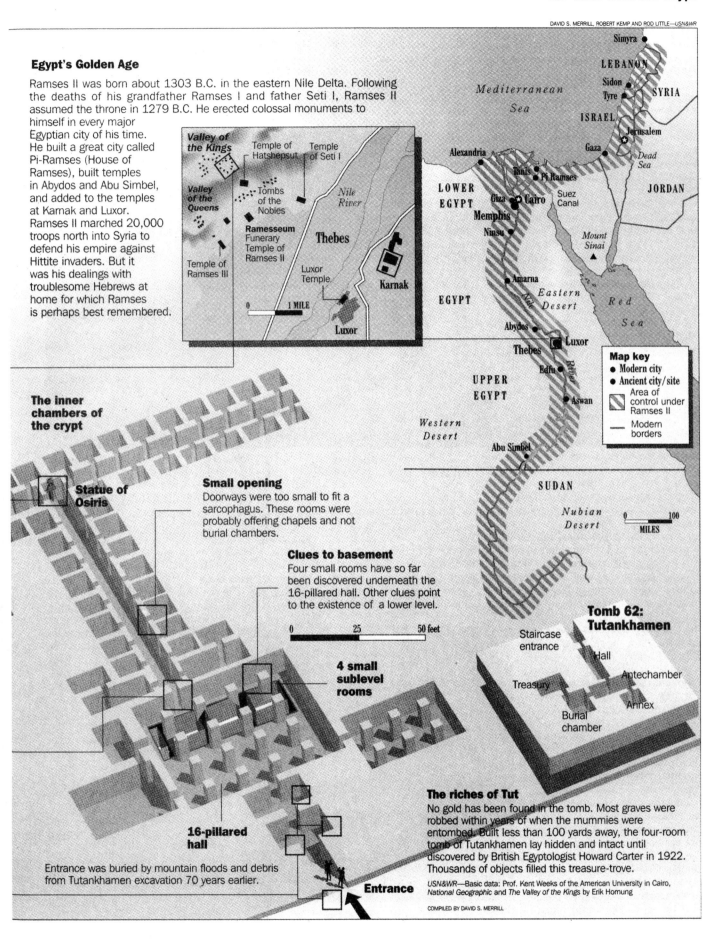

Egypt's Golden Age

Ramses II was born about 1303 B.C. in the eastern Nile Delta. Following the deaths of his grandfather Ramses I and father Seti I, Ramses II assumed the throne in 1279 B.C. He erected colossal monuments to himself in every major Egyptian city of his time. He built a great city called Pi-Ramses (House of Ramses), built temples in Abydos and Abu Simbel, and added to the temples at Karnak and Luxor. Ramses II marched 20,000 troops north into Syria to defend his empire against Hittite invaders. But it was his dealings with troublesome Hebrews at home for which Ramses is perhaps best remembered.

Valley of the Kings
Temple of Hatshepsut
Temple of Seti I
Valley of the Queens
Tombs of the Nobles
Nile River
Ramesseum Funerary Temple of Ramses II
Thebes
Temple of Ramses III
Luxor Temple
Karnak
Luxor
0   1 MILE

Simyra
LEBANON
Sidon
Tyre
SYRIA
Mediterranean Sea
ISRAEL
Jerusalem
Alexandria
Gaza
Dead Sea
Tanis
Pi Ramses
JORDAN
LOWER EGYPT
Suez Canal
Giza
Cairo
Memphis
Mount Sinai ▲
Ninsu
EGYPT
Amarna
Eastern Desert
Red Sea
Abydos
Luxor
Thebes
UPPER EGYPT
Edfu
Aswan
Western Desert
Abu Simbel

Map key
● Modern city
● Ancient city/site
▨ Area of control under Ramses II
— Modern borders

SUDAN
Nubian Desert
0   100
MILES

The inner chambers of the crypt

Statue of Osiris

Small opening
Doorways were too small to fit a sarcophagus. These rooms were probably offering chapels and not burial chambers.

Clues to basement
Four small rooms have so far been discovered underneath the 16-pillared hall. Other clues point to the existence of a lower level.

0   25   50 feet

4 small sublevel rooms

16-pillared hall

Entrance was buried by mountain floods and debris from Tutankhamen excavation 70 years earlier.

Entrance

Tomb 62: Tutankhamen

Staircase entrance
Hall
Treasury
Antechamber
Annex
Burial chamber

The riches of Tut

No gold has been found in the tomb. Most graves were robbed within years of when the mummies were entombed. Built less than 100 yards away, the four-room tomb of Tutankhamen lay hidden and intact until discovered by British Egyptologist Howard Carter in 1922. Thousands of objects filled this treasure-trove.

USN&WR—Basic data: Prof. Kent Weeks of the American University in Cairo, *National Geographic* and *The Valley of the Kings* by Erik Hornung

COMPILED BY DAVID S. MERRILL

limestone bedrock so soft that a kitchen knife can shape it. The god—a traditional adornment of the tombs of the great—was there to judge the dead and guard the crypt.

Beyond the statue, the dig has uncovered 67 chambers, most of them decorated with paintings and inscriptions. Weeks says he is "90 percent sure" there is another, deeper level. At the end of one corridor, he says, the ceiling slopes down, which is a sign that it is a staircase. His hypothesis: The chambers he has uncovered so far served as a ceremonial area for prayers and offerings, and the level below must contain the burial chambers with their sarcophagi. He notes that he found five more doorways, and the spaces behind them are waiting to be explored.

The team will be back at work in early July. The top priorities are to keep clearing and sifting the rubble and to conserve items such as segments of plaster walls with inscriptions that fell into the rubble. Another, long-range study will involve matching body parts and determining their identities through DNA testing and the inscriptions found on linen mummy bindings and the walls.

Rewriting the books. For Weeks, who decided to become an archaeologist at age 9, this is the big find that all archaeologists dream about—a treasure-trove of precedent-shattering data that sends scholars back to their desks to rewrite their books. He has a ready smile, and lets out a belly laugh when asked what would happen if he found the body of Ramses's firstborn son with his skull cracked, thus confirming the truth of the tenth biblical strike that finally persuaded the pharaoh to let the people of the Hebrew God go. "We don't know how he died," he adds, turning somber. "But he was in his 20s or 30s." Then spurting scholarly cold water, he explains that Egyptian inscriptions do not concede defeats, nor do they mention people as unimportant to them as a band of Asiatic slaves.

Weeks figures that the tomb will require at least 30 years of work to piece together not only artifacts but the theological and social order it was designed to express. "This kind of a mausoleum does not reflect the whim of an architect," he says. "Its unique size, location and function had to be endorsed by priests who had to develop a long series of theological arguments first." Weeks is looking forward to working on his find for the rest of his life.

CHARLES FENYVESI

New Finds Suggest Even Earlier Trade on Fabled Silk Road

A silken thread in a mummy's tomb is a key piece of evidence.

John Noble Wilford

New archeological discoveries suggest that trade across the sweep of Eurasia may have begun in some form many centuries earlier than thought. The findings, coupled with a widening range of scientific and historical research, could write a fascinating new chapter in the epic of the legendary Silk Road.

The latest and most surprising discovery is strands of silk found in the hair of an Egyptian mummy from about 1000 B.C., long before regular traffic on the Silk Road and a good millennium before silk was previously thought to be used in Egypt. Other research may extend human activity along this route back even further, perhaps a million years to the migrations of human ancestors into eastern Asia.

The official origin of East-West commerce along the road is usually placed in the late second century B.C. An agent of the Chinese Emperor Wu-ti returned from a dangerous secret mission across the western desert into the remote high country of Central Asia. The agent, Zhang Qien, traveled as far as Afghanistan and brought back knowledge of even more distant lands like Persia, Syria and a place known as Li-jien, presumably Rome. Historians have called this one of the most important journeys in antiquity.

His journey opened the way for what have been thought to be the first indirect contacts between the ancient world's two superpowers, China and Rome. Chinese silk, first traded to Central Asian tribes for war horses and to the Parthians of old Persia in exchange for acrobats and ostrich eggs, was soon finding its way through a network of merchants to the luxury markets of Rome. All this effort, the historian Pliny wrote, was "so Roman women may expose their charms through transparent cloth."

Thus began more than 1,500 years of active commerce in goods and ideas along what is now known as the Silk Road. From Xian, the capital of the Han Dynasty, the caravan tracks ran west across the bleak Taklamakan Desert to the oasis city of Kashgar, through mountain passes to Samarkand and Bukhara, thence eventually to Byzantium, today's Istanbul, or the Mediterranean ports at Antioch and Tyre to meet ships bound for Alexandria and Rome. By this route, Christianity, Buddhism, Islam and Marco Polo reached China, and Genghis Khan conquered much of Eurasia.

But the new discoveries reveal that Chinese silk was apparently present in the West long before the Han emperor started organized trade over the Silk Road. The research could revise thinking about the early history of world trade and provide insights into the mystery of just how and when Europe and the Mediterranean lands first became aware of the venerable culture at the other end of Eurasia.

After microscopic, infrared and chemical analyses, scientists at the University of Vienna determined that the material from the mummy was clearly silk and almost certainly from China. The scientists, writing in the journal Nature two weeks ago, said their work "would shed new light on ancient trading practices."

Although Egyptologists were cautious in their first reactions, other archeologists said the discovery, if confirmed by further testing, gave greater credibility to previous reports of silk fabrics being excavated in seventh-century B.C. graves in Germany and fifth-century B.C. burials in Greece. The presence of silk at the most thoroughly studied site, in the southwestern German state of Baden-Württemberg, was already beginning to influence interpretations of long-distance contacts between East and West in prehistory.

"I'm glad to see people finding silk outside China at this early date," said Irene Good, a specialist in the archeology of silk at the University of Pennsylvania's University Museum. "After all, this was the end of the Bronze Age and the beginning of the Iron Age in the Near East. Trade was expanding by sea and overland by camel and cart and horse. We are seeing a world economy emerging at this point."

By coincidence, the mummy silk discovery comes at a time of renewed scholarly interest in the Silk Road. Many lands along the route, gaining independence with the collapse of the Soviet Union, are welcoming outsiders to explore archives, art treasures and archeological ruins. International art experts are to meet this fall to plan the conservation of paintings at Buddhist shrines along the Silk Road.

Geologists plan new radar surveys from space to map ruins of long-abandoned caravan stations half buried in desert sands. Teams of anthropologists have been searching for stone tools and fossils that could reveal traces of the first humans to migrate to eastern Asia, showing that they probably followed the route that became the Silk Road.

The Silk Roads Project, begun in 1990 by Unesco, is bringing together a variety of scholars from 90 countries for field trips along parts of the route and seminars to exchange research findings. One program, for example, is to collect and analyze the oral and written epic traditions of the Silk Road countries.

SHIFTING NETWORK OF CARAVAN TRAILS

"The Silk Road has become fashionable," said Dr. Denis Sinor, a historian of Central Asia at Indiana University in Bloomington and coordinator of a Unesco study of the languages used in communicating along the trade route.

The allure of the Silk Road through history is not hard to understand. It was not so much a road as a way, a shifting network of caravan trails between remote kingdoms and oasis trading posts. No one, until the Mongols in the 13th century, traversed the entire route. People at one end were only dimly aware of what lay more than 4,000 miles away at the other end. Exotic goods seemed to arrive as if from nowhere.

Egyptian discovery indicates the silk trade may have existed as early as the tenth century B.C.

Caravans headed east with gold, woolens, ivory, amber and glass. From China the camels were laden with furs, ceramics and lacquer, as well as silk. By the first century B.C., the Romans could not get enough of this commodity, which to them was synonymous with China. The Romans had learned of the Chinese from the Greeks, who called them "Seres," and the Latin word for silk became "serica."

Silk is produced by caterpillars of several moth species belonging to the genus Bombyx. Domesticated silkworms feeding on white mulberry leaves build a cocoon out of a fine thread running to lengths of 2,000 to 3,000 feet. The filament can be unwound by softening the cocoon with water.

Tradition has it that the process was discovered by accident in the third millennium B.C. by the Chinese Empress Hsi Ling-shi. She was sitting in a garden when a cocoon fell from a tree into some hot water, perhaps her tea. As she withdrew the cocoon, it came out as a long delicate thread of silk.

However that may be, silk production became a national industry and was thriving by 1500 B.C. The process was such a carefully kept secret that 1,500 years later China's eager customers, the Romans, remained in the dark, thinking that silk somehow grew on trees. Pliny called silk "the down from leaves." Not until the sixth century A.D. did the secret get out. Two Christian monks are said to have concealed silkworm eggs in the hollows of their wooden staffs and smuggled them out of China by the Silk Road.

UNAUTHORIZED TRADING?

Any silk fibers in the West before that time, Ms. Good said, must be closely examined to separate the inferior products of some Mediterranean silkworms from the genuine Chinese articles. If chemical tests show a virtual absence of the gummy protein sericin, then the silk is assumed to have undergone Chinese processing.

In a telephone interview, Dr. Gert Lubec, a chemist who directed the mummy examination and whose next project is to study the hair of the 5,000-year-old man found in the Alpine ice two years ago, said the Vienna tests were thorough and convincing. "If people go and examine the hair and cloth of other Egyptian mummies," he said, "they will probably find more silk."

The mummy in question, a woman of 30 to 50 years of age, was found at the burial ground of the king's workers at Thebes. It was one of many mummies and artifacts removed by Russian and Eastern European archeologists to save them from flooding by the Aswan Dam.

The Vienna researchers noted that silk was not widely used in Egypt until the fourth century A.D., although a descrip-

tion of Cleopatra four decades earlier did dwell on "her white breasts resplendent through" a fabric that was "wrought in close texture by the skill of the Seres."

If Chinese silk reached the West as early as 1000 B.C., as indicated, Ms. Good said it was undoubtedly the result of unauthorized trading. Chinese border officials may have bribed nomad warriors with silk, and then some of the goods changed hands many times across Asia into the Mediterranean region. Archeologists have surmised that the seventh-century silk in Germany came over the usual trade route into the Middle East and by sea to Massalia, today's Marseilles, then up river valleys into the heart of Europe. Other evidence, Ms. Good said, suggested that the silk could have traveled across the Russian steppes into central Europe.

Other scientists are trying to extend the history of trans-Asia traffic back even further. Judging by fossil remains, early human ancestors, Homo erectus, migrated out of Africa at least a million years ago and later showed up in China and other parts of eastern Asia. It is the informed hunch of Dr. John W. Olsen, an anthropologist at the University of Arizona, that they traveled the route of the future Silk Road.

"Many of the same geographical factors that made the Silk Road a useful means of communications—mountain passes, level terrain and oases—may have also influenced prehistoric travel," Dr. Olsen said.

In several expeditions into the Central Asian deserts, Dr. Olsen has been digging for stone artifacts and fossils, any sign that Homo erectus passed this way. Some 20,000-year-old stone tools he found represented, he said, "the earliest-known evidence of human populations in Chinese central Asia." Russian geologists may be having better luck. They have encountered artifacts buried in the Pamir Mountains that seem to be traces of humans 800,000 years ago. Dr. Olsen said this was "potentially a very important find."

Ever since spaceborne radar systems helped uncover the "lost city" of Ubar in the Arabian peninsula in 1991, archeologists and remote-sensing experimenters have been eager to apply the technology to identifying buried settlements on the Silk Road. The imaging radar system tested on space shuttle flights is capable of penetrating the desert to reveal everything from ancient river beds to city ruins.

Parts of the Taklamakan were surveyed in this way in 1985 and will be investigated in greater detail by upgraded versions of the radar scheduled for shuttle flights in April and December next year, officials of the Jet Propulsion Laboratory said.

"Some day we really need to do a radar job on the entire Silk Road," said Dr. Ronald G. Blom, a specialist in remote sensing at the laboratory in Pasadena, Calif.

The last time Westerners showed a keen interest in the Silk Road was early this century. In a highly competitive race into the previously unknown, explorers and archeologists from all the major Western nations retraced the old trade route and uncovered lost cities with a wealth of art and ancient manuscripts, much of which wound up in European museums. In "Foreign Devils on the Silk Road," the British writer Peter Hopkirk described these adventures as the "great archeological raids of the Silk Road."

The approach is different this time. In October, international art experts will be meeting in the Chinese desert, near the Mogao Grottoes, to develop a program to save the priceless Buddhist paintings and carvings there and at other Silk Road sites. The conference is being convened by the Chinese Government and the Getty Conservation Institute of Santa Monica, Calif.

As earlier archeologists discovered, art on the Silk Road was, like the travelers, a blending of East and West. In his pre–World War I reconnaissance, the British archeologist Sir Aurel Stein came upon murals depicting followers of the Buddha with the long faces and aquiline noses of the West and a two-sided tablet showing on one side a figure in the Indian Buddhist yoga position and on the other side figures with Chinese and Persian features. It was the face and story of the Silk Road, now being explored anew as one of the great avenues of adventure, commerce and human communication.

Herodotus

Roving reporter of the Ancient World

Carmine Ampolo

Carmine Ampolo, of Italy, teaches Greek history at the University of Pisa. He has carried out research on the origins of ancient Rome, on Greek politics and society, and on the relationship between myth and history. Among his published works are La citta antica *(1980; "The Ancient City") and, with M. Manfredini,* Le vite di Teseo et di Romolo *(1988; "The Lives of Theseus and Romulus").*

Herodotus of Halicarnassus, his *Researches* are here set down to preserve the memory of the past by putting on record the astonishing achievements both of our own and of other peoples . . . that the great deeds of men may not be forgotten . . . whether Greeks or foreigners: and especially, the causes of the war between them."*

In this introduction to his *Histories,* Herodotus (c. 490–425 BC) provides us with perhaps the earliest definition of the historian's aims and concerns. Some sixty years earlier, his precursor Hecataeus of Miletus, who had sought to inquire rationally into the mythical legends of the Greeks, explained his intentions in the following terms: "Thus speaks Hecataeus of Miletus: I write these things inasmuch as I consider them to be truthful; in fact, the legends of the Greeks are numerous and, to my mind, ridiculous." In this tetchy assertion of the author's role we can already see the two requirements of historiography in the Hellenic world: it must be written and it must be truthful.

With Herodotus the tone changes. He does not seek to give his own personal interpretation of what he relates, and usually he compares the different versions of stories he has collected. He wants to talk about his researches, tell of his inquiries. History as he understands it is at once the gathering of information and the recounting of a story. He thus inaugurated the two main trends in Greek historiography for centuries to come. Sometimes one would be given prominence, sometimes the other, but the prime imperative was always truthfulness, even in the case of historians who attached very great importance to narrative.

THE ART OF STORYTELLING

When Herodotus describes his work as an "exposition of his researches, the narration of an inquiry", these ambivalent terms must be taken to mean both the oral transmission of a story and its written formulation. The blending of oral and written styles in the *Histories* can be explained by the fact that Herodotus would give public readings of the various stories *(logoi)* making up his work. This is confirmed by the allusions in the text to audience reaction, and by the circular structure of the writing.

This practice had a marked effect on the composition of the work, which may seem to be something of a patchwork, with its countless digressions that sometimes fit into one another like Chinese boxes or Russian dolls. More a painter than a sculptor, Herodotus excels in the art of storytelling and possesses the gift of enthralling his audience, whether listener or reader, by his descriptions of a detail, an episode or an individual.

He often tells a story which he has heard at second or third hand. For example, after describing the victory of the Athenians over the Persians at Marathon, he tells what happened to the Athenian soldier Epizelos, who lost his sight while fighting in the battle, though nothing had hit him: "I am told that in speaking about what happened to him he used to say that he fancied he was opposed by a man of great stature in heavy armour, whose beard overshadowed his shield; but the phantom passed him by, and killed the man at his side." It would be a mistake to see this as Herodotus directly reporting what he has heard, but rather as an example of the mirror play that is a common feature of the *Histories:* Epizelos tells his story, others repeat it, Herodotus hears it and tells it in his turn.

This is not simply a taste for the fantastic or the marvellous, for which Herodotus is so often criticized, but a delight in intriguing and surprising his audience. He is able to arouse people's curiosity because his own is so great. He is interested in all kinds of out-of-the-way details, the customs of each people and all the wonders of the world, whether events, inventions or monuments like the pyramids of Egypt, the labyrinth above Lake Moeris and the walls of Babylon. In his quest for knowledge, Herodotus would travel and make inquiries of those who might have information about the countries visited—scholars, priests or people whose names are not recorded: "I learn by inquiry."

The reason for this passion for research emerges clearly in the introduction to the *Histories:* it is the historian's task to combat time, to preserve what he considers to be memorable. In the Greek cities and sanctuaries there were already "memorizers" *(mnemones)* responsible for recollecting and recording divine and human occurrences. But the historian's concerns are much loftier than the purely administrative, legal and religious functions of the *mnemones.* All the illustrious deeds and labours *(erga)* that he relates must retain their *kleos,* their aura of glory, their renown. In some ways Herodotus seems to carry on where the epic

---

*Quotations from *Herodotus: The Histories,* translated by Aubrey de Sélincourt, Penguin Classics, 1954.

poets left off. They recounted the deeds of heroes, the historian recounts the deeds of men.

The insatiable curiosity shown by Herodotus in his investigations and travels considerably broadened the scope of written history, which ceased to consist solely of myths, genealogical lists and ethno-historical material relating to particular peoples or communities. Although he wanted to preserve as much as possible, he had to select which of the facts to save. For the historian who takes as his subject "great and marvellous actions", not everything is memorable.

Herodotus was aware of the amount of space given in his *Histories* to the long parentheses of the storyteller. On one occasion he even confesses: "I need not apologize for the digression—it has been my plan throughout this work." To understand this attitude, we should not use modern criteria nor even refer to later Greek authors whose works, which were designed exclusively to be read, seem to be better constructed. In a work addressed primarily to listeners and only subsequently to readers, not only the form but the choice of material were determined by the exigencies of spoken communication. It is not enough for details to be historically revealing or admirable; they must also be entertaining and, whether glorious or despicable, arouse the curiosity of the narrator and strike a chord in the minds of his audience.

AN INVESTIGATOR AT WORK

What was Herodotus' raw material? Much of the *Histories* records the history and customs of peoples incorporated in the Persian empire (or those of peoples like the Scythians which were unsuccessfully fought by the empire) as well as facts about the Greek cities in the sixth and fifth centuries BC. The culmination is confrontation between the Greeks and the Persians, which accounts for less than half the work.

Herodotus does not speak of a single people, nor even of a single Greek city, nor of Greece in its entirety. He erects no barriers, shows no scorn. He does not really differentiate between the Greeks and other peoples, the "Barbarians". Born at a time which, under the influence of the Sophists, saw the development of cultural relativism, and originating from a region at the meeting-point of East and West, he showed curiosity, consideration and even respect for other cultures.

He nevertheless viewed them through Greek eyes. In keeping with a typically Hellenic way of seeing the foreigner as a reversed image of oneself, he depicted the behaviour of other peoples as the antithesis of that of the Greeks. Among the "strange practices" of the Egyptians, for example, he mentions that "women attend market and are employed in trade, while men stay at home and do the weaving. . . . Men in Egypt carry loads on their heads, women on their shoulders. . . ." His enumeration of their differences ends as follows: "In writing or calculating, instead of going, like the Greeks, from left to right, the Egyptians go from right to left—and obstinately maintain that theirs is the dexterous method, ours being left-handed and awkward."

This comparative method can be seen as a way of classifying and hence of understanding. But Herodotus also observes similarities, which he scrupulously notes, as in the case of the Spartans. Customs on the death of a king, he reports, "are the same in Sparta as in Asia", and "the Spartans resemble the Egyptians in that they make certain callings hereditary: town-criers (heralds), flute-players and cooks are all, respectively, sons of fathers who followed the same profession."

Although he does not go as far as Thucydides in saying that the Greeks lived formerly in the same way as the Barbarians today, and although he maintains a distance between the two worlds, he does not regard them as two monolithic blocks, one of which is in certain respects inferior to the other or culturally backward. Different though they may be,

he acknowledges the many qualities of the Barbarians, considering, for example, that the Greek gods have Egyptian origins, that Egyptian civilization is older than that of the Greeks, and that the Persians have numerous virtues.

The *Histories* end with a revealing anecdote. To convince his people not to attempt to settle in more fertile lands, the Persian King Cyrus the Great declares to his troops that "soft countries breed soft men", pointing out that the Greeks have preferred to keep their freedom on a harsh land rather than to be slaves cultivating fertile plains for others. It is thus a Persian sovereign who enunciates a truth applying chiefly to the Greeks. Herodotus also sets among the Persians a discussion on the best form of government—democracy, oligarchy or monarchy. They are foreigners, enemies, but not completely different. They could even, in theory at least, be like the Greeks, in the same way that the Greeks in some respects resemble them.

Herodotus does not try to describe a series of mythical or historical events since their origins or even from one of the traditional milestones in Greek history, as other historians were to do after him. His field of study—the Median wars and the events that led up to them—covers a fairly recent period. That which is remote in time is left to poets and genealogists. He displays the same attitude towards Egypt, distinguishing what he has witnessed personally from the information he has collected from the Egyptians. If he consults Persian, Phoenician or Egyptian scholars about mythical episodes, such as the abduction of Helen and the Trojan War, it is mainly in order to retrace and understand the causes of the Median wars.

In choosing as his area of investigation recent history of which he could have direct knowledge, Herodotus had a decisive influence on the development of historiography. Thucydides, half a generation younger, would go even further than his great predecessor, directing his gaze to current events.

The Later Civilizations to 500 C.E.

Life in the ancient world was likely to be short and brutal. Poor nutrition, disease, hazards of childbirth, warfare, and violence all took their toll. In the Roman Empire, for instance, only one child in eight could expect to reach 40 years of age. Since people were often judged for their usefulness, long life was not necessarily a blessing. Women were often subservient and mistreated, criminals and slaves were publicly slaughtered, and unwanted children were abandoned to die. Yet, at the same time, humanity built splendid cities, formed empires, wrote history, invented sports, and created art treasures. Aspects of this growing diversity is examined in this section.

In the New World, civilization evolved later than in the Old World, perhaps due to the pattern of migration to the hemisphere and the later development of agriculture. The Aztecs and Incas, nonetheless, constructed stone cities, invented their own form of writing, and developed a complex social and economic system. Unfortunately, much of this accomplishment was destroyed during the European invasions. Forerunners of these groups have been discovered at Teotihuacán in Mexico (see unit 4) and along the western coast of Peru. Funeral art from the Moche culture, rescued from modern looters, gives an indication of the rich life and skill of this prehistoric group in the New World. Interestingly, it may have been climatic changes that brought their downfall.

Athens, one of the most interesting of the ancient Greek city-states, was important for the origin of modern ideas about government, art, and sport. At the center of the city was the Agora, a plaza surrounded by civic and religious buildings. The modern word agoraphobia, fear of open space, comes from this place in Greek cities. In Athens the Agora served as a meeting place for trading goods and ideas, as John Fleischman explains in his report. It was the focal site of Athenian life. Women were a part of the scene, but men dominated politics and military affairs. As in most places in the ancient civilizations, the place of women was at home where they cooked, reared children, and made clothing, as Susan Cole notes in "Women and Politics in Democratic Athens."

Warfare was a common part of life for men in the ancient world, and the long conflict between Rome and Carthage is a central part of the history of Rome. The Romans persevered and eventually won the wars, then went on to rule the Mediterranean for 500 years. To maintain their interest in bloodshed and to condition the Roman public to violence, the gladiator games of Rome, supported by the rulers, provided sports of brutality where killing was common. Most gladiators died in the arena of combat.

Other sports of a more benign nature can also be found throughout this Mediterranean world. Author Allen Guttmann, a leading sports historian, notes the murals found in Egypt showing wrestling, Minoan frescoes of boxing, and Etruscan chariot racing. The most important sports development, however, was the Olympic Games of Greece that endured from the eighth century B.C.E. to the third century C.E. Even with the Greek emphasis on the harmony of body and mind, most of the early sports have a basis in military or survival skills. It was these old competitions of throwing, running, and wrestling, however, that inspired the modern Olympics of the present time.

Looking Ahead: Challenge Questions

Compare the artifacts found in the tombs of the Moche with those of Egypt. Is there evidence of interest in art and religion? What effect has looting had on the study of these peoples?

Are there places in modern life that serve the purposes of the Agora of Athens?

Compare the lives of women in ancient Athens, Rome, and Greece.

How can Carthage and Rome be considered superpowers of the Mediterranean? What was the reason for their conflict?

What do the sports of a society tell you about the attitudes of the society?

What is the purpose of sports in the ancient world? What sorts of sports can be found?

Unit 4

Tales from a Peruvian Crypt

The looting of a prehistoric pyramid stimulates an operation in salvage archeology, with unexpected scientific dividends

Walter Alva and Christopher B. Donnan

Walter Alva, a native of Peru, has participated in numerous excavations on that country's north coast and is the director of the Museo Brüning at Lambayeque. Coauthor Christopher B. Donnan is a professor of anthropology and director of the Fowler Museum of Cultural History at the University of California, Los Angeles. They are the coauthors of Royal Tombs of Sipán *(Los Angeles: Fowler Museum of Cultural History, University of California, 1993).*

In the fertile river valleys that relieve Peru's arid coastal plain, mud-brick pyramids stand as the most visible evidence of the prehistoric Moche civilization, which flourished between the first and eighth centuries A.D. Rising out of agricultural fields in the Moche River valley, the massive Pyramid of the Sun was the largest structure ever built in South America. With a ramp that led up to small buildings on its flat summit, it stood about 135 feet high and sprawled over 12.5 acres at its base. It once contained more than 130 million sun-dried bricks. Some of it has eroded away naturally, while part was demolished in the seventeenth century by Spanish entrepreneurs in search of rich burials or other treasures.

About ninety-five miles north of the Pyramid of the Sun, in the Lambayeque River valley, the Moche ceme-

teries and three pyramids near the village of Sipán have long been the target of looters. Over the years they have dug many deep holes with picks and shovels in hopes of locating intact tombs containing ceramic vessels, shell and stone beads, and rarer ornaments of silver and gold. By November 1986, they had nearly exhausted the cemeteries, and one group of treasure seekers decided to focus on the smallest pyramid. Working at night to avoid police detection, they dug a series of holes, but found little of value. Then, on the night of February 16, 1987, at a depth of about twenty-three feet, they suddenly broke into one of the richest funerary chambers ever looted, the tomb of an ancient Moche ruler.

The looters removed several sacks of gold, silver, and gilded copper artifacts. They also took some ceramic vessels, but they broke and scattered many others in their haste. Almost immediately, the looters quarreled over the division of the spoils, and one of them tipped off the police. The authorities were able to seize some of the plundered artifacts, but only a pitiful amount was salvaged from the find. The rest disappeared into the hands of Peruvian collectors or was illegally exported for sale in Europe, Japan, and the United States.

Building on civilizations that preceded them in coastal Peru, the Moche developed their own elaborate society, based on the cultivation of such crops as corn and beans, the harvesting of fish and shellfish, and the exploitation

of other wild and domestic resources. They had a dense, socially stratified population, with large numbers of workers devoted to the construction and maintenance of irrigation canals, pyramids, palaces, and temples. Their lords apparently received food and commodities from their subjects and distributed them to lesser nobles and to the potters, weavers, metalworkers, and other artisans who created luxury objects for the elite. In sculptures, decorated ceramics, and murals, archeologists have glimpsed many complex scenes of Moche life, including hunting, combat, and ceremonial practices.

The luxury items from Sipán that were confiscated by the police, including hollow gold beads of various shapes and sizes, hinted at the magnificence of the plundered burial, which must have belonged to one of the Moche elite. More fortune-hunters descended on the site in search of overlooked valuables. They hacked at the tomb walls and sifted through the excavated dirt. By the time the police secured the area, little was left except a boot-shaped hole. Nevertheless, with armed guards stationed around the clock, we hastily organized an archeological survey to learn everything possible of scientific value (author Walter Alva directed the project; coauthor Christopher B. Donnan was one of the many participants.)

We began by making a contour map of the three pyramids and what remained of their ramps and adjacent plazas. The small pyramid, where the

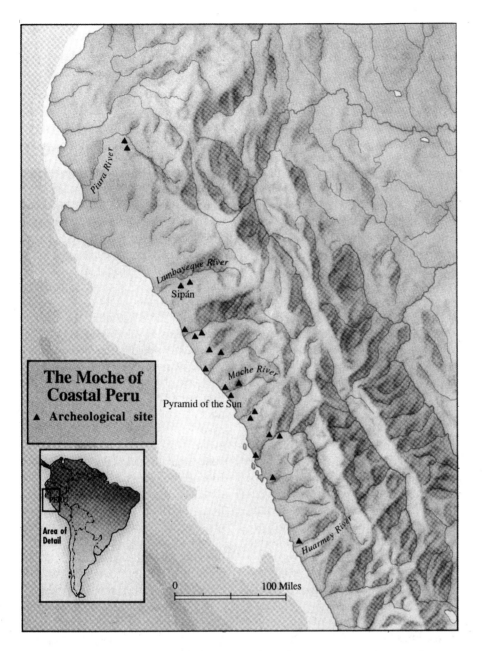

The Moche of Coastal Peru

▲ **Archeological site**

Area of Detail

0   100 Miles

Piura River

Lambayeque River

Sipán

Moche River

Pyramid of the Sun

Huarmey River

platform with a balustrade, surrounding an open-front building with one back wall and a peaked roof supported by posts. Seventeen double-faced human heads decorated the roof ridge, while depicted in relief on the wall was a supernatural creature, half feline and half reptile, copulating with a woman on a crescent moon.

Knowing that the pyramid would be further plundered once we left, we decided to open up a new section to methodical excavation, choosing a ten-by-ten meter (1,076-square-foot) area near the summit. Here we came upon a place where the mud brick had been carved out and refilled in ancient times. Digging down, we found eight decomposed wood beams, similar to those that had roofed the looted burial chamber. Buried beneath these, in the debris of what had been a small rectagular chamber, we found 1,137 ceramic bowls, jars, and bottles. They portrayed a variety of human figures: warriors holding war clubs and shields, nude prisoners with leashlike ropes around their necks, musicians with drums, and seated figures wearing beaded pectorals (biblike coverings). Some were arranged in symbolic tableaux, for example, musicians and prisoners ringing and facing noble personages.

As we removed the ceramics, we found several pieces of copper and, finally, a man's skeleton lying jack-knifed on its back, with chin, knees, and arms pulled in toward the torso. Since the Moche customarily buried their dead in a fully extended position, we interpreted this individual to be a sacrificial victim, whose body had been shoved into the small chamber as part of the ritual offering.

Even as these offerings were being excavated, we discovered a second, larger rectangular area that appeared to have been carved into the pyramid and refilled. As we carefully excavated this, we found, about thirteen feet below the original surface of the pyramid, the skeleton of a man wrapped in a cotton shroud. He lay stretched out on his back and wore a gilded copper helmet. Over the right forearm, which rested on his chest, was a round copper shield. A little below we found the

tomb had been found, was riddled with looters' tunnels, but in some places, the piles of dirt they had excavated helped preserve the original contours. The tunnels also enabled us to examine the internal construction. The pyramid and the rest of the complex evidently had been built and rebuilt over a long period of time, undergoing many changes as the various parts were enlarged. The small pyramid seems to have gone through six phases, beginning in the first century A.D. and ending about 300.

Although the burial chamber had been gouged out of shape, we were able to determine that it had originally

been roofed with large wood beams, which had decomposed. To our great surprise, we were able to uncover some of the tomb's contents that had been missed by the original looters and the subsequent gleaners. Clearing along one side of the chamber, we found the remains of a large, gilded copper crown decorated with metal disks; four ceramic jars modeled in the shape of human figures; and a copper mask with inlaid turquoise eyes. In excavating these, we also discovered a heavy copper scepter forty inches long, pointed at one end and bearing a three-dimensional architectural model on the other. The model depicted a remains of seventeen parallel beams that, we dared hope, lay over a major, undisturbed burial chamber.

The discoveries that subsequently emerged surpassed our dreams. Buried in the chamber were the remains of a wood coffin that contained the richest grave offerings ever to be excavated scientifically in the Western Hemisphere. The body of a man between thirty-five and forty-five years of age had been laid to rest with a feathered headdress, banners of cloth with gilded copper decorations, beaded pectorals, nose ornaments and necklaces of gold and silver, ear ornaments of gold and turquoise, face coverings of gold, a gold backflap and a silver backflap that would have been hung from the belt, and countless other precious objects. In his right hand the deceased had held a gold and silver scepter topped with a large rattle, and in his left hand, a smaller scepter of cast silver. In relief on the rattle, which was shaped like an inverted pyramid, were scenes of an elaborately dressed warrior subjugating a vanquished opponent. The sculpted head of the smaller scepter echoed this theme.

Working six days a week, it took us four months to document and safely empty the delicate contents of the tomb. As our original budget became exhausted, we received some partial funding from a brewery and a truckload of noodles donated by a pasta manufacturer. At one point we were paying the fieldworkers with a combination of cash and noodles. We eventually secured new support from the Research Committee of the National Geographic Society and were able to proceed with further excavation.

All the while we had been working and moving equipment around the coffin burial, we had been walking only inches above hundreds of ceramic vessels, two sacrificed llamas, a dog, and the burials of two men, three women, and a child of nine or ten. Although we do not know this for sure, the men and the child might have been buried as sacrifices to accompany the principal figures. The remains of the females, however, were partly decomposed at the time they were placed in the tomb,

as evident from the way the bones were somewhat jumbled. They had probably died years earlier and their remains maintained elsewhere until this final interment.

As we excavated the tomb and cataloged its contents, we couldn't help wondering who was the important personage buried there. The key to the answer was a major photographic archive of Moche sculpture and drawings at the University of California at Los Angeles. As the tomb was being excavated, photographs of the objects were sent to UCLA for comparative study.

Many of the objects in the coffin suggested the man buried there was a warrior. The archive of Moche art contains hundreds of depictions from which we can reconstruct a sequence of Moche militarism and ceremonial activity. We can see processions of warriors carrying war clubs, spears, and spear throwers, perhaps on their way to battle. We can see warriors in combat, apparently away from settled areas. The essence of Moche combat appears to have been the expression of individual valor, in which warriors engaged in one-on-one combat, seeking to vanquish, rather than kill, an opponent. The victor is often shown hitting his opponent on the head or upper body with the war club, while the defeated individual is depicted bleeding from his nose or losing his headdress or other parts of his attire. Sometimes the victor grasps his adversary by the hair and removes his nose ornament or slaps his face.

As far as we can tell, the Moche warriors fought with one another, not against some foreign enemy. Once an opponent was defeated, he was stripped of some or all of his clothing and a rope was placed around his neck. The victor made a bundle of the prisoner's clothing and weapons and tied it to his own war club as a trophy. After a public parading of the spoils, the prisoners were arraigned before a high-status individual and finally brought back to the Moche settlements or ceremonial precincts. There the priests and their attendants sacrificed them, cutting their throats and drinking the

blood from tall goblets. The bodies were then dismembered and the heads, hands, and feet tied individually with ropes to create trophies.

Many representations of the sacrifice ceremony exist in Moche art. Although they vary, not always depicting all personages in the ceremony, apparently three principal priests and one priestess were involved, each associated with specific garments and ritual paraphernalia. The most important was the "warrior priest," generally depicted with a crescent-shaped nose ornament, large circular ear ornaments, a warrior backflap, a scepter, and a conical helmet with a crescent-shaped ornament at its peak. A comparison of these and other details with the contents of the tomb convinced us that the individual buried there was just such a warrior priest.

When the sacrifice ceremony was first identified in Moche art, in 1974, no one could be sure it was a real practice, as opposed to a mythical event. Now we had archeological evidence that this was an actual part of Moche life. Here was one of the individuals who presided over the sacrifices. Further, because the limited numbers of objects salvaged from the looted tomb were similar to some of those we had excavated, we could conclude that the looted tomb also must have belonged to a warrior priest.

As if this were not enough, during the excavation of the warrior priest's tomb, we located another suspected tomb elsewhere on the pyramid. We held off excavation until work on the earlier find was nearly complete. The knowledge we gained made it easier to anticipate the sequence of excavation. Again we found the residue of a plank coffin containing the rich burial of a man between thirty-five and forty-five years old. Among his grave goods was a spectacular headdress ornament of gilded copper, in the form of the head and body of an owl from which arched long banks with suspended bangles, representing the feathered wings. Nearby we found the remains of four other individuals: a male between fourteen and seventeen years of age, two females in their late teens or early twenties, and an eight- to ten-year-old child. Buried with the child were a dog and a snake.

The contents of this tomb were only a little less lavish than those of the warrior priest. They suggest that the principal individual was another of the priests depicted in the sacrifice ceremony—one we call the "bird priest." The major clue was the large owl headdress. He was also buried with a copper cup near his right hand, similar in proportion to the cups portrayed in pictures of the sacrifice ceremony.

Having identified these individuals as participants in the sacrifice ceremony, we began to wonder if such ceremonies took place in Sipán itself. The answer was soon revealed when, about eleven yards from the bird priest's tomb, we found several small rooms that contained hundreds of ceramic vessels, human and llama bones, and miniature ornaments and implements, mixed with ash and organic residues. Among the human remains were hands and feet, quite possibly the trophies taken from dismembered sacrificial victims. Altogether these looked to be the residue of sacrifice ceremonies, which the Moche apparently carried out at Sipán, as no doubt they did at their other centers.

The looted tomb, the two excavated tombs, and the sacrificial offerings all seem to date to about A.D. 290. While excavating the offerings, we found a fourth, somewhat earlier tomb containing the remains of a man between forty-five and fifty-five years old, also richly endowed with grave goods, including a necklace of gold beads in the form of spiders on their webs, anthropomorphic figures of a crab and a feline, scepters, an octopus pectoral with gilded copper tentacles, and numerous other ornaments and objects. Nearby we found the body of a young, sixteen- to eighteen-year-old woman next to a sacrificed llama. This tomb may also have belonged to a warrior priest, but not all the identifying elements are there. Possibly, this is simply because it dates to an earlier period than the depictions we have of the sacrifice ceremony, which are all from after A.D. 300.

Moche civilization collapsed suddenly, probably as a result of one or more of the natural cataclysms that periodically devastate coastal Peru—earthquake, flooding, or drought. The Moche had no writing system, so they left no records we can hope to decipher. They disappeared before Europeans reached the New World and could leave us eyewitness accounts. Yet with the scientific excavation of these royal tombs, we have gained an intimate portrait of some of their most powerful lords. Work at Sipán continues, now at a promising location near the tomb of the bird priest. As we dig more deeply, we look forward to our next encounter.

In Classical Athens, a market trading in the currency of ideas

For 60 years, archaeologists have pursued secrets of the Agora, where Socrates' society trafficked in wares from figs to philosophy

John Fleischman

John Fleischman, who wrote about the excavation of the legendary site of Troy in Smithsonian *last year, braved Athens' summer heat on the trail of his story.*

Athens on an August afternoon: the clear radiant light of Greece suffuses every stone and walkway. From my vantage point, I squint upward to the outcropping of the Acropolis, crowned by Athena's temple, the Parthenon; hordes of tourists lay constant siege to the site. Standing at the base of that fabled rampart, I begin to traverse a quiet, heat-baked square, crisscrossed by gravel paths, dotted with the stubs of ancient walls and scrubby pomegranate and plane trees.

This dusty archaeological park, a sanctuary amid the roar of overmotorized Athens, is in fact one of the most remarkable sites in Classical archaeology. I am crossing the Agora—or central marketplace—of ancient Athens. That this place still exists seems nothing short of miraculous. I am walking in Socrates' footsteps.

The gadfly philosopher frequented this very square—as did his compatriots in the extraordinary experiment that was Classical Athens. Shades of Pericles, Thucydides, Aristophanes, Plato. They all strolled in this place—the Agora, where philosophy and gossip were retailed along with olive oil. And where Classical Athens actually lived, traded, voted and, of course, argued. The Agora was the city's living heart. Here, politics, democracy and philosophy (their names, after all, are Greek) were born.

For every ten tourists who climb to the Parthenon, only one discovers the precincts of the serene archaeological site at its base. Those visitors are in fact missing an excursion into history made palpable, as well as a glimpse into what must be acclaimed as one of this century's most triumphant urban archaeology undertakings.

Since 1931, the American School of Classical Studies has been digging here, unearthing a dazzling array of artifacts from the layers of history compacted under this earth: Neolithic, Mycenaean, Geometric, Classical, Hellenistic, Roman, Byzantine and more—all collected from this 30-acre site. Still, it is the objects from Classical Athens that seem to speak with greatest resonance.

And fortunately for those of us unable to make it to Athens anytime soon, we have a chance to see for ourselves some of the Agora's most celebrated artifacts. The occasion of this opportunity is a striking anniversary: 2,500 years ago, the Athenian reformer Cleisthenes renounced tyranny and proclaimed the birth of a radically new form of government, democracy. His genius was to offer a straightforward plan. To diffuse powerful political factions, Cleisthenes reshuffled the Athenian city-state into ten arbitrary tribes and called 50 representatives from each to a senate, or boule, of 500. This, then, was the beginning of democracy, however imperfect and subject to subversion and strife it might have been.

Hence the arrival of the exhibition "The Birth of Democracy," which opened recently in the rotunda of the National Archives in Washington, D.C. and continues there through January 2, 1994. A few steps from our own Declaration of Independence, Constitution and Bill of Rights lie the humble tools of Athenian self-government, nearly all of them unearthed in the Agora over the past 60 years by American excavators.

You can look upon actual fourth-century B.C. Athenian jurors' ballots, discovered still inside a terra-cotta ballot box. The ballots, stamped "official ballot," look like metal tops. Each juror was handed two; the spindle shafts designated the vote, solid for acquittal and hollow for guilty. Taking the spindle ends between thumb and forefinger, an Athenian juror was assured that no one could see which spindle he deposited in the ballot box.

For the too powerful, a decree of exile

Also on view are ostraca, pottery fragments on which Athenians inscribed the names of persons they felt too powerful for the good of the city and deserving of ostracism, or ten years' exile, a procedure formalized by Cleisthenes. More than 1,300 ostraca, condemning many famous figures–Pericles, for instance, and Aristides and Themistocles–have been found in the Agora. Looking closely at the sherds, you can spell out the names straight from the history books and realize that these ostraca were written out by contemporaries who knew these men personally. And in some cases hated them.

Ostracism was not the worst punishment the democracy could decree. The National Archives also displays a set of distinctive pottery vials uncovered from the fifth-century B.C. Athenian state prison. These tiny vials were used to hold powerful drugs, such as lethal doses of hemlock. Socrates swallowed just such a dose, voted for him in 399 B.C. by his fearful fellow citizens. Archaeologists say the death scene of Socrates described in Plato's *Phaedo* fits the layout of a precise location in the Agora–a building near the southwest corner of the market square.

Plato recounts that after Socrates took the poison, he walked about, then lay down, telling his friends to stop

weeping "for I have heard that one ought to die in peace." When the numbness spread from his legs upward to his abdomen, he covered his face. His last words were, as always, ironic. Socrates claimed he had a debt to the god of medicine. "I owe a cock to Asclepius," he informed a companion, "do not forget, but pay it."

The exhibition contains several other objects associated with Socrates, including part of a small marble statue, thought to be of the philosopher, that was also recovered from the prison. Visitors can find, as well, actual hobnails and bone eyelets from the Agora shop of one Simon the cobbler. Socrates is known to have met at such a shop with young students and prominent Athenians alike.

The boundaries of the Agora were clearly marked, and entrance was forbidden to Athenian citizens who had avoided military service, disgraced themselves in the field–or mistreated their parents. Around the open square, but outside its actual boundaries, lay the key civic buildings–courts, assembly halls, military headquarters, the mint, the keepers of the weights and measures, commercial buildings and shrines to the city gods. One such shrine, the Altar of the Twelve Gods, stood within the Agora and marked the city's center.

On business days, the square was filled with temporary wicker market stalls, grouped into rings where similar wares were offered. There was a ring for perfume, for money changing, for pickled fish, for slaves. The Agora was a constantly changing mix of the mundane and the momentous–pickled fish and the world's first democracy. The comic poet Eubulus described the scene: "You will find everything sold together in the same place at Athens: figs, witnesses to summonses, bunches of grapes, turnips, pears, apples, givers of evidence, roses, medlars, porridge, honeycombs, chickpeas, lawsuits, beestings-puddings, myrtle, allotment machines, irises, lambs, water clocks, laws, indictments."

"The Agora was a place for hanging out," according to archaeologist John M. Camp, who is my patient guide this afternoon. "You'd have men of affairs doing a little business, conducting a little politics and stirring up a little trouble." Camp has spent most of his adult life digging here, and he's tireless even in the heat. (He's also the author of *The Athenian Agora*, an erudite and delightful guide to the site, written for a general audience.) The real pleasure of studying this site, he says, is the shock of recognition. "Our own ideas, our own concepts originated right *here*," he told me, gesturing toward the bright open square of the Agora. "It's not only democracy, it's virtually all of Western drama, law–you name it. Over and over again, you find the only thing that's really changed is the technology. Everything else, they thought of it before. They did it before, and it all happened *here*."

In the beginning, archaeologists banked on hope

The open Agora at midday is suited only for mad tourists and foreign archaeologists, both on tight schedules. The tourists can see the Agora today because American archaeologists (funded in large part by American philanthropists–principally John D. Rockefeller jr. and the David and Lucile Packard Foundation) saved the site from total obliteration. At the outset, the archaeologists who began nosing around here in the late 1920s were banking on educated hope. Although the memory of the Agora was preserved by sources such as Plato and the historian Xenophon, tantalizing description was all that remained. That celebrated site had vanished at least 1,400 years before, lost to waves of pillaging barbarians, buried under layers of settlement from medieval times on.

In short, no one knew for sure where the ancient Agora really was. (Greek and German archaeologists had made some tentative beginnings in the 19th century, but their efforts had shed little light on the actual location.) The most likely site, authorities agreed, was at the foot of the northwestern slopes of the Acropolis. That area, however, was buried beneath a dense neighborhood of 19th-century houses and shops.

The debate remained largely academic until 1929, when the Greek government offered to the American School of Classical Studies a dig-now-or-forever-hold-your-peace deal. The Americans would have to demolish 300 houses and relocate 5,000 occupants. The Greek government required that a permanent museum be built for any finds and that the Agora be landscaped as a park.

The American School finally commenced excavations in 1931. As archaeologists have labored here for more than 60 years, we can read the life and times of Classical Athens in the spaces they have cleared and excavated.

Take the Panathenaic Way, for example, a diagonal street running uphill to the Acropolis. The roadway is packed gravel today, as it was in the days of the Panathenaia, the city's great religious festival. The celebrations began with the Athenian cavalry leading a procession of priests, sacrificial animals, chariots, athletes and maidens across the Agora to the temples of the gods above. All of Athens would have gathered along this route to witness the splendid parade wending across the marketplace. One Panathenaic event, the *apobates* race, in which a contestant in full armor leapt on and off a moving chariot, continued in the Agora well into the second century B.C.

With or without armor, walking uphill is not a recommended Athenian summer-afternoon activity. But taking your time and picking your shade, you can cut across the square to the base of a sharply inclined hill and look upward at a large Doric temple just beyond the western limit of the Agora. This is the Hephaisteion–a temple dedicated to Hephaestus, the god of the forge, and to Athena, patron deity of the city and of arts and crafts. Excavations have shown that it was once surrounded by shops where bronze sculpture, armor and fine pottery were made. Today the world's best-preserved Classical temple, it is a marvel unto itself. Somehow it has survived from Pericles' time onward, a marble monument to the miracle of Athens.

The temple's friezes are carved with scenes that spoke to the imagination of every Athenian. Theseus battling the Minotaur, the labors of Hercules, the Battle of the Centaurs–all images from a world where gods and men resided in a kind of rarefied complicity.

Below the Hephaisteion stood the most important buildings of the Athenian city-state. Here was the Bouleuterion where the 500 representatives of the tribes met. (An older assembly hall stood next door.) Nearby was the round, beehive-shaped Tholos where the 50 members of the executive committee of the Boule served 35- or 36-day terms of continuous duty, living and dining in the Tholos at state expense. (Those early practitioners of democracy apparently subsisted on simple fare–cheese, olives, leeks, barley, bread and wine. No lavish state dinners yet.)

In front of the Bouleuterion stood the statues of the Eponymous Heroes, the ten tribal namesakes chosen by the Delphic Oracle (and the source of our word for a group or thing named after a real or mythical person). Athenians tended to throng before this monument–not out of piety but because this was the site of the city's public notice board, a kind of proto-daily-paper for ancient news junkies. Nearby lay the Strategeion where the ten military leaders of the tribes made their headquarters (and gave us a Greek word for military planning).

North of the Bouleuterion complex rose the Stoa, or covered colonnade, of Zeus, a religious shrine but apparently an excellent place to practice philosophy. Both Plato and Xenophon said that the Stoa of Zeus was a favorite teaching post of Socrates. No one is more closely associated with the Agora than Socrates. He lived his life here. He met his death here. Xenophon remembered his former teacher moving among the market tables and stoas: "he was always on public view; for early in the morning he used to go to the walkways and gymnasia, to appear in the agora as it filled up, and to be present wherever he would meet with the most people."

As much as Socrates enjoyed the public scene in the Agora, he made it clear, according to Plato, that he was not a "public" person, that is, he was not interested in politics. This was a scandalous opinion to hold in Athens, where the real work of every Athenian citizen was just that–being a citizen. In Plato's *Apology*, Socrates rounded on his critics: "Now do you really imagine that I could have survived all those years, if I had led a public life, supposing that . . . I had always supported the right and had made justice, as I ought, the first thing?"

He had learned the hard way. Allotted to a turn in the Bouleuterion in 406-05 B.C., he was assigned to the Tholos as a member of the executive committee. And thus it fell to Socrates to preside over a wild meeting of the mass Athenian Assembly when word arrived of the sea battle at Arginusae. It was an Athenian win, but the victorious generals were accused of leaving their own dead and dying behind. The majority moved to condemn the generals to death as a group without individual trials. Socrates resisted. "Serving in the Boule and having sworn the bouleutic oath [to serve in accordance with the law], and being in charge of the Assembly, when the People wished to put all nine [actually eight of the ten] generals to death by a single vote, contrary to the laws, he refused to put the vote," according to Xenophon. "He considered it more important to keep his oath than to please the People by doing wrong."

That was the sort of behavior that could earn you a great many enemies. Eventually, three citizens brought charges against Socrates for mocking the gods and corrupting Athenian youth. The exact location of the courtroom where Socrates stood trial still eludes identification, but the place of his indictment, the Royal Stoa, has been excavated. As for the place of his death, if you hunt carefully on the rising slope beyond the Tholos, you can find the low precinct of exposed stones that archaeologists believe was the site of his demise.

The precise forces and circumstances that led to the jury's death sentence have never been elucidated completely. What is clear is that the questions raised by that trial so long ago are not dead letters. Dissent versus consent, public good versus private conscience, they still buzz about the ears of modern democracies. "I am the gadfly which the god has given the state," Socrates told his jury in the *Apology*, "and all day long and in all places am always fastening upon you, arousing and persuading and reproaching you."

The Athenian Agora still buzzes with surprises and mysteries. In 1981, on the northern edge of the Agora, Princeton archaeologist T. Leslie Shear jr. hit the corner of one of the most famous buildings of ancient Athens, the Poikile, or Painted, Stoa. This discovery was stunning good news for Agora archaeology. The structure had been renowned throughout the ancient world for its spectacular wall paintings. The glowing images, covering enormous wooden panels, lionized Athenian victories both mythological (over the Amazons, for instance) and historical (over the Persians at Marathon).

The fabled paintings were removed by the Romans in the fourth century A.D. but survived long enough to have been described by the second-century A.D. chronicler Pausanias. "The last part of the painting," he recorded, "consists of those who fought at Marathon. . . . In the inner part of the fight the barbarians are fleeing and pushing one another into the marsh; at the extreme end of the painting are the Phoenician ships and the Greeks killing the barbarians who are tumbling into them."

For Athenians, the Painted Stoa was the arena of their triumphs made visible. It was also a hotbed of philosophical speculation, eventually turning up as the gathering place of the third-century B.C. followers of Zeno of Citium. Zeno preached that the wise man should remain indifferent to the vanities of the transient world. The people of Athens associated the school of thought with the building, calling Zeno's disciples Stoics and their philosophy Stoicism. And 2,300 years later, so do we.

Stoicism is a necessity in Agora archaeology. As Leslie Shear explains, his father had, in some ways, an easier time of it here. The elder Shear supervised the original excavations during the 1930s. He had a squad of colleagues and 200 paid workmen to take down a whole neighborhood at a time. This summer, Shear has John Camp, his coinvestigator and colleague of 25 years, a nine-week season, and 33 student volunteers (American, Canadian and British) in addition to a small crew of Greek workmen who handle the heavy machinery and earthmoving. And he has his wife, Ione, a highly trained archaeologist in her own right, who has also worked at the site for 25 years.

Pursuing the Agora in the present Athens real estate market is tedious and expensive. It is house-to-house archaeology–negotiation, demolition and then excavation. While he has been busy elsewhere on the site, Shear is still waiting patiently to acquire the five-story building that is standing on the rest of the Painted Stoa.

Meanwhile, every water jug, bone or loom weight excavated anywhere in the Agora must receive a numbered tag. Every number goes into the dig's records, meticulously kept in special 4-by-6-inch clothbound notebooks. When in use in the field, these notebooks reside in an old, cheap suitcase that sits on a rough wooden desk that looks even older and cheaper. With a folding umbrella for shade, this is the nerve center for the dig. The senior archaeologists sit here, drawing tiny diagrams of the strata and the find location for every tagged item.

May 28, 1931: "H. A. Thompson commenced . . ."

It is, as Camp puts it, "dinosaur-age" archaeology in the era of field computers, but it works. Completed notebooks go into filing cabinets in offices inside the Stoa of Attalos. (This colonnade, originally a great commercial arcade in the second century B.C., was completely reconstructed in the 1950s to house the excavation's museum, laboratories, offices and storage vaults.) There the records march back in unbroken order through the decades to May 28, 1931, and the very first entry: "In the afternoon, H. A. Thompson commenced the supervision of Section A."

Looking back over more than 60 years, from the other side of the Atlantic, Homer Thompson smiled when he heard again that clipped description of the first day. He was a young, relatively inexperienced archaeologist then. Today he is a vigorous professor emeritus at the Institute for Advanced Study in Princeton, New Jersey. He oversaw the Agora excavations from 1947 to 1967.

Back in the '30s, he recalls, it took seven years to find the first boundary stone that used the word "Agora." It wasn't a thrill so much as a relief, says Thompson, who was in charge of the crew that uncovered the marker, wedged in by the wall of Simon the cobbler's shop. "We believed we were working in the Agora, but we had so little to show for it–in inscriptions–that some of our colleagues would come by and ask 'How do you know that you're in the Agora?' Well, this settled it."

Finding the second boundary stone took another 30 years. The marker lies on the southwest corner of the square. Ione Shear uncovered it one afternoon in 1967.

It is a very ordinary marble block. The faintly visible lettering runs across the top and then down one side. The important thing, says Leslie Shear, is that this block and the one found near Simon's shop have not been moved in 2,500 years. Other boundary stones have been found uprooted, buried in rubble fill. "But these two stand where they've stood since the sixth century B.C.," he observes. "They were set out at about the time the democracy was founded. In a very real sense, democracy as we understand it was invented in the Agora of Athens." He leaned down to trace the letters.

Stones can speak, although they rarely speak in the first person. This one spoke loud and clear: "I am the boundary of the Agora." There was no dispute after that. This was the word. This was the place.

Additional reading

The Athenian Agora: Excavations in the Heart of Classical Athens by John M. Camp, Thames and Hudson (London), 1986

The Birth of Democracy: An Exhibition Celebrating the 2500th Anniversary of Democracy, edited by Josiah Ober and Charles W. Hedrick, American School of Classical Studies at Athens (Princeton, New Jersey), 1993

The Athenian Agora: A Guide to the Excavation and Museum, American School of Classical Studies at Athens, 1990

The Agora of Athens, The Athenian Agora, Volume XIV by H. A. Thompson and R. E. Wycherley, American School of Classical Studies at Athens, 1972

WOMEN AND POLITICS IN DEMOCRATIC ATHENS

Susan Guettel Cole is Associate Professor of Classics and History at the State University of New York at Buffalo. She has written about the Samothracian mysteries, the literacy of Greek women, Greek sanctions against sexual assault, and the cult of Dionysos; she is presently working on a comprehensive study of female rituals in the ancient Greek city.

The Athenians maintained that Erichthonios, the king from whom they believed they were descended, was born from the earth herself. This myth of autochthony rationalised claims to the territory of Attica, expressed a strong relationship with the land, and recognised male dependence on the female as nurturer of life. Even in the classical period, when many people lived in the urban area of Athens, families maintained agricultural property in the countryside and therefore continued to have strong economic and emotional ties to the land of Attica, the agricultural territory of Athens. Linguistic distinctions preserved this identification of the people with the land. Terms for the collective population were 'Attikoi/Attikai', 'people of Attica', or 'astoi/astai,', 'having a share in the city', used for both males and females. 'Athenaioi', from which we derive the English term 'Athenians' was almost always reserved for the male population eligible for citizenship. Females seem to have been called by the feminine form of this term ('Athenaiai') only when the issue was the religious office of a public priesthood, as 'Attikai' females were defined in terms of the land. Official documents are very precise,

The deity from whom the city was named and who was Athens' protector may have been female, but formally women were excluded from the democratic process. Susan Cole examines how nevertheless they were visible through the cracks and made their mark.

distinguishing those with political authority from their dependents when they refer to the whole population of Athens as 'the people (*demos*) of the Athenians and their wives and children'. The usual term for 'citizen' (*polites*, masculine singular) referred only to men; its rare feminine form (*politis*) defined a woman as daughter of an Athenian citizen or resident of the polis, but not as a political actor.

In the early Greek polis, political responsibility entailed military service, a fact that tended to sharpen the distinction between the lives of men and women. The lives of men were spent in public; women lived, for the most part, in the private domestic world of the home. Male and female roles were represented, paradoxically, by the two great female divinities

of the city. Athena was represented as Promachos, armed for battle, her perennial virginity a necessary sign of the city's invulnerability. Demeter, on the other hand, goddess of grain and symbol of motherhood, was identified with the establishment of agriculture and civilised life. The Thesmophoria, a secret festival celebrated by the wives of the city's citizens, honoured Demeter and encouraged her protection of the city's crops. Athenian democracy evolved in the context of an agricultural community, a fact recognised by the oath sworn by young men during the military training that would qualify them for full political rights. They vowed to protect the boundaries of the land of Attica and invoked as witnesses the products of the land: the wheat, the barley, the vines, the olives, the figs. Wars were fought to protect the agricultural territory and the wives and children of the Athenians, an idea reflected in a vocabulary of war that described the rape of women with the same terms used for destruction of land and crops. Full political rights were originally predicated upon possession of land, but even after they were eventually extended to men without land, the Athenian political system did not outgrow the hierarchy of wealth and privilege based on and derived from the land.

The basic social unit was the family (*oikos*, 'household'), a unit defined originally in terms of possession of land for farming (*kleros*, 'allotment'). Stability was represented by the land, and success was measured by the transfer of land from a father to a son. Males remained in the oikos of their birth (unless adopted by a childless family), but females had to move to a new oikos at the time of marriage, when they took property away from the natal household in the form of dowry. This movement of women between families provoked anxiety because the allegiance of a married woman could always be divided between a father's and a husband's oikos. The transmission of land from one generation to the next was another source of anxiety for husbands and fathers; first, because it required marriage and the reception of a female from another (perhaps competing) oikos; second, because it required the production of legitimate sons (but not too many); and third, because the birth of daughters, who took land away from the oikos in the form of dowry at marriage, posed a risk to the economic security of sons. This last problem could be avoided if a father had received a generous dowry with his wife at marriage. A wife's dowry enriched her husband's oikos during her lifetime and passed to her children later; to her daughters in the form of dowry, to her sons in the form of inheritance. Land, with which women were identified because of their own procreative power, could come into the oikos with women, but there was always a certain tension because it could also be lost to an oikos when the females of the next generation left to marry.

The earliest stages of participatory politics at Athens were brought about by land reform in the early sixth century, when Solon created a hierarchical system of public offices with the highest offices rotated annually among the males with the largest agricultural production. Under Solon's system, the highest political, military, and religious authority went to the men whose families possessed the best and most land, those whose families had traditionally made the best marriages. Solon's reforms rewarded the more economically successful male members of the political community with the highest political offices, but because he also restricted public displays of family wealth, he directly affected the public lives of women, especially those of prestigious families. His regulations are said to have included restrictions on the clothing and behaviour of women in public, at festivals, funerals, visits to cemeteries, and during travel at night.

When a law sponsored by Perikles changed requirements for citizenship in 451 BC, women assumed a greater political importance to their sons (without gaining any for themselves). Before Perikles' law, participation in the Athenian political community was open to any man whose father belonged to that community. After 451 (except for a brief period during the Peloponnesian War), both parents had to be from Attic families. The democratic polis recognised women's contribution to the reproduction of the citizen body by defining citizenship according to the status of mothers as well as fathers and protected this relationship by linking the political status of husbands to the sexual fidelity of their wives. Athenian political language preserved the archaic terminology of honour and shame, and infractions of the code of sexual honour could have political consequences. Citizenship (epitimia)

Equal partners? Zeus and Hera represented together on the Parthenon frieze c.440 BC. The reality of Athenian marriage was of a highly asymmetrical relationship of authority – harmony but with male dominance accepted.

was described in terms of rights and privileges (timai, 'honours'); loss of these rights and privileges and loss of rights of political participation were described in terms of dishonour and disgrace (atimia). The polis protected the transfer of property at the level of the oikos by protecting the legitimacy of children and by requiring the appearance of sexual fidelity of citizens' wives. A citizen's political status could depend on his wife's sexual reputation. A husband who caught another man alone with his wife could kill the offender with impunity, but if he continued to live with a woman whose sexual reputation had been compromised, he could lose the rights and privileges of citizenship, be permanently excluded from the political community, and described as dishonoured (atimos). As a consequence, restrictions on citizens' wives tended to increase in proportion to a husband's political activity or public prominence. The woman held to the highest public sexual standard was the wife of the most important ritual official in Athens, the basileus. She not only had to maintain sexual fidelity to her husband, but was required to have been a virgin (parthenos) at marriage and never to have been married to any other man.

Women were invisible as individuals. In Perikles' famous Funeral Oration, Thucydides defines good reputation for women in terms of the least possible celebrity among males. As a result of this attitude, it was not considered proper for men to name in public women from families of citizen status. If it was necessary to mention them at all, they were identified not by name, but in terms of a relationship to a male relative or husband. This convention was followed in lawcourt speeches (unless the status of the woman herself was the issue under discussion), as well as in conversations represented in comedy. When Demosthenes went to court to obtain his inheritance, he had to discuss his mother's status after his father's death without mentioning her name. If it were not for a remark in Plutarch, we would never have known that her name was Kleoboule. Women could call each other by name and name themselves in public, but even in comedy a free Athenian male did not mention a citizen's wife by name. A woman's personal name was mentioned in public speech outside her family only if she were a slave, *hetaira* (prostitute), priestess in a public priesthood, or dead. Official naming practices differed for males and females. Athenian men had three names when named officially in public: personal name, patronymic, and demotic (the name of the family's original deme or place of residence, indicating registration in the deme and therefore eligibility for citizenship). Women had personal names and were identified further by a father's or husband's name in the possessive case, but they did not have demotics and were not recorded on lists of phratries (hereditary kin groups for males) or on deme registers. The protocol persisted even in death. Attic grave inscriptions for women from citizen families give the demotic of a woman's father or husband.

In classical Athens women inhabited a negative political space. Essential to the reproduction of the citizen body, they were nevertheless passive participants in a society based on public competition between males. In the fifth century BC the priestess of the city goddess Athena Polias had a front row seat in the theatre, a privilege called *proedria* and reserved for those who performed extraordinary service to the city, but public honours for women were granted only for their role in religious activities. It is uncertain whether other Athenian women besides the special priestess even attended the plays. When the women of the chorus in Aristophanes' *Thesmophoriazusai* make a joke about honours for women whose sons performed great service to the city, they do not propose proedria at the Great or City Dionysia, but proedria at their own much smaller festivals, the secret Stenia or the Skira.

The judicial system recognised occasions when a woman's testimony might be needed in a dispute, usually in paternity cases where only a mother could identify her son's father. However, women did not appear as formal witnesses in court. Women had access to the judicial system only through a male guardian or authority (Kyrios), and may not have appeared in court even when charged with a crime. In a well known case where a woman was charged with murder, it was her son, not she herself, who swore that she was innocent.

Asymmetry between male and female in the public political life of the city was directly related to asymmetry of authority within the family. Marriage itself was the result of an agreement between two men without participation of the female involved. The father of a bride promised a dowry and daughter to a potential husband with an agricultural metaphor: 'I give you this girl for the ploughing of legitimate children'. This metaphor reflects the Greek terminology for verbs of sexual intercourse, used in the active voice of the male, and in the equivalent of the passive for the female. A significant bridal gesture suggests a similar relationship. At the time of marriage the bride gave her body to her new husband for the first time by lifting her veil away from her face with her hand, a gesture of submission called *anakalypteria* (uncovering). Xenophon describes Athenian marriage as a partnership, but relations between husband and wife were never like a relationship between equals. The marriage relationship was sometimes described in terms of mutual affection (*philia*), but a bride's first experience of sexual intercourse was often described in literature in terms of dominance and submission with language used elsewhere for the taming of animals. The image of the *anakalypteria* of Hera for Zeus was enshrined on the Parthenon to symbolise the harmony of marriage, but it also represented the unequal relationship between the divine husband and his wife.

In the fourth century, the city of Athens used the same image to illustrate the text of the alliance between the *demos* of the Athenians and the *demos* of the Corcyreans. The relief shows the goddess Athena with her hand held out in a gesture signifying advice, directing a wedding between a seated male and a standing female figure. The scene is reminiscent of similar scenes showing the *anakalypteria* of Hera, but the seated male figure also resembles representations of the personified demos of the Athenians. If he represents Athens, then the female figure represents the land of Corcyra, seductive but submissive as she lifts her veil away from her face in the bride's gesture of anakalypteria. The ritual of diplomacy defined the relations between cities joined in alliance in terms of friendship (also philia), but the relief exploits the ambiguity of the imagery of marriage to represent more accurately the reality of diplomatic agreements.

The nature of women's contribution to the city was directly related to the role of women within the family as wives and mothers, providers of nourishment, and producers of clothing. Unlike the variation of the countryside, the uniformity of the urban landscape, where the patterns of intersecting streets determined the size of houses, created a new domestic equality for the women of the city whose work was located inside the home. Rich and poor, the women of Athens worked side by side with their female slaves to produce at home the textiles that clothed their families.

A pair of matched vases, possibly once a gift to a bride, recognises the link between the two primary roles of a citizen's wife: reproduction of the oikos and production of clothing. The first vase shows the bride moving by wedding cart from her father's house to her husband's home, already making the gesture of anakalypteria, which symbolised sexual union with her husband. The second vase shows the domestic labour of married women on the warp-weighted loom where Athenian housewives painstakingly made by hand every item of clothing worn by themselves, their children, and their husbands. The other side of the vase shows a woman taking the unspun wool from a wool basket, another woman spinning the wool with her spindle, and a second pair of women folding the finished cloth. The shoulders of both vases are decorated with a circle of dancing figures, probably representing the wedding dances performed by the bride's friends. The bride herself takes the central position, seated directly above the centre of the loom, her veil held out in the suggestive gesture of anakalypteria.

Public civic ritual recognised the contribution of citizens' wives and daughters to the prosperity of the city. Athena was goddess of women as well as goddess of men. As protector of weaving she received dedications from women in her sanctuary on the acropolis. The original ritual of her major festival, the Panathenaia, required a select group of women and girls to weave a new robe (*peplos*) for her statue. The frieze of the Parthenon depicts the procession that brought the citizens of Athens to the acropolis for the central sacrifice, and as the only known temple frieze

to represent mortals, manages to raise the Athenian experience to a mythical plane. Included in the procession are the Ergastinai, the women and girls who made the robe. Together with the female libation bearers for sacrifice, these are the only mortal females represented on the frieze, far outnumbered by the males in the procession. Their gift points in two directions, to the divinity whose robe they bestow, and to the women of Athens whose labour they represent.

Public images, like that of the Parthenon, carried dignified political messages that linked domestic life with the public life of the city. Messages moved in the opposite direction as well. For example, Athenian coins carried the imagery of Athens throughout the Mediterranean. They showed Athena Promachos on one side and her owl on the other, a predator with keen vision whose chilling stare, like that of the gorgon on Athena's breast, was meant to paralyse the enemy. Byzantine commentators tell us that ancient Greek women sang as they worked at their looms. We do not know the songs they sang or the stories they told, but we do have thousands of the ceramic loomweights to which they tied the warp of their simple movable looms. Some were even inscribed with the name of the woman who used them in her work, others were decorated with simple images. One such loomweight from Tarentum, decorated with the owl of Athena, translates the political imagery of Athens into a domestic setting. The owl of Athena

imitates the owls of her coins, faces the same way, with her feet in the same position. A simple tool, but decorated for a female audience, the loomweight makes its own political statement. Here the owl is transformed into a spinner, equipped like the spinner on the wedding vase. She has acquired two hands to manipulate the distaff; at her feet is her wool basket (*kalathos*) and her spindle. She cocks her head and turns her face to the viewer, demure, yet open, and unmistakably feminine. A symbol of Athenian public life, famous at home and abroad, has been appropriated for the private, constricted world in which most women lived out their lives, a contrast to Athena herself, endowed with the paraphernalia of war in the male realm. Here we find Athena's owl domesticated, a sly challenge, perhaps, and an affirmation of women's worth.

FOR FURTHER READING:
Lin Foxhall, 'Household, Gender and Property in Classical Athens', *Classical Quarterly* 39 (1989) 22-43. Jane Gardner, 'Aristophanes and Male Anxiety', *Greece and Rome* 36 (1989) 51-61. Virginia Hunter, 'Women's Authority in Classical Athens', *Echos du Monde Classique/Classical Views* 8 (1989) 39-48. Jenifer Neils, *Goddess and Polis: The Panathenaic Festival in Ancient Athens* (Princeton, 1992). Cynthia Patterson, '*Hai Attikai*: The Other Athenians', in *Rescuing Creusa*, ed. Marilyn Skinner, *Helios* 13.2 (1987) 49-67. Pauline Schmitt Pantel (ed.) *A History of Women I: From Ancient Goddesses to Christian Saints* (Cambridge MA, 1992).

Dido was its old flame, and Hannibal called it home

But the ancient city of Carthage is still being rediscovered, bit by bit, 2,100 years after the Romans thought they had expunged it

Robert Wernick

The author writes frequently for Smithsonian. *His last article was on Conspiracy Theory (March 1994).*

When the ancient Romans thought of Carthage, the picture that came to their minds was of fire. They had all heard of the terrible brazen image of Ba'al Hammon, which dropped infants from its red-hot outstretched arms onto blazing altars. They had heard of Hamilcar, the commander who, after losing all but one of his 251 vessels in a fight with Syracuse at Himera, built a fire and jumped into it. They had heard especially of Dido, the queen who founded Carthage, and how, when she saw her faithless lover Aeneas sailing off on his divine mission to found Rome, built a pyre on the beach, stabbed herself and plunged into the flames.

The Dido story was Virgil's version; Aeneas sees the dark pillar of fire from the deck of his ship. Other accounts follow what is most likely an older tradition of the Dido story. Half-myth but perhaps half-history as well, it tells how a princess of the Phoenician port city of Tyre named Elisha (Elissa in Greek) flees the city after her brother Pygmalion murders her husband. With a group of Tyrian aristocrats and a cache of gold, she reaches a Tyrian colony on nearby Cyprus called Qart Hadasht, or New City. They rescue 80 virgins from ritual prostitution at the temple of Astarte, and then head westward in their ships. Sailing when the winds are favorable but mostly rowing along the north coast of Africa, they come to what is now the Gulf of Tunis and find a superb site for a settlement. It offers a fine natural harbor near a promontory that can easily be defended against attacks from the mainland, and is an ideal place for trade, strategically located at the narrowest part of the Mediterranean Sea.

Here Elisha gets a new name, Dido (meaning, says one ancient author, "the Wanderer"; meaning, says another, "husband killer"). She founds a second new city, the Qart Hadasht twisted on Greek and later Latin tongues to become Carthago.

Mythic and scholarly consensus holds that all this happened sometime around 800 B.C. Some 650 years later, in 146 B.C., when the Romans, after more than a century of sporadic though savage war by land and sea, finally conquered the city Dido founded, they destroyed it utterly, letting fires rage for ten days until not one building was left upright.

"Great Carthage made war three times," Bertolt Brecht once wrote, summing up seven centuries of Carthaginian history. "After the first, she was powerful. After the second, she was rich. After the third, no one knew where Great Carthage had been."

The last phrase was a slight exaggeration. Everyone had heard about Great Carthage, and about Hannibal and his elephants crossing the Alps in 218 B.C. to start the Second Punic War with Rome ("Punic" comes from the Roman word for "Phoenician"). It was, after all, Roman history. Everyone knew where Great Carthage had been because the Romans built a city of their own on the site, a new Carthage that became a center of industry, learning and luxury, arguably the second city of the Roman Empire. But until less than a century ago, no one had any real idea of the size of the original Punic city, its boundaries, its layout or its architecture.

It was only in 1921 that a local public servant and an archaeologist named Count Byron Khun de Prorok tracked a shady trafficker in classical antiquities and caught him digging up funerary stelae in the adjacent countryside, now part of the modern seaside resort of Carthage. Their discovery led to the unearthing of thousands of urns and tombstones. The urns held the bones and ashes of infants who had been ceremonially burned in the place to which scholars have given the name of its counterpart outside biblical Jerusalem, the tophet. It is only in the past 20 years that archaeologists, working as part of a ten-nation international team directed by UNESCO (Smithsonian, February 1977), have proved that a nondescript, brackish pond by the shore of the Gulf of Tunis was once the military port where 220 warships of the Carthaginian navy could be sheltered in covered slips and drydocks. Nearby they found traces of the great commercial port as well.

For more than a century archaeologists had been digging into the Byrsa Hill, which tradition held to be the center of old Carthage, in the hope of finding some trace of the magnificent temples and palaces that ancient authors say once crowned it. Every time they were sure they had come upon a wall of its most celebrated monument, the temple of the god Eshmoun (whom the Greeks and Romans identified with the god of medicine, called Aesculapius by the Romans), their triumph turned to dust as the masonry was shown to be Roman. Only the gigantic work undertaken since 1972 under UNESCO has at last dug up the reason for their failure.

The Byrsa excavations have revealed the appalling extent of destruction at Carthage. The Romans left the blackened ruins alone for a century and would not let anyone live there. (They did not, however, sow salt into its soil, as all the schoolbooks say. Salt was valuable; and anyway, the work of scattering it would have taken thousands of man-hours). That story got its start in 1902 when Professor B. L. Hallward, in the *Cambridge Ancient History*, compared Scipio Aemilianus, the Roman commander in the Third Punic War, to Abimelech in the Old Testament (IX Judges 45) who took the Canaanite city of Shechem "and slew the people that were therein; and he beat down the city, and sowed it with salt."

In 44 B.C. Julius Caesar decided to build a new city on the site of the old, but he was killed before the plan was fully developed. Eventually, to make sure that no vestige of the old city remained to pollute this creation, Emperor Augustus had the Byrsa Hill decapitated, lowering its summit by 16 feet or more to make a ten-acre plateau on which to lay out a proper Roman city. More than 245,000 cubic meters of earth, rock, masonry (including the foundations of the temples of Eshmoun and Apollo/Reshef), were hacked out and either used as landfill or spilled down the sides of the hill.

Digging into the remains, UNESCO teams have cleared about four city blocks in what appears to have been a prosperous neighborhood, with apartment houses constructed around central courtyards, a few shops, paved streets, sewers, and cisterns for collecting rainwater. According to one Roman author, some of these buildings were six or seven stories high. But nothing is left of the buildings but fragments of ground-story walls,

Map includes Tyre, where Dido originally came from, Spain (New Carthage), the Alps and Cannae, the site of a great victory by Hannibal over Rome.

dwarfed into insignificance by the immense pillars the Romans raised to hold in place the city they were building. Beneath the ancient Roman road that led from the Byrsa Hill to the sea, a German team of archaeologists, led by Hans Georg Niemeyer of Hamburg University's Archaeological Institute, has recently unearthed remains of Punic housing that date back as far as the eighth century B.C.–the time of the legendary founding of Carthage.

A current show devoted to the arts of ancient North Africa, on view through May 29 at Emory University's handsome new museum in Atlanta, has a Carthaginian section assembled from a collection in the Louvre. The rich variety of objects illustrates the cultural crosscurrents–from Egypt, from Syria, from Greece–that naturally swept through the greatest trading center of the ancient world.

There were once great libraries of books in the Punic language. Not a page, not a line, remains. The works of a Carthaginian named Mago, the greatest agronomist of antiquity, were translated and studied by Roman landowners, but now even the translations are lost. What remains of the language, a variety of the Phoenician spoken in Tyre, a near relative of ancient Hebrew, are mostly grave inscriptions (some 6,000 of them) with the names of parents offering children to Ba'al

Hammon, or the goddess Tanit, and some lines of comic dialogue put into the mouths of Carthaginian merchants and slaves in the work of a Roman playwright.

One consequence is that practically everything known about the Carthaginians comes from the Greeks and Romans, who made war on Carthage for centuries. Their historians naturally tended to present a biased picture of the enemy as cruel, untrustworthy Orientals. This was the picture touched up with lurid highlights by Gustave Flaubert, whose novel *Salammbo* portrays a Carthage of glittering opulence and unspeakable vice, where rivers of Oriental perfume mingle with rivers of blood from torture chambers and infant holocaust. Flaubert had sometimes the soul of a naughty schoolboy; he was never happier than when offering such tidbits as the claim that high-born maidens used a paste made of crushed flies' legs to touch up their eyebrows. But there is no reason to think the people of ancient Carthage were any more addicted to cruelty than the Romans, who thought nothing of crucifying prisoners along the public highways and leaving them there till their bones were picked clean by birds. Some scholars challenge the whole idea of Carthaginian infant sacrifice, claiming that the charred bones in the urns, when they are not those of lambs and calves, are of infants who were stillborn or died of natural causes. But tophet excavator Lawrence Stager, director of Harvard's Semitic Museum, thinks there is no doubt that some form of infant sacrifice took place. According to the gloomy prophet Jeremiah, the custom was being practiced in Jerusalem in the sixth century B.C. The early church father Tertullian, who spent most of his life in North Africa, wrote in A.D. 200 that "to this day that holy crime persists."

At one time or another, Rome fought with many of the other peoples of the Mediterranean world, occasionally taking cruel vengeance, but eventually absorbing them into the Roman state or making them allies. Only Carthage was utterly destroyed, because it was the only foe the Romans genuinely feared, the only trade rival that might have supplanted Rome.

From 262 B.C. to 146 B.C. these two states, which started out as small towns, groped and then clawed their way toward mastery of the known world. Sometimes the story of those centuries sounds like a dress rehearsal for modern times. Just as the expansion of the Western European world began in the 1400s with Portuguese captains pushing their solid oceangoing ships farther and farther down the coast of West Africa in search of gold, spices and slaves, so the Phoenicians, 2,400 years earlier, at the beginning of the first millennium B.C., developed sturdier, faster ships than had ever been built before and began sending them on trading or raiding voyages to what was then the wild west end of the Mediterranean. Homer's *Odyssey* (dated by current scholarship to the latter part of the eighth century B.C.) describes them as "pirates in black boats laden with a thousand *arhythmata*," that is to say, beads and bowls and wine and metalware and all sorts of bric-a-brac. The Phoenicians traded for produce of the iron mines of Elba, the gold mines of Andalusia and later the tin mines of Cornwall, growing rich on such commerce (SMITHSONIAN, August 1988). They also invented an alphabetic script, which made it easier to keep business records.

For hundreds of years the competition was fierce between Phoenicians and island Greeks, mainland Greeks, Sicilian Greeks and the Etruscans of western Italy, where Aeneas and his Trojans landed. They all established trading posts or spheres of influence scattered over hundreds of miles of coastline; the posts became commercial ports and sometimes fortified cities. The cities made alliances, propped up satellite states, quarreled over tariffs and monopolies and eventually fought "world" wars. By the fifth century B.C., Rome (which had expelled the loosely confederated Etruscans) and Carthage (which had long outgrown its mother city of Tyre) were emerging as superpowers.

They were briefly allied against the Greeks, then came to blows in 264 B.C. and over the next 118 years fought the three Punic Wars for the domination of the world. They were complex wars on a scale unknown before, bringing into play vast amounts of weaponry, strategic movements of fleets and armies over hundreds of miles of water, the juggling of alliances and the large-scale hiring of mercenaries.

At first the Carthaginians took command of the sea with big battleships—98-foot-long triremes with tusk-shaped timber battering rams on their prows. When a ship was propelled at full speed by three banks of oarsmen (as many as 170), it could ram and sink an enemy vessel. Carthage even developed a quinquereme, with five banks of oars, though no one in modern times has figured out how such a complicated conveyance could operate in real water with real rowers.

After salvaging a wrecked Punic trireme, the Romans were soon building their own. Then, since their sailors had not enough experience to sail them as well as their enemies, they came up with an innovation that revolutionized war at sea. It was called the *corvus*, or crow, a special boarding bridge at the bow of the ship that could be lowered onto the deck of an enemy vessel alongside. At its end was a heavy piece of iron with a sharpened point like a crow's beak, which would fasten onto an enemy deck like a grappling hook. Then naval war became

land war—which the Romans were good at—as heavily armed Roman infantry, using the *corvus* as a gangplank, swarmed aboard the enemy vessel and massacred its crew.

At Mylae in 240 B.C. in the first Roman naval victory of the Punic Wars, the *corvus* pecked the Carthaginian fleet to death. In the peace that followed the ensuing Roman victory that ended the First Punic War in 241 B.C., Carthage lost some of its overseas empire. It also found itself with 20,000 mercenaries still on its hands in Sicily, mostly wild Gauls, Numidians, Iberians, black Africans and Mauretanians. Having to pay a huge tribute to Rome for the next 50 years because Carthage had lost the war (our more enlightened century speaks of "reparations"), the Carthaginian senate did not see its way clear to pay the mercenaries what they had been promised. Gisco, the commander in Sicily, proposed sending them back a few boatloads at a time so that the senators could negotiate a mutually agreeable sum with each group. But someone (an MBA from the Punic School of Business Administration, perhaps) persuaded them that they could make a better deal by settling on a lump sum payment for the whole force, and the 20,000 were shipped back together. A child could have predicted what would happen when all those fierce, fully armed men, camped just outside Carthage, learned that they were going to be shortchanged. They started a spree of burning and killing that lasted for three years and almost destroyed the state.

Defeat only sharpened hatred of Rome. Hamilcar Barca, leader of the Carthage war party, built up a new empire among the old Phoenician colonies in Spain, where he founded a "New Carthage," now Cartagena. Lacking the support at home to rebuild a navy, he created an army to challenge Rome on land. The Greek historian Polybius tells us that Hamilcar had his son Hannibal swear a solemn oath to be forever an enemy of Rome.

It was Hannibal who, at the age of 25, started the Second Punic War and began the campaign that led him to within a hair's breadth of destroying Rome and making Carthage master of the world. He came so close that, for generations, Romans would exclaim "Hannibal is at the gates!" to express fear or anxiety. Hannibal, the greatest of all captains, according to Napoleon, could not only outmaneuver the Romans in the field, he could handle the logistical problems of moving a huge army and a horde of elephants through Spain and hostile Gaul and eventually over the Alps in winter, hoping to take Rome by surprise.

He tried to make strategic alliances and to plant fifth columns behind the Roman lines. He was a master of what today is called psychological warfare: the elephants, of which only a few survived the Alpine crossing, were of limited military value, but their image haunted every soldier's imagination as German Tiger tanks did in World War II.

Both sides used mercenaries, but in the 15 years Hannibal fought in Italy he was steadily outnumbered because Rome could always count on a reservoir of sturdy patriotic peasants. Hannibal had mauled two numerically superior Roman armies, at Lake Trasimene and Cannae, but the Romans raised a third. In the end, Hannibal was called back to North Africa to help repel a counterinvasion led by Scipio Africanus, who defeated him in 202 B.C. at the Battle of Zama.

The Roman historian Livy records how Hannibal, after the loss of the Second Punic War, rebuked the rich senators who had watched with dry eyes while their country's navy was towed out to sea and set afire under the draconian terms of the peace treaty, but began to wail and tear their clothes when they learned that there was so little gold in the national treasury that the yearly tribute would have to be paid out of their own pockets.

Military disaster did nothing to break the entrepreneurial spirit of Carthage. While the taxpayers of Rome were pouring out gold along with their blood to expand and police their empire, the Carthaginians, reverting to their primal role as Levantine traders, were shamelessly prosper-ing. Cato the Elder, sternest of the noble old Romans, on a diplomatic mission to Carthage in 175 B.C. to make sure that the provisions of the peace treaty were being honored, was horrified by all the bustle and industry he saw around him. To his eye the city was "teeming with a new generation of fighting men, overflowing with wealth, amply stocked with weapons and military supplies . . . and full of confidence at the revival of its strength." Cato thenceforward added to every speech he made in the senate on any subject the words *Delenda est Carthago*– "Carthage must be destroyed."

One group in Rome was perfectly willing to go on living in peaceful coexistence. But a war party was in power in the year 149 B.C. when the Carthaginians gave Rome a pretext to act by repeatedly taking up arms to repel the Numidians who were seizing their lands. Roman forces were deployed, and the Third Punic War was launched. The Carthaginians, who were in fact ill prepared and fearful, soon agreed to hand over 600 hostages to guarantee their good behavior and braced themselves for another heavy tribute. The Romans first insisted that the Carthaginians surrender every instrument of war in the city. Two hundred thousand weapons and 2,000 pieces of artillery–catapults and ballistae–were duly loaded on wagons and delivered.

Only then were the rest of the impossibly harsh conditions of surrender revealed: Carthaginians must abandon international trade, leave their city and build another at least ten miles inland from the coast. It would be for their own good, the Roman consul Censorinus piously told them, for had not the sea brought them all their woes? Only their temples and tombs would remain undesecrated.

For a people who had lived almost 700 years by overseas commerce, this was a decree of forced suicide. All Carthage united in passionate defiance. The gates of the city were closed, arsenals were improvised and soon were turning out 300 swords and 500 spears a day. Women cut off their hair to make braided ropes for catapults. The Romans had expected a quick surrender by the disarmed foe. They were slow to assault a city with a triple line of walls extending for some 22 miles. The highest wall reached 65 feet and was 98 feet deep, with space dug into it sufficient to stable 300 elephants and 4,000 horses. It took the forces of Rome, eventually commanded by Scipio Aemilianus, three years just to breach the walls. Then they had to fight their way, street by street and house by house–including the streets and houses whose remains can still be seen—crossing from housetop to housetop on beams that straddled the 15-foot-wide streets, stopping occasionally to allow troops of street cleaners to clear off the dead bodies and rubble.

Polybius served as a Roman staff officer in Carthage. He left an eyewitness account of the slow, bloody climb up the Byrsa Hill. With all Carthage burning in front of them, he was amazed to see Scipio with tears in his eyes. He was recalling, Scipio said, the lines of the *Iliad* in which Hector has a premonition of the death of his country: "The day shall be when holy Troy shall fall, and Priam, lord of spears, and Priam's people." When Polybius asked him why he would be thinking such thoughts on a day like this, Scipio answered: "Oh, Polybius . . . I feel a terror and dread, lest someone someday should give the same order about my own native city."

It took many centuries for Scipio's premonition to be fulfilled. Roman arms would ensure peace and prosperity to millions for hundreds of years. By supplying wheat, olive oil and wild beasts for the arena, the province of Africa created out of the Carthaginian homeland would become the most prosperous in the empire. Traces of it remain everywhere in today's Tunisia. You cannot drive long in any direction without coming across the ruins of a Roman town, provincial places with elegant theaters, temples and forums. Between the broken walls of their homes, as well as in the vast chambers of the Bardo National Museum in Tunis, you can see acres and acres of mosaic floors–jolly hunters, piping shepherds, frolicking deer, amorous gods in all the rich, colorful gaiety of Greco-Roman art in its happiest years. Roman dominion in Africa ended with the Vandal incursions of the fifth century A.D., Byzantine dominance in the sixth century, and the arrival of a wave of Semitic invaders, the Arabs, in the seventh century. The latter preferred to build new capital cities of their own, first at Kairouan, then at Tunis. Gradually, the Roman city of Carthage was drained of people. Its palaces and temples and mansions provided a quarry from which pillars and hewn stones could be carted off for the monuments of the new masters of the land. Most of what was left was taken off by raiding parties of Italian sailors and used to build the churches and palaces of Genoa and Pisa.

The ancient Carthaginians would have preferred their way–a quicker and less-agonizing death. At the end of the six-day battle for the Byrsa Hill, 50,000 Carthaginians marched out to give themselves up and be sold into slavery. Everyone else in what had been a city of several hundred thousand souls was dead, except for a desperate handful clustered in the temple of Eshmoun, resolved to die rather than surrender. At the last moment the Carthaginian leader Hasdrubal lost his nerve and left the temple to grovel before Scipio, begging for his life. His wife, Sophonisbe, dressed as for a feast, was standing on the wall of the temple, which was burning behind her. She howled down a curse upon Hasdrubal for his cowardice, seized her two little sons in her arms and jumped into the purifying fire.

Additional reading

Carthage by David Soren, Aicha Ben Abed Ben Khader and Hedi Slim, Simon & Schuster, 1991

Carthage: A Mosaic of Ancient Tunisia, edited by Aicha Ben Abed Ben Khader and David Soren, American Museum of Natural History in association with W.W. Norton, 1987

New Light on Ancient Carthage, edited by John Griffiths Pedley, University of Michigan Press, 1980

Carthage by B. H. Warmington, Frederick A. Praeger (New York), 1960

Ancient Roman Life

John Woodford

Life in the Early Roman Empire (roughly the first two centuries A.D.) was indeed nasty, brutish and short, according to Bruce W. Frier, professor of classical studies, whose article on the demography of that era will be published in the forthcoming edition of *The Cambridge Ancient History.*

"We look at this ancient civilization as a wellspring of Western civilization, for we find a similarity of values between ancient authors and ourselves," Frier notes. "And we also acknowledge its organizational and administrative achievements. But despite these facts, when we examine something like life expectancy at birth—one of the fundamental measures of human welfare—we may conclude that in certain important respects, the Roman Empire's achievements were nil."

But Frier adds that in these respects, the Empire did not differ from contemporaneous societies. The picture of mortality, fertility and migration in the Early Roman Empire "generally corresponds," he says, "to what we'd expect of a pre-industrial society with limited medical development."

His and other scholars' "informed conjectures" about the far-flung empire that stretched from Egypt to Britain rest upon such scanty reliable data as tax documents, skeletal evidence and cemetery inscriptions, explains Frier, whose specialty is Roman law and social history.

Despite the lack of detailed local records like those that exist for the Middle Ages and Renaissance, it is probable that life expectancy for newborn females was around 25 years and 23 years for males, Frier reports. On the average, a year-old child would survive only to age 35, a 10-year-old to 46, and a 20-year-old to 50. A 40-year-old was likely to reach 60—but only one newborn in eight could expect to reach 40.

The odds against living that faced any newborn can be expressed another way: Of a cohort of 1,000 newborn girls, fewer than half would live past 15; and of a similar cohort of boys, fewer than half would live much past 5.

These estimates are based on evidence that is somewhat skewed, Frier adds, "because the data tend to over-represent upper-class persons and families; for the population as a whole, life expectancy at birth was probably lower than these estimates put it."

Exploring why life was so short in the Early Roman Empire also reveals its nasty and brutish aspects.

The very high annual death rate of 40 to 44 per thousand resulted to a great extent from the population's virtual defenselessness against typhus, typhoid, Malta fever, malaria, tuberculosis, pneumonia, childhood diarrhea and other ailments.

Poor nutrition—brought on by very low wages and by an inability to transport food overland from thriving areas to the famine-stricken in nearby cities—was probably a greater factor in the high death rate than was poor medical care. The latter, according to Frier, "probably had no effect on mortality one way or the other."

Filth, plagues and infanticide could make it nasty and short

"The population also suffered a very high violence rate, and a high level of death by accident," he continues. "One reads on epitaphs, for example, of a man of 22 from Ephesus who died of a hemorrhage after drinking a massive dose of wine. Or of a 35-year-old African who died after being 'deceived by a bull,' as his widow put it." Surprisingly, violent

deaths did not, in the main, result from military activity, which was extremely low. Less than half of a percent of the empire's population was in the army (about 350,000 men.)

Sanitation practices took their toll, too, especially the dumping of a million cubic meters of human waste into the Tiber River each year. "That gives one pause," Frier comments, "when one reads of people bathing in the Tiber River. In fact, during the later years of this period, the physician Galen warned against eating fish caught in the Tiber."

At about this same time (A.D. 164), when the population of the Empire had presumably reached 60 million (a fifth of the world's total), Roman diplomatic and trading missions contacted China's Han Empire and also the Kushana Empire on the Indian subcontinent.

Roman traders may have imported more than silk and other luxuries upon their return. "Many scholars think smallpox, measles and the other plagues that afflicted the Later Roman Empire for several centuries were introduced into the Mediterranean by these contacts with Asia," Frier reports.

Whatever its cause, when Avidius Cassius and his army returned from Parthia (present-day Iran) in A.D. 165, the first smallpox pandemic struck, exacerbating the problem of everyday pestilence. "The plague rose and fell across the entire empire for 25 years," Frier says. "By 190, the city of Rome, which had a population of 700,000 to a million, was losing 2,000 residents a day to smallpox."

From the birth of Jesus to this time, the Empire's population had grown from 45 million to 60 million, but the scourge reduced it by 5 million over the next three decades.

Countervailing these overwhelming agents of disease and death, however, was the fertility of the Empire's adults.

"For any population to endure over a long period," Frier notes, "each genera-

From *Michigan Today*, a publication of the University of Michigan, December 1985, pp. 1-3. © 1985 by John Woodford.

tion of women must reproduce itself, which means that, on the average, each woman who reaches menarche must have a daughter who does so."

It appears that the average woman in the Early Roman Empire, bore five to six children if she reached menopause, or 2.5 to 3 daughters per woman, a very high reproduction rate by modern standards.

Unwanted daughters were far more often the victims of infanticide and exposure than were sons, who tended to be accepted if they weren't unhealthy or deformed. Neither of these family-planning practices was considered immoral; they weren't outlawed until the late Empire.

Various methods of contraception and abortion also were practiced. Some were likely to have been effective, others were dangerous, but most were folk-magical practices with no effect—like the effort of teen-age girls to induce a miscarriage by tying wool around their ankles.

"The 'advantage' of infanticide and exposure to the Romans," Frier says, "was that it gave parents control in determining whether they would rear a male or female child in instances where a female child was unwanted. However, Jews, and the Christians who followed Jewish law, did not practice direct forms of contraception or abortion, but unlike most Romans, they did know about, and practice, *coitus interruptus.*"

Taken as a whole, the several family-planning practices may have resulted in a population of 107 men for every 100 women.

"We read many complaints from men about their difficulty in finding marriageable women," Frier says. "This disproportion also shows up in the high number of girls who married early and in the many men who married women of lower status. According to evidence on inscriptions, 30 percent of the females were married by age 13, and 50 percent by 15. Men tended to be 10 years older than their first wives, many of whom were prepubescent. Records indicate that 95 percent of women of marriageable age were married or had been married. Celibacy was rare; Rome had no spinster class."

These estimates reflect statistics about women from well-off families that prized legal marriages and who were important enough to reach the tallies of census-takers and other data-keepers. Many imperial residents, however, were barred from legal marriage: slaves, soldiers and sailors during the entire 20 years of their tour of duty and others. In addition, some Romans, such as freed slaves, were restricted in their marriage opportunities.

Men and women in these non-marriageable categories often entered into a relationship of concubinage, the Roman version of significant otherhood. The children of these unions were illegitimate.

Although the lack of data on illegitimate births is a problem for historical demographers, Frier says that there was probably no great difference in mores, fertility rates or other mating indices between persons living in concubinage versus those who were married.

"The Romans were relentlessly monogamous," he reports. "A married man was unlikely to have a concubine. But men and women who lived in concubinage weren't seen as 'living in sin.' Divorce was unregulated and could be initiated by a woman as well as a man, but it was uncommon, nonetheless, except among the upper classes. A man with a concubine seems to have been no more likely to leave his mate than was a married man. On the whole, the image of Roman life as riotous is false. Stable domestic life was the norm."

From a demographic standpoint, Frier concludes, the Early Roman Empire's mortality and fertility rates may have influenced its population growth far less than did the migration that gradually shifted the center of gravity of its population from east to west.

The scope and direction of this migration was made possible by Rome's political unification of the Mediterranean," Frier says, "and it was undoubtedly the most important and enduring demographic achievement of the Empire."

Even if a larger population gave no other edge to the Western Empire than greater numbers to survive the decimating plagues, that advantage alone was profound, Frier says. In fact, however, the population shift had a qualitative significance as well.

"The Empire had few formal barriers to movement within its borders," Frier points out. "As a result, many Easterners from the commercial and intellectual classes—Greeks, Syrians, Jews and others—headed westward to Italy, Spain and Gaul in hope of gain. They spread Eastern religions including Christianity, which we can trace in the New Testament as Paul visits Jewish merchant communities on his way to Rome."

Slavery and slave migrations also greatly affected the Empire's growth and development. The chief suppliers of these "involuntary immigrants," who made up 10 to 15 percent of the Empire's population, were slave traders; next came the military.

Demographers theorize, Frier says, that the growth rate of the West Empire's population over its Eastern half "may have been accomplished entirely through migration."

During the first two centuries A.D., the Western portion of the Empire gradually assumed a population density comparable to that of the East. Regions like modern Spain, France and Britain, thinly populated by local tribes at the time of the Roman conquest, began to emerge as important centers of urban life and culture. Not even the great plague of 165 undid this fundamental change.

There is no doubt, Frier sums up, that the plague "ushered in or immensely complicated a host of social and economic problems, to cope with which a new imperial dynasty was ultimately required."

**Bronze sculpture
of a retiarius – a
fighter with a trident.**

Murderous Games

Gladiatorial shows in Ancient Rome turned war into a game, preserved an atmosphere of violence in time of peace, and functioned as a political theatre which allowed confrontation between rulers and ruled.

Keith Hopkins

Rome was a warrior state. After the defeat of Carthage in 201 BC, Rome embarked on two centuries of almost continuous imperial expansion. By the end of this period, Rome controlled the whole of the Mediterranean basin and much of north-western Europe. The population of her empire, at between 50 and 60 million people, constituted perhaps one-fifth or one-sixth of the world's then population. Victorious conquest had been bought at a huge price, measured in human suffering, carnage, and money. The costs were borne by tens of thousands of conquered peoples, who paid taxes to the Roman state, by slaves captured in war and transported to Italy, and by Roman soldiers who served long years fighting overseas.

The discipline of the Roman army was notorious. Decimation is one index of its severity. If an army unit was judged disobedient or cowardly in battle, one soldier in ten was selected by lot and cudgelled to death by his former comrades. It should be stressed that decimation was not just a myth told to terrify fresh recruits; it actually happened in the period of imperial expansion, and frequently enough not to arouse particular comment. Roman soldiers killed each other for their common good.

When Romans were so unmerciful to each other, what mercy could prisoners of war expect? Small wonder then that they were sometimes forced to fight in gladiatorial contests, or were thrown to wild beasts for popular entertainment. Public executions helped inculcate valour and fear in the men, women and children left at home. Children learnt the lesson of what happened to soldiers who were defeated. Public executions were rituals which helped maintain an atmo-sphere of violence, even in times of peace. Bloodshed and slaughter joined military glory and conquest as central elements in Roman culture.

With the accession of the first emperor Augustus (31 BC–AD 14), the Roman state embarked on a period of long-term peace (*pax romana*). For more than two centuries, thanks to its effective defence by frontier armies, the inner core of the Roman empire was virtually insulated from the direct experience of war. Then in memory of their warrior traditions, the Romans set up artificial battlefields in cities and towns for public amusement. The custom spread from Italy to the provinces.

Nowadays, we admire the Colosseum in Rome and other great Roman amphitheatres such as those at Verona, Arles, Nîmes and El Djem as architectural monuments. We choose to forget, I suspect, that this was where Romans regularly organised fights to the death between hundreds of gladiators, the mass execution of unarmed criminals, and the indiscriminate slaughter of domestic and wild animals.

The enormous size of the amphitheatres indicates how popular these exhibitions were. The Colosseum was dedicated in AD 80 with 100 days of games. One day 3,000 men fought; on another 9,000 animals were killed. It seated 50,000 people. It is still one of Rome's most impressive buildings, a magnificent feat of engineering and design. In ancient times, amphitheatres must have towered over cities, much as cathedrals towered over medieval towns. Public killings of men and animals were a Roman rite, with overtones of religious sacrifice, legitimated by the myth that gladiatorial shows inspired the populace with 'a glory in wounds and a contempt of death'.

Philosophers, and later Christians, disapproved strongly. To little effect; gladiatorial games persisted at least until the early fifth century AD, wild-beast killings until the sixth century. St Augustine in his *Confessions* tells the story of a Christian who was reluctantly forced along to the amphitheatre by a party of friends; at first, he kept his eyes shut, but when he heard the crowd roar, he opened them, and became converted by the sight of blood into an eager devotee of gladiatorial shows. Even the biting criticism quoted below reveals a certain excitement beneath its moral outrage.

Seneca, Roman senator and philosopher, tells of a visit he once paid to the arena. He arrived in the middle of the day, during the mass execution of criminals, staged as an entertainment in the interval between the wild-beast show in the morning and the gladiatorial show of the afternoon:

All the previous fighting had been merciful by comparison. Now finesse is set aside, and we have pure unadulterated murder. The combatants have no protective covering; their entire bodies are exposed to the blows. No blow falls in vain. This is what lots of people prefer to the regular contests, and even to those which are put on by popular request. And it is obvious why. There is no helmet, no shield to repel the blade. Why have armour? Why bother with skill? All that just delays death.

In the morning, men are thrown to lions and bears. At mid-day they are thrown to the spectators themselves. No sooner has a man killed, than they shout for him to kill another, or to be killed. The final victor is kept for some other slaughter. In the end, every fighter dies. And all this goes on while the arena is half empty.

You may object that the victims committed robbery or were murderers.

So what? Even if they deserved to suffer, what's your compulsion to watch their sufferings? 'Kill him', they shout, 'Beat him, burn him'. Why is he too timid to fight? Why is he so frightened to kill? Why so reluctant to die? They have to whip him to make him accept his wounds.

Much of our evidence suggests that gladiatorial contests were, by origin, closely connected with funerals. 'Once upon a time', wrote the Christian critic Tertullian at the end of the second century AD, 'men believed that the souls of the dead were propitiated by human blood, and so at funerals they sacrificed prisoners of war or slaves of poor quality bought for the purpose'. The first recorded gladiatorial show took place in 264 BC: it was presented by two nobles in honour of their dead father; only three pairs of gladiators took part. Over the next two centuries, the scale and frequency of gladiatorial shows increased steadily. In 65 BC, for example, Julius Caesar gave elaborate funeral games for his father involving 640 gladiators and condemned criminals who were forced to fight with wild beasts. At his next games in 46 BC, in memory of his dead daughter and, let it be said, in celebration of his recent triumphs in Gaul and Egypt, Caesar presented not only the customary fights between individual gladiators, but also fights between whole detachments of infantry and between squadrons of cavalry, some mounted on horses, others on elephants. Large-scale gladiatorial shows had arrived. Some of the contestants were professional gladiators, others prisoners of war, and others criminals condemned to death.

Up to this time, gladiatorial shows had always been put on by individual aristocrats at their own initiative and expense, in honour of dead relatives. The religious component in gladiatorial ceremonies continued to be important. For example, attendants in the arena were dressed up as gods. Slaves who tested whether fallen gladiators were really dead or just pretending, by applying a red-hot cauterising iron, were dressed as the god Mercury. Those who dragged away the dead bodies were dressed as Pluto, the god of the underworld. During the persecutions of Christians, the victims were sometimes led around the arena in a procession dressed up as priests and priestesses of pagan cults, before being stripped naked and thrown to the wild beasts. The welter of blood in gladiatorial and wild-beast

shows, the squeals and smell of the human victims and of slaughtered animals are completely alien to us and almost unimaginable. For some Romans they must have been reminiscent of battlefields, and, more immediately for everyone, associated with religious sacrifice. At one remove, Romans, even at the height of their civilisation, performed human sacrifice, purportedly in commemoration of their dead.

By the end of the last century BC, the religious and commemorative elements in gladiatorial shows were eclipsed by the political and the spectacular. Gladiatorial shows were public performances held mostly, before the amphitheatre was built, in the ritual and social centre of the city, the Forum. Public participation, attracted by the splendour of the show and by distributions of meat, and by betting, magnified the respect paid to the dead and the honour of the whole family. Aristocratic funerals in the Republic (before 31 BC) were political acts. And funeral games had political implications, because of their popularity with citizen electors. Indeed, the growth in the splendour of gladiatorial shows was largely fuelled by competition between ambitious aristocrats, who wished to please, excite and increase the number of their supporters.

In 42 BC, for the first time, gladiatorial fights were substituted for chariot-races in official games. After that in the city of Rome, regular gladiatorial shows, like theatrical shows and chariot-races, were given by officers of state, as part of their official careers, as an official obligation and as a tax on status. The Emperor Augustus, as part of a general policy of limiting aristocrats' opportunities to court favour with the Roman populace, severely restricted the number of regular gladiatorial shows to two each year. He also restricted their splendour and size. Each official was forbidden to spend more on them than his colleagues, and an upper limit was fixed at 120 gladiators a show.

These regulations were gradually evaded. The pressure for evasion was simply that, even under the emperors, aristocrats were still competing with each other, in prestige and political success. The splendour of a senator's public exhibition could make or break his social and political reputation. One aristocrat, Symmachus, wrote to a friend: 'I must now outdo the reputation earned by my own shows; our family's recent generosity during my consulship and the official games given for my son allow us to present nothing mediocre'. So he set about enlisting the help of various powerful friends in the provinces. In the end, he managed to procure antelopes, gazelles, leopards, lions, bears, bear-cubs, and even some crocodiles, which only just survived to the beginning of the games, because for the previous fifty days they had refused to eat. Moreover, twenty-nine Saxon prisoners of war strangled each other in their cells on the night before their final scheduled appearance. Symmachus was heart-broken. Like every donor of the games, he knew that his political standing was at stake. Every presentation was in Goffman's strikingly apposite phrase 'a status bloodbath'.

The most spectacular gladiatorial shows were given by the emperors themselves at Rome. For example, the Emperor Trajan, to celebrate his conquest of Dacia (roughly modern Roumania), gave games in AD 108–9 lasting 123 days in which 9,138 gladiators fought and eleven thousand animals were slain. The Emperor Claudius in AD 52 presided in full military regalia over a battle on a lake near Rome between two naval squadrons, manned for the occasion by 19,000 forced combatants. The palace guard, stationed behind stout barricades, which also prevented the combatants from escaping, bombarded the ships with missiles from catapults. After a faltering start, because the men refused to fight, the battle according to Tacitus 'was fought with the spirit of free men, although between criminals. After much bloodshed, those who survived were spared extermination'.

The quality of Roman justice was often tempered by the need to satisfy the demand for the condemned. Christians, burnt to death as scapegoats after the great fire at Rome in AD 64, were not alone in being sacrificed for public entertainment. Slaves and bystanders, even the spectators themselves, ran the risk of becoming victims of emperors' truculent whims. The Emperor Claudius, for example, dissatisfied with how the stage machinery worked, ordered the stage mechanics responsible to fight in the arena. One day when there was a shortage of condemned criminals, the Emperor Caligula commanded that a whole section of the crowd be seized and thrown to the wild beasts instead. Isolated incidents, but enough to intensify the excitement of those who attended..

The handle of a knife with the figure of a gladiator carved in ivory.

Imperial legitimacy was reinforced by terror.

As for animals, their sheer variety symbolised the extent of Roman power and left vivid traces in Roman art. In 169 BC, sixty-three African lions and leopards, forty bears and several elephants were hunted down in a single show. New species were gradually introduced to Roman spectators (tigers, crocodiles, gi-

Graffiti of gladiators from the walls of Pompeii, showing their 'show-biz' appeal.

raffes, lynxes, rhinoceros, ostriches, hippopotami) and killed for their pleasure. Not for Romans the tame viewing of caged animals in a zoo. Wild beasts were set to tear criminals to pieces as public lesson in pain and death. Sometimes, elaborate sets and theatrical backdrops were prepared in which, as a climax, a criminal was devoured limb by limb. Such spectacular punishments, common enough in pre-industrial states, helped reconstitute sovereign power. The deviant criminal was punished; law and order were re-established.

The labour and organisation required to capture so many animals and to deliver them alive to Rome must have been enormous. Even if wild animals were more plentiful then than now, single shows with one hundred, four hundred or six hundred lions, plus other animals, seem amazing. By contrast, after Roman times, no hippopotamus was seen in Europe until one was brought to London by steamship in 1850. It took a whole regiment of Egyptian soldiers to capture it, and involved a five month journey to bring it from the White Nile to Cairo. And yet the Emperor Commodus, a dead-shot with spear and bow, himself killed five hippos, two elephants, a rhinoceros and a giraffe, in one show lasting two days. On another occasion he killed 100 lions and bears in a single morning show, from safe walkways specially constructed across the arena. It was, a contemporary remarked, 'a better demonstration of accuracy than of courage'. The slaughter of exotic animals in the emperor's presence, and exceptionally by the emperor himself or by his palace guards, was a spectacular dramatisation of the emperor's formidable power: immediate, bloody and symbolic.

Gladiatorial shows also provided an arena for popular participation in politics. Cicero explicitly recognised this towards the end of the Republic: 'the judgement and wishes of the Roman people about public affairs can be most clearly expressed in three places: public assemblies, elections, and at plays or gladiatorial shows'. He challenged a political opponent: 'Give yourself to the people. Entrust yourself to the Games. Are you terrified of not being applauded?' His comments underline the fact that the crowd had the important option of giving or of withholding applause, of hissing or of being silent.

Under the emperors, as citizens' rights to engage in politics diminished, gladiatorial shows and games provided repeated opportunities for the dramatic confrontation of rulers and ruled. Rome was unique among large historical empires in allowing, indeed in expecting, these regular meetings between emperors and the massed populace of the capital, collected together in a single crowd. To be sure, emperors could mostly stage-manage their own appearance and reception. They gave extravagant shows. They threw gifts to the crowd—small marked wooden balls (called *missilia*) which could be exchanged for various luxuries. They occasionally planted their own claques in the crowd.

Mostly, emperors received standing ovations and ritual acclamations. The Games at Rome provided a stage for the emperor to display his majesty—luxurious ostentation in procession, accessibility to humble petitioners, generosity to the crowd, human involvement in the contests themselves, graciousness or arrogance towards the assembled aristocrats, clemency or cruelty to the vanquished. When a gladiator fell, the crowd would shout for mercy or dispatch. The emperor might be swayed by their shouts or gestures, but he alone, the final arbiter, decided who was to live or die. When the emperor entered the amphitheatre, or decided the fate of a fallen gladiator by the movement of his thumb, at that moment he had 50,000 courtiers. He knew that he was *Caesar Imperator,* Foremost of Men.

Things did not always go the way the emperor wanted. Sometimes, the crowd objected, for example to the high price of wheat, or demanded the execution of an unpopular official or a reduction in taxes. Caligula once reacted angrily and sent soldiers into the crowd with orders to execute summarily anyone seen shouting. Understandably, the crowd grew silent, though sullen. But the emperor's increased unpopularity encouraged his assassins to act. Dio, senator and historian, was present at another popular demonstration in the Circus in AD 195. He was amazed that the huge crowd (the Circus held up to 200,000 people) strung out along the track, shouted for an end to civil war 'like a well-trained choir'.

Dio also recounted how with his own eyes he saw the Emperor Commodus cut off the head of an ostrich as a sacrifice in the arena then walk towards the congregated senators whom he hated, with the sacrificial knife in one hand and the severed head of the bird in the other,

(Above) Clay lamp showing gladiators' weapons. (Right) A clay pot depicting gladiators fighting.

clearly indicating, so Dio thought, that it was the senators' necks which he really wanted. Years later, Dio recalled how he had kept himself from laughing (out of anxiety, presumably) by chewing desperately on a laurel leaf which he plucked from the garland on his head.

Consider how the spectators in the amphitheatre sat: the emperor in his gilded box, surrounded by his family; senators and knights each had special seats and came properly dressed in their distinctive purple-bordered togas. Soldiers were separated from civilians. Even ordinary citizens had to wear the heavy white woollen toga, the formal dress of a Roman citizen, and sandals, if they wanted to sit in the bottom two main tiers of seats. Married men sat separately from bachelors, boys sat in a separate block, with their teachers in the next block. Women, and the very poorest men dressed in the drab grey cloth associated with mourning, could sit or stand only in the top tier of the amphitheatre. Priests and Vestal Virgins (honorary men) had reserved seats at the front. The correct dress and segregation of ranks underlined the formal ritual elements in the occasion, just as the steeply banked seats reflected the steep stratification of Roman society. It mattered where you sat, and where you were seen to be sitting.

Gladiatorial shows were political theatre. The dramatic performance took place, not only in the arena, but between different sections of the audience. Their interaction should be included in any thorough account of the Roman constitution. The amphitheatre was the Roman crowd's parliament. Games are usually omitted from political histories, simply

because in our own society, mass spectator sports count as leisure. But the Romans themselves realised that metropolitan control involved 'bread and circuses'. 'The Roman people', wrote Marcus Aurelius' tutor Fronto, 'is held together by two forces: wheat doles and public shows'.

Enthusiastic interest in gladiatorial shows occasionally spilled over into a desire to perform in the arena. Two emperors were not content to be spectators-in-chief. They wanted to be prize performers as well. Nero's histrionic ambitions and success as musician and actor were notorious. He also prided himself on his abilities as a charioteer. Commodus performed as a gladiator in the amphitheatre, though admittedly only in preliminary bouts with blunted weapons. He won all his fights and charged the imperial treasury a million sesterces for each appearance (enough to feed a thousand families for a year). Eventually, he was assassinated when he was planning to be inaugurated as consul (in AD 193), dressed as a gladiator.

Commodus' gladiatorial exploits were an idiosyncratic expression of a culture obsessed with fighting, bloodshed, ostentation and competition. But at least seven other emperors practised as gladiators, and fought in gladiatorial contests. And so did Roman senators and knights. Attempts were made to stop them by law; but the laws were evaded.

Roman writers tried to explain away these senators' and knights' outrageous behaviour by calling them morally degenerate, forced into the arena by wicked emperors or their own profligacy. This

Fresco showing riots between men of Pompeii and Nuceria in and around the amphitheatre in AD 59.

explanation is clearly inadequate, even though it is difficult to find one which is much better. A significant part of the Roman aristocracy, even under the emperors, was still dedicated to military prowess: all generals were senators; all senior officers were senators or knights. Combat in the arena gave aristocrats a chance to display their fighting skill and courage. In spite of the opprobrium and at the risk of death, it was their last chance to play soldiers in front of a large audience.

Gladiators were glamour figures, culture heroes. The probable life-span of each gladiator was short. Each successive victory brought further risk of defeat and death. But for the moment, we are more concerned with image than with reality. Modern pop-stars and athletes have only a short exposure to full-glare publicity. Most of them fade rapidly from being household names into obscurity, fossilised in the memory of each

generation of adolescent enthusiasts. The transience of the fame of each does not diminish their collective importance.

So too with Roman gladiators. Their portraits were often painted. Whole walls in public porticos were sometimes covered with life-size portraits of all the gladiators in a particular show. The actual events were magnified beforehand by expectation and afterwards by memory. Street advertisements stimulated excitement and anticipation. Hundreds of Roman artefacts—sculptures, figurines, lamps, glasses—picture gladiatorial fights and wild-beast shows. In conversation and in daily life, chariot-races and gladiatorial fights were all the rage. 'When you enter the lecture halls', wrote Tacitus, 'what else do you hear the young men talking about?' Even a baby's nursing bottle, made of clay and found at Pompeii, was stamped with the figure of a gladiator. It symbolised the hope that the baby would imbibe a gladiator's strength and courage.

The victorious gladiator, or at least his image, was sexually attractive. Graffiti

from the plastered walls of Pompeii carry the message:

Celadus [a stage name, meaning Crowd's Roar], thrice victor and thrice crowned, the young girls' heart-throb, and Crescens the Netter of young girls by night.

The ephemera of AD 79 have been preserved by volcanic ash. Even the defeated gladiator had something sexually portentous about him. It was customary, so it is reported, for a new Roman bride to have her hair parted with a spear, at best one which had been dipped in the body of a defeated and killed gladiator.

The Latin word for sword—*gladius*—was vulgarly used to mean penis. Several artefacts also suggest this association. A small bronze figurine from Pompeii depicts a cruel-looking gladiator fighting off with his sword a dog-like wild-beast which grows out of his erect and elongated penis. Five bells hang down from various parts of his body and a hook is attached to the gladiator's head, so that the whole ensemble could hang as a bell in a doorway. Interpretation must be speculative. But this evidence suggests that there was a close link, in some Roman minds, between gladiatorial fighting and sexuality. And it seems as though gladiatorial bravery for some Roman men represented an attractive yet dangerous, almost threatening, macho masculinity.

Gladiators attracted women, even though most of them were slaves. Even if they were free or noble by origin, they were in some sense contaminated by their close contact with death. Like suicides, gladiators were in some places excluded from normal burial grounds. Perhaps their dangerous ambiguity was part of their sexual attraction. They were, according to the Christian Tertullian, both loved and despised: 'men give them their souls, women their bodies too'. Gladiators were 'both glorified and degraded'.

In a vicious satire, the poet Juvenal ridiculed a senator's wife, Eppia, who had eloped to Egypt with her favourite swordsman:

What was the youthful charm that so fired Eppia? What hooked her? What did she see in him to make her put up with being called 'The Gladiator's Moll'? Her poppet, her Sergius, was no chicken, with a dud arm that prompted hope of early retirement. Besides, his face looked a proper mess, helmet scarred, a great wart on his nose, an unpleasant discharge always trickling from one eye. But he was a Gladiator. That word makes the whole breed seem handsome, and made her prefer him to her children and country, her sister and husband. Steel is what they fall in love with.

Satire certainly, and exaggerated, but pointless unless it was also based to some extent in reality. Modern excavators, working in the armoury of the gladiatorial barracks in Pompeii found eighteen skeletons in two rooms, presumably of gladiators caught there in an ash storm; they included only one woman, who was wearing rich gold jewellery, and a necklace set with emeralds. Occasionally, women's attachment to gladiatorial combat went further. They fought in the arena themselves. In the storeroom of the British Museum, for example, there is a small stone relief, depicting two female gladiators, one with breast bare, called Amazon and Achillia. Some of these female gladiators were free women of high status.

Behind the brave façade and the hope of glory, there lurked the fear of death. 'Those about to die salute you, Emperor'. Only one account survives of what it was like from the gladiator's point of view. It is from a rhetorical exercise. The story is told by a rich young man who had been captured by pirates and was then sold on as a slave to a gladiatorial trainer:

And so the day arrived. Already the populace had gathered for the spectacle of our punishment, and the bodies of those about to die had their own death-parade across the arena. The presenter of the shows, who hoped to gain favour with our blood, took his seat . . . Although no one knew my birth, my fortune, my family, one fact made some people pity me; I seemed unfairly matched. I was destined to be a certain victim in the sand . . . All around I could hear the instruments of death: a sword being sharpened, iron plates being heated in a fire (to stop fighters retreating and to prove that they were not faking death], birch-rods and whips were prepared. One would have imagined that these were the pirates. The trumpets sounded their foreboding notes; stretchers for the dead were brought on, a funeral parade before death. Everywhere I could see wounds, groans, blood, danger . . .

He went on to describe his thoughts, his memories in the moments when he faced death, before he was dramatically and conveniently rescued by a friend. That was fiction. In real life gladiators died.

Bronze tintinnabulum of a gladiator from Pompeii.

Gladiator's dress helmet found at Herculaneum.

Why did Romans popularise fights to the death between armed gladiators? Why did they encourage the public slaughter of unarmed criminals? What was it which transformed men who were timid and peaceable enough in private, as Tertullian put it, and made them shout gleefully for the merciless destruction of their fellow men? Part of the answer may lie in the simple development of a tradition, which fed on itself and its own success. Men liked blood and cried out for more. Part of the answer may also lie in the social psychology of the crowd, which relieved individuals of responsibility for their actions, and in the psychological mechanisms by which some spectators identified more easily with the victory of the aggressor than with the sufferings of the vanquished. Slavery and the steep stratification of society must also have contributed. Slaves were at the mercy of their owners. Those who were destroyed for public edification and

113

entertainment were considered worthless, as nonpersons; or, like Christian martyrs, they were considered social outcasts, and tortured as one Christian martyr put it 'as if we no longer existed'. The brutalisation of the spectators fed on the dehumanisation of the victims.

Rome was a cruel society. Brutality was built into its culture in private life, as well as in public shows. The tone was set by military discipline and by slavery. The state had no legal monopoly of capital punishment until the second century AD. Before then, a master could crucify his slaves publicly if he wished. Seneca recorded from his own observations the various ways in which crucifixions were carried out, in order to increase pain. At private dinner-parties, rich Romans regularly presented two or three pairs of gladiators: 'when they have finished dining and are filled with drink', wrote a critic in the time of Augustus, 'they call in the gladiators. As soon as one has his throat cut, the diners applaud with delight'. It is worth stressing that we are dealing here not with individual sadistic psycho-pathology, but with a deep cultural difference. Roman commitment to cruelty presents us with a cultural gap which it is difficult to cross.

Popular gladiatorial shows were a by-product of war, discipline and death. For centuries, Rome had been devoted to war and to the mass participation of citizens in battle. They won their huge empire by discipline and control. Public executions were a gruesome reminder to non-combatants, citizens, subjects and slaves, that vengeance would be exacted if they rebelled or betrayed their country. The arena provided a living enactment of the hell portrayed by Christian preachers. Public punishment ritually re-established the moral and political order. The power of the state was dramatically reconfirmed.

When long-term peace came to the heartlands of the empire, after 31 BC, militaristic traditions were preserved at Rome in the domesticated battlefield of the amphitheatre. War had been con-

Terracotta relief of a gladiatorial circus.

verted into a game, a drama repeatedly replayed, of cruelty, violence, blood and death. But order still needed to be preserved. The fear of death still had to be assuaged by ritual. In a city as large as Rome, with a population of close on a million by the end of the last century BC, without an adequate police force, disorder always threatened.

Gladiatorial shows and public executions reaffirmed the moral order, by the sacrifice of human victims—slaves, gladiators, condemned criminals or impious Christians. Enthusiastic participation, by spectators rich and poor, raised and then released collective tensions, in a society which traditionally idealised impassivity. Gladiatorial shows provided a psychic and political safety valve for the metropolitan population. Politically, emperors risked occasional conflict, but the populace could usually be diverted or fobbed off. The crowd lacked the coherence of a rebellious political ideology. By and large,

it found its satisfaction in cheering its support of established order. At the psychological level, gladiatorial shows provided a stage for shared violence and tragedy. Each show reassured spectators that they had yet again survived disaster. Whatever happened in the arena, the spectators were on the winning side. 'They found comfort for death' wrote Tertullian with typical insight, 'in murder'.

FOR FURTHER READING:

An expanded version of this article with references appears in K. Hopkins, *Death and renewal, Sociological Studies in Roman History,* Volume 2 (Cambridge University Press, May 1983, £19.50). The most extensive review of the evidence on gladiatorial games is by L. Friedlaender, *Roman Life and Manners, Volume 2 with references in Volume 4* (London, 1913). A more accessible and readable account is given by M. Grant, *Gladiators,* (Weidenfeld and Nicolson, 1976). On the methods used here, see C. Geertz, *The Interpretation of Cultures* (Weidenfeld and Nicolson, 1973).

Old Sports

The Olympic Games were not the earliest athletic rituals in the eastern Mediterranean

Allen Guttmann

Guttmann recently completed an English translation of *Sports and Games of Ancient Egypt,* by Wolfgang Decker. A professor of English and American studies at Amherst College, he now plans to examine the diffusion of modern sports from England and America as a case of cultural imperialism.

Every four years at Olympia, the athletes of ancient Greece paid homage to Zeus by demonstrating their *arete,* their excellence of mind and body. According to Hippias of Elis, the nearby city-state that organized the competitions, the Olympic Games began in 776 B.C. with a simple footrace, and other events were subsequently added. But the list of victors Hippias compiled, sometime about 400 B.C., exaggerated the age of the games, apparently to aggrandize the glory of his native city. Plutarch admonished that Hippias "had no fully authoritative basis for his work," and historians now believe that the games began, with as many as five different sports, about 600 B.C., more or less at the same time as the sacred games at Delphi, Corinth, and Nemea, which rounded out the four-year cycle of Greek athletics. (Isaac Newton anticipated modern scholars, estimating the games' later origin by recalculating the duration of royal reigns and accurately dating eclipses referred to by ancient astronomers.)

The true precursors of the sixth-century games remain elusive, but we do know that the Greeks were not the only people of the eastern Mediterranean to emphasize athletic ritual as a religious and political statement. In ancient Egypt, for example, from at least 3000 B.C., physical prowess was a necessary sign of a pharaoh's fitness to rule. As a representative of divinity on earth, his role required him to maintain order against the forces of chaos. A pharaoh commemorating the thirtieth anniversary of his enthronement would formally prove his fitness by executing a ceremonial run in the jubilee known as the Festival of Sed. The course, from one mark to another and back, symbolized the boundaries of the kingdom he protected. The earliest known turn markers, at the pyramid of Djoser (ca. 2600 B.C.), lie about sixty yards apart.

There were numerous other occasions for a pharaoh to display his strength and stamina. Inscriptions and reliefs testify to almost superhuman demonstrations of hunting skill, events that may or may not have actually occurred. Tuthmosis III, for example, one of the monarchs of the Eighteenth Dynasty (1552–1306 B.C.), boasted, "In an instant I killed seven lions with my arrows." Similarly, he and several other monarchs of that dynasty were said to have so mastered the composite bow (made of hardwood, softwood, and horn) that their arrows were able to transfix sheets of copper "three fingers thick."

(Modern attempts to replicate this feat have failed.) The pharaoh had to be seen as the mightiest archer, most successful hunter, and swiftest runner. An American president can lose a tennis match without unleashing the forces of chaos, but Tuthmosis III was required to surpass all mortal achievements.

In the biography of Cheti, prince of Siut, who lived during the Eleventh Dynasty (2134–1991 B.C.), we read that "he learned to swim together with the children of the pharaoh." But despite the central role of the Nile in Egyptian life, there is no evidence that the pharaoh was expected to demonstrate his prowess at swimming. Or perhaps Egyptian artists considered the physical movements too undignified to show in a representation of divinity. There is, however, an inscription telling of the amazing boating exploits of the Eighteenth Dynasty monarch Amenophis II, who was said to have steered his "falcon ship" for three *itrw* (about 18.6 miles), when others gave up in exhaustion after a mere half *itrw*. And according to Egyptian legend, the gods Horus and Seth, both of whom claimed the right to rule the universe, agreed to settle their dispute with a diving contest.

If the quantity of visual evidence is any indication, wrestling was among the most popular Egyptian sports. Murals discovered in the eleventh-century tombs at Beni Hasan depict nearly every hold known to modern wrestlers. Although the sport has a religious character in many cultures, including those of Africa south of the Sahara, for the ancient Egyptians it seems to have been a purely secular contest. A pharaoh thrown roughly to the ground would have been a terrifying portent of disaster.

The pharaohs most celebrated for their athletic achievements were the martial monarchs of the Eighteenth Dynasty, especially Tuthmosis III, Amenophis II, Tuthmosis IV, and Amenophis III. These were the immediate successors of the Hyksos, a seminomadic people whose warriors swept from the northeast into the valley of the Nile about 1650 B.C. Their war chariots spread terror among the Egyptians of the time, for whom this was an unknown weapon. For more than a century, the Hyksos usurpers ruled Egypt; once they were expelled, more emphasis than ever was placed on the pharaoh's physical prowess. Even Queen Hatshepsut, an Eighteenth Dynasty monarch who ruled as if she were a man, had to prove her fitness with the time-honored ceremonial run. A relief discovered at Karnak depicts her in the middle of the ceremony, accompanied by the bull-god Apis. The great exception was the pacific Amenophis IV (who ruled as Akheneten), best remembered for his heretical monotheistic religious views.

The Hyksos were expelled; the chariot remained. It was used for hunting as well as for waging war, and pharaohs were often portrayed wielding spears or drawing bows from the basket of a chariot. Chariot races as such were not part of ancient Egyptian culture, despite the suitability of the terrain. But later, during the Hellenistic age (fourth to first centuries B.C.), when Alexander the Great and his successors spread Greek culture throughout the eastern Mediterranean, chariot races became immensely popular in Alexandria and elsewhere in Egypt.

The Egyptians seem never to have been as passionate about horses as were the Hyksos, the Hittites (of what is now central Turkey), the Assyrians of Mesopotamia (modern Iraq), and other peoples of the Near East, who devoted enormous amounts of time and energy to their care and breeding. An obscure fourteenth-century Hittite named Kikkuli has left us a detailed account of these matters in writings sometimes referred to as *The Book of Horses*. The later Persian empire, which came close to overwhelming Greek civi-

lization in 490 B.C., had similar roots. As Xenophon and other Greek historians made clear, equestrianism was an essential aspect of the education of a Persian prince, whose skill as a rider and hunter was a warranty of fitness to rule.

We know little about the role of sports in the great Minoan civilization, which reached its height on the island of Crete between 2200 and 1400 B.C. The written language remains mostly a mystery. But few frescoes have engendered more speculation than the one excavated at the Palace of Minos in Knossos, which shows adolescents, a boy and two girls, seizing the horns of a charging bull and somersaulting over its back. Ever since Arthur Evans discovered the image in 1900, scholars have wondered whether people really performed this dangerous stunt and, if so, what it signified. Was it a contest in which youths competed against each other, like modern gymnasts, or was the bull their adversary, as in a Spanish *corrida de toros?* Another fresco from Knossos, now at the National Museum in Athens, depicts a group of male and female spectators arranged on terraces, or tiers. Whether the audience consists of assembled worshipers or sports enthusiasts is not clear, but some scholars believe they are attending a bull-vaulting performance.

Vases, statuettes, coins, and other remains of Minoan culture attest to the popularity of hunting, boxing, and wrestling. Among the most tantalizing discoveries is a fresco from the island of Thera, a Minoan outpost, that shows two boys wearing some kind of boxing gloves, squaring off as if in a modern ring. The guides in Thera call them the "boxing princes," but whether they really were princes proving their fitness for rule or merely two boys at play remains the artist's secret.

The Etruscans, whose civilization flourished during the seventh century B.C. in the region north and west of Rome, were enthusiastic about sports, perhaps as a result of Greek influence. The murals inside the so-called Tomb of the Monkey and other burial sites feature Etruscan wrestling and boxing, while chariots race across the walls of the Tomb of the Olympics, Tomb of the Two-Horse Chariots, and others. The murals of the chariot races include the spectators and perhaps the officials, at least one of whom seems to have been female. Jean-Paul Thuillier, the leading authority on Etruscan sports, argues that these types of murals represented fu-

neral games, traditionally held to honor the dead. This is plausible for many sports, but one wonders about the scenes in the Tomb of Hunting and Fishing, which include a fine picture of a man diving.

A mysterious Etruscan sport appears in the Tomb of the Augurs and Tomb of the Olympics. Known as the Phersu combat, from a word inscribed in the latter tomb, it pitted a masked man against a dog held on a leash by a second man. It may have inspired the later Roman combats of men and animals (*venationes*).

Scholars once believed that the Etruscans also gave the Romans the idea for their *munera,* combats between pairs of armed gladiators. An origin in Campania, south of Rome, or Samnia, east of Rome, now seems more likely. The precedent may have been a deadly funeral contest that had evolved from a still earlier ritual of human sacrifice. Such sacrifices would have been made to provide dead heroes with an entourage and appease the gods of the underworld. Eventually, death in combat might have been deemed a better offering than the less thrilling sacrifice of a passive victim. The Romans took the ultimate step of making a fight to the death a gruesome form of entertainment. (The religious trappings of Rome's pagan games, incidentally, were what horrified Christian theologians like Tertullian, who deplored idolatry more than the martyrdom of his fellow believers.)

Funeral games may also have been the chief precursors of the Greek Olympics. Our best early source is not visual art or archeology but literature: Homer's *Iliad,* a ninth-century account of the Trojan War, which probably occurred in the thirteenth century B.C. In Book XXIII, the Greeks, who have not yet captured the city of Troy, celebrate funeral games for Patroklos, who has been slain by the Trojan hero Hektor. Lavish prizes are offered by the great Achilles, Patroklos's bosom friend.

The first event of the games is a chariot race, for which Achilles offers five prizes, chief of which is "a woman skilled in fair handiwork." Although Greece was not the ideal place to breed horses, chariot races were apparently common in Attica, Thessaly, and other places where the terrain was not too forbidding. The plain before "the topless towers of Ilium" provides a suitable course, but the race is a rough one, with the goddess Athene intervening to assure victory for her favorite, Diomedes. (Fair play, which requires that everyone compete under the same rules, is as much a nineteenth-century concept as the nearly defunct amateur rule of the modern Olympics.)

The chariot race is followed by the boxing and wrestling contests. The first is won by Epeius, who fells his opponent with a mighty blow to the cheek. The second is declared a draw when neither Odysseus nor Ajax can throw the other. Then comes the footrace, in which Athene again intervenes, this time to favor Odysseus, whose limbs she lightens. The oafish Ajax she causes to slip and fall on offal left from the ritual slaughter of oxen.

When Ajax recovers, he is matched against Diomedes in potentially deadly armed combat, but the spectators stop the fight when Diomedes thrusts fiercely at Ajax's throat. Ajax has apparently suffered enough for a single day. The games conclude with the hurtling of the discus and with an archery contest in which the target is a dove tethered to a ship's mast. (The javelin contest, which was supposed to end the games, is canceled when Achilles, deciding that Agamemnon is certain to win anyway, gives him the prize.)

In Homer's dramatization, we can see that the games were a form of religious ritual, an appropriate way to worship the gods and to honor a fallen warrior. The contests also emphasized the skills and accomplishments of warriors. Both themes were eventually incorporated in the Greek Olympics, although the nature of the contestants changed somewhat. At first they were aristocratic warriors, but later, ordinary Greek men also competed and the role of the full-time athlete grew.

Pelops, a local hero said to be buried at Olympia, may have been honored by funeral games, and subsequent commemorative contests may explain why the site was chosen when the official games were instituted about 600 B.C. Originally, the Olympics probably consisted of a number of events, foremost of which was the short-distance race, or stade, from one end of the field to the other (a stadium for the footrace built later at Olympia may still be visited). The other events may have included a chariot race and the pentathlon or its constituents—a footrace, the discus, long jump, javelin, and wrestling. Other contests added over the years included longer footraces, a race in armor, and boys' events.

Neither the *Iliad*'s archery contest nor its armed combat were a part of the Olympic Games. Nor, despite the location of most Greek cities on the shores of the Aegean or on the banks of a river, were there swimming events at Olympia or any of the other sacred games. This was true even of the Isthmian Games, held at Corinth in honor of Poseidon, god of the sea.

Although the Greek athletic festivals were not the only, or even the earliest, ritualized sports of antiquity, they, more than any others, characterized an entire culture and embodied many of its people's highest aspirations. When, nearly a century ago, Pierre de Coubertin championed ancient Greece as an inspiration for modern games, he chose his model wisely. Amenophis II proved his divinity by his superhuman (and probably imaginary) athletic performance. Olympic victors, true exemplars of human physical excellence, won their immortality the hard way.

The Great Religions

Presently there are approximately 1.9 billion Christians, 1 billion Muslims, 751 million Hindus, 334 million Buddhists, 20 million Sikhs, 19 million Jews, and 6 million Confucians in the world. Most people profess some sort of religion. Although it is often difficult to ascribe religious motivation to people and events, the world religions, nonetheless, provide a moral foundation for human interaction. In some instances the role of religion is obvious, such as in the conflict between Jews and Muslims in the Middle East, Protestants and Catholics in Ireland, or Muslims and Hindus in India. In other situations the role of religion is not obvious, but in any historical analysis, the possible religious motivation should not be ignored.

Despite the various subdivisions and numerous denominations today, the great religions originated in premodern times. In the stories of their development there are common themes—the relationship of one person to another and the relationship of people to a higher entity. Since development happened so long ago, there are unsolved historical questions. North of Mexico City at Teotihuacán, for example, an imposing pyramid dedicated to a goddess, apparently, was the center of a thriving city-state that led cultural development in Mesoamerica. The culture then disappeared suddenly for unknown reasons in the eighth century. Goddess religions seem to have preceded all others, as Caroline Malone explores in "The Death Cults of Prehistoric Malta," where, "fat lady" icons were found amidst the ruins of temples.

There are mysteries in the Bible as well. Archaeologists have used the Old and New Testaments as historical maps to guide exploration. Sometimes the Bible is the only source of information, such as about the Hebrew escape from Egypt, the conquest of Canaan, and Sodom and Gomorrah. On the other hand, other evidence has confirm accounts about the Temple, Hebrew Kings, the Exodus, the use of crucifixion, and Pontius Pilate. Although historical proof tends to give credence to the Bible stories, the quest for Jesus as a historical character persists, as the essay "Who Was Jesus?" points out.

There are inconsistencies in the gospels, no one knows what Jesus looked like, and there is uncertainty about the miracles. The story of Christ, as one scholar notes, is wonderful theology and poor history. The power of his message, nevertheless, spawned the largest religion in the world. There is a strong belief in Jesus' promise that he will return to establish the kingdom of God on earth. This has resulted in human attempts at prediction and doomsday prophecies about the end of the twentieth century.

Much more is known about Muhammad, who in the seventh century sent the Arab tribes on a spiritual quest and established the religion of Islam. The Bible became a sacred book for the Muslims, and so did the Koran, a collection of Muhammad's statements. Islam's similarity to Christianity has disturbed Westerners, as well as Muslims, who generally resist challenges to their faith.

Hinduism is older than the others and embraces hundreds of deities, some more powerful than others. Dominating the Indian subcontinent, Hinduism has shown an ability to absorb foreign religious concepts. Ideas involving the circular movement of time, reincarnation, and Karma, however, remain strange to Westerners. Out of Hinduism came Buddha, a religious leader who described the path to Nirvana, a place of peace and unity with the cosmos. Buddha, like Muhammad, never claimed to be more than a man, but as a great teacher he pointed the way to a better life for human beings. Buddhism died out in India, but it migrated to Sri Lanka, China, and Japan where it became a predominant religion. In "The Koran, Gita, and Tripitaka," Thomas Coburn compares the holy books of Islam, Buddhism, and Hinduism, while in the previous article of an interview with Charles Malamoud, the belief and history of Hinduism are explained.

Confucianism is often counted as a religion, but sometimes it is listed as a belief system, or philosophy, for life on earth. Confucious thought that the question of life after death would lead to no conclusion and thus did not spend time on it. Jonathan Spence, one of the foremost contemporary scholars of China, finds in the historical Confucious, however, much to be admired because of his decency and humanity.

Spiritual matters have long been of interest to human beings and they cannot be lightly dismissed or cynically disregarded in the study of world history. Even in nations that profess religious freedom and emphasize the separation of religion from government, such as the United States, religion has a permeating effect. Therefore, in evaluating any nation or society, this dimension of human existence merits consideration.

Looking Ahead: Challenge Questions

What is the purpose of religion in human life?

Why is there concern about the historical Jesus, historical Buddha, or historical Muhammed?

What is the message of the various religions about the treatment of fellow human beings?

Why does a person of one religion sometimes distrust someone of another?

On what points are the major religions alike and different? What do they say about life after death?

Why is it difficult to examine religion in a scientific or historical manner?

Mysterious Mexican Culture Yields Its Secrets

Scientists explore the ancient enigma of Teotihuacan.

John Noble Wilford

SAN FRANCISCO

The brooding pyramids that rise from the high basin north of Mexico City have long mystified archeologists. Even the Aztecs, awestruck at their first sight of the monuments seven centuries ago, could not come up with an earthly explanation. Deciding that something so grand could only have been built by the gods, they called the site Teotihuacan, "the place of the gods" in their language.

The culture of Teotihuacan (pronounced Tay-oh-tee-wha-KAHN) flourished from the first century A.D. until its abrupt collapse, for as yet unknown reasons, in A.D. 750. But almost nothing has been known about the people, their origins, the language they spoke or what they called themselves. Compared to them, the other large civilizations of the region—the Olmecs before them, the Zapotec and Maya who were contemporaries, and the Toltecs and Aztecs who followed—are an open book.

Only now, after decades of plodding research and excavation, have American and Mexican archeologists begun to crack the enigma of Teotihuacan and develop an image of the first urban state in the Americas.

A thorough survey of buried ruins surrounding the monuments has revealed that this was not just a religious ceremonial center, as had been thought, but a densely populated, multi-ethnic city. At its zenith in A.D. 600, Teotihuacan was one of the largest cities in the world, with possibly as many as 200,000 people. Constantinople, with half a million people, was the largest.

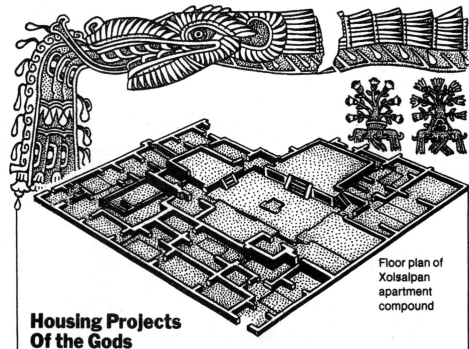

Housing Projects Of the Gods

The Teotihuacan culture invested heavily in housing, eventually building 2,000 stone and adobe compounds, with apartments of several rooms arranged around open courtyards. The compounds may have housed groups of related families or people with similar occupations or ranks. The images above the floor plan are detail of a mural depicting a feathered serpent and flowering trees, from a compound believed to have housed military leaders.

Floor plan of Xolsalpan apartment compound

Sources: "Teotihuacan," (Fine Arts Museums of San Francisco); "Feathered Serpents and Flowering Trees," (Fine Arts Museums of San Francisco)

The New York Times; Illustration by Patricia J. Wynne

Most of the Teotihuacanos lived in elaborate apartment compounds built of stone and adobe, some of which appeared to be so spacious and comfortable that archeologists at first mistook them for small palaces. More than 2,000 such multifamily compounds have been mapped, and recently several have been excavated in work that has been going on continuously since the early 1960's. No other ancient culture in Mesoamerica is known to have invested so much in the housing of its population.

Another aspect setting the civilization apart from most other prehistoric American cultures is the fact that its supreme deity was a goddess. In mural paintings and other art, the goddess is always shown with her face either missing or covered with a mask and her hands giv-

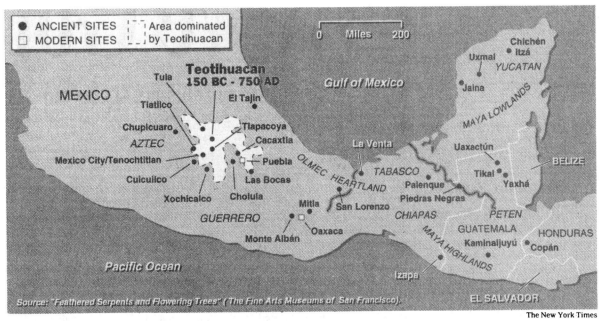

The Teotihuacan culture built a major market and pilgrimage center with influence extending to sites throughout Mesoamerica. It had trading colonies as far south as what is now Guatemala.

ing, in various versions, water, seeds or treasures.

In some less beneficent poses, the supreme goddess is associated with military imagery, heart sacrifice and destruction. Evidence of the mass sacrifice of more than 200 young soldiers has been discovered at the Temple of the Feathered Serpent. So much for earlier ideas of Teotihuacan as a peaceful theocracy run by priests.

A notable absence in the ruins may also be revealing. So far no lavish tomb or burial has been found that could be attributed to a powerful ruler. Nor does the art glorify any specific rulers; power is represented in mythic beings, like the supreme goddess, a storm god and the feathered serpent, a symbol of wealth and fertility. The celebration of the larger society in art and the construction of substantial housing for the general population, scholars say, could mean that Teotihuacan was guided by an ideology of collective power, with rulers subject to checks and balances—quite a contrast to the dynastic rule of other Mesoamerican societies.

"It's increasingly clear that there was no other early city like Teotihuacan anywhere," said Dr. René Millon, professor emeritus of anthropology at the University of Rochester and leader of the three-decades-long mapping project.

Dr. Esther Pasztory, an art historian at Columbia University and authority on the Teotihuacan culture, said, "It was

probably one of the most fascinating and unique civilizations that ever existed."

While the Maya, Aztecs and Incas continue to dominate most pre-Columbian studies, the nature and importance of Teotihuacan have emerged slowly from the new archeological findings. A dramatic expression of this new knowledge is the collection of stone sculptures and masks, colorful ceramics and mural paintings being exhibited here at the M. H. De Young Memorial Museum. The exhibition, "Teotihuacan: City of Gods," will run through Oct. 31. Dr. Pasztory and Kathleen Berrin, an art historian at the museum, are co-curators of the exhibition.

At a symposium in connection with the exhibition, scholars said the new research has produced a revised chronology for Teotihuacan, showing the culture to have been older than once thought and divided into at least two periods architecturally and perhaps politically.

As early as the first or second century B.C., scholars say, some charismatic leaders probably drew together various clans to establish a religious center. The largest monument, the Pyramid of the Sun, was erected at about that time over a natural cave, probably the focus of a creation myth and the dwelling place of the supreme goddess. There is a ritual cave inside the pyramid.

"I imagine that the rulers of Teotihuacan created a powerful religious cult that

either attracted, urged or forced people to move to Teotihuacan and build its monuments," Dr. Pasztory said, adding that the people were probably promised that they were "finding and creating paradise on earth."

By the first century A.D., Dr. Millon said, this city was on its way to being a major market and pilgrimage center with influence extending throughout Mesoamerica. The city appeared to have a few trading colonies as far south as what is now Guatemala.

Teotihuacan's splendor and power would eventually be enhanced by the addition of two other imposing monuments—the Pyramid of the Moon and the Temple of the Feathered Serpent. This mythic creature carved in stone, a serpent covered with the feathers of the quetzal bird, is familiar in many Mexican cultures, scholars point out, but may have been largely a creation of Teotihuacan.

ELABORATE APARTMENT COMPLEXES

Dr. Millon attributed Teotihuacan's enduring success in Mesoamerica to "the instrumental way its leaders used the attraction of its holy places and the prestige of its religion to make it so significant to so many for so long a time."

A great change came over the culture in the third century A.D. The construction of religious architecture on a grand scale came to an end. Nearly all effort began to be directed at building permanent living quarters for the people. Since there are no archeological remains of the previous housing, it is assumed that it consisted of huts made of thatch and other perishable materials, as was the case with many other prehistoric cultures.

From A.D. 250 on, as the ruins indicate, dwellings of stone and adobe clustered in compounds behind high walls were built along avenues laid out in a grid pattern. The apartment compounds were alike in concept. As Dr. Linda Manzanilla, an archeologist at the National University of Mexico, said, each compound enclosed several apartments, each of which presumably was occupied by a nuclear family. Each apartment included an area for food preparation and consumption, sleeping quarters, storage rooms, a patio and a burial area.

A religious shrine, with decorative incense burners and sometimes mural paintings, would occupy a courtyard used by all the families. The compounds varied in size to accommodate from 50 to 100 people, usually related families. Noting that there were about 230 temple complexes and 2,000 apartment compounds, Dr. Pasztory suggested that the city was organized so that there was a temple complex for every 100 compounds.

Other archeological research suggests that in some cases the compounds were organized along occupational lines, with obsidian knappers, potters and lapidaries concentrated in certain sections. Other compounds were reserved for foreigners, one barrio in the south of the city for people from Oaxaca and one in the east for people from Vera Cruz.

In the last six months, Rubén Cabrera Castro, an archeologist with the National Institute of Archeology and History in Mexico City, has excavated an older section of the city, known as La Ventilla, situated near the civic and religious center. He reported finding evidence of a sewer system with drains running from the apartment compounds to the streets, where bigger drains gathered water and channeled it to a river. He also found traces of canals that brought drinking water to the compounds.

AVOIDANCE OF HERO WORSHIP

Many of the buildings in La Ventilla, Mr. Cabrera said, were decorated with red borders on the floors, in moldings, on stairways and at doorways. Even the murals emphasize red hues. The significance of this has so far eluded archeologists. But in a religious-civic compound, he noted, buildings were crowned with roof ornaments made of clay from which project clay simulations of three drops of liquid, possibly blood.

The layout of the city implied effective centralized control of growth and construction, and the similarities of the apartment compounds suggested that they were part of a planned state endeavor.

Gertrude Stein once wrote, "Every civilization insisted in its own way before it went away." That is, each society has its own character and approach to life, qualities she called "insistence" because they are so often repeated.

According to Dr. Pasztory, the Teotihuacan insistence can be inferred from the city's art and architecture. The early colossal architecture was created without any accompanying images of gods or rulers. When the people began to express themselves in sculpture, murals and figurines, from A.D. 250 on, much of the art was abstract or included human figures all dressed alike.

In the book "Feathered Serpents and Flowering Trees: Reconstructing the Murals of Teotihuacan," edited by Ms. Berrin, Dr. Pasztory wrote that the art expresses values that are impersonal, corporate and communal. The art, she said, "suggests that the ideology that held Teotihuacan together for 700 years as a state and a city was one that stressed the relationship of various groups to one another and avoided dynastic personality cults with a fervor comparable to the American democratic abhorrence of monarchy."

But the society was probably not egalitarian, Dr. Pasztory said. In all likelihood, it had powerful rulers and social stratification, though, she added, "Teotihuacan must have maintained a delicate balance between power, control, hierarchy and a sense of collective belonging."

MYSTERIOUS MASKS AND FIGURES

The insistence on a communal ideology may also be reflected in the culture's apparent lack of writing on a large scale. Only a few murals contained glyphs, archeologists said, and their nonstandardized forms suggest that they were too idiosyncratic to be writing.

The development of writing usually went hand in hand with the rise of urban societies, and in other Mesoamerican cultures like the Maya it was employed on pottery and stone as a form of political propaganda, describing and celebrating the exploits of warrior kings. Since nothing like this has been found at Teotihuacan, scholars take this as another indication that the culture had a different system of government from most Mesoamerican dynastic kingships.

Another defining characteristic of the Teotihuacanos may have been their stone masks. Mr. Cabrera recently excavated several of these masks in temple complexes rather than in burials, and none have been found in the apartment compounds. For this reason, it is assumed that their use was restricted to the elite or in political or religious ceremonies.

Archeologists have also been intrigued by what Dr. Warren Barbour of the State University of New York at Buffalo calls "host figures," so called because the ceramic hollow figures had "guests" inside them.

Some scholars are beginning to think of the host figures, unlike anything in other early American cultures, as representing the Teotihuacan view of the world: a sheltering deity protecting and nourishing the diverse society of Teotihuacan.

The Death Cults of Prehistoric Malta

New archaeological excavations reveal that as the ancient island societies suffered from environmental decline, they developed an extreme religious preoccupation with life and death.

Caroline Malone, Anthony Bonanno, Tancred Gouder, Simon Stoddart and David Trump

Caroline Malone, Anthony Bonanno, Tancred Gouder, Simon Stoddart and David Trump have extensively explored the ruins of ancient Maltese culture and contributed to the modern understanding of it. Malone and Stoddart are both lecturers in archaeology at the University of Bristol in England. Bonanno is professor of archaeology at the University of Malta. Gouder is director of museums at the National Museum of Malta. Trump is a lecturer in extramural studies at the University of Cambridge. Between 1958 and 1963 he was also curator of archaeology at the University of Malta.

The Mediterranean region is a fine laboratory for the scientific study of early religions because so many emerged there. Everyone has heard of the mythology of Greece and the cults surrounding the Roman emperors. Yet those were the religions of city-states not far removed from our own modern societies. Far less well known are the religions of the agricultural communities that preceded the advance of Greco-Roman civilization.

In several of the latter, images of corpulent human figures played an important role. Because some of these figures are recognizably female in shape, archaeologists sometimes refer to them as "fat ladies" and associate them with the celebration of fertility, both human and agricultural. On one small group of islands, those of Malta, such figures became the object of an infatuation that was closely linked to the construction of the earliest free-standing public stone buildings in the world.

Those temples and the underground burial chambers related to them contained many images of obese humans—some no larger than a few centimeters, others the size of giants—as well as of animals and phallic symbols. A collaborative project between British and Maltese archaeologists, of which we are the directors, has recently made spectacular discoveries about the artistic representations of the so-called mother goddesses. These findings have cast new light on how certain religious practices evolved on Malta and perhaps on why they eventually disappeared. They suggest the religion itself encompassed much more than a worship of human fecundity. They also tell a cautionary tale about what happens when a people focus too much energy on worshiping life rather than sustaining it.

Traditionally, archaeological discoveries in Malta have been interpreted—or perhaps we should say misinterpreted—against a backdrop of broad conjecture about the significance of mother goddesses. Figurines fitting that general description date from the Upper Paleolithic era (about 25,000 years ago) to the dawn of metal-using societies in the Neolithic era. A few have been found in western Europe, but the yields have been much richer at sites in Egypt, the Levant, Turkey, Greece, Cyprus and the Balkans. The most elaborate figures come from the islands of Malta in the third millennium B.C.

Unfortunately, many of these figurines are far less informative than they might once have been because of the unscientific ways in which they were collected. The dating of the figures is often inaccurate. The records of where and how they were situated are often incomplete, so we cannot know whether the figures were peculiar to burial sites, shrines or houses. We do know that in the Balkans such figures were kept in houses inside specially constructed niches in the walls. In Turkey, at the site of the eighth millennium B.C. settlement Çatal Hüyük, the finest figurines of clay and stone were associated with the burials of high-status people in special shrines, whereas cruder figurines were found in houses. The discovery of similar figurines at far-flung sites and from disparate eras inspired a long tradition of scholarly speculation about a widespread prehis-

5. THE GREAT RELIGIONS

toric religion based on the worship of the mother goddess. In the middle decades of this century, for example, some archaeologists tried to show that a cult of the Eye Goddess (so called because of eye motifs on Mesopotamian idols) diffused throughout the entire Mediterranean. More recently, claims have been made that the Balkans were the center of an Old European religion.

Most modern scholars appreciate that the early cults were radically different in each prehistoric society and that the cults of domestic life were distinct from the cults of death and burial. The example of Malta demonstrates that variation most emphatically. Elsewhere in the Mediterranean, the cults generally involved simple domestic rituals; little effort was invested in religious art or architecture. In Malta, however, the worship of corpulent images gradually blossomed into a consuming passion. That fixation may have been able to take root because conditions there enabled a closed, isolated, introverted society to develop.

Today the dry, rocky, hilly islands of Malta seem inhospitable to farming communities. Little soil or vegetation is present, and obtaining fresh water is a problem. Yet the geologic evidence suggests that between 5,000 and 7,000 years ago, a far more inviting scene greeted the early inhabitants. Those people probably cleared the fragile landscape of its natural vegetation fairly rapidly. Thereafter, severe soil erosion gradually robbed the islands of their productivity. The resulting environmental fragility may have caused agricultural yields to be unpredictable. That stress may well have shaped the strange and often extreme society that one finds portrayed in the archaeological record of ancient Malta.

The prehistoric archaeology of the Maltese islands is famed for its many huge stone temples. The number of them is staggering: some 20 groups of temples dot the islands, most containing two or three individual massive structures. Radiocarbon dating has indicated that they developed over roughly a millennium, from approximately 3500 to 2500 B.C. Because of their prominence in the landscape of Malta and Gozo, the two largest and most populous of the islands, the temples were always obvious targets for enthusiastic archaeological investigations, particularly during the 19th century. Those early workers cleared the rubble and other deposits from the

temples long before scientific archaeology had developed. Little effort was made to specify the exact positions of the unearthed artifacts; in particular, the contexts of the cult idols were rarely recorded. Not much can be done now with that incomplete evidence, other than to appreciate the sculptors' high level of skill.

Although mostly stripped of its cult images and other decoration, the architecture of the Maltese temples still survives. The design of the temples is regular: each consists of a curved stone façade overlooking an open forecourt. The façade usually has a formal entrance, marked by enormous carved stones and a capstone, that leads to a central corridor. Lobe-shaped apses open onto this corridor at either side and ahead, as in a cloverleaf. The apses often had stone altars (which were frequently carved with spiral or animal designs), carefully plastered floors and walls and other decorations painted with red ocher, a pigment probably imported from Sicily. They also feature tie-holes, which in some cases were perhaps for fastening animals to the walls, and holes in the ground that were evidently for draining liquids. In many instances, substantial quantities of animal bones, particularly those of sheep and goats, were found together with drinking vessels and sharp flint knives. All these details suggest that sacrifices and feasting may

have played an important part in the rituals performed in the temples.

Some information about the layout of the furnishings survived in the temples of Tarxien, which were excavated between 1915 and 1919. The lower half of an enormous statue of a "fat lady" was found in the temple precinct. Next to it is an altar within which the remains of food were found. The altar faced the carved figures of animals that may have represented sacrifices. Deeper within the recesses of the temple, excavators found the images of people who may have been priests, caches of precious pendants and even architectural models of the temples themselves.

The discovery in 1902 of the hypogeum, or subterranean burial chamber, at Hal Saflieni added another dimension to the cults of early Malta. Construction workers stumbled across this remarkable site while excavating cellars and foundations for new buildings in the surrounding town of Pawla. Before any skilled archaeologist was called to the scene, most of the chambers were emptied without documenting their contents; the rich assemblage of human remains and grave goods they must have contained probably ended up as fertilizer in nearby fields. A proper study of the hypogeum was finally conducted a few years later by Themistocles Zammit, the curator of the National Museum of Malta and the father of Maltese prehistory. He attempted to salvage what information he could from the near-empty chambers cut in the rock.

Zammit estimated that a fantastic number of individuals—between 6,000 and 7,000—had been buried in the 32 chambers of the hypogeum complex. They had been interred along with grave gifts of pots, obsidian and flint tools, jewelry consisting of beads and stone pendants, and clay and stone figures of obese people and animals. One of the most striking figures is the Sleeping Lady of the Hypogeum. This statuette shows a rotund female lying on her side on an elaborate woven bed. She is clothed in gathered skirts, and her hair is dressed in a small neat bun.

The various passages and chambers of the site strongly resembled the temples aboveground, with upright stone blocks spanned by lintels, steps, hinge holes for barriers and perhaps painted decorations. Nevertheless, the primary function of the hypogeum was clearly for burial, as the thousands of bones attest. Yet it may have been more than

simply a huge tomb. Its elaborately carved form, so similar in design to the temples, hints that it was also a temple for the dead, central to the rituals of death, burial and the afterlife.

The great number of figurines from both the temples and the ornate burial hypogeum of Hal Saflieni have fueled ideas (some plausible, some fantastic)

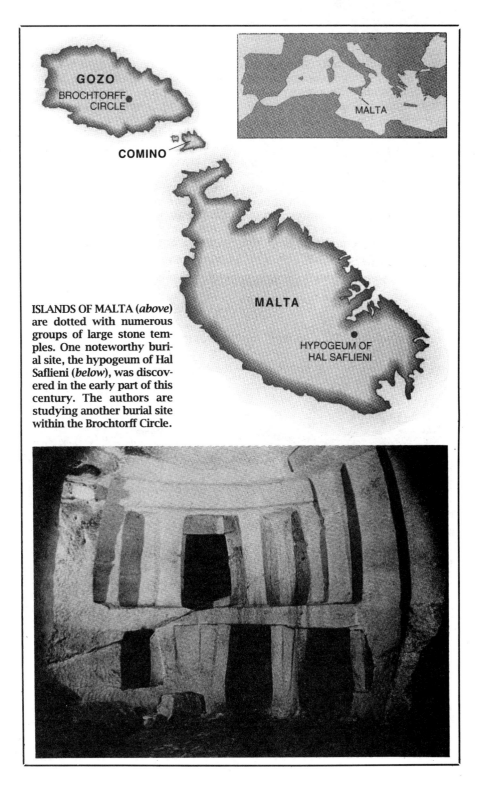

ISLANDS OF MALTA (*above*) are dotted with numerous groups of large stone temples. One noteworthy burial site, the hypogeum of Hal Saflieni (*below*), was discovered in the early part of this century. The authors are studying another burial site within the Brochtorff Circle.

that consists of a stone wall and entrance that encircle a huge rough hole at the center; several megaliths also stand within the enclosure. In one drawing, a man is shown climbing from the hole, holding an object shaped like a human skull.

That series of pictures was the only clue left to suggest that an archaeological site was located on the plateau. It served as a starting point for our team, which set out to rediscover whatever remained underneath the flat field. Using the most up-to-date scientific techniques, such as ground-penetrating radar, we conducted topographic and geophysical surveys of the area to assess the nature of the buried rock. In 1987 we succeeded in once again locating the Bayer excavation within a circle that had been found 20 years earlier.

Since then, months of hard reexcavation have been spent at the site. Over an area of about a quarter acre, we needed to remove not only the 19th-century backfill but also the rubble from cave collapses that had filled several deep natural cavities to a depth of more than four meters. By the end of five work seasons, the true nature of the site was clear, and the rich array of recovered artifacts and human remains testified to its importance.

After the previous depredations at the site, we wanted to ensure that it was reexcavated with all the care and precision available to late 20th-century science. We therefore recorded and photographed every item at the base level of the caves in situ from several directions for a three-dimensional record of its position and appearance. Samples were taken for dating and also for studies of the local environment and subtle stratigraphy of the site. Paleoanthropological methods helped us to reconstruct a profile of the buried

about the supposed fertility cults and rituals of Malta. Some archaeologists have hypothesized that Maltese society may have been a powerful matriarchy dominated by priestesses, female leaders and mother goddesses. Those theories were always based on an implicit faith in the meaning of the artifacts—a faith as devout, in its way, as the prehistoric religion itself but lacking much scientific foundation.

During the past five years, a new excavation at the site of the Brochtorff Circle on Gozo has uncovered important evidence about

the prehistoric rituals of death. The Brochtorff Circle, a megalithic enclosure on the summit of the Xaghra plateau, was first discovered in the 1820s by Otto Bayer, the lieutenant governor of Gozo. Vague historical records suggest that a typically haphazard treasure hunt at the site followed, from which no findings or documentation survived. Those efforts obliterated all surface traces of the structure. Fortunately, though, a roving Maltese artist, Charles Brochtorff, made several sketches of the work while it was in progress. His accurate, detailed watercolors and engravings show a site human population. We kept scrupulous computer records.

Unlike the great hypogeum of Hal Saflieni on Malta, which consists mainly of artificial carved chambers, the Brochtorff site on Gozo is fundamentally a series of natural caves with numerous interconnecting chambers. Erosion and perhaps earthquakes have cracked the thin rocky roof of the caves, resulting in several meters of rockfall and jumbled archaeological deposits. The caves were crumbling even 5,000 years ago. The prehistoric community, which by that time had already been using the caves for the burial of the dead for perhaps 1,000 years, began to insert carved stone supports under the cave roof in a vain attempt to control the collapse.

The burial complex at the Brochtorff site was in use for about 1,500 years, a period spanning several stages in the evolution of Maltese religion and society. In the early Zebbug period between 4000 and 3500 B.C., burial rituals were simple. The dead were placed in collective chambers that were either in caves or in tombs cut into the rock. Each chamber may have held the members from a single family or lineage group. One such tomb was found inside the circle in 1988. The burial rites evidently included the progressive removal of bones from earlier burials to allow space for later ones; the large removed bones may have been dumped in other parts of the caves.

A variety of gifts were interred with the dead: pottery, bone and stone beads and pendants, stone axes made of metamorphic rocks, flint and obsidian blades, shell pendants, and shell and bead necklaces. The bone pendants often have budlike appendages suggestive of arms and heads. Red ocher was spread lavishly over the grave goods and also over the dry white bones of the dead (perhaps in a symbolic attempt to restore them to life). At the entrance to one of the chambers stood a small upright monolith, a so-called menhir, bearing a crudely carved face that guarded the doorway.

The later burials, which were contemporary with the great Tarxien period of temple building, were different.

SMALL CERAMIC POT was used to hold red ocher, a pigment daubed on ritual figures and human bones during Maltese burial rites.

The emphasis on small family groups appears to have been supplanted by a more ritualized and elaborate cult of the dead. Part of the evidence for that conclusion comes from the megalithic construction of the Brochtorff Circle itself. The builders enclosed the opening to the cave with a wall and oriented its entrance eastward through the massive upright stones. In so doing, they integrated the entire site with the Ggantija temple, 300 meters away and on a lower terrace of the plateau.

Inside the caves the Tarxien builders leveled the earlier burials to provide a fresh (albeit bone-riddled) surface for the installation of stone monuments. The niches and smaller caverns were subdivided with pairs of upright stones and rough walls, which created additional, enclosed places for burials. At the center of the main cavern, the Maltese builders set up megalithic slabs in a semicircle, at the heart of which was a huge carved stone bowl. The stonework surrounding this bowl

was elegant, and there is evidence that some of it included animal figures and pitted patterns. The builders did not apply red ocher as liberally as their predecessors did, and they painted only a few of the nearby slabs.

Bodies were buried in the compartments around this central shrine. One noteworthy burial site was a natural cavity in the cave floor where hundreds of bodies were laid to rest. At first sight, the remains seemed incomplete and in confusion. Our further work has shown, however, that the bones from many bodies had been carefully sorted and stacked by type: skulls in one place, femurs in another and so on. This pattern suggests that as part of the burial ritual, old bodies being removed from compartments were disarticulated.

The thousands of human bones, which probably represent hundreds if not thousands of individuals, are now being studied. The early results paint the ancient Maltese as a typically Mediterranean people—stockily built and

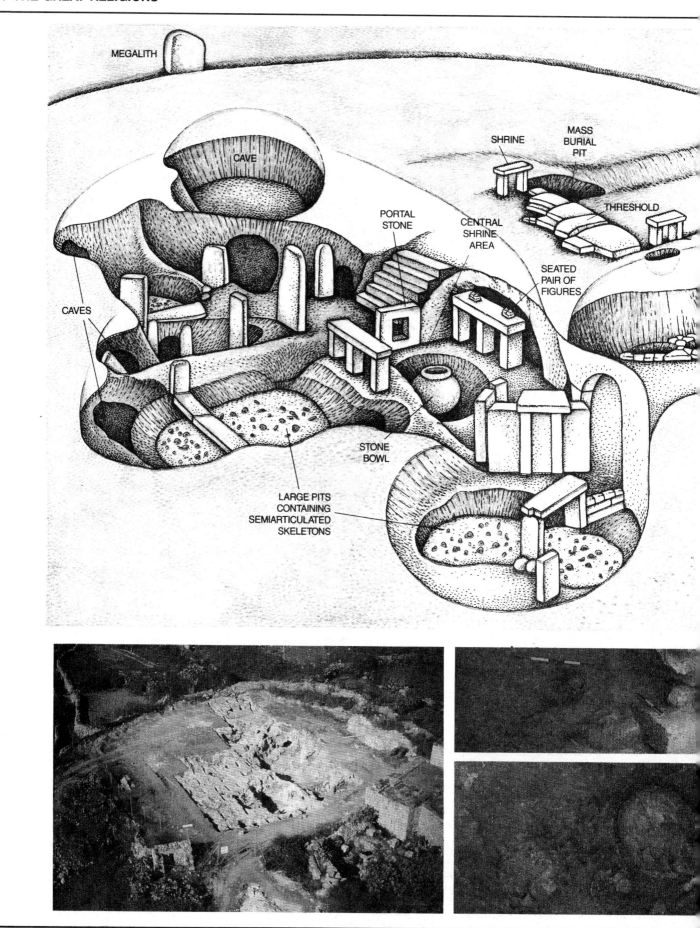

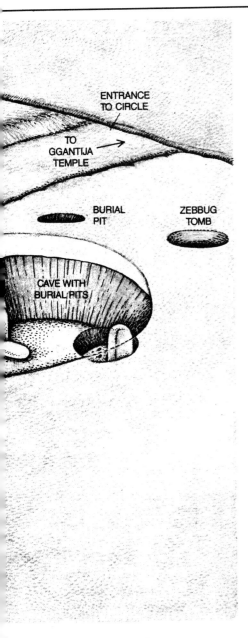

ENTRANCE TO CIRCLE

TO GGANTIJA TEMPLE

BURIAL PIT

ZEBBUG TOMB

CAVE WITH BURIAL PITS

Underground Burial Chambers

Brochtorff Circle marks a cave complex that the inhabitants of Gozo used for burials between 4000 and 2500 B.C. Treasure hunters found the site and then obliterated it in the 19th century, but in 1987 the authors and their colleagues found it again and re-excavated it. An aerial photograph (*far left*) shows the site as it appears today. The drawing (*above*) shows a partial reconstruction of the burial complex based on the most recent work. Thousands of human remains, many still adorned with ceremonial red ocher pigment, are clearly identifiable within certain pits in the cave floor (*near left*).

of medium height. They show some distinctive characteristics, such as a digastric fossa, a well-formed groove on both sides of the skull that is found in some other populations. Their health was apparently very good, with few dental problems or other detectable illnesses. The same anthropological features are present from the earliest Zebbug people to the late Tarxien population, which evinces little or no change in the genetic makeup of the early Maltese community. The changes in their customs and cults were therefore probably not the result of foreign immigration. Scientific studies of the bones will continue for the next few years, providing one of the first and possibly the biggest samples of research on an early Mediterranean population ever undertaken.

The only grave goods with these Tarxien people (which have been dated by the radiocarbon method to around 2800 B.C.) were small, carefully modeled ceramic statuettes of obese human figures. These figurines are almost certainly female because of the distinctive accumulations of fat on the buttocks. Their discovery in that location was highly significant: it marked the first secure association of "fat ladies" with burial sites instead of shrines or temple altars.

On the ground surface, at the monumental entrance leading down into the caverns, another pit was also filled with human remains. Among them were many males whose body parts had been rearranged after being taken from some other burial place. Almost no grave gifts accompanied the bones. Small altars at either end of the megalithic pavement beside the burial pit may have been used for preliminary sacrifices and obeisances before the priest and the assembled mourning community ventured down into the foul, reeking caves of the dead.

The most exciting discoveries from the Brochtorff site, aside from the human remains themselves, are small stone sculptures that have changed our views about the role of art in the ancient local religion. The prehistoric Maltese of the Tarxien pe-

riod seem to have invested most of their artisanship and craft into cult objects that were more than mere grave gifts. For example, a ceramic strainer and a unique stone sculpture were unearthed from near the stone bowl in the megalithic shrine. The strainer was probably meant to be used with the bowl, perhaps for straining out unwanted objects or for sprinkling liquids onto bodies.

The sculpture shows a beautifully carved and painted pair of obese figures. They are seated on an intricately carved bed, daubed with red ocher, that shows woven struts on the underside and curvilinear designs on the upper. The fat figures are not explicitly male or female. They wear the familiar pleated skirts, painted black, of the finest Maltese cult figures. The head of one figure sports a haircut that includes a pigtail at the back. The other's head is missing, and we can only hope to find it in future seasons of excavation. Both figures hold objects on their laps: one a tiny dressed person (who may be a baby), the other a cup.

Aside from the sculpture's fine craftsmanship, it is astonishing because the portrayal of several humans together is almost unknown from that period in Europe: even individual figures, other than the "fat ladies," are uncommon. A few artifacts with features that are reminiscent of this sculpture have been found elsewhere in ancient Malta, such as the fragments of carved beds and the terra-cotta Sleeping Lady of the Hypogeum. Nevertheless, this discovery is one of the earliest and most thought-provoking groups of sculpture from European prehistory.

The other major find was a cache of nine carved stone idols, which were also closely associated with the stone bowl in the central shrine. The objects must originally have been wrapped tightly in a bag or box: when they were discovered in 1991, they were all lying one above the other, having fallen from the structures surrounding the bowl. Six of the objects represent human figures: flat, triangular shapes attached to carvings of human heads. The six range from poorly detailed rough-outs

SMALL STONE IDOLS were probably used by priests or other specialists in burial rituals at the Brochtorff Circle during the Tarxien period. The three on the left representing human figures show very different levels of detail and artistic execution. The other three, which invoke animal and phallic imagery, are more fanciful and individualized.

to skillfully executed cult idols. Two of the most detailed figures have pleated skirts and belts, and one wears an elaborate crested circlet, seemingly of metal, around its head. The faces of both these figures show eyes and lips and well-defined noses. A third figure is simpler and has no costume other than an exquisitely sculpted cowl headdress. Two more have plain bodies and bobbed hair. The last of the six is a crude rough-out that shows only the lines that the finished sculpture was to follow.

The three other idols of the nine are small and individual. One has a pig's head, the second a well-carved human head on a phallus-shaped pedestal and the third a head supported by two legs. Along with these extraordinary objects was a miniature Tarxien pot filled with ocher, perhaps for smearing on idols.

No parallels for any of these strange objects have ever been found elsewhere in Malta or the central Mediterranean. Even so, our knowledge of the context in which they appear is informative. Whereas the figures associated with the dead in their burial chambers are "fat ladies," those from the central shrine are much more complex. One cannot find an emphasis on images of female fertility in the shrine. Indeed, where the imagery is interpretable, it

seems to be male and animal. The context of their discovery suggests that the shrine objects were the paraphernalia employed by the ritual specialists or priests and that their symbolism was meant to evoke much more than just a mother goddess.

Unprecedented discoveries at the Brochtorff Circle have encouraged us to reconsider the whole basis of ancient cults and religions in prehistoric Malta and Gozo. As the old ideas had supposed, the worship of fertility may well have been a component of the prehistoric religion. But the recent findings argue that it would be a mistake to concentrate exclusively on any one facet or historical period: the prehistoric religion of Malta was not only an infatuation with fat females.

During the Zebbug period between 4000 and 3500 B.C., the cult focused on the provision of caves and underground tombs as burial places. Accurate depictions of people do not seem to have played a part in the local rituals: the closest representations of human forms in the tombs are the very crude faces on the menhirs and the curious bone pendants with budlike arms and heads. Red ocher was the predominant decoration. Exotic axes of green stones and

other objects made of flint and obsidian were also used as grave goods. In many ways, the early ritual developments appear to have paralleled similar trends in Sicily, where rock-cut tombs and simple collective burial rites were developing at the same time. The Maltese islands during this early period were still relatively fruitful and may not have been overpopulated.

But by half a millennium later Malta seems to have been shaken by major changes. The erosion of the soil and other signs of environmental degradation may have become apparent; in this environment, population levels almost certainly began to pose problems. Artifacts from that period—the obese human and animal figurines and the phallic symbols carved in stone or bone and modeled in clay—point to the idea that the people had an obsession with the living world and its successful propagation. Malta seems to have become an island world under powerful economic and environmental stress, where the communities were struggling to maintain their former standards of living and to feed the population. Yet fewer materials were imported into the islands during this time of crisis than in the more fruitful era. The prehistoric Maltese society seems to have let a fixation on sculpture and art replace contact with the world beyond the islands' rocky coasts.

That debilitating fixation may explain why the temples are so numerous on so small a group of islands. Some scholars have theorized that they were built by perhaps half a dozen rival clans or tribes, each competing for land and water. The colossal size of the temples, and the later architectural additions that made them even more prominent, could have been inspired by such a competitive spirit. Religious and cult influence and social control over the population may also have been influential.

Cult activities seem to have reached a feverish pitch in the final phases of the Tarxien period around 2500 B.C. The society was becoming increasingly dominated by a religious hierarchy in which cult specialists or priests controlled much of the industry of the people. Vast amounts of human time and energy were invested in temple building, artistic endeavors and ritual feasts. The dead were honored within cults and linked to animals and human obesity. The people seem to have expended relatively little effort on the building of villages or domestic structures, on terracing or on farming methods. The obsession with the cults of the temples seems to have been complete.

Such obsessions are dangerous, and so it proved to be on ancient Malta. By about 2500 B.C. the community of the temple builders had ceased to build and perhaps even to use the monumental burial sites prepared by earlier generations. By 2000 B.C. the entire culture had disappeared and been replaced by very different religious practices that favored cremation burials. The burial hypogea, the cult of the "fat ladies" and the other symbols of the living and the dead were completely abandoned.

The prehistoric religion of Malta might appear to be a failed experiment in the Mediterranean laboratory. Like many failures, however, it tells us more than a success might have. The extreme religious fervor of ancient Malta shows one of the possible results when societies are placed under severe pressures. Further careful excavations and reconstructions on Malta and at other Mediterranean sites should extend our understanding of the complexities and diversity of prehistoric society. To that end, the excavations at the Brochtorff Circle continue.

FURTHER READING

THE PREHISTORIC ANTIQUITIES OF THE MALTESE ISLANDS: A SURVEY. J. Evans. Athlone Press, London, 1971.

MALTA AND THE CALIBRATED RADIOCARBON CHRONOLOGY. Colin Renfrew in *Antiquity*, Vol. 46, No. 182, pages 141–144; June 1972.

THE COLLAPSE OF THE MALTESE TEMPLES. D. H. Trump in *Problems in Economic and Social Archaeology*. Edited by G. Sieveking, I. Longworth and K. E. Wilson. Duckworth, 1977.

MONUMENTS IN AN ISLAND SOCIETY: THE MALTESE CONTEXT. A. Bonanno, T. Gouder, C. Malone and S. Stoddart in *World Archaeology*, Vol. 22, No. 2, pages 190–205; October 1990.

CULT IN AN ISLAND SOCIETY: PREHISTORIC MALTA IN THE TARXIEN PERIOD. S. Stoddart, A. Bonanno, T. Gouder, C. Malone and D. Trump in *Cambridge Archaeological Journal*, Vol. 3, No. 1, pages 3–19; April 1993.

WOMEN IN GREEK MYTH

MARY R. LEFKOWITZ

Mary R. Lefkowitz, Andrew W. Mellon Professor in the Humanities at Wellesley College, is co-editor of Women's Life in Greece and Rome.

THE GREEKS' MOST IMPORTANT LEGACY is not, as we would like to think, democracy; it is their mythology. Even though in the second century A.D. a mysterious voice was heard exclaiming "great Pan is dead," the Greek gods and many obscure and irrational stories about them lived on in the imaginations of artists and writers, no matter how often or in how many different ways Christians and philosophers tried to dismiss the myths as frivolous or harmful. And even in the twentieth century, when man has acquired greater power than ever before to alter the natural world, the old myths continue to haunt us, not just in the form of nymphs and shepherds on vases or garden statuary, but in many common assumptions about the shape of human experience. The notions—now presumably obsolete—that a man should be active and aggressive, a woman passive and subject to control by the men in her family, are expressed in virtually every Greek myth, even the ones in which the women seek to gain control of their own lives. That the most important phase of a woman's life is the period immediately preceding her marriage (or remarriage) is preserved in the plot of many novels, as is the notion that virginity, or at least celibacy, offers a woman a kind of freedom that she is no longer entitled to when she becomes involved with a man.

Here I intend to describe how the Greeks portrayed female experience in myth. I also want to suggest why, in the hands of the great poets, the portrayal of women was not as restrictive as I have made it sound. The Greeks at least attributed to women a capacity for understanding not found in the other great mythological tradition that has influenced us—namely, the Old and New Testaments. One reason the Greeks receive too little credit for their relatively balanced view of women's abilities is that most of us encounter Greek mythology only in a condensed and filtered form, usually in a translation of some work of literature, but more often as stories retold in a modern handbook. Inevitably, in the process of condensation and translation, the original meaning can easily get lost. But Edith Hamilton and D'Aulaire have done far less damage to the intended meaning of the myths than psychiatric theory or, more recently, feminist theory.

Psychologists tend to assume that human nature has for all time remained basically the same. They therefore conclude that the ancients were preoccupied with much the same problems that we are, namely, sex and the definition and role of the sexes. But it is another question whether the ancients themselves would have understood or accepted interpretations that place such disproportionate emphasis on desire and incest. The text of Sophocles' *Oedipus Tyrannus* gives no indication that Oedipus was sexually attracted to Jocasta; he married her because marriage to the king's widow was the reward for ridding Thebes of the Sphinx. Similarly, I think, Thyestes does not have intercourse with his daughter because he is in love with her but because the Delphic oracle told him that the son born from this union would take revenge on Thyestes' brother, Atreus, for murdering Thyestes' other children. The son, Aegisthus, seduces Clytemnestra and murders Atreus's son, Agamemnon, and so reclaims his father's kingdom. In each generation, inheritance and power were more compelling motives than sex.

Feminists tend to reject the psychologists' premise that man's preoccupations have not changed over time, and prefer instead to discover in the myths evidence of the persistent limitations of human imagination. In particular, the myths have a tendency to portray polar opposites and to organize experience into restricted channels, much in the same way as a language forbids some grammatical usages in favor of others that are inherently no more worthy than those it has excluded. Page DuBois has recently argued in *Centaurs and Amazons* that Sophocles' *Oedipus Tyrannus* is primarily concerned with incest, or at least with an excessive endogamy that ends in sterility and the extinction of his family. It is true that Oedipus's sons Eteocles and Polynices kill each other in combat and that his daughter Antigone dies because she seeks, against her uncle Creon's orders, to bury her brother Polynices' body. But in the *Antigone* Sophocles speaks only about the inexorable progress of the family curse, from which no generation can free itself and which he calls "folly in speech and a fury in the mind." In other words, where modern critics emphasize either sexual or social issues, the poet himself speaks of *perceptual* and *ethical* problems: will man know what is right, and even if he does, will he do it? Sophocles' answer is unequivocally negative:

Hope in its many wanderings is a help to some men, but to others it is the deception that comes from vain passions. It comes on a man who knows nothing until he burns his foot in the hot fire. In wisdom once—from some unknown person—a famous statement came to light: "evil seems good to the person whose wits the god is leading toward delusion (*ate*); he acts only for the shortest time apart from delusion."

The chorus does not say specifically that these lines apply to any particular character in the play, but since it is talking about the house of Oedipus, it is natural to assume that it has Antigone in mind, though it soon turns out that the chorus's words apply equally well to Creon, the king who has condemned Antigone to death for trying to bury her brother against his orders. Creon's decision will cause the death of his family as well. The point is that, at least as far as the Greeks were concerned, the human condition—not gender—causes problems that both men and women are bound to experience, especially when they try to accomplish something out of the ordinary.

I wish to suggest that it may not be profitable to regard the myths as a kind of code that could be reliably deciphered were we to apply the right modern methodology: Whatever the story of Oedipus may have meant when it was first told (whenever that was), by the time the poems of Homer were composed, it and virtually every other myth were presumed to belong to a distant past. The myths had become a kind of history, and they were retold both for entertainment and for instruction, often with the conclusion first (since everyone knew how the story would end). Even an extraordinarily long narrative like the *Odyssey* begins by stating that Odysseus returned home after wandering and learning much, but having lost his companions because of their own folly. Modern critics may discern in Odysseus's adventures a covert description of the development of the human psyche, but the Greeks themselves understood it first as a moral tale, where the evil suitors were defeated by the courage and intelligence not only of Odysseus but also of his wife Penelope, to whom—in spite of an offer of immortality from the goddess Calypso—he was eager to return.

What would ancient Greek women have thought about Greek mythology? The ancients tell us very little about their education. In general, we only know what male writers tell us about what women thought, because there are so few women writers. But certainly everyone, men and women, free and enslaved, knew the stories. In Euripides' *Ion*, a group of slave women who had been brought to Delphi eagerly identify in the temple of Apollo the representations of gods, heroes, and monsters that they recognized from stories that were told to them as they worked at their looms. It is unlikely that women, at least in the fifth century, attended the theater. But I doubt in any case that women (or men) regarded the stories of Oedipus and Jocasta or Agamemnon and Clytemnestra as "norms," since the stories belonged to a heroic past that no longer existed.

The myths did, however, place emphasis on the kind of experiences and problems—although in idealized or exaggerated forms—that most ancient women encountered in the course of their lives. In myth, there were essentially two main courses of female existence: celibacy or involvement with males and (inevitably) childbearing. The two paths were of course mutually exclusive, though a woman (or goddess) could return to celibacy after her children were born. For mortal women, involvement with males was the more usual and probably the more promising alternative, since virginity offered freedom only to goddesses like Athena and Artemis, who as goddesses had the power to defend themselves and by definition were ageless and immortal. Virgin goddesses who remained fixed in one place, like Hestia and Hecate, were guaranteed protection and honor by Zeus. Other goddesses who had been wives or lovers of the gods could gain power temporarily by withdrawing from the males and by withholding something essential to men or to the gods. Demeter, for example, long since estranged from Zeus, won back her daughter Persephone from Hades by keeping the seeds of grain within the earth so that humans began to starve and the gods received no sacrifices. But to mortal women, who by definition as humans can be destroyed and will grow old, disengagement offered fewer rewards and posed greater dangers. Daphne refused to have sexual relations with Apollo and ended up fixed in one place—as a laurel tree. Only in one respect—the dependence on males—does the existence of the virgin goddesses correspond to that of mortal women. Although the virgin goddesses were worshiped for their power over so many aspects of human life, they acted only within limits defined by Zeus and with his approval, or with the cooperation of another god. Hesiod, in a passage that describes and virtually advertises a local cult, explains how Zeus honors the virgin goddess Hecate beyond all others and gave her shining gifts. Zeus permits her to help or hinder kings, soldiers in battle, or athletes in competition; with Poseidon she can help the fisherman, and with Hermes she can aid the herdsman.

The great majority of myths about goddesses or women concentrate on their relations with males, particularly the first union with a male, which, in the case of ordinary mortals at least, was marriage. The great epic about the origin of the gods, Hesiod's *Theogony*, is a chronological catalogue of divine unions, in which the virgin goddesses, like Hecate and Athena, appear as rare exceptions; virtually every other goddess is the mother of children. Earth, who with her husband, Heaven, is the ancestress of Zeus and the most important gods and many primeval

forces, asks her son Cronus to castrate his father because he hides all his children back in Earth as soon as they are born, and she "groans because she is oppressed." But Cronus, too, swallows his children as soon as they are born. His wife Rhea has to devise a means of keeping one son, Zeus, away from him so that Zeus can drive Cronus out of power by force and rule over the gods himself. But Zeus prevents a recurrence of this cycle by having several wives. He swallows Metis, his first wife, so that he could bear Athena himself from his own head, and thus keep her and her mother under his control. Zeus has six other wives, the last of whom is Hera, and he has many temporary liaisons with both goddesses and women. Thus a patriarchal order is established, with both women and children kept subordinate, although with particular rights and responsibilities.

Hesiod doesn't say how Zeus tricked Metis into letting him swallow her or what she might have said when she discovered that she had been tricked. But Homer, in the first book of the *Iliad*, makes it clear that Hera very much resents Zeus's granting favors to other goddesses and opposing her plans without consulting her. Hesiod, in the *Theogony*, says nothing about the fate of the mortal women, Semele and Alcmene, with whom Zeus had relations, but later poets speak poignantly about the perils and pleasures of intercourse with a god. Perhaps the most vivid description of a union of this type is spoken by Creusa in Euripides' *Ion*. Apollo had fallen in love with Creusa, but he immediately abandoned her; years later, as queen of Athens, unable to bear another child, she complains that she can neither ask for the god's help nor tell her story because even associating with a woman who bore a bastard child might disgrace her. Like Persephone when she was carried off to the Lower World by Hades, or like Europa who was approached by a beautiful white bull who later turned out to be the god Zeus, Creusa was gathering flowers when Apollo—his hair glittering with gold—drew her into a cave, as she cried out in vain to her mother:

You brought me there in shamelessness as a favour to the Goddess of Love. And I in my misfortune bore you a son, and in fear of my mother I left him in the couch where you compelled me, in misfortune, in my sorrow, on a bed of sorrow.

When she speaks these lines she is angry at the god, who has—as she believes—both abandoned her and failed to protect their son. Only after she attempts and fails to kill him does she discover that the boy her husband thought to be his son is, in fact, her and Apollo's lost child, who is destined to be king of Athens. Similarly, in *Prometheus Bound*, the chorus hears the story of Io's involvement with Zeus and sees her head horned like a cow's. After listening to her hysterical ravings, the female chorus exclaims that they would not want to "marry" one of the gods:

Let my marriage be humble, may the passion of the powerful gods not cast on me an eye none can escape; that is a war I could not fight, a source of resourcelessness. I do not know who I would become. For I do not see how I could escape the mind of Zeus.

Their words make it clear that they are afraid not only of the gods' power but of the physical changes in themselves that sexual union with a god might cause. Ancient medical treatises confirm that girls in the first stages of puberty (the time when they would ordinarily be married off) became hysterical and suicidal, like Io; the prescription and cure for them, as it was for her, is pregnancy. Also, neither Io nor the chorus can see that for her, as for Creusa, what she presumes to be misfortune will ultimately bring her fame and happiness: the birth of a son who will be the ancestor of a famous race and whose descendants will include another son of Zeus, Heracles.

Like Antigone, Io and Creusa are victims of *ate*, "folly of speech and a fury in the mind," because they do not understand the consequences of their actions, and they fear as disaster what will ultimately bring them fame and guarantee them a place in history. Judged by standards of what Christianity promises to the good, at least after the Day of Judgment, the Greek reward for endurance may seem slight indeed. But in Greek religion no human being, male or female, could live entirely without sorrow; from Zeus's two jars of good and of evil, a person can get either a mixed portion or *all evil*, but there is no possibility of *all good*. For a woman the best available "mixture" would seem to be marriage—however temporary—and family, particularly if her children are heroes or the mothers of great men.

Perhaps because the life of any human being was perceived as essentially temporary and fragile, the myths tend to emphasize the continuity, not just of families, but of whole peoples. Creusa's son by Apollo is Ion, ancestor not only of the Athenians but of the Ionians in Asia Minor. Virtually every village and town claimed descent from a god, often through a hero for whom the town was named. The Ionians, for example, were said to have been named after Ion. Hesiod's *Theogony* ends with a long catalogue of marriages and extramarital unions between gods and goddesses, gods and women, and goddesses and men, all of which resulted in the birth of gods, goddesses, heroes, and women who married heroes. Another epic attributed to Hesiod, *The Catalogue of Women*, described the unions that produced all the famous heroes, nations, and races; each new heroine was introduced with the words "And like her was. . . ."

For centuries, only short quotations from the *Catalogue* survived and some prose summaries that could give but little impression of the shape of the original epic; but in this century a number of long fragments were discovered on tattered strips of papyrus, and from these we can get at least a partial sense of the pacing and emphasis of the original narrative. Although Greek bards could describe brilliantly the excitement of sexual passion and the verbal and physical prelude to making love—the *Homeric Hymn to Aphrodite* is the best example—the *Catalogue of Women* seems to have been valued, and recited, even in the Hellenistic Age, not for its power to engage the emotions, but as historical information, like the *begats* in Genesis or at the beginning of Matthew, or the fascinating list of the different types of whales that interrupts the grim story of Melville's *Moby-Dick*. The ancient Greeks seem to have been particularly fond of such catalogues—book 2 of the *Iliad* contains a list of all the cities that sent ships and men to Troy—and they attribute to women a significant role in this formal history. Each "founding mother" is listed by name; none is merely an anonymous bearer of divine seed.

Like the *Theogony*, the *Catalogue* is organized by genealogies, and within each family tree Hesiod concentrates on explaining why certain women captured the attention of gods or of heroes. In the first book Demodike (about whom virtually nothing is said in any other surviving text) is wooed by numerous suitors, as were Helen and Penelope, because of her "unbounded beauty, but they didn't persuade her." She held out, apparently, for a god instead. Ares, by whom she became the mother of Thestius, was the father of Leda, who in turn was the mother of the most beautiful woman in the world, Helen. Mestra, daughter of Erysichthon, who had an insatiable appetite, was able to change into every type of animal; each day her father sold her in exchange for food, and each night she changed back into human shape and returned to him. Finally, Sisyphus bought her for his son and demanded arbitration when she ran away. But even then, Sisyphus wasn't able to keep her, because "Poseidon broke her [*edamassato*, the same verb denotes both taming of animals and the taking of a virgin], far away from her father in sea-girt Cos, carrying her across the wine-faced sea, even though she was very clever" [*polyidris*, a term that always seems to imply, both for men and for women, that one is tricky, or too clever for one's own good]. By Poseidon, Mestra became the mother of the great hero Bellerophontes. Another fragment describes the contest for the athletic and beautiful Atalanta from the point of view of her successful suitor, Hippomenes: "The prize that awaited them both was not the same; swift-footed god-like Atalanta raced refusing the gifts of golden Aphrodite; for him the race was for his life, whether he should be captured [by Atalanta's father] or escape; and so he addressed her with crafty intention, 'daughter of Schoeneus, with your relentless heart, accept these shining gifts of golden Aphrodite.'" He threw an apple on the ground, "and she snatched it swiftly like a Harpy on delaying feet; but he threw a second apple to the ground . . . then swift god-like Atalanta had two apples, and she was near the goal, but he threw a third to the ground, and with this he escaped death and dark fate. He stood there catching his breath."

In this and every other case, the males win, which could be

interpreted as an illustration of the inferiority of women, were no struggle to capture them involved. In Atalanta's case, the women's skill is quite obviously superior. The mother of a hero clearly must be more beautiful than other women, but she must also be more clever or swift than most men and, in the end, can be subdued only by or with the assistance of the gods. Perhaps the best example is Alcmena, the mother of Heracles, the greatest hero of all. Her brothers were all killed, and she "alone was left as a joy to her parents"—after which, immediately, the next lines refer to Zeus, who wanted Alcmena to be the mother of his greatest mortal son, Heracles. According to the epic the *Shield of Heracles*—another work attributed to Hesiod but probably composed at least a century later than the *Catalogue of Women*—Alcmena was more beautiful, more clever, and (in our terms) sexier than anyone. She was also so faithful that on her wedding night Zeus had to pretend that he was her husband. That occasion had been postponed until Amphitryon had avenged the death of Alcmena's brothers, but "when [Amphitryon] had accomplished the great deed he returned to his home, and he did not go to his slaves or the shepherds in the fields until he had gone up to his wife's bed—such great desire ruled the heart of the leader of the army; and he lay with his wife all night rejoicing in the gifts of golden Aphrodite." This should be noted, lest anyone argue that Greek men had all their sexual pleasure in extramarital or homosexual relationships.

The moral superiority of women like Alcmena is significant, because the heroic age is brought to an end by the three daughters of Tyndareus, "twice and thrice married and leavers of husbands": Timandre who left her husband Echemus for Phyleus, Clytemnestra who "after she deserted her husband Agamemnon slept with Aegisthus and chose a worse husband, and then Helen disgraced the bed of fair-haired Menelaus." It is important to note that Helen, unlike Atalanta, is won not by the most daring man but by the one who offered the most gifts, and one who was not even present himself but rather was represented by his brother; the poet observes that "Menelaus could not have won Helen nor would any other mortal suitor, if swift Achilles returning home from Pelion had encountered her when she was a girl; but before that warlike Menelaus had her, and she bore fair-ankled Hermione in his halls—though the birth had been despaired of" (*aelpton*). At this point the gods were divided by strife, and Zeus wanted to destroy the race of men. The Trojan War followed and, with it, a kind of *Heldendämmerung*: apparently, the race of heroes cannot exist without women of heroic caliber.

Since Greek myth glorified the role of mother, it also tended to condemn to infamy those who in some way rebelled against it. A confirmed mortal virgin who resisted the advances of a god might be punished simply by metamorphosis into a tree or flower. But women who consciously denied their femininity, like the Amazons, or ones who killed their husbands and fathers, like the women of Lemnos, were regarded as enemies and monsters. The expected outcome of any sexual encounter between a mortal woman and a god was a notable child—as Poseidon reassures Tyro both in the *Odyssey* and in Hesiod's *Catalogue*: "You will bear glorious children, since the embraces of a god are not fruitless." But in the *Catalogue*, when Poseidon had intercourse with the daughter of Elatus, king of the Lapiths in Thessaly, and promised to grant her any favor she wished, she asked to be turned into a man and made invulnerable. This man, Caineus, proved to be a threat to the gods because he did not respect the limitations of mortality, like Ixion, who tried to seduce Hera, or like Tantalus, who stole nectar and ambrosia from the gods to try to make his friends immortal. Caineus instead set up his spear in the marketplace and asked people to worship it; so Zeus arranged to have the Centaurs drive Caineus into the ground.

According to the prose genealogy of Acusilaus, Poseidon allowed the sex change of Caineus because "it wasn't holy for them to have children by him or by anyone else." Compare the story of Thetis, whose son was destined to be greater than his father and who was therefore married to a mortal man, or the story of Metis, whom Zeus swallowed in order to produce her offspring Athena from his own head. The notion seems to be that by completely preventing rather than somehow mitigating the outcome of her pregnancy, Poseidon makes Caineus dangerous and undesirable. Coronis, who has intercourse with another of Elatus's sons,

Ischys, while she was pregnant with Apollo's son, is allowed to die, but the child Asclepius is saved only to be killed when he too oversteps mortal boundaries. Medea, who kills her children to take revenge on their father, Jason, who has deserted her, gets away with her life, but she knows she will live unhappily ever after. Clytemnestra, who helped to murder her husband, Agamemnon, in order to live with her lover Aegisthus, is murdered by Orestes, her son by Agamemnon. Throughout the *Odyssey* Clytemnestra's evil actions are contrasted with those of the faithful Penelope. Modern feminists may admire these destructive women because they took action and used their great intelligence to right what they considered to be personal wrongs against themselves. But even the chorus of Corinthian women, who at first sympathize with Medea's desire to punish Jason for deserting her, condemn the form that her revenge takes.

Even though so few options in life seem to have been available to Greek women (or men), the Greeks did not hesitate to give "equal time" to descriptions of the problems of human existence from a woman's point of view. We can tell from the titles of lost plays that women were the central figures of many tragedies, as they are in the ones that have come down to us. The poets, even though they were men, and their plays, even though they were performed by male actors, allow female characters to describe their predicaments in detail. It is as if the actors had listened with a sympathetic ear to the complaints of women in their own families. Euripides shows with particular clarity how the conditions of ancient marriage could be both restrictive and frustrating. As Medea says, when a man is bored with his family, he can go out and put an end to his heartache, but a woman must stay behind, inside the house, and "look towards him alone." Phaedra complains of the aristocratic wife's problem of having too much time on her hands to think. She cannot even have the man she loves because adultery would bring disgrace not only to her but to her children. Sophocles depicts the plight of Heracles' wife Deianira no less sympathetically. She is abandoned year after year by her husband as he goes about his labors and sleeps with other women. Heracles sees his children "like a farmer who sees a distant field only at sowing-time and harvest." In a fragment of Sophocles' lost play *Tereus*, the king's deserted wife complains that women are happy only in girlhood, in their father's house, after which they are "thrust out and sold" to strangers or foreigners, in joyless or hostile houses, "—and all this once the first night has yoked us to our husband we are forced to praise and say that all is well." Sophocles' and Euripides' dramas were often produced in competition with one another, so throughout the last decades of the fifth century (from the beginning until the disastrous end of the Peloponnesian War), Athenian men who comprised the audiences were compelled to reflect on how their customs and actions affected (or afflicted) women's lives.

It has recently been suggested both by Freudian and feminist critics that the destruction of Athenian society was predicted in dramas like Euripides' *Bacchae*, which describes how Pentheus, the king of Thebes, is murdered by his mother in a Bacchic frenzy. The Greeks' habitual misogyny, it is suggested, compelled them to seek the company and love of other men and to restrict and repress the females in their family. Euripides, it would then seem, is saying that women are confined to "the loom and the shuttle" inside their houses. Pentheus's cruel death and the disgrace and exile of his mother are particularly vivid reminders of the universal power of *ate*. The deception that leads men to ignore the worship of the gods (and of the vital forces in nature that the gods represent) and the "folly in speech and fury in the mind" will drive men to bring about their own destruction. Pentheus, his mother, and his aunts refused to recognize the existence of the god Dionysus, so the god whom they dishonor causes them all to go mad and ultimately to destroy themselves. As in the *Antigone*, both men and women are equally subject to *ate*, and both are equally responsible for their actions. When Euripides suggests that, if the women abandon their homes and infant children and the responsibility of caring for the family that is represented by the loom, they will harm not only others but themselves, he is recommending, not that women enjoy the role society has assigned to

them, but simply that women accept that role as the least destructive possibility. Men, too, are compelled to play roles that they would not willingly choose. For example, Cadmus, Pentheus's grandfather, had to abdicate his throne when he was too old to defend himself. He was forced to pretend that he was young again in the ritual required by the god. At the end of the play, he is but an old man who has done nothing himself to offend the god, but he nonetheless must leave the city he founded and end his days in the form of a snake.

Rather than claim that Greek men were misogynists because they did not give women "equal rights"—rights that women have yet to acquire even in the most advanced democracies of this century—I would suggest that they be regarded as pioneers. Greek men recognized and described with sympathy both the life and the central importance to their society of women. Women, to whom society assigned the task of lamenting and burying the dead, are very often the last commentators on the war or murders described in an epic or a drama, and male poets did not hesitate to allow them to make articulate and poignant observations about the futility of all that their men had prized so highly. Women assume an important role in drama because they are passive and required to remain at home or away from the scene of the action, as natural victims, and thus they are able to represent the human condition in general, and man's true powerlessness before the gods and the fact of his own mortality.

Even though male Greek writers of the fifth century created brilliant descriptions of the problems of women's lives, they were not equally good at offering solutions. Even the philosophers of the fourth century were better at explaining how the world worked than at proposing any *practical* change. In the Hellenistic period, when the Macedonian conquests had imposed more efficient governance and caused Greek culture to come in contact with new ideas, the law, centuries behind the facts as always, granted women in name some of the rights they had already had in practice. Despite greater physical comfort and freedom of movement, women had the same basic role in life, and the old myths continued to be told and retold, even by the best and most sophisticated court poets in Alexandria. Medea, in Apollonius's epic *The Voyage of the Argo*, has the run of the palace, and with her handmaids, the city of Colchis; but she is still dependent on her father and, later on, her lover Jason. The destructive powers of Medea's magic and her selfish desires lead to her exile, the death of her brother, and the unhappiness of both Jason and herself.

At least by stressing the importance of the family and of women's role within it as nurturers and continuers of the race, the Greeks attributed to women a vital function that the Church fathers were later to try to deny them when they placed an even higher value on celibacy and offered virgins a new subservience rather than an increased independence. Comparison with narratives about women in the early church reveals that the Greeks—however immoral their tales from the point of view of Christian ethics—at least placed a higher value on women's initiative and intelligence. In the Gospel of Luke, Mary is chosen to be the mother of God's son because she is a virgin and thus fulfills the prophecy in Isaiah 7:14: "Behold the maiden [*parthenos*] shall conceive in her womb and she shall bear a son, and they shall call his name Immanuel." We hear nothing about her other qualities, though she does, in the course of the narrative, display both piety and common sense: "How can this be," she asks, "since I know no man?" The sexual encounter that .invariably marks the culmination of the episodes in Hesiod's *Catalogue* is of course missing in the Gospel of Luke 1:35–37: "The Holy Spirit will come to you and the power of the highest will overshadow you." The incident emphasizes instead the power of God: "and behold, Elizabeth your kinswoman, she has also conceived a son, in her old age, and this is the sixth month for her who had been called barren." Here the angel cites Genesis 18:14—"because nothing at all will be impossible for God." In Greek mythology gods choose women because of their distinguished genealogy—Io, for example, was the daughter of the river Inachus—or for their beauty—for example Cassandra, who, because of her ability to prophesy accurately, was the "most beautiful of Priam's daughters"—or for their courage—Apollo sees Cyrene wrestling alone with a lion—or for their intelligence—Poseidon finally outwitted the "very clever" Mestra.

Of course I do not mean in any way to deny that from a modern point of view women's experience as described in Greek myth is severely limited. We cannot really blame the Greeks for not having been able to envisage the advantages for women that the industrial and scientific revolutions would bring. At the same time it would be foolish to claim that the traditional roles of women in Greek myths have lost all their influence or even appeal. If feminists now seek to concentrate instead on those relatively few myths and authors whose heroines assert themselves, even if only to hasten their own or another's death, that is to be expected and possibly even applauded. But at the same time I would like to stress that the original myths, with their original emphases, also have something to teach us; *ate* is still with us, and perhaps nowhere more obviously than in the belief that the ambitious career woman can "have it all," without divine intervention, or at least without the creation of new narrative patterns to help chart some of the crises, other than marriage and childbearing, that may arrive as the result of a longer, more complex life. In addition to reminding us of the limits of human vision, the ancient texts also emphasize the importance of "nature" as opposed to "nurture" in human life. In their concentration on certain critical moments, the myths also suggest that in some respects human existence is perceived episodically, even though it is lived chronologically. But perhaps the most important notion that Greek mythology has helped fix in our minds is that women have not only the right but the power to comment on the events that shape their lives, even if they cannot control them; and because they have a voice, women are able to speak not only for themselves, but for humankind in general.

Mysteries of the Bible

It is holy land to three world religions, the setting of a primordial drama of humanity's encounter with the divine. From the fertile valley of the Euphrates to the desolate sands of the Sinai, it is a land of ancient civilizations whose material history lies buried in the rocky hills and deserts but whose stories of patriarchs and prophets have survived the centuries in sacred Scriptures.

Now the sands of the Middle East are yielding secrets hidden for thousands of years that shed surprising new light on the historical veracity of those sacred writings. In this decade alone, archaeologists in Israel have unearthed amazing artifacts pertaining to two important figures from the Bible: a ninth-century B.C. stone inscription bearing the name of David, the ancient Israelite warrior-king who killed the giant Goliath, and a first-century A.D. tomb believed to be that of Caiaphas, the Jerusalem high priest who presided over the trial of Jesus. In both cases, it was the first archaeological evidence ever discovered suggesting that the two existed beyond the pages of the Bible. "These are tremendously important finds," says James K. Hoffmeier, chairman of archaeology and biblical studies at Wheaton College in Illinois. "They will certainly cause anxiety for the skeptics." Some have even hailed the discoveries as the beginning of a new "golden age" of biblical archaeology.

Yet for many scholars, such exuberance raises profound questions. Just how far can archaeological evidence go in "proving" the accuracy of the Bible? To what extent can, and should, Bible texts be used to interpret data and to guide archaeologists to important historical sites? Most in the field today agree with archaeologist Kenneth Holum of the University of Maryland: "The point of our work is no longer to try to prove or disprove the Bible. It is to help scientists understand the ancient cultures." Even so, many consider the Bible to be an invaluable tool in understanding and interpreting artifacts and ru-

ins. Notes Trude Dothan, an expert on Philistine sites at Jerusalem's Hebrew University: "Without the Bible, we wouldn't even have known there *were* Philistines."

Biblical archaeology has changed drastically from 100 years ago, when its focus was on treasure hunting and finding artifacts to "prove the Bible true." By the 1960s, observes William G. Dever, a professor of Near Eastern archaeology at the University of Arizona, many scholars realized that the approach centered on biblical history had left much evidence "overlooked, discarded or even destroyed." Excavation staffs began adding experts in other fields—geologists, climatologists, zoologists, anthropologists and even statisticians and computer programmers—to address questions that had never previously been asked.

The pace of exploration and the number of teams have grown recently. The result has been an upsurge in discoveries that have enormous and mixed implications for biblical history. Some seem to affirm the general historical accuracy of Scripture. But many others have posed severe challenges to traditional understandings of biblical narratives or opened up brand-new areas of knowledge. The findings have nonetheless illuminated the distant times and places that shaped Judaism and Christianity.

THE PATRIARCHS

Who were the ancient Israelites? How did they come to possess a land torn, then as now, by territorial conflict? For nearly a century, historians and Bible scholars have debated the veracity of the biblical account of Israel's begin-

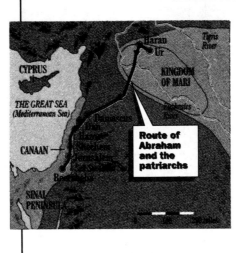

THE PATRIARCHS
CIRCA 2000–1550 B.C.

DAN. An Ancient Canaanite city at the foot of Mount Hermon, known in its early days as Laish. In Genesis 14:14, Abraham is said to have come here with a small army to free his captured nephew. They would have passed through a mud-brick gate, dating to the 18th century B.C., that was discovered here in 1978.
HARAN. A major commercial city in Mesopotamia when Abraham and his father came here. It was later abandoned for hundreds of years.
SHECHEM. A fortified Canaanite city where Abraham is said to have built an altar to God. Earliest settlements date to 4500 B.C.

MAPS BY ROD LITTLE – USN&WR

From *U.S. News & World Report*, April 17, 1995, pp. 60-64, 66-68. © 1995 by U.S. News & World Report. Reprinted by permission.

nings. And the latest archaeological evidence has not helped those who argue that there is a solid historical core behind the stories of the patriarchs.

The Book of Genesis traces Israel's ancestry to Abraham, a nomadic chieftain who God promised would be "father of many nations" and whose children would inherit the land of Canaan as "an everlasting possession." God's promise and Israel's ethnic identity are passed from Abraham to Isaac and then to Jacob, whose name is changed to Israel ("contender with God") after he wrestles with a divine being. Then Jacob and his sons—the progenitors of Israel's 12 ancient tribes—are forced to leave Canaan and move to Egypt, where the Israelite people emerge over some 400 years.

But modern archaeology has found little tangible evidence from the Middle Bronze Age (2000-1500 B.C.)—roughly the period many scholars consider to be the patriarchal era—to corroborate the biblical account. Nor are there extrabiblical references to the early battles and conflicts reported in some detail in Genesis as Abraham and his descendants claimed their inheritance.

Even so, many scholars point to other evidence suggesting that Abraham was a historical person whose memory was preserved through generations of oral tradition. Writing in the current issue of *Biblical Archaeology Review,* Prof. Kenneth A. Kitchen, an Egyptologist at the University of Liverpool in England, notes that archaeology and the Bible match well in depicting the backdrop of the patriarch stories. In one of the stories, for example, Joseph, a son of Jacob, is sold into slavery for 20 shekels. That, notes Kitchen, matches precisely the going price of slaves in the region during the 18th and 19th centuries B.C., as contained in documents recovered from ancient Mesopotamia and from Mari, in modern Syria.

The patriarch stories also seem generally consistent with what archaeologists and historians now know about the form of treaties, contracts and other social conventions of the ancient world. And the ruins of a number of sites that figure in the patriarch stories—including Ur, Shechem, Ai and Hebron—have been located. One ancient city, Haran in upper Mesopotamia, appears to have been a major commercial hub in the period when Abraham and his father would have arrived there after leaving Ur. The site, now being excavated by archaeologists from the University of Chicago, was abandoned shortly after the patriarchal period in about 1800 B.C. and remained unoccupied until about the seventh century B.C., experts say. "It's highly improbable," says Barry Beitzel, an archaeologist at Trinity Evangelical Divinity School in Deer-field, Ill., that someone inventing the story later "would have chosen Haran as a key location when the town hadn't existed for hundreds of years."

Yet scholars remain divided over just how strongly this kind of evidence supports the biblical narrative. "After nearly 100 years" of research on Israel's origins, says Dever of the University of Arizona, "we are further than ever from a consensus of scholarly opinion."

THE EXODUS

The escape of Israelite slaves from Egypt under the leadership of Moses has been called the "central event of the Hebrew Bible." Much of the story is still cloaked in mystery, "since slaves, serfs and nomads leave few traces in the archaeological record," Dever notes. But some modern archaeological finds seem to buttress elements of the biblical story.

The dating of the Exodus has long been a point of contention. In the Old Testament, 1 Kings 6:1 indicates it occurred 480 years before Solomon began building the temple in Jerusalem, or in about 1446 B.C. But most Bible scholars argue that date conflicts with other biblical texts. The Book of Exodus (1:11), for example, notes that Hebrew slaves were building "treasure cities, Pithom and Ramses," for the Egyptian pharaoh. Many scholars now think Raamses was Pi-Ramesse, a Nile delta city built by Ramses II, presumably the pharaoh of the Exodus, in the late 13th century B.C.

A 13th-century B.C. exodus also is compatible with the earliest-known reference to Israel outside of the Bible—a line of hieroglyphics in the Merneptah Stele, a monument commemorating the military conquests of Pharaoh Merneptah, son of Ramses II. The granite monument, found in Merneptah's funerary temple in Thebes, boasts that Israelites were "laid waste" during a campaign in the central highlands of Canaan around 1200 B.C. In order for the Israelites to be established there, writes Nahum Sarna, professor emeritus of biblical studies at Massachusetts's Brandeis University, the Exodus "would therefore have taken place about half a century earlier."

Recent archaeological data, scholars note, also are consistent with the Bible's explanation, in Exodus 13:17, about why Moses and the Israelites took the long way to Canaan through the desolate Sinai wilderness rather than following the shorter coastal route: Enemy military posts lay on that path. Egyptian hieroglyphics from about 1300 B.C. at the temple of Amun in Karnak depict a series of Egyptian installations along the coastal route. And modern excavations

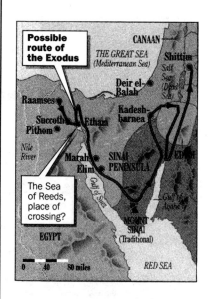

THE EXODUS
CIRCA 1440–1270 B.C.

MOUNT SINAI. Archaeologists are uncertain about the location of the mountain where God is said to have given his law to Moses. Christian tradition recognized a craggy peak in the southern Sinai Peninsula as the probable site.

PITHOM. According to the Book of Exodus, the pharaoh used the Hebrew slaves to build the great storehouse cities of Pithom and Raamses.

RAAMSES. It is from these two cities that the Israelites, led by Moses, are said to have begun their Exodus journey. Experts disagree about the exact location and about the route they took to where Moses "parted" the sea.

DEIR EL-BALAH. Archaeologists have found this site of one of five Egyptian fortresses that guarded the coastal route from Egypt to Canaan (Israel) during the period of the Exodus. Some scholars believe these fortifications help explain why the Israelites chose the circuitous southern route of escape through the forbidding Sinai.

have uncovered a string of Egyptian citadels strikingly similar to those in the Karnak relief, stretching from the Nile delta to Gaza. The presence of the forts "is perfectly compatible with the Exodus," says Dothan, the Hebrew University archaeologist, who excavated there.

She notes that compatibility is not proof. And scholars say there is no confirming archaeological evidence that Hebrews were slaves to the Egyptians, that the Egyptians suffered deadly plagues and military catastrophe when the slaves fled or that there was a clear-cut Exodus route that included miraculous passage through the Red Sea, or perhaps the Sea of Reeds to the north. Nor have scholars found the biblical Mount Sinai where Moses is said to have received the Commandments from God.

THE CONQUEST

After wandering 40 years in the Sinai wilderness, according to the Bible, the Israelites crossed the Jordan River and invaded Canaan, launching military attacks on city after city until the Promised Land was theirs. Citing a lack of evidence of sudden destruction at several key sites, many scholars now flatly reject the biblical description of Joshua's leading the Israelites in the military takeover. Instead, some argue that ancient Israel more likely arose out of a gradual and peaceful infiltration, or as a result of internal social rebellion.

Ruins of hundreds of small settlements recently have been found in the northern Negev Desert, the central highlands and Galilee, dating from the late 13th century B.C. to the 11th century B.C. But scholars so far have been reluctant to hastily link the sites to early Israelites. Whatever the explanation, says Israel Finkelstein, a prominent archaeologist at Tel Aviv University, "archaeology has pushed aside a military conquest. It's not a possibility. It's over." Not everyone agrees, of course. But even those who regard a military conquest as historical concede the archaeological record has raised a serious challenge.

The Book of Joshua, for example, describes an early and important battle at the fortified city of Jericho, where the Israelites marched and the trumpets sounded and the walls came tumbling down. Yet Kathleen Kenyon, a British archaeologist who excavated Jericho during the 1950s, concluded that there was no wall there during the period many scholars associate with the Israelite conquest—the Late Bronze Age III (1300-1200 B.C.). The city, which had existed since about 8000 B.C., appeared to have been destroyed in about 1500 B.C. and was uninhabited until the eighth century B.C. Some experts suggest Kenyon might have misdated the debris. But hers is still the accepted interpretation in most archaeological circles.

After the defeat of Jericho, Joshua is depicted as turning to Ai, where he "utterly destroyed all the inhabitants" and "burned Ai, and made it forever a heap of ruins." But archaeologists have found no evidence of a Late Bronze Age occupation at Ai. "The site was in ruins for centuries before the Israelites came to Canaan," observes Leslie J. Hoppe, an archaeologist and assistant professor of the Old Testament at Catholic Theological Union in Chicago.

Of 16 sites said in the Bible to have been destroyed by invading Israelites, evidence of Late Bronze Age destruction has turned up in three, observes Dever of the University of Arizona. He says seven of the remaining 13 sites "were not even occupied in the period or show no trace of a destruction." At the other six sites, he says, "archaeology is simply silent."

While the dispute over how the Israelites emerged in Canaan continues, there is no archaeological evidence disputing the central assertion of the Bible about this period. "The significant message of the Bible," Dever notes, "is not that the Israelites took Caanan by military might" but rather the theological claim "that God miraculously gave them the land."

THE KINGDOM

The reigns of Kings David and Solomon over a united monarchy mark the glory years of ancient Israel. The period, roughly from 1000 B.C. to 920 B.C., is described in detail in the Old Testament Books of Samuel, Kings and Chronicles. It also marks the beginning of an era of strong links between biblical history and modern archaeological evidence.

Faced with a growing military threat from Philistine warriors and filled with a renewed resolve to follow Yahweh, the Israelites began to unite, according to the Bible—first under Saul and then David, who forged the disparate Israelite tribes into a powerful nation with Jerusalem as its capital. Given David's amazing deeds, some modern scholars have suggested he was a mythical character—a theory largely based on the absence of nonbiblical references to him or to his throne.

But the discovery of a broken monument at Tell Dan in northern Israel in 1993 may have changed all that. Scholars say the monument refers to the defeat of the "House of David" by the king of

---

THE CONQUEST
CIRCA 1400–1200 B.C.

AI. Experts have not found evidence yet of the Israelites' purported destruction of this city.

JERICHO. The Bible says Joshua conquered this fortified oasis city after its walls miraculously crumbled. Archaeological evidence suggests there was no walled city at the time.

BETHEL. Originally known as Luz, this city is said to have been captured by Joshua and then lost again. Archaeologists so far have been unable to authenticate the traditional site.

LACHISH. Joshua is said to have captured this large Canaanite stronghold during the second millennium B.C. It was rebuilt and later captured by the Assyrians in a siege described in 2 Kings. In the 1930s, archaeologists discovered 21 inscribed potsherds, two of which mention a prophet believed to be Jeremiah. Later, ancient coins were discovered that helped clarify a mistranslated biblical text.

NEGEV DESERT. Archaeologists surveying this vast wasteland have found evidence of what may be early Israelite settlements.

HAZOR. The Bible says this Canaanite royal city was burned by Joshua's Army, rebuilt and fortified by King Solomon. Archaeologists have found ashes suggesting the city was destroyed about 732 B.C. An ancient archive may still lie at the site.

THE KINGDOM
CIRCA 1050–920 B.C.

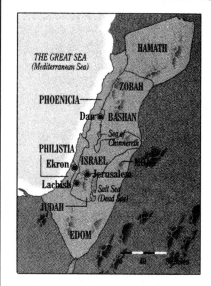

DAN. Originally known as Laish, the city was captured by the Israelite tribe of Dan. Later, it became a sanctuary for worshipers of a golden calf. In 1993, a research team discovered a stone inscription believed to bear the first reference to King David ever found outside the Bible.

JERUSALEM. A small ivory pomegranate from the eighth century B.C., discovered in the possession of an antiquities dealer in Jerusalem in 1979, is thought to be the head of a scepter used by priests in Solomon's Temple. If so, it is the only temple artifact known to have survived antiquity.

DAYS OF JESUS
CIRCA 4 B.C.– A.D. 40

church that many believe was built over the site of Peter's home.

SEPPHORIS. A regional capital and major cosmopolitan trade center just an hour's walk from Jesus's boyhood home. Though is it not mentioned in the Bible, it is almost certain that Jesus would have spent some time here, exposed to the Hellenistic culture. The town also is believed to be the birthplace of Jesus's mother, Mary. Now a major archaeological site.

JERUSALEM. Site of the trial and Crucifixion of Jesus. The tomb and an ossuary, or bone box, of Caiaphas, the high priest who reportedly presided at Jesus's trial, were found here in 1990.

CAESAREA MARITIMA. The apostle Paul was imprisoned in this ancient port city, which was built by Herod the Great. An inscription mentioning Pontius Pilate, the Roman governor at the time of Jesus's Crucifixion, was found here.

QUMRAN. Site of the discovery of the Dead Sea Scrolls in caves near the ruins of a first-century community probably inhabited by Essenes, a monastic Jewish sect.

CAPERNAUM. According to the Gospels, Jesus taught here and stayed briefly, probably in the home of the apostle Peter. Archaeologists have uncovered an ancient synagogue that may have been the site where Jesus taught and the ruins of a

Damascus in a battle that could be the one mentioned in 1 Kings 15:20. Avraham Biran, an archaeologist at Hebrew Union College in Jerusalem, who found the stone, sees the Aramaic inscription as "the first reference to David outside of the Bible." There is some dispute about it, but critics are in the minority.

From the end of Solomon's reign in about 920 B.C., through the Babylonian exile, about 540 B.C., much of biblical history is supported by numerous inscriptions and other archaeological sources. Excavations near modern-day Baghdad, Iraq, for example, turned up lists of ration allowances granted by Nebuchadnezzar to, among others, "Yaukin, king of Judah." That is believed to be a reference to Jehoiachin, an exiled king of Judah whose release is recorded in 2 Kings 25.

At Tell el-Husn in Beth-Shan, ruins of several temples have been uncovered. One from the 12th century B.C. was dedicated to Ashtaroth, a Canaanite goddess. Archaeologists say this is almost certainly the temple referred to in 1 Samuel 31:10 where after King Saul's death, soldiers "put his armor in the temple of Ashtaroth."

Discoveries from the kingdom era also have solved longstanding mysteries regarding some previously unintelligible biblical texts. Modern excavations at David's City outside the present Old City of Jerusalem, for example, have helped clarify the meaning of the word *millo* in 2 Samuel 5:9 and 1 Kings 9:15. Most English translations simply transliterate the Hebrew word, which means "filling." Excavations have revealed a large stepped-stone structure that probably supported a large building, perhaps a citadel. These are now widely believed to be the *millo* mentioned in the Bible.

Meanwhile, archaeologists recently have raised an intriguing question concerning ancient conceptions of the Hebrew God, Yahweh. Two storage jars with inscriptions and drawings were found at Kuntillet Ajrud, a remote site in southern Judah. One inscription reads: "May you be blessed by Yahweh and his Asherah." Asherah is a female deity of Canaan. Below it is a drawing of three figures, two of which are assumed to represent Yahweh and Asherah. This discovery, says Hoppe of Catholic Theological Union, "has opened for study and discussion an issue never raised by the biblical text: Did ancient Israel, at one point in its religious quest, believe that Yahweh had a consort?" This would add a vast new dimension to ancient Jewish life if further evidence is unearthed.

DAYS OF JESUS

A wealth of modern archaeological data is providing a revealing glimpse into the times of Jesus and early Christianity. In some cases, but not all, the picture that emerges matches the historical backdrop of the Gospels.

In 1968, for example, explorers found the remains of a crucified man outside Jerusalem whose wounds were strikingly similar to those described in the Gospel account of the Crucifixion of Jesus and the thieves. The discovery in 1990 of the tomb of the high priest Caiaphas at Jerusalem added another name to the list of Gospel figures whose historical existence has been attested to by physical artifacts. In 1961, an inscription found at Caesarea Maritima confirmed that Pontius Pilate was the Roman prefect in Judea at the time of Jesus's Crucifixion.

Meanwhile, current excavations at ancient cities in Galilee, Judea and elsewhere are casting new light on everyday life in the Roman-occupied land then. At Sepphoris, an ancient capital just an hour's walk from Nazareth, experts have found evidence of a cosmopolitan city, suggesting that Jesus did not grow up in rustic surroundings, as is often thought, but would have been exposed to Greek ideas and other cultures. And the Dead Sea Scrolls are still providing surprising

---

INTO THE FUTURE

HIGH HOPES. New technology, like satellite imagery of the Jordan River and the Dead Sea, could speed exploration. Regional peace would open up vast areas to archaeologists.

---

insights into religious thinking within first-century Judaism that some scholars say may have been reflected in early Christianity.

Yet while scores of sites in modern Israel, from the Church of the Nativity in Bethlehem to the Church of the Holy Sepulchre in Jerusalem, are venerated as settings of key events in the life of Jesus and the early church, few locations have been verified with solid physical evidence. And reconstructing the events themselves, say scholars, is well beyond the reach of archaeologists. Says Edwin Yamauchi, history professor at Miami University in Ohio: "Archaeology may give us a better understanding of the Crucifixion and tomb of Jesus Christ, but it can say nothing of his Resurrection."

INTO THE FUTURE

If, indeed, a new golden age of biblical archaeology awaits, scholars say it will be helped along by long-term peace in the Middle East, which could open lands now closed to international explorers. New technologies may speed the process. Radar imaging, for example, already shows promise in scanning beneath the earth's surface for buried ruins. And vast new resources—human and financial—will be needed to excavate and analyze the hidden treasures.

Many more mysteries wait to be solved. Where, for example, are the lost "Annals of the Kings" cited in the Old Testament Book of 1 Kings, and the five Books of Papias, mentioned in early church writings as a collection of the sayings of Jesus? Where is the tomb of Herod the Great, the imperious ruler of Palestine at the time of Jesus's birth? "There's so much out there, waiting to be found," says Hoffmeier of Wheaton College. "It's just a matter of time."

JEFFERY L. SHELER

WHO WAS JESUS?

He is depicted as an eloquent preacher and skilled healer, an exorcist and miracle worker. Now scholars are unearthing the historical truth of his life and times

⬚ ⬚ ⬚

He walked out of the Judean desert nearly 2,000 years ago, an unknown itinerant preacher, proclaiming to all who would listen that the Kingdom of God was at hand. It was said that he was a healer and a gifted teacher who challenged conventional wisdom and spoke with authority and wit. In the villages and hillsides of Galilee, curious crowds would gather to witness his deeds and hear his teachings. Some followed him, believing he was God's anointed one, while others dismissed him as a pretender and a troublemaker. Less than three years after he began, he was arrested in Jerusalem and executed on a Roman cross. His death, and the testimony of his followers that he arose from the dead, would change the course of history.

Today, as in his own time, Jesus of Nazareth remains one of history's most intriguing and enigmatic figures. The religion founded on his teachings counts nearly a third of the world's population as members, yet his words and deeds and the meaning of his life, death and Resurrection are subjects of intense debate and sometimes surprising interpretations. Many still ask the question of the ages: "Who is Jesus?"

For more than two centuries, biblical scholars and historians have sought to discern to what extent the Christ of faith, as perceived and experienced by Christian believers, resembles Jesus of Nazareth, the man who lived and died in Roman-occupied Palestine at the turn of the era. Using the tools of modern textual research, archaeology and social science, they seek to reconstruct a portrait of the historical Jesus, unembellished by nearly 2,000 years of church devotional tradition.

Judging from the number of recent books on the subject, the quest for the

Sermon on the Mount

⬚ ⬚ ⬚

Jesus proclaimed that the Kingdom of God had arrived, but his view of the Kingdom defied conventional wisdom.

historical Jesus is getting a new surge of scholarly energy. In just the past two years, Jesus has been depicted variously as a magician and healer, as a religious and social revolutionary and as a radical peasant philosopher. One author has even theorized that Jesus was the leader of the Dead Sea Scrolls community at Qumran, that he survived the Crucifixion and went on to marry twice and father three children. While such theories make for provocative reading, none has been widely accepted by biblical scholars and some have been quickly dismissed by the academic community as not much more than fanciful speculation.

Ever since the quest for the historical Jesus began in earnest during the Enlightenment, it has focused as much on the veracity of the New Testament Gospels as on the figure of Jesus himself. The late-18th-century skepticism dramatically altered the scholarly view of the Gospels. They came to be viewed not as pure biography or objective historical documentation, but as theological proclamation based on historical events believed to have occurred decades earlier. In going back to those events, says Anthony Tambasco, professor of theology at Georgetown University, the Gospel writers went searching for specific kinds of stories from the oral traditions concerning the life of Jesus—stories that would illustrate what a resurrected Christ and son of God would accomplish through the church. "They did not attempt," says Tambasco, "to reconstruct a complete account of his life and all that he spoke."

Many consider the search for the "real" Jesus in historical documents to be a quixotic task. A more reasonable objective, they say, is to learn who his contemporaries thought he was and what he thought of himself. Did he claim to be the Messiah, the divine Son of God? Did his audiences think of him in those ways?

Holy roots? In the Gospels, Jesus frequently refers to himself ambiguously as the Son of Man and to God as Father. Yet he shies away from publicly proclaiming himself Israel's Messiah. Only in the Gospel of Mark, when asked after his arrest if he is Israel's Promised One, does Jesus respond "I am." Some scholars doubt Jesus ever spoke these words. They argue instead that the declaration reflects the views of his followers as they came to understand the meaning of his life, death and Resurrection.

Even those who take the words as authentic say it is impossible to be certain what Jesus meant by those terms or to determine when he came to recognize himself as God's promised Messiah. "The texts don't tell us," says Don Carson, professor of New Testament at Trinity Evangelical Divinity School in Deerfield, Ill. Yet what seems clear, says Carson, is that by the time Jesus begins his public ministry he knows his special status, "and he knows he is going to be a different Messiah from what is expected."

Indeed, scholars are turning up evidence that the term *Messiah* itself had many and varied meanings in Jesus's time: Some expected a military conqueror, others a prophetic teacher and still others an apocalyptic figure who would bring down God's wrath. Recently published texts from the Dead Sea Scrolls suggest that in the Jewish milieu there may also have been an expectation of a "suffering Messiah" who would be killed by his enemies.

In large measure, those seeking the historical Jesus must base their judgments of the man's authenticity on his words and deeds, much as his Galilean audiences had to do at the time. In his sermons and discourses recorded in the Gospels of Matthew, Mark and Luke, Jesus often speaks in parables and pithy aphorisms. At the center of his teachings was the Kingdom of God—its arrival, its future fulfillment and its implications for human conduct. He

Casting the nets

✠ ✠ ✠

When they followed Jesus's command, the disciples' nets were filled, symbolic of their new calling as "fishers of men."

declared love the greatest of the Old Testament commandments and spoke reassuringly to the poor, the powerless and the peacemakers. Yet he also warned of divine judgment and declared paradoxically that he had come "not to bring peace, but a sword" that would divide nations and families.

To his curious Jewish listeners, chafing under Roman rule and longing for a restoration of the glory days under Israel's great kings, historians say, the arrival of God's Kingdom would have been a tantalizing but puzzling message. In the Gospels, Jesus seldom spoke explicitly concerning the nature of God's Kingdom, but instead described it in parables with sometimes hidden meanings.

In fact, to many of his listeners, says N. T. Wright, chaplain at Worcester College, Oxford, England, it is likely that Jesus's message would have sounded subversive. He seemed to challenge the bounds of the Jewish law by declaring, for example, "the Sabbath was made for man, not man for the Sabbath," and "not what enters into the mouth defiles the man, but what proceeds out of the mouth." He often accused the Pharisees, the leaders of the synagogues, of hypocrisy for following the letter of the law but not its spirit.

The Kingdom of God that Jesus described would include the gentiles, and many of Israel's cherished traditions would be seriously challenged by this egalitarian vision. "It would be like announcing in a Muslim country that one was fulfilling the will of Allah while apparently vilifying Muhammad and burning a copy of the Koran," says Wright in his new book, *Who Was Jesus?* "It's no wonder Jesus needed to use parables to say all this." While some of Jesus's listeners were prepared to follow him, forsaking all, says Edwin Yamauchi, professor of history at Miami University of Ohio, "many more were either skeptical or aghast at his apparent disregard of Moses's teachings and his claim of a special relation with God the Father."

Feats of wonder. More astounding than his words, then and now, are the miracles of Jesus. The Gospels report 35 of them directly and allude to 12 others, from healings and exorcisms to walking on water and raising the dead. Implied in the modern debate over whether or not Jesus performed such feats is the ultimate question of his identity: Was he the divine Son of God, as the church would come to believe, or was he just a uniquely gifted teacher and perhaps a prophet?

The significance of the issue was recognized early on by leaders of the church. The Christian apologist Justin Martyr, writing in about A.D. 160, referred to the healing miracles of Jesus as the fulfillment of Messianic prophecies in the Book of Isaiah, written about 700 years before Jesus's lifetime:
. . . the eyes of the blind will be opened, and the ears of the deaf unstopped; then the lame shall leap like a deer, and the tongue of the speechless sing for joy.
Jesus performed healing miracles, Justin wrote, to elicit recognition that he was indeed the prophesied Messiah.

But many who witnessed Jesus's miraculous feats, he said, drew the opposite conclusion: "They said it was a display of magic art, for they even dared to say he was a magician and deceiver of the people." To label someone a magician and a deceiver in antiquity, explains Graham N. Stanton, professor of New Testament Studies at King's College, University of London, England, "was an attempt to marginalize a person who was perceived to be a threat to the dominant social order." Jesus's criticisms of the legalistic excesses of Judaic law could easily have been perceived as a threat to the religious customs and traditions of his time, Stanton contends in the forthcoming book *Jesus of Nazareth,* and would certainly have set the Temple priests and the leaders of the synagogues against him.

Today, there is broad consensus among even the most skeptical of scholars that Jesus probably did perform feats that would have been perceived as miracles at the time. They find considerable evidence, for example, that Jesus's reputation as a healer and miracle worker extended beyond his own circle of followers. The Jewish historian Josephus, writing near the end of the first century, wrote that Jesus was known as "a doer of startling deeds" and a teacher who "gained a following both among many Jews and many men of Greek origin." The Jewish Talmud relates that "on the eve of Passover, Yeshu was hanged . . . because he has practiced sorcery and led Israel astray."

Yet many biblical experts are convinced that Jesus did not perform all the miracles ascribed to him in the Gospels. Some in fact argue that his performance of "startling deeds" does not make him entirely unique in his place and time.

The healing touch. Among the most common of Jesus's recorded miracles were his healings. Yet theologians point out that every culture—before, during and after Jesus's time—has had stories of healings. To declare, therefore, that Jesus was a healer, and to tell stories of healings by Jesus, says Stevan Davies, New Testament scholar at College Misericordia in Pennsylvania, is "no more exciting than to say he was a carpenter."

Davies, who has written on the subject of Jesus's healings, concludes that he undoubtedly was known by his contemporaries as having healed people of

Healing the lame

⌘ ⌘ ⌘

Scholars say the weight of historical evidence supports the Gospels' depiction of Jesus as a healer of physical maladies.

some maladies. Even without believing in the supernatural, says Davies, one could conclude that Jesus successfully healed certain psychosomatic illnesses—rashes, lameness and some types of blindness, for example. Some Gospel accounts of his healings seem to involve his use of primitive medical arts—the application of mud to the eyes of a blind man, for instance—and his appropriation of conventional religious practices, such as Jewish purification rites for those suffering from skin diseases.

The fact that Jesus was widely known as a healer makes it likely that he did indeed engage in such activity, says Robert Funk, director of the Westar Institute in Sonoma, Calif., and leader of the Jesus Seminar, a group of liberal scholars examining the words and deeds of Jesus. "To say that Jesus was known for engaging in these types of events," says Funk, "is far different than saying he healed this particular man in this particular way, as recorded in the Gospels."

Ousting demons. Jesus also was widely known as an exorcist. The Gospels record four instances in which the Nazarene preacher came upon people said

to be possessed by demons. In one story, he casts out a "legion" of demons, sending them into a herd of pigs that throw themselves off a cliff. "There is little doubt that Jesus performed exorcisms as they were understood in his time," says John J. Rousseau, an archaeologist and member of the Jesus Seminar. "It was just a natural thing to do for an itinerant charismatic healer and teacher . . . and he was not the only one to do it."

Exorcisms clearly were a part of the Jewish milieu in first-century Palestine. The Judaism of Jesus's time, observes Rousseau, had been influenced by Babylonian, Persian, Egyptian and Greek cultures. The Persian belief that demons could possess individuals and cause diseases, says Rousseau, "had gained wide acceptance, and techniques of exorcism were used for the treatment of illnesses."

Often those techniques involved use of magical devices such as amulets, rings, stones and other artifacts, which have recently been discovered at archaeological sites. One tradition, mentioned by both the first-century Jewish historian Josephus and the third-century Christian writer Origen of Alexandria, held that the ancient Israelite King Solomon, who lived in the 10th century B.C., was himself an exorcist.

Besides the several accounts of Jesus casting out demons, the Acts of the Apostles—the New Testament book that chronicles the early growth of Christianity after the Resurrection—notes that Jesus's disciples also performed exorcisms. Many scholars conclude that such a preponderance of reports indicates that Jesus probably did set the example for his followers. Yet as with healings, whether or not the specific exorcisms recorded in the Gospels are factual accounts of actual events remains a matter of dispute.

Fooling with nature. Among the most sensational of Gospel stories, and the most problematic for historians, are those that depict Jesus performing so-called nature miracles—calming a stormy sea, walking on water, changing water into wine at a wedding feast and feeding 5,000 people with five loaves and two fish. Also in that category are two stories that depict Jesus raising the dead.

Such feats pose little trouble for theologians and scholars who believe Jesus was God and, therefore, capable of suspending the laws of nature. Some scholars, however, find it much more likely that these were literary inventions of the Gospel writers intended to illustrate a theological belief about the divinity of Jesus and the ongoing activity of the risen Christ.

Dennis MacDonald, a professor of New Testament and Christian origins at Iliff School of Theology in Denver, sees a connection between stories of Jesus walking on water and calming the seas and Homer's *Odyssey*, in which the god Poseidon is depicted as walking on water and controlling the wind and waves. The Gospel writers, says MacDonald, would have been familiar with Homer's writings, which were in common use as school texts in the ancient world. The Christian writers drew upon the familiar motif, argues MacDonald, to construct stories "in which Jesus revealed his divine identity."

Clearly the most astounding of Jesus's reported miracles are the accounts of his raising the dead. The Gospel of Luke tells of Jesus reviving a widow's son in Nain: "And he said, 'Young man, I say to you, arise!' And the dead man sat up and began to speak." And the Gospel of John records Jesus raising his friend Lazarus, who was dead for three days in Bethany, near Jerusalem. While many scholars also reject these stories as pure fiction, some have suggested that the stories may reflect honest mis-

Loaves and fishes

⌘ ⌘ ⌘

Jesus miraculously feeding the multitudes may be a metaphor for the Risen Christ feeding the faith of his followers.

understandings—that the victims were mistakenly thought to be dead and were simply revived.

Ultimately, says Paul Maier, professor of ancient history at Western Michigan University, "there is no way for historians to prove or disprove" the resuscitation stories. But he finds some historical corroboration in the subsequent history of Bethany. The town, destroyed when the Romans attacked Jerusalem in A.D. 70, was later rebuilt and was renamed by the Arabs who settled there. "The Israelis today call it Bethanya but the Arabs call it el-Azariyeh, 'the place of Lazarus,'" says Maier. "I find that fascinating. Why would they change the name of the town unless something spectacular happened there?"

Dangerous game. Though it is not depicted as a miracle, Jesus's chasing of the money-changers from the Temple in Jerusalem is clearly one of the most dramatic and significant of his reported deeds. Beyond the religious symbolism of the act—purifying what the Gospels said had become "a den of thieves"—it was a definitive event leading to his arrest and Crucifixion. But the account in the Gospels of Matthew, Mark and Luke of Jesus doing this after his final entry into Jerusalem, just days before his arrest, conflicts with John's Gospel, which seems to have him performing the deed at the very beginning of his ministry. Is either of the accounts accurate?

Again, there is wide disagreement on the historicity of the specific details. The story, says Paula Fredriksen, professor of ancient Christianity at Boston University, "is excellent theology. It's just terrible history." Selling of sacrificial animals in the Temple court, she notes, was a long-standing practice that enabled pilgrims to meet their religious obligations. And portraying Jesus as chasing the money-changers from the

Walking on water

⊠ ⊠ ⊠

Accounts of Jesus walking on water and calming the seas parallel Greek stories of gods who had power over wind and waves.

Temple, says Funk of the Westar Institute, "is not a realistic picture. There

must have been hundreds of them, especially on a festival day."

Nonetheless, there is broad consensus that underlying the Gospel anecdote is some Temple incident that is somewhat akin to the Gospel accounts of Jesus's bold and decisive act. Some have suggested that he protested the Temple tax or the use of coins with pa-

The raising of Lazarus

⊠ ⊠ ⊠

The Gospel story of Jesus raising Lazarus from the dead is doubted by many scholars but is memorialized in ancient history.

gan images. Others theorize he was angered that the selling of animals had taken over the only area in the Temple where gentiles were permitted to pray.

Whatever the exact nature of Jesus's deed, says Bruce Chilton, professor of religion at Bard College in Annandale-on-Hudson, N.Y., "an act against the Temple would have been perceived by the Romans as an attack on the status quo." And that would have made him a prime candidate for arrest.

Whether or not the miracle accounts are more symbolic stories than biogra-

phy, it appears to most scholars that Jesus probably did perform some miracles. "We may not be able to ascertain which miracles are authentic," says Professor Tambasco of Georgetown University, "and we do have a sense that all of the stories are reworked. We can, however, be reasonably sure that all of the healings taken together witness to the fact of miracles in the life of Jesus."

Regardless of the controversy it generates and the lack of consensus over what it may produce, the quest for the historical Jesus is certain to continue. If some clearer, purer vision of Jesus of Nazareth is to be found, it may very well come not from some obscure text or ancient scroll buried in the Judean desert. Perhaps it will be as the scholar and humanitarian Albert Schweitzer wrote early in this century, after he concluded his own search of the evidence and found the historical Jesus as elusive and mysterious as ever. "He comes to us as One unknown, without a name," Schweitzer concluded, "as of old, by the lakeside, he came to those men who knew Him not. He speaks to us the same word: 'Follow thou me!' and sets us to the tasks which He has to fulfill for our time."

JEFFERY L. SHELER

THE CHRISTMAS COVENANT

Was Jesus's birth part of a divine plan leading to a golden age? Scholars are re-examining the biblical prophecies

The Advent season, in church tradition, is a time of sacred anticipation as Christians prepare to celebrate the birth of Jesus Christ some 2,000 years ago in a Bethlehem stable. For believers through the ages, the joy of Advent lay in their understanding of that humble birth as a divine promise fulfilled, the swaddled baby in the manger as the long-awaited Messiah.

But for many Christians, the comforting images of the Christmas season are inexorably linked to another, more mysterious prophecy: that of the apocalyptic Second Coming of Christ. Ancient liturgies and modern Advent observances alike point to the promised return of Jesus in what many Christians believe will be a cataclysmic event that will end history and inaugurate a divine kingdom on Earth.

Although Jesus is quoted in the Gospel of Matthew as saying no one will know "the day nor the hour" of his return, the approach of a new millennium in the year 2000 is unleashing a flood of doomsday prophecies, not only from zealous Christians who are convinced that Christ's return is imminent but also from those in cultural and religious settings far removed from Christian belief (see accompanying boxes). There is a broad expectation that "when the world's odometer ticks over to three zeros, it will have cosmic significance," says Ted Daniels, editor of *Millennial Prophecy Report,* a Philadelphia-based newsletter that tracks about 1,100 groups and individuals.

One result, Daniels and others note, has been a bizarre and sometimes deadly intensification of cultlike behavior. The tragic inferno at the Branch Davidians' "Ranch Apocalypse" in Waco, Texas, last year and the recent ritualistic deaths of members of the Solar Temple cult in Switzerland and Canada are just two of the most dramatic examples of modern millennial expectations run amok. They may not be the last. In the run-up to the year 2000, predicts University of Southern California Prof. Stephen D. O'Leary in his book *Arguing the Apocalypse,* "we will see more religious groups who are willing to martyr themselves" because of tragically distorted millennialist views.

Challenging TV preachers. Hoping to avert such tragedies, biblical scholars from a variety of Christian traditions have begun rethinking some popular views of the Second Coming. Some are openly challenging the imaginative end-of-the-world scenarios espoused by TV preachers and Bible teachers who view current events as fulfillment of end-times prophecies. Their objections are sparking a debate that is sure to intensify and that could dramatically alter some popular views of the apocalypse.

But belief in an apocalyptic end to history is by no means limited to the religious fringe. A new *U.S. News* poll has found that nearly 60 percent of Americans think the world will end sometime in the future; almost a third of those think it will end within a few decades. And more than 61 percent say they believe in the Second Coming of Christ. The poll, conducted by Market Facts Inc., found that self-described born-again Christians and frequent churchgoers subscribe to millennial views by significantly greater margins than others.

The embrace of millennialism

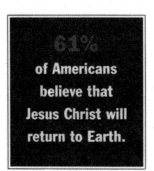

61% of Americans believe that Jesus Christ will return to Earth.

comes as little surprise to social scientists. "We no longer need poets to tell us it could all end with a bang, or a whimper, or in the agony of AIDS," explains Charles B. Strozier, a psychoanalyst and professor of history at the City University of New York. With the looming possibility of nuclear or environmental destruction, says

Of those who believe Jesus will return, the percentage who think he will come within:	
a few years; few decades	34%
longer than that	37%

Americans who believe the world will come to an end	59%

Of those, the percentage who believe the end will occur within:	
a few years	12%
a few decades	21%
a few hundred years	16%
longer than that	28%

Americans who believe the Bible should be taken literally when it speaks of:	
a final Judgment Day	60%
the Antichrist	49%
a battle of Armageddon	44%
the Rapture of the church	44%

Americans who believe some world events this century fulfill biblical prophecy	53%

Of those, the percentage who believe these specific events fulfill prophecy:	
world wars	16%
conflict between Israel and its enemies	10%
establishment of Israel	6%
AIDS epidemic	6%

U.S. News poll of 1,000 American adults conducted by Market Facts' TELENATION Dec. 2–4, 1994, Margin of error: +/− 3 percentage points. Percentages may not add up to 100 because some respondents answered, "Don't know."

Strozier, "it now takes an active imagination *not*' to think about human endings."

Early prophecy. Similar apocalyptic turmoil surrounded the year 1000. In a historical psychological study, *The Year 1000,* Henri Focillon says artistic and cultural activity in Europe's monasteries nearly ground to a halt as the year 999 wound down toward what was widely viewed as "an evening of the world." One legendary account has it that on the stroke of midnight, Jan. 1, 1000, the entire country of Iceland converted to Christianity out of apocalyptic anxiety.

Indeed, the mystery and promise of the Second Coming of Christ have fired Christians' imaginations from their earliest days, often inspiring hopeful piety and artistic and theological creativity but sometimes destruction and violence as well. Jesus is quoted in the Gospel of John as saying, "I will come again and receive you unto myself; so that where I am there ye may be also." Most biblical scholars believe the first disciples were convinced Jesus would return in their lifetime. When he did not, the church began developing a more detailed eschatology, or theology regarding the "last things."

Belief that the Second Coming was imminent pervaded early Christian writings, scholars note. But only Hippolytus of Rome (A.D. 170-235) tried to pinpoint the timing: He guessed A.D. 500 based on the dimensions of Noah's ark. Meanwhile, Augustine of Hippo, the pre-eminent theologian of the fourth and fifth centuries, argued against literal readings of prophecy and detailed speculation concerning Christ's return. His eschatological views were endorsed by the Council of Ephesus in 431 and set the tone for Roman Catholicism.

Even so, and despite Jesus's warning in Acts 1:7 that "it is not for you to know the times or the seasons," the history of the church is filled with self-proclaimed prophecy experts who think they have cracked the biblical code and pieced together precise timetables for the end of the world. Over the centuries, religious movements have risen and fallen on such speculation. In the 1840s, for example, Baptist Bible teacher William Miller set four successive dates for Christ's return. At the time, some followers dressed in white robes and waited on a hillside for the Lord to take them away. When it didn't pan out, some of his disciples left, disillusioned, while others adjusted his teachings and founded a new denomination, the Seventh-Day Adventists—who now refer to Miller's failed predictions as "the Great Disappointment."

Despite such failures, the doctrine of the Second Coming remains a part of mainstream Christian belief in both Catholic and Protestant traditions.

There have been major disagreements, however, especially over how and when Christ's 1,000-year reign of peace known as the millennium, mentioned in Revelation 20, will occur. The church has long been divided into contentious camps:

■ Postmillennialists were strong among 19th-century Protestants but have faded in this century. Their optimistic creed proclaims that Christ will return after an earthly golden age of peace that is brought about by God working through the human efforts of the church. Adherents tend to encourage Christian activism in world affairs, according to Stanley Grenz, theology professor at Carey/Regent College in Vancouver, in his book *The Millennial Maze.*

■ Amillennialists do not anticipate a literal, 1,000-year golden age but interpret the millennium as a period in which Christ reigns in and through the church and in the lives of individual believers. They include Roman Catholics, some evangelicals and much of mainline Protestantism, and they tend, says Grenz, to be realists: They expect that "victory and defeat, success and failure, good and evil will be our experience until the end."

■ Premillennialists, who include most evangelical and fundamentalist Christians, take a much more pessimistic view of history. For them, says Grenz, the world will grow nastier. Only "the catastrophic return" of Christ, he says, will "inaugurate the golden age on Earth."

The dispensations. It is the premillennialist view, with its elaborate timetables and graphic end-of-the-world scenarios, that has captured the most attention in recent years and that now has become the focus of scholarly scrutiny. While there are differences of opinion within the tradition, the dominant view, called dispensationalism, has its roots in the teachings of John Nelson Darby, a 19th-century Englishman and founder of the Plymouth Brethren. He taught that history is divided into seven ages, or dispensations, which will culminate in the final judgment and the end of the world. The dispensationalist scenario, popularized recently in evangelical writer Hal Lindsey's 1970 bestseller, *The Late Great Planet Earth,* and by Dallas Theological Seminary Chancellor John Walvoord's *Armageddon, Oil and the Middle East Crisis,* is drawn largely from the Old Testament prophecy books of Ezekiel, Zechariah and Daniel and the enigmatic New Testament book of Revelation.

The doomsday script begins with Christians suddenly being pulled out of the world in an event called the Rapture. Nonbelievers are left behind to face the great tribulation, a seven-year period during which the world is ruled by the Antichrist, a charismatic but duplicitous world leader who makes peace with Israel only to break the pact and persecute the Jews.

The major world powers then are drawn into a Middle East war and face off in the battle of Armageddon. At the climax of the battle, Christ returns in "power and great glory" to defeat the evil forces, judge the godless nations and set up his earthly kingdom of 1,000 years. Then comes the new Jerusalem, final judgment and eternal bliss.

NEW AGE
THE NEXT PLANE OF CONSCIOUSNESS

All our institutions are failing, says Solara — the single name she uses. But amid the chaos, a "doorway" she has helped open gives earthlings until Dec. 31, 2011, to "step into the next dimension of consciousness." If we fail, she warns, Earth could explode.

Spoken by a popular leader of the growing New Age movement, the millenarian message is taken seriously by many thousands. Solara has taught sold-out seminars around the world and written five books, two of which have brought movie offers. Her favorite answer to 20th-century angst — that "we are angels, descended from the stars" — has sustained her own publishing house, Star-Borne Unlimited, and she pens a newsletter, the "Starry Messenger," for 5,000 devotees.

But Solara is best known for organizing "the 11:11 event," a kind of sequel to the 1987 "Harmonic Convergence" when more than 100,000 people prayed over a weekend for world peace. In 1992, convinced that the flash of "11:11" on digital clocks holds mystical significance, tens of thousands of participants worldwide wore only white and at 11:11 a.m., 11:11 p.m. and 11:11 Greenwich Mean Time on January 11 performed dances she designed as "a sign to those on high" to open the door. Her next move: to sell her Charlottesville, Va., home and go to French Polynesia to start a "community of light."

A hallmark of premillennialism, and a major target of scholarly criticism, has been its inclination to view current world events as prophetic signs of the end times. No single event in the 20th century has excited apocalyptic fervor as much as the rise of the state of Israel in 1948. When the United Nations created Israel, premillennialists exulted that the final countdown had begun. In 1950, a youthfully exuberant Billy Graham told a rally in Los Angeles, "Two years and it's all going to be over." Since then, Graham has become more cautious regarding apocalyptic timetables.

The embodiment of evil in most end-times story lines is the Antichrist, a powerful and charismatic dictator who, some Christians believe, will rule over a reconstituted Roman Empire, enforce a "false peace" and a heretical worldwide religion and ultimately declare himself to be God. One identifying sign of the Antichrist, according to dispensationalists drawing from Revelation 13:3, will be his recovery from a mortal head wound: "And his deadly wound was healed: and all the world wondered after the beast." Another will be his association with the number 666, described in Revelation 13:18 as the "mark of the beast."

In almost every generation, Christians have tried to identify the Antichrist from among their contemporary enemies, from the murderous Roman emperor Nero in the first century to Napoleon Bonaparte, Benito Mussolini and Saddam Hussein. More recently, some Christians even suspected Ronald Wilson Reagan, in part because each of his names has six letters. Fear of the Antichrist has prompted some fundamentalist preachers to denounce electronic bar codes and the increasing use of credit and debit cards as precursors of the "mark of the beast," which Revelation says the Antichrist will place on his followers, and without which "no man might buy or sell."

Such views are often dismissed by more liberal academicians as fanciful inventions based on a too-literal reading of the Bible. But now some conservative evangelical scholars are beginning to challenge them as well. Professors at such bastions of premillennialism as Dallas Theological Seminary, Moody Bible Institute in Chicago and Wheaton College in Wheaton, Ill., recently have raised strong objections to the literal interpretation of some apocalyptic texts and to the intense search for "signs of the times" in current events.

In their forthcoming book, *Doomsday Delusions*, Moody Professors C. Marvin Pate and Calvin B. Haines Jr. argue that premillennial doomsday preachers often "misinterpret and misapply" bibli-

[handwritten margin note: What if Jesus comes w/o an anti christ? People think he's the antichrist]

WHITE BUFFALO
AN OMEN STIRS HOPE

Native American legends tell of a magical "White Buffalo Woman" who brought spiritual knowledge to a starving tribe, allowing its members to hunt buffaloes across the Great Plains. Now, says revered Oglala Lakota medicine man Floyd Hand, she has returned and a great human reconciliation will occur.

Others also think the birth of an all-white buffalo named Miracle last August has great meaning. More than 32,000 people have made the pilgrimage to Janesville, Wis. — even though her coat is now fading. Some wept as they adorned Miracle's fence with protective offerings of sage, tobacco and small round nets called dream catchers. In September, leaders from many tribes took the unusual step of consecrating the farm as holy land.

The American Bison Association says that the odds against this birth are in the millions. But they cannot explain Hand's other prediction that the calf's father would die shortly after Miracle was born. Days later, the bull, which had seemed healthy, died.

In spite of the attention, Miracle's owner, Dave Heider, 45, said he won't charge admission or sell the animal — even after receiving an offer from rocker Ted Nugent, who wrote the 1974 hit, "Great White Buffalo." "I'm not a churchgoer," Heider says, "but folks walk out of here like they've looked upon Christ."

---

cal prophecies by ignoring their historical context. They note that apocalyptic texts such as the book of Revelation and some of the Old Testament prophecies were a common literary genre in New Testament times and were often written during periods of oppression to reassure persecuted believers of God's faithfulness. Imaginative symbols and images generally were employed to evoke people and events known to the readers of that time.

JERUSALEM TEMPLE
PREPARING FOR THE MESSIAH

The rebuilding of Solomon's Temple in Jerusalem's Old City has been so important to Jews that they have prayed for it for centuries and they end each wedding with the breaking of a glass to remind participants of the Temple's destruction—first by Babylonians over 2,500 years ago and then again 656 years later by Rome after it was rebuilt. Its reconstruction is unthinkable because it stands on the same location as the Dome of the Rock Mosque, the site believed by Muslims to be where Mohammed ascended to heaven in the early seventh century.

While stressing they have no plans to displace the mosque, a small group believes that if proper preparations are made, a miracle will occur, enabling the Temple to be rebuilt. The first step, says Chaim Richman of the Temple Institute, is replication down to the precise detail of Temple objects, half of which have now been made. In addition, a Mississippi cattle farmer has agreed to provide special unblemished red heifers, the ashes of which are required for a purification ritual.

Others also prepare for the miracle. Rabbi Nahman Kahane of the Old City has created a database of all Jews descended from Aaron, the priestly brother of Moses. They will be called into service if the Temple is rebuilt.

Richman says he is not messianic: "[We hope] the Temple will be again the spiritual center of all mankind."

Literary legends. The Antichrist in Revelation, for example, says Pate, was no doubt "intended to signify Nero," a persecutor of Christians who committed suicide by falling on a sword. Later literary legends depicted Nero returning from the dead to plague his enemies, much as Revelation describes the Antichrist. Passages in Ezekiel that premillennialists say predict a future Armageddon probably refer to the inva-

sion of Israel by Scythian hordes in pre-Christian times, according to the scholars. Imaginative doomsday preachers ignore this. Instead, says Haines, "the locusts of Revelation become Cobra helicopters" and the northern invader of Israel in Ezekiel becomes the Russian Army. "This is anachronism."

Other evangelical scholars take premillennialism to task for drawing extreme conclusions from biblical text. Dallas seminary Profs. Craig A. Blaising and Darrell L. Bock argue for a more moderate view of the end times in their new book *Progressive Dispensationalism.* While they, too, await the Second Coming and fulfillment of prophecy, they contend that God's agenda evolves in history and is not abruptly compartmentalized, as some dispensationalists teach.

At Wheaton College, growing faculty disaffection with the school's rigid adherence to premillennialist doctrine prompted school officials recently to drop the view from its doctrinal statement. "It's just not an essential part of the Christian faith," explains New Testament Prof. Alan Johnson. Even at Jerry Falwell's fundamentalist Liberty University in Lynchburg, Va., New Testament Prof. D. Brent Sandy challenges the notion that details of future events can be extracted from the Bible. Prophecy's primary purpose, Sandy writes in the evangelical journal *Christianity Today*, is simply "to assure readers that God is going to accomplish his plans in unique and amazing ways."

Aside from concerns about faulty interpretation, critics also worry that some Christians may be getting so wrapped up in deciphering prophecy and awaiting divine deliverance that they ignore other missions. "If God's timepiece for this present age is rapidly ticking off the remaining seconds," says Paul Boyer, history professor at the University of Wisconsin, "what is the point of battling social issues?" Some scholars see an even greater danger. "What scares me is that people who believe that Israel must go through terrible trouble will stand by and let them be crushed," says James Tabor, a religion professor at the University of North Carolina at Charlotte.

Beyond the theological debate, some social scientists and religion scholars have sought to explain why apocalyptic thinking strikes such a resonant chord in a modern age. Norman Cohn, history professor emeritus at the University of Sussex, England, in his often-cited book, *The Pursuit of the Millennium*, explained apocalyptic thinking as a "paranoid" response to economic deprivation and political persecution and said that its adherents throughout history largely have been social and economic outcasts

who take comfort in assurances that the tables soon will be turned. That might be true in other places, but it does not seem to apply to many American evangelicals in the 1990s who are comfortably middle-class and politically active.

Search for meaning. Another explanation focuses on psychological forces. Bernard McGinn, theology professor at the University of Chicago Divinity School,

RADIO PREACHER
FORESEES DOOM SOON

Radio evangelist Harold Camping admits he is "slightly disappointed" that the world did not end last September.

A civil engineer by training and now president of Family Radio Inc.'s network of 39 Christian radio stations and 14 shortwave transmitters, Camping figured that he had deciphered the Bible's chronological blueprint: The world began with Adam in 11013 B.C. and was scheduled to end some 13 millenniums later, almost certainly in the first jubilee year after the birth of modern Israel. September 1994, to be exact. That's the time his book "1994?," which sold 70,000 copies, predicted that skies would darken at midday and graves would fly open as the dead joined the living to face God's fiery judgment.

Camping's critics say he ignored, or misinterpreted, the well-known passage (Matthew 25:13) where Jesus admonishes his disciples that no man can know "the day nor the hour" of his return. But Camping, whose radio network will take in some $12 million this year, up 20 percent since "1994?" was published two years ago, brushes off the criticism. The 73-year-old father of six says that he is in fact "delighted" to have a little more time, because he has many friends and family members who are "not yet saved." He adds: "I still believe we are very near the end. Are you ready?"

says apocalyptic eschatology "always involves a sense of psychological imminence—a belief that the most important thing about the present is that it is witnessing events that must inexorably lead to the end." This provides "meaning in a time of historical uncertainty." There's an ominous side, as well, says McGinn in his book *Antichrist*. The apocalyptic worldview, he says, "has no room for moral ambiguity, for any shades of gray." By viewing opponents as adherents of absolute evil, apocalypticism "allows for total opposition and dire vengeance of the wicked."

Despite millennialism's destructive potential, it is the ultimate optimism of the apocalypse that many through history have found so compelling. It is a "primary task of religion," observes Strozier of the City University of New York, "to provide a meaningful sense of endings and beginnings." For nearly 2,000 years, Christians have found such meaning in the promise of Advent and their visions of the apocalypse. For them, as for others, the greatest challenge of the new millennium may well be in discovering spiritual satisfaction in the ordinary times that lie before the end—whatever that is and whenever it comes.

The World of Islam

THE MESSENGER OF ALLAH

In a cave at the foot of Mount Hira near Mecca, where he had spent six months in solitary meditation, the vision came to Muhammad. The Angel Gabriel roused him from his bed with the stern command: "Proclaim!" Rubbing his eyes, the startled Muhammad gasped, "But what shall I proclaim?" Suddenly his throat tightened as though the angel were choking him. Again came the command: "Proclaim!" And again the terrified Muhammad felt the choking grip. "Proclaim!" ordered the angel for a third time. "Proclaim in the name of the Lord, the Creator who created man from a clot of blood! Proclaim! Your Lord is most gracious. It is he who has taught man by the pen that which he does not know."

Thus it was, according to Islamic tradition, that an unremarkable Arab trader from Mecca was inspired to preach God's word in the year A.D. 610. Compared with Jesus or the Buddha, information about the life of the man who became known as the Messenger of Allah is relatively abundant, although the facts have been embellished with pious folklore. Some have claimed that at Muhammad's birth the palace of the Persian emperor trembled, or that a mysterious light ignited at his mother's breast, shining all the way to Syria, 800 miles away. It was said that his body cast no shadow and that when his hair fell into a fire it would not burn. Muhammad himself disdained any miraculous claims, insisting that he was merely the all-too-human conduit through which God had revealed himself.

It is known that the Prophet was born about A.D. 570 to a member of the respected Meccan clan of Hashim. His father died shortly before Muhammad was born, and his mother when the boy was only six. Two years later, his doting grandfather Abd al-Muttalib died, leaving the orphan in the care of a poor uncle, Abu Talib. As a youth, Muhammad was set to work tending his uncle's herds; he later recalled that task as a mark of divine favor. "God sent no prophet who was not a herdsman," he told his disciples. "Moses was a herdsman. David was a herdsman. I, too, was commissioned for prophethood while I grazed my family's cattle."

As a young man, Muhammad was exposed to the currents of religious debate then swirling through the Middle East. He would listen avidly as Jews and Christians argued over their faiths. Those discussions may have fed his dissatisfaction with the traditional polytheistic religion of the Arabs, who believed in a panoply of tribal gods and jinn, headed by a deity known as Allah. Says Muhammad's French biographer, Maxime Rodinson: "Both Jews and Christians despised the Arabs, regarding them as savages who did not even possess an organized church."

At 25, Muhammad accepted a marriage proposal from Khadijah, a rich Meccan widow 15 years his senior, for whom he had led a successful caravan. With his financial security assured by Khadijah's wealth and business, he began to venture into the desert, to contemplate and pray, as had other Arab holy men before him.

According to legend, Muhammad had earned a reputation as a wise and saintly man even before his first revelation from the angel on Mount Hira. Looking out from the balcony of his Mecca home one day, he saw the members of four clans arguing over which of them should be allowed to carry the Black Stone, a huge meteorite that the Arabs regarded as sacred, to its new resting place in a rebuilt shrine called the Ka'ba. Unknown to Muhammad, they had resolved to let the first man who walked into the sanctuary decide the matter. Entering the holy place, Muhammad proposed a satisfactory compromise: placing the Black Stone on a blanket, he instructed each tribe to lift one corner. Then he personally laid the meteorite in its new niche.

At 40, Muhammad began to preach the new faith of Islam, which was gradually being revealed to him on his sojourns in the desert. Some of this religion was familiar to Arabs who knew about the monotheistic teachings of Jews and Christians. His countrymen, for example, could readily accept Muhammad's assertion that Allah, long regarded as the highest of the desert gods, was the same God worshiped by Jews and Christians. But Meccan traders felt threatened by Muhammad's growing power. Both Jews and Christians questioned his claim that he was revealing the true word of God to the Arabs, in effect joining them as "People of the Book." In 622, after being harassed by his opponents, Muhammad and his followers escaped to Medina in a migration known as the hegira.

To a growing body of converts, Muhammad began to elaborate on his new religion. Revelations came to him in trances; his descriptions of those encounters, memorized and recorded by his adherents, were later collected as the Koran. As his followers grew in strength and numbers, Muhammad began a series of raids on Meccan caravans, which led to several indecisive battles with their avenging war parties. In 628 the Meccans agreed to let Muhammad's followers make their pilgrimage to the Ka'ba, which the new faith continued to regard as a sacred shrine. Muslims believe it is the spot where Abraham prepared to sacrifice his son Ishmael at God's command. Two years later the prophet led an army of 10,000 into his former city, taking control in a bloodless victory.

For all the pious legends that grew up even in his lifetime, Muhammad remained a humble and, in some ways, unfulfilled man. He occasionally incurred the wrath of his wives and concubines. All of his sons died in childhood, leaving him with no male heir. In 632 he led a pilgrimage to Mecca, where he declared, "I have perfected your religion and completed my favors for you." Three months later he fell ill in Medina and died. To his zealous followers went the task of spreading the word of Allah, not only throughout Arabia but far beyond it as well.

A FAITH OF LAW AND SUBMISSION

God's grandeur, and a path to follow

Eight words in Arabic sum up the central belief of the world's 750 million Muslims: "There is no god but God, and Muhammad is the Messenger of God." Five times a day, from Djakarta to Samarkand to Lagos, this *shahada* (confession of faith) is recited by the devout as meµzzins (callers to prayer) summon them to worship God.

In the prescribed daily prayers, a pious Muslim does not beseech God for favors, either material or spiritual, so much as for guidance and mercy. The word Islam means submission, and the true Muslim submits his life to the divine will of a deity who is the Compassionate, the All Knowing, the Strong, the Protector, the All Powerful—to cite only a few of the traditional 99 "most Beautiful Names" of God.

Muslims believe that God decrees everything that happens in the cosmos. Some critical Western scholars contend that this doctrine leads to a kind of passive fatalism, but Islamic theologians strongly deny that *qadar* (divine will) negates a person's freedom to act. It merely means, says Muhammad Abdul Rauf, director of the Islamic Center in Washington, that "when some misfortune befalls us, we resign ourselves to it as something coming from God, instead of despairing."

Islam stresses the uniqueness of the Creator, and strictly forbids *shirk*—that is, the association of anyone or anything with God's divinity. Along with Moses and Abraham, Jesus is revered by Muslims as one of the 25 scriptural prophets of God, and Islam accepts both his virgin birth and his miracles. But Muslims believe that Christian faith in the divinity of Jesus is polytheism. They resent being

called "Muhammadans," which suggests that Muhammad's role in Islam is similar to that of Jesus in Christianity. The Prophet is revered as God's final Messenger to mankind, but is not worshiped as a divine being.

Because they accept the Bible, Jews and Christians have a special status in Islam as "People of the Book." Muslims also believe that the Bible in its present form is corrupt and that the true faith was revealed only to Muhammad. Those revelations are contained in the Koran, the Arabic word for recitation. Slightly shorter than the New Testament, the Koran has little narrative. There are evocations of divine grandeur in rhymed prose, florid descriptions of the harsh fate that awaits those who knowingly ignore God's will, and detailed instructions on specific ways that man must submit to his maker.

The basic spiritual duties of Islam are summed up in the so-called five pillars of faith. They are: 1) accepting the *shahada;* 2) the daily prayers to God while facing Mecca; 3) charitable giving; 4) fasting during the daylight hours of Ramadan, a 29- or 30-day month in Islam's lunar calendar* and 5) making the hajj, or pilgrimage, to Mecca at least once in an individual's lifetime—if he or she is financially and physically able. Some Muslims argue that there is a sixth pillar of the faith, namely jihad. The word is frequently translated as "holy war", in fact, it can refer to many forms of striving for the faith, such as an inner struggle for purification or spreading Islamic observance and justice by whatever means.

During the hajj, pilgrims throng Mecca, the men clad in two seamless white garments and sandals, the women in white head-to-toe covering. The pilgrims walk seven times around the Ka'ba, a cubical stone building covered by a gold-embroidered black canopy, in the exterior wall of which is set the Black Stone. The interior, now empty, once housed pagan idols, which Muhammad destroyed. The pilgrims also visit other holy sites, act out the search for water by Hagar, the mother of the Arab nation, perform a vigil on Mount 'Arafat (site of the Prophet's last sermon) and conduct a ritual sacrifice of goats, sheep and camels.

___

*By the Islamic calendar, this is the year 1399, dated from Muhammad's Hegira to Medina.

The devout Muslim is also expected to observe the Shari'a, which means "the path to follow." Based on the Koran, the deeds and sayings of Muhammad and the consensus of Islamic scholars, the Shari'a is not just a compilation of criminal and civil law, but a complex, all embracing code of ethics, morality and religious duties. It is a sophisticated system of jurisprudence that summarizes 1,400 years of experience and constantly adapts, in subtle ways, to new circumstances.

In Western eyes, however, the Shari'a all too often is denigrated as a relic of the Dark Ages. Some of its provisions do seem awesomely harsh: habitual thieves are punished by having a hand cut off; adulterers are either scourged or stoned to death; falsely accusing a woman of adultery calls for 80 lashes—the same penalty imposed on a Muslim caught drinking alcohol. The equivalence of the two punishments exemplifies the time-honored logic of the Shari'a. The Koran forbade the drinking of wine, but did not specify a punishment; 80 lashes, however, was decreed for those who bore false witness. Making the analogy that drink leads to hallucination and to telling untruths, Islamic sages decided that the punishment for the two sins should be the same.

Muslim jurists contend that stoning is no more typical of Islamic justice than extra-tough state laws against the possession of drugs are representative of the American legal tradition. Beyond that, the threat of the Shari'a is usually more severe than the reality. As in Western common law, defendants are presumed innocent until proved guilty. To convict adulterers, four witnesses must be found to testify that they saw the illicit act performed. Moreover, there are loopholes in the law and liberal as well as strict interpretations of it. For example, a thief can lose his hand only if he steals "in a just society"; the provision has been used by Islamic courts to spare men who steal because they are poor and have no other means to feed their families.

In Iran particularly, the reintroduction of the Shari'a under an Islamic republic is seen as a threat to rights that women won under the monarchy. Feminists do have reason to complain. Islamic law tolerates polygamy, so long as a husband treats his wives equally, and he can end a marriage simply by saying "I divorce thee" three times in front of witnesses. A woman may request a divorce under certain circumstances—for example, if she is mistreated or her husband is impotent. Women must dress modestly, and their inheritance is limited to a fraction of that of men. In defense of these sexist inequities, scholars of the Shari'a note that Islamic law was advanced for its time. Before Muhammad, women in Arabia were mere chattel. The Koran emphatically asserts a husband's duty to support his wife (or wives), who are allowed to keep their dowries and to own property—rights that did not emerge until much later in Western countries.

All Muslims accept the Koran as God's eternal word, but Islam to some extent is a house divided, although its divisions are not as extensive as those in Christianity. About 90% of all Muslims are Sunnis (from *sunna,* "the tradition of the Prophet"), who consider themselves Islam's orthodoxy. In Iran and Iraq, the majority of Muslims are Shi'ites ("partisans" of 'Ali), who differ from the Sunnis in some of their interpretations of the Shari'a and in their understanding of Muhammad's succession. The Prophet left no generally recognized instructions on how the leadership of Islam would be settled after his death. The Sunnis believe that its leader should be nominated by representatives of the community and confirmed by a general oath of allegiance. Shi'ites contend that Muhammad's spiritual authority was passed on to his cousin and son-in-law, 'Ali, and certain of his direct descendants who were known as Imams. Most Iranian Shi'ites believe that 'Ali's twelfth successor, who disappeared mysteriously in 878, is still alive and will return some day as the Mahdi (the Divinely Appointed Guide), a Messiah-like leader who will establish God's kingdom on earth. Meanwhile, Shi'ite religious leaders, such as Iran's Ayatullah Khomeini, have wide powers to advise the faithful on the presumed will of the "Hidden Imam." Sunni religious scholars, the ulama, have less authority, though both branches of Islam consider their leaders to be teachers and sages rather than ordained clergymen in the Western sense.

Both Sunni and Shi'ite Islam include Sufism, a mystical movement whose adherents seek to serve God not simply through obedience to the law but by striving for union with him through meditation and ritual. Sufism is considered suspect by fundamentalist Muslims like the puritanical Wahhabis of Saudi Arabia, because it allows for the veneration of *awliya*—roughly the equivalent of

Christianity's saints. Islam also has spawned a number of heretical offshoots. One is the Alawi sect, a Shi'ite minority group to which most of Syria's leaders belong. The Alawis believe in the transmigration of souls and a kind of trinity in which 'Ali is Allah incarnate. Another is the secretive Druze sect of Israel, Lebanon and Syria, which split away from Islam in the 11th century. America's so-called Black Muslims were once generally regarded by Sunni Muslims as followers of a new heresy. By adopting orthodox beliefs and discarding a rule that limited membership to black Americans, the World Community of Islam in the West, as the movement is now known, has been accepted as being part of the true faith.

Islam is not a collection of individual souls but a spiritual community; its sectarian divisions, as well as the man-made barriers of race and class that Islam opposes, dissolve dramatically at the hajj. Once a pilgrimage made mostly by Muslims of the Middle East and North Africa, the hajj has become a universal and unifying ritual. For those who have taken part in it, the hajj acts as a constant testament to Islam's vision of a divine power that transcends all human frailties.

SOME SAYINGS FROM A HOLY BOOK

The grandeur of the Koran is difficult to convey in English translation. Although Islam's Holy Book is considered God's precise word only in Arabic, a generally recognized English text is that of Abdullah Yusuf 'Ali.

THE OPENING PRAYER. In the name of God, Most Gracious, Most Merciful. Praise be to God, the Cherisher and Sustainer of the Worlds; Most Gracious, Most Merciful; Master of the Day of Judgment. Thee do we worship, and Thine aid we seek. Show us the straight way, the way of those on whom Thou hast bestowed Thy Grace, those whose (portion) is not wrath, and who go not astray.

THE NATURE OF GOD. God! There is no god but He—the Living, the Self-subsisting, Eternal. No slumber can seize Him, nor sleep. His are all things in the heavens and on earth. Who is there can intercede in His presence except as He permitteth? He knoweth what (ap-

peareth to His creatures as) Before or After or Behind them. Nor shall they compass aught of His knowledge except as He willeth. His Throne doth extend over the heavens and the earth, and He feeleth no fatigue in guarding and preserving them.

DRINKING AND GAMBLING. They ask thee concerning wine and gambling. Say: "In them is great sin, and some profit, for men: but the sin is greater than the profit."

THEFT. Male or female, cut off his or her hands: a punishment by way of example, from God, for their crime: and God is Exalted in Power. But if the thief repent after his crime, and amend his conduct, God turneth to him in forgiveness; for God is Oft-forgiving, Most Merciful.

POLYGAMY. If ye fear that ye shall not be able to deal justly with the orphans, marry women of your choice, two, or three, or four; but if ye fear that ye shall not be able to deal justly (with them) then only one, or (a captive) that your right hands possess.

CHRISTIANS. They do blaspheme who say: "God is Christ the son of Mary." But said Christ: "O Children of Israel! Worship God, my Lord and your Lord." Whoever joins other gods with God—God will forbid him the Garden, and the Fire will be his abode.

THE DAY OF JUDGMENT. When the sun is folded up; when the stars fall, losing their lustre; when the mountains vanish; when the she-camels, ten months with young, are left untended; when the wild beasts are herded together; when the oceans boil over with a swell; . . . when the World on High is unveiled; when the Blazing Fire is kindled to fierce heat; and when the Garden is brought near;—(Then) shall each soul know what it has put forward.

PARADISE. (Here is) a Parable of the Garden which the righteous are promised: In it are rivers of water incorruptible; rivers of milk of which the taste never changes; rivers of wine, a joy to those who drink; and rivers of honey pure and clear. In it there are for them all kinds of fruit, and Grace from their Lord. (Can those in such bliss) be compared to such as shall dwell forever in the

Fire, and be given, to drink, boiling water, so that it cuts up their bowels?

ISLAM, ORIENTALISM AND THE WEST

An attack on learned ignorance

In an angry, provocative new book called Orientalism *(Pantheon; $15), Edward Said, 43, Parr Professor of English and Comparative Literature at Columbia University, argues that the West has tended to define Islam in terms of the alien categories imposed on it by Orientalist scholars. Professor Said is a member of the Palestine National Council, a broadly based, informal parliament of the Palestine Liberation Organization. He summarized the thesis of* Orientalism *in this article.*

One of the strangest, least examined and most persistent of human habits is the absolute division made between East and West, Orient and Occident. Almost entirely "Western" in origin, this imaginative geography that splits the world into two unequal, fundamentally opposite spheres has brought forth more myths, more detailed ignorance and more ambitions than any other perception of difference. For centuries Europeans and Americans have spellbound themselves with Oriental mysticism, Oriental passivity, Oriental mentalities. Translated into policy, displayed as knowledge, presented as entertainment in travelers' reports, novels, paintings, music or films, this "Orientalism" has existed virtually unchanged as a kind of daydream that could often justify Western colonial adventures or military conquest. On the "Marvels of the East" (as the Orient was known in the Middle Ages) a fantastic edifice was constructed, invested heavily with Western fear, desire, dreams of power and, of course, a very partial knowledge. And placed in this structure has been "Islam," a great religion and a culture certainly, but also an Occidental myth, part of what Disraeli once called "the great Asiatic mystery."

As represented for Europe by Muhammad and his followers, Islam appeared out of Arabia in the 7th century and rapidly spread in all directions. For almost a millennium Christian Europe felt itself challenged (as indeed it was) by this last monotheistic religion, which claimed

to complete its two predecessors. Perplexingly grand and "Oriental," incorporating elements of Judeo-Christianity, Islam never fully submitted to the West's power. Its various states and empires always provided the West with formidable political and cultural contestants—and with opportunities to affirm a "superior" Occidental identity. Thus, for the West, to understand Islam has meant trying to convert its variety into a monolithic undeveloping essence, its originality into a debased copy of Christian culture, its people into fearsome caricatures.

Early Christian polemicists against Islam used the Prophet's human person as their butt, accusing him of whoring, sedition, charlatanry. As writing about Islam and the Orient burgeoned—60,000 books between 1800 and 1950—European powers occupied large swatches of "Islamic" territory, arguing that since Orientals knew nothing about democracy and were essentially passive, it was the "civilizing mission" of the Occident, expressed in the strict programs of despotic modernization, to finally transform the Orient into a nice replica of the West. Even Marx seems to have believed this.

There were, however, great Orientalist scholars; there were genuine attempts, like that of Richard Burton (British explorer who translated the *Arabian Nights*), at coming to terms with Islam. Still, gross ignorance persisted, as it will whenever fear of the different gets translated into attempts at domination. The U.S. inherited the Orientalist legacy, and uncritically employed it in its universities, mass media, popular culture, imperial policy. In films and cartoons, Muslim Arabs, for example, are represented either as bloodthirsty mobs, or as hook-nosed, lecherous sadists. Academic experts decreed that in Islam everything is Islamic, which amounted to the edifying notions that there was such a thing as an "Islamic mind," that to understand the politics of Algeria one had best consult the Koran, that "they" (the Muslims) had no understanding of democracy, only of repression and medieval obscurantism. Conversely, it was argued that so long as repression was in the U.S. interest, it was not Islamic but a form of modernization.

The worst misjudgments followed. As recently as 1967 the head of the Middle East Studies Association wrote a report for the Department of Health, Education and Welfare asserting that the region including the Middle East and North

Africa was not a center of cultural achievement, nor was it likely to become one in the near future. The study of the region or its languages, therefore, did not constitute its own reward so far as modern culture is concerned. High school textbooks routinely produced descriptions of Islam like the following: "It was started by a wealthy businessman of Arabia called Muhammad. He claimed that he was a prophet. He found followers among other Arabs. He told them that they were picked to rule the world." Whether Palestinian Arabs lost their land and political rights to Zionism, or Iranian poets were tortured by the SAVAK, little time was spent in the West wondering if Muslims suffered pain, would resist oppression or experienced love and joy: to Westerners, "they" were different from "us" since Orientals did not feel about life as "we" did.

No one saw that Islam varied from place to place, subject to both history and geography. Islam was unhesitatingly considered to be an abstraction, never an experience. No one bothered to judge Muslims in political, social, anthropological terms that were vital and nuanced, rather than crude and provocative. Suddenly it appeared that "Islam" was back when Ayatullah Khomeini, who derives from a long tradition of opposition to an outrageous monarchy, stood on his national, religious and political legitimacy as an Islamic righteous man. Menachem Begin took himself to be speaking for the West when he said he feared this return to the Middle Ages, even as he covered Israeli occupation of Arab land with Old Testament authorizations. Western leaders worried about their oil, so little appreciated by the Islamic hordes who thronged the streets to topple the Light of the Aryans.

Were Orientalists at last beginning to wonder about their "Islam," which they said had taught the faithful never to resist unlawful tyranny, never to prize any values over sex and money, never to disturb fate? Did anyone stop to doubt that F-15 planes were the answer to all our worries about "Islam"? Was Islamic punishment, which tantalized the press, more irreducibly vicious than, say, napalming Asian peasants?

We need understanding to note that repression is not principally Islamic or Oriental but a reprehensible aspect of the human phenomenon. "Islam" cannot explain everything in Africa and Asia, just as "Christianity" cannot explain Chile or

South Africa. If Iranian workers, Egyptian students, Palestinian farmers resent the West or the U.S., it is a concrete response to a specific policy injuring them as human beings. Certainly a European or American would be entitled to feel that the Islamic multitudes are underdeveloped; but he would also have to concede that underdevelopment is a relative cultural and economic judgment and not mainly "Islamic" in nature.

Under the vast idea called Islam, which the faithful look to for spiritual nourishment in their numerous ways, an equally vast, rich life passes, as detailed and as complex as any. For comprehension of that life Westerners need what Orientalist Scholar Louis Massignon called a science of compassion, knowledge without domination, common sense not mythology. In Iran and elsewhere Islam has not simply "returned"; it has always been there, not as an abstraction or a war cry but as part of a way people believe, give thanks, have courage and so on. Will it not ease our fear to accept the fact that people do the same things inside as well as outside Islam, that Muslims live in history and in our common world, not simply in the Islamic context?

CHARLES MALAMOUD

talks to Tony Lévy

The French scholar Charles
Malamoud, a specialist in the
history and religions of India,
describes in this interview the
characteristics of Vedism and
Hinduism, the great Indian
religions, as revealed in their
scriptures, rites and gods. A
linguist by training, Malamoud
started his career by studying the
Sanskrit language before turning
his attention to the Sanskrit
classics and in particular to the
patterns of thought underlying the
oldest of these, the *Veda*. His
published works include *Le
Svâdhyâya, récitation personnelle
du Veda, Taīttirîya-Aranyaka II*
(Boccard, Paris, 1977), *Lien de
vie, nœud mortel, les
représentations de la dette en
Chine, au Japon et dans le monde
Indien* (EHESS, Paris, 1988) and
*Cuire le monde, Rite et pensée
dans l'Inde ancienne*
(La Découverte, Paris, 1989).

■ *Could you give an overview of the religious history of India?*

—If you leave aside the so-called Indus Valley civilizations, which are only known to us through rather scanty material remains that are difficult to interpret and even to date—I'm thinking of the sites of Moenjodaro and Harappa, from the third millennium B.C.—the religious history of India can be divided, in a very schematic way, into a "Vedic" period, from about 1500 to 500 B.C., and a "Hindu" period, starting in about 500 B.C. and continuing to the present day. These dates are intended as no more than a rough guide.

■ *Have other religions been involved?*

—Indeed. Two movements that took the form of a critique of Vedism and Hinduism made their appearance in India around 500 B.C. On the one hand there was Buddhism, a universally-minded religion (perhaps it would be more accurate to describe it as a world view) founded by the Buddha, a legendary figure who probably also really existed. Then there was Jainism, founded by another half-real, half-mythical figure, Mahavira, the Jina. Buddhism was to play a major cultural and philosophical role in India, but it disappeared almost entirely from the mainland by about 1000 A.D., while spreading to and taking root in the Himalaya region, Sri Lanka, and central, east and south-east Asia. Jainism was confined to India, where it has survived to the present day. Jainists now make up a small, prosperous and well-organized minority of the Indian population.

Another major event in Indian history was the conquest of much of the sub-continent by Muslims from Iran and Afghanistan, again around the year 1000 A.D. Once they had seized power, the conquerors made many converts—so many that Islam became one of the great religions of the subcontinent. After Inde-

pendence and Partition in 1947, Pakistan, later to be divided in its turn when its eastern part became Bangladesh, was set up as an almost entirely Muslim state. But in the Indian Union itself, 10 per cent of the population are Muslim, which means more than 100 million people today. Another religion that came from outside is Christianity in its various forms, which began to be introduced into India by Europeans in the sixteenth century.

But the most ancient and characteristic religion of India, the one that can be said to be indigenous to the country, is the Vedic-Hindu complex. It has by far the greatest number of adherents, and it is the faith most closely linked to traditional Indian ways of thought and forms of social organization.

■ *How are Vedism and Hinduism linked?*

—Well, Vedism and Hinduism are two successive phases or aspects of the same religion rather than two separate religions. To put it another way, there was never a clean break between Vedism and Hinduism, for all their very obvious differences and even contradictions. There wasn't even a deliberate or consciously undertaken movement of radical reform. Even now in very orthodox circles, Vedism is still considered the source of Hinduism and its ultimate authority, as valid now as ever.

What's more, there is a third term in the vocabulary of historians of religion that underlines the continuity between Vedism and Hinduism. This is the word "Brahmanism". It has more than one meaning, referring both to the form of religion codified in the texts known as the *Brahmana*, which date from the end of the Vedic period, and also to the orthodox core of early Hinduism.

■ *Does each phase have its own scriptures?*

—Vedism is known to us through the vast

corpus of texts called the *Veda*. These were composed at various dates between 1500 and 500 B.C. There is no similar body of literature for Hinduism proper—certainly not one that is as clearly defined or that carries the same authority. Even so, as the word "epico-Puranic" that is sometimes applied to Hinduism suggests, the two great epics of the *Mahabharata* and the *Ramayana*, along with the vast mass of encyclopaedic writings known as the *Purana*, are in a certain sense the sacred books of Hinduism, containing ideas that all Hindus accept. These epics were composed in the closing centuries of the 1st millennium B.C., the *Purana* about a thousand years later. These dates are approximate.

■ *Where does the Bhagavad Gita fit in?*
—It's a fragment of the *Mahabharata*.

■ *Is there any link between the* Purana *and the Vedic hymns?*
—They belong to two very different literary forms, and their content is also different. The *Veda* is often quoted in the *Purana*, and is spoken of with reverence. But the *Purana* (the term means "antiquities") are first and foremost creation myths and genealogies of gods and men, mixed with dissertations on cosmology, ritual, social organization, summaries of various sciences, descriptions of places of pilgrimage and so on. Some of these elements also exist in the Vedic corpus, but the format and the diction, if I may use that word, are quite different. The *Purana* are long-winded, jumbled, loosely expressed. The Vedic hymns, on the other hand, are dense, profound, often hermetic: they are great poetry.

■ *Could you describe the* Veda *more precisely?*
—As I said, the *Veda* is a corpus of texts. It is our only source of information about India from 1500 to 500 B.C. There are no other written sources, no external evidence, no archaeological remains to speak of. The texts themselves are composite, varying greatly in age, content and form. Yet they are all linked, the latest elements presupposing a knowledge of the earlier ones, since they quote them. But orthodox Hindus today see the *Veda* as homogeneous, in the sense that they regard the whole work as a revealed text. The revelation concerns gods as well as human beings, and although it was not delivered in one piece it does not assume a chronological framework implying a before and after.

■ *In using the word "revealed" you suggest comparisons with other religions founded on holy scripture.*
—There is a great difference between the *Veda* and revelation in the religions based on the Bible. The *Veda* is not generally viewed as the word of a god addressed to humanity but as a text outside of time that exists of itself and reveals itself by itself. Strictly speaking, the *Veda* has no author. But men of exceptionally powerful vision "saw"—that is the word that is used—different fragments, different versions of the text, put their vision into words and passed it on to other men. These visionaries are known as *rishi*, a word usually translated as "seer".

Yet even though the revelation has been "seen", the *Veda* is primarily sound-oriented. It is a collection or sequence of sounds formed into meaningful words. The text of the *Veda* is a manifestation of the word; words are oral, made up of the sounds of language, and all their power comes from vibrations of the sound-waves. Furthermore rhythm, as determined by the number of syllables and the arrangement of long and short syllables, plays an important part in the symbolism of the work. A final point: the usual word to designate the *Veda* as revelation is *çruti*, literally "hearing".

What is so extraordinary about the Vedic revelation, then, is that the knowledge it contains (for *veda* means "to know") was "seen", yet it consists of sounds. Nor can one resolve the paradox by imagining that the "seers" viewed a written text they subsequently translated into spoken words, for the very notion of writing is completely foreign to the *Veda*. Even in later times when India had writing, the very idea that the *Veda* could be learned otherwise than by repeating the words of a master was vigorously rejected.

■ *Does this Word without an author have its own specific intercessor?*
—Only the *rishi*, the seers who transmitted the text to humankind through the medium of sound. But they are not strictly speaking intercessors, for they only put the *Veda* into words, rather than interpreting it. What's more, there is no question of them operating in the other direction by transmitting the thoughts or desires of human beings to the *Veda*. They are simply the mouthpiece of the *Veda*. The *Veda* is a text they discover and

that was there before them, not one they have shaped themselves.

■ *So it is an oral message that over the centuries has been committed to writing and transmitted in written form. How much do we know about the transmission process?*
—We don't know exactly when or how India acquired writing. The oldest inscriptions date from the third century B.C., and their technique is so fine as to indicate a long previous history. But there is no doubt that the corpus of Vedic texts, or at least the oldest part of it, was constituted and transmitted from generation to generation over many centuries without the aid of writing. And I would repeat that even when writing became common in India, even when the *Veda* could be written down, the text was still usually passed on orally from master to pupil. To all intents and purposes this process continued until our own day. Studying the Veda means learning it by heart by repeating it after the master. Highly elaborate techniques are used to memorize such long and difficult texts. But then even scholars for whom reading and writing are everyday activities habitually learn religious and even non-religious texts they consider important by heart, however long these texts may be.

■ *How would you describe the Vedic corpus itself?*
—Two principal layers can be discerned in the text. The older consists of collections of poems in the form of prayers, or more often hymns, glorifying a god or a group of gods, or the sacrificial act and its various elements, or the people who carry it out. The most important of these collections is the *Rig-Veda*, the "Veda of Laudatory Stanzas", which comprises about a thousand poems. The other important group is the *Atharva-Veda*, part of which consists of magical texts. One of the main themes of the Vedic hymns is a celebration of the power of the word, which means ultimately a celebration of Vedic poetry by the *Veda* itself. The hymns are composed in an archaic form of Sanskrit. The style is often obscure, marked by figures of speech, particularly metaphors, of great power and boldness.

The more recent layer consists of the prose treatises known as the *Brahmana*, which explain what the various sacrificial rites of the Vedic religion are and how they should be understood. They provide liturgical instruction, but also information on the symbolism of the rites and on their links with mythology. Furthermore, since the performance of the rites calls for the recitation, in whole or in part, of Vedic poems, the *Brahmana* explain why specific ritual gestures are associated with specific texts. In this respect, the *Brahmana* can be considered as a commentary on the Vedic poems.

The *Brahmana* themselves have appendices, the *Upanishads*. The *Upanishads* come right at the end of Vedic literature, and Indians like to say that they contain the *Veda*'s deepest meaning. The content of the *Upanishads* consists of speculations whose starting-point is a meditation on ritual. But this meditation ends by going beyond ritualism: rituals are no longer considered in themselves but as symbols of the cosmos and of the organization of the spirit. This "meta-ritualism" lays the foundations for a metaphysical world view.

To sum up, the hymns, the *Brahmana* and the *Upanishads* jointly make up the Vedic revelation.

To make learning and understanding the *Veda* easier, India developed very early on, towards the end of the Vedic period, auxiliary sciences known as the *Vedanga*, literally "members" added to the body of the Veda. These are phonetics, grammar, etymology, astrology, the study of metre, and the analysis and use of ritual. Despite their Vedic origins, some at least of these disciplines came to be studied for their own sake and became non-religious fields of study.

One should add that literal commentaries exist for most of the Vedic texts. These are for the most part quite late, but they are considered authoritative.

■ *The word* brahman *seems to crystallize certain links, particularly the necessary one between the divine word and human speech.*

—The word *brahman* is without any doubt the most mysterious in the Sanskrit language. In the speculative tradition that begins with the *Upanishads*, *brahman* links up with *atman*. The *brahman*, the Absolute of the universe, corresponds to the *atman*, which is the Self, the Absolute as revealed in the reflexivity of the individual soul.

The term *brahman* lies at the root of a whole complex of derivations that need some

explanation. First and foremost we have the word *brahman* itself, which is neuter in gender. Its principal meaning is "essential content of the *Veda*". Because the Vedic poems contain many statements in the form of riddles, *brahman* also comes to have the secondary meaning of "riddle" or "enigma".

The first derivation is *brahman*, gender masculine, which designates men who are particularly well-versed in knowledge and use of the neuter *brahman* in its first sense. In Vedic ritual the *brahman* is the priest whose job is to check that exactly the right formulas are employed. As the "doctor of the sacrifice" he says next to nothing but is, as it were, the incarnation of the Vedic text on the sacrificial ground. In post-Vedic Hinduism, Brahman in its masculine form can also be a proper name, for Brahman or Brahma is one of the great gods who, with Vishnu and Shiva, makes up the supreme triad, the triple figuration known as *Trimurti*.

Then there's the word *Brahmana*, which means "that which has reference to *brahman*" and designates the sacrificial treatises I spoke of earlier. *Brahmana* has another meaning in Sanskrit, and that is what we think of when we use the word "brahmin", which is to say a man born into the highest of the four "classes" of the Indian social hierarchy, the priestly one. Brahmanism is the religion that considers the brahmins to be the repositories of Vedic knowledge, and that they alone are entitled to officiate during sacrifices.

■ *Can one say that the* Veda *created the world?*
—Yes, certainly. The role of the Vedic texts in the Creation is one of the themes of the *Veda*. It is both a poetic motif and a principle of the Vedic religion.

■ *How does sacrifice fit into what might be called the geography of the sacred?*
—The sacrificial rite is one element among others in the Vedic religion. Not all Vedic ritual is sacrifice, just as not all the religion is ritual. It is true, though, that sacrifice is the main subject of the Vedic texts, and their expositions of mythology and the creation of the universe, their speculations on the correspondences between the macrocosm and the microcosm and so on, are presented in the context of sacrificial instructions. They also tend to analyse such other rites as prayer,

funerals and marriages as though they too were forms of sacrifice, organized in the same way and with the same division of roles between the participants.

Furthermore, as Louis Renou has pointed out, one can see the idea developing that the Vedic compilations are nothing more than collections of mantras, forms of words to recite during ceremonies. The gestures and objects involved in rites become sacred and effective insofar as they are "sacralized" by the recitation of appropriate mantras.

It should be said that the clearest and most vigorous creation stories present genesis itself as a sacrifice, with the different elements of the cosmos and of society coming from the dismemberment of a primordial victim, and also that the core of Vedic mythology hinges on the efforts made by the gods to take possession of the sacrificial procedures and instruments or to put them to their own exclusive use.

But another characteristic of Vedic civilization is that it produced thinkers, true intellectuals in my view, who reflected on the formal structure of the sacrifice, on the way in which the various parts are linked and on how all the acts of which it consists are joined and separated. And since you mentioned "geography", I would add that sacrifices take place in the open, in a space equipped with fire-altars and poles. Vedic ritualists devised a whole system of geometry to make sure that this equipment is set up in conformity with the canons of shape and size. Yet the sites themselves are considered "abstract", in the sense that we know of none that was marked out to serve exclusively as the stage for any particular rite.

■ *To whom are the sacrifices offered up?*
—To the gods or, using different procedures, to ancestors. There is a whole mythology of sacrifice, which can itself be seen as a divine being, just as the word can. Various gods of the Vedic pantheon have a double aspect, a twofold reality. For instance fire—*Agni*—is both a god to whom prayers are addressed and the flame lit in the altars to receive offerings. Soma is a god, but also a plant whose juice is considered the drink of immortality and is therefore itself offered up to the immortal ones.

Vedic speculation, particularly in the *Brahmana*, tends to suggest that the gods depend on the sacrifices made to them and in a sense are even raised up by these sacrifices. The right order of the world, prosperity in our present existence and salvation in the after-life can all be achieved by correct execution of rites, much more than by any kind of divine acquiescence or grace.

■ *If sacrifice, in conjunction with the word, helped to create the world and even the gods themselves, is it possible to say that there are established correspondences between the macrocosm and the microcosm, the divine and human worlds?*

—Yes, such correspondences exist, but it is up to humans to discover them, to become aware of them, to formulate them—and in so doing, to confirm them. Solving the Vedic riddles I referred to earlier, which are one of the aspects of *brahman*, involves linking similar elements from the different levels of existence. There are not just two of these, but more often three: the level of the gods, which is that of the cosmos; the level of the individual human being (body and soul); and, between the two of them, the ritual level. A ritual object, a particular moment in a ceremony, is thought to have a replica or counterpart in some specific spatial or temporal element of the universe, and also in some aspect of human activity or an organ of the human body.

This network of correspondences is not static. The Vedic authors, particularly in the *Upanishads*, give much thought to finding new, more refined and complex equivalences. Several Sanskrit words convey this idea, words that mean "connection", "link", even "kinship". In Vedic India the idea of correspondences is more important than the concept of causality—whereas Buddhism insists on the sequence of cause and effect. Louis Renou admirably clarified the difference between Vedism and Buddhism on this point in one of the articles collected in his book *L'Inde fondamentale*, which came out in 1978.

■ *What differentiates Hinduism from the Vedic religion?*

—We've already noted the differences with relation to the nature and status of the holy writings. If we turn to religious beliefs and practices, and first and foremost to the pantheon of gods, we find that some Vedic gods survive into Hinduism, though in a weaker and more obscure form, while others disappear completely. On the other hand, gods that play only a secondary role in the *Veda* move to centre-stage. Vishnu and Shiva are the principal Hindu gods, co-existent and venerated by all believers. But Hindus divide into "sects" devoted to different aspects of Vishnu or Shiva, for another important characteristic of Hinduism is that there are an infinite number of divinities, but each is a special manifestation of one of the principal gods.

This is where the doctrine of avatars comes in. At different times, depending on the cosmic problems he had undertaken to resolve, the god Vishnu made himself manifest by "descending" to Earth in various guises, while always remaining himself. Each of the personalities he adopted, and there are canonical lists of these, has a mythology built around it and is the object of a specific cult. Rama and Krishna, for example, who are both gods and heroes, are among the avatars of Vishnu. It is extraordinary that these avatars, destined to intervene in cosmic eras earlier than our own, are still the object of fervent devotion today. I would also point out that the theory of cosmic cycles, and the division of each cycle into a similar number of successive eras separated from one another by catastrophes, is also a Hindu innovation.

Unlike the Vedic gods, who are primarily receivers of offerings, the Hindu gods are seen as beings with whom humans can have an intense emotional relationship. One of the most remarkable aspects of Hinduism is the appearance, in about the sixth or seventh century A.D., of the concept of *bhakti*, or fusional devotion, according to which worshippers seek to be absorbed into and fused with the divinity they adore. Unity with the god is the expected outcome of the love they bear and the grace they hope for.

The Hindu conception of divinity is both the cause and the effect of forms of worship that are unknown to the *Veda*. In Hinduism gods are represented by images—or, more accurately, they are present, alive and active, in the images that represent them. These images are permanently housed in sanctuaries or temples, clearly defined places where they are the masters.

The gods are present in every image of themselves, but this presence has different degrees of completeness and intensity, so that there is a kind of hierarchy among images. Worship consists of treating the image as a living person whom one can contemplate, revere and care for, and whose goodwill one hopes to win. In Hinduism devotion to the image of a god in his sanctuary or temple occupies the place that the sacrificial rite held in Vedism. Not that Hinduism did away with sacrifices entirely; it shifted them from the centre of life and religious thought and gave them a secondary role.

■ *What is asked of the Hindu gods?*

—The things of this world, first and foremost: health, prosperity, above all offspring. Wisdom and all kinds of success. On a wider scale, the gods are expected to provide good harvests, the normal round of the seasons, order in society and the world. But also personal salvation in the after-life. And this raises the question of what salvation is and what it is that one needs to be saved from. The answer is: from unpleasant forms of life after death. People want to avoid hell and go to heaven. Such a desire was already expressed in Vedism. When Hinduism emerged, however, a new concept was added, and that was the famous doctrine of *karma* (or *karman*).

The idea is that people are caught up in an endless stream of successive lives. Death is simply the unending passage from one life to the next. The type of existence a person enters at the end of each life is determined by his or her actions in previous lives. Which is to say that we always have the life we deserve. If it is pleasant, it is to allow us to enjoy the fruits of meritorious acts accomplished in some previous existence. If it is disagreeable, it is the result of bad deeds committed in past lives.

One's *karma* or stock of acts is of course constantly renewed, as long as one passes through lives in which taking action of some sort is unavoidable. But Indian Hindus see the necessity of rebirth in a series of lives that are always deserved, through the workings of an autonomous mechanism, as a misfortune or rather as a state of subjection from which they seek release. Salvation in the context of *karma* is not a matter of seeking to obtain a happy life in a heavenly abode after death, for such a destiny would itself inevitably be temporary. Real salvation lies in deliverance, the possibility of reaching the end of this mechanism and so concluding the process of rebirth.

■ *How can this be brought about?*

—It can only be achieved by individuals who have exhausted their *karma* by various methods that involve on the one hand a very difficult process of mental awakening and on the other various kinds of asceticism. As to the condition of those who achieve deliverance and the attitude to be adopted towards them, different schools have different views, though none has very much to say on the matter. In popular Hinduism, however, deliverance is thought to lead to eternal happiness, which is another blessing expected from the gods, or more accurately from the god one entrusts oneself to in *bhakti.*

In speaking of Hinduism I have concentrated on what distinguishes it from Vedism, and I have also stressed the great diversity of beliefs, doctrines and forms of worship contained within it. But I should also point out that from a different viewpoint what is striking is the continuity of certain fundamental principles that are always present. These include the idea that there is an order that englobes nature as well as society. The division of society into "classes" is not a human institution but a fact associated with the structure of the cosmos. Since the individual soul subjected to the laws of *karma* passes not only through human existences but also those of animals and gods, one might well ask if there is anything special about the role humankind plays in the cosmos. In fact it is distinguished from all the other life-forms by the fact that only humans act in such a way as to produce *karma.*

■ *Buddhism is thought to have emerged from Brahmanism around the fifth or sixth century B.C. What are the links, and the differences, between Brahmanism and Buddhism?*

—It is by no means certain that Buddhism did grow out of Brahmanism, nor that it should be explained as a deviation or an innovation in relation to a pre-exisiting Brahmanic faith, even though this is often said. It might be more accurate to think that Buddhism is rooted in the religious traditions of the eastern part of the Ganges Valley, a region which was perhaps not exclusively given over to Brahmanism.

It is true nevertheless that the Buddhist texts presuppose the existence of Brahmanic society and religion and are in fact a critique of certain Brahmanic concepts. But the fact that the Brahmanic texts are in Sanskrit, while the earliest Buddhist texts are in Pali, a Middle Indo-Aryan language, is evidence of early Buddhism's autonomy of Brahmanism.

The distinctive characteristic of early Buddhism seems to be the belief that suffering is ever-present, and that it is linked to the impermanent nature of things. One has to become aware of suffering, recognize its causes and discover the means of deliverance from it. From that flows a sentiment of universal compassion, and a critique of both the Brahmanic rites and the pretentions of the brahmans, the masters of ritual. Then again,

Buddhism is the creation of a human founder who lived in a known time and place. The story of his life, his ordeals, the way he was "illuminated" by the truth, his efforts to build up the community of his first disciples—all these events make up a story that is an essential part of Buddhist doctrine.

■ *Without forcing the comparison, what would you say about the similarities and differences between Vedism and Hinduism and the religions of the Book?*

—I wouldn't overemphasize the gap between Indian polytheism and the monotheism of the religions of the Book. There is a difference, obviously, but stressing it tends to lead to oversimplification. On the one hand one could point to the divine plurality of Christianity; on the other to the idea, so often repeated by Hindus, that all their countless gods are only aspects of a single God. What seems more important to me is that for the religions of the Book, human beings are radically different from the rest of creation. Humanity is destined to have a history, and that history is oriented and punctuated by successive moments of revelation. We've seen that in Vedism and Hinduism humanity and society cannot be said to have existed before the event of revelation—and that revelation cannot even properly be described as an event. In my view, the most significant difference between the two groups of religions lies in this relationship to time.

The Koran, Gita, and Tripitaka

Islam, Hinduism, and Buddhism have their own distinct approaches to their sacred writings

Thomas B. Coburn

Special to The Christian Science Monitor. *Thomas B. Coburn is Charles A. Dana professor of religious studies and classical languages at St. Lawrence University in Canton, N.Y.*

Since all of the world's major religious traditions have produced written documents, it is possible and legitimate to ask: What are the equivalents of the Christian Bible in those different traditions? What and where are the historic copies of their scriptures?

Answers to these questions, however, quickly indicate not only the expected diversity of documents, but also very different *significances* that have been ascribed to the documents.

The written word does not always have the same function in the lives of Buddhists, Hindus, Muslims or others as it does for Christians—even acknowledging that there is variety among Christians themselves.

Verbal literacy has been variously valued in different times and places, and the unique authority that Christians, particularly Protestants, ascribe to a book is elsewhere: in a charismatic individual, in certain ritual behavior, in a self-authenticating mystical experience.

In short, to ask a seemingly simple and obvious question is to move immediately into the fascinating field of the comparative study of religion.

Questioning our assumptions

The first step in attempting to answer these questions is to reexamine the assumptions that lead us to ask them.

As William A. Graham, a historian of religion, has noted, we in the modern West "stand on this side of the epochal transition accomplished to large degree by about 1800 in the urban culture of Western Europe, and now still in progress elsewhere, from a scribal . . . and still significantly oral culture to a print-dominated . . . primarily visual culture. Our alphabetic 'book culture,' like our 'book religion,' is not even the same as the 'book culture' (or 'book religion') of sixteenth- or seventeenth-century Europe, let alone that of classical antiquity, the Medieval or Renaissance West, or the great literary civilizations of Asia past and present."

It is therefore impossible for us to find any "book religions" precisely parallel with those of the modern West, because the quite specific conditions that have produced our "book culture" have not existed elsewhere.

Even as literacy rises around the globe, its significance is shaped by local cultural factors, which are virtually always very different from those of European and American life of the past two centuries.

The following brief overview of Muslim, Hindu, and Buddhist "Bibles," therefore, can only hint at what the relevant documents are—and at the more interesting and complex matter of their religious significance for those who value them.

Islam: the 'corrective' scripture

The Muslim situation is closest to that of Jews and Christians, and for good reason: The religion of Islam sees itself as the fulfillment of the two older traditions, which, like Islam, are rooted in the faith of Abraham. This fulfillment focuses explicitly on scripture, the Koran (or Qur'an; meaning "the recitation").

In Muslim understanding, this scripture was revealed piecemeal to the Prophet Muhammad, in the Arabian cities of Mecca and Medina, between AD 610 and 632. The words are understood as the flawless word of God himself, not as Muhammad's personal utterances.

The Koran stands as the corrective to the faulty scriptures of other "People of the Book": the one God (Allah) had previously spoken through a series of prophets to Jews and Christians, but his message was distorted in the course of writing it down.

The Koran serves to amend these previous partial misunderstandings and to provide comprehensive guidance for human conduct, both individual and social.

Islam is in many ways the most "scriptural" of the world's religions, not just in the comprehensive significance it ascribes to the Koran, but in the rapidity with which a definitive version was assembled.

Within 20 years of Muhammad's death, the third caliph, Uthman, had a definitive codex completed, thereby setting a norm for recitation.

Oral transmission remained crucial, however, because of the incomplete system of writing Arabic, and it was nearly three centuries later that a text with vowel pronunciation was produced.

The Uthmanic version, with very minor variant readings, remains standard throughout the Muslim world. So, too, does emphasis on the Koran's oral, recited quality; a great many Muslims who are functionally illiterate carry the entire "text" verbatim within their hearts.

Hinduism: primacy of oral tradition

The Hindu situation could not be more different. The symbolic center of the tradition is the Rig Veda, a collection of 1,028 Sanskrit hymns, composed for liturgical use over 3,000 years ago. They are among the earliest compositions in any Indo-European language.

Yet Indian culture has consistently affirmed that the power of these (and most other) words lies in their oral and aural quality, and so has resisted reducing them to writing.

The Rig Veda was not, in fact, publicly accessible until its first published edition appeared in the mid-1800s. That work, significantly, was accomplished by an Oxford professor, F. Max Müller, and is of virtually no religious consequence for Hindus themselves: The Rig Veda's significance is symbolic, a cultural and religious reference-point, not literal or applicable to daily life.

In modern times, partly in response to imported Western ideas about "religions" having "scriptures," efforts have been made to present the Bhagavad Gita, Krishna's instruction on knowledge, morality and devotion, as the "Bible" of Hinduism. This text has become, after the Christian Bible, the second-most translated book in world history.

The Gita has doubtless been widely prized over the course of the past 2,000 years, but it has never commanded the exclusive attention of Hindus as a whole.

As it is with gods in Hinduism, so it is with scriptures: There are a very great number, and which one is in the ascendant depends on region, time of year, family tradition, caste, language, century, and so on.

Certain texts may attain a near-canonical status in particular contexts, but the core of Hindu religion lies, not in its texts, but in its stories about deities: Rama, Shiva, the Goddess, Krishna, and others.

It is these stories that lie in Hindu hearts and that get told, and retold, interpreted, and amended, and reinterpreted over and over and over again.

Buddhism: melding the word and experience

Buddhists lie somewhere between Muslims and Hindus in their attitudes toward holy writ. Like Muslims, they have a notion of a standard text, a canon, but like Hindus, they have an open-ended and expansive attitude toward what may appropriately be considered standard.

The decisive measure is what is consistent with "the word of the Buddha," but this does not mean slavish fidelity to the historical founder, Siddhartha Gautama (563 to 483 BC). Rather, it means teachings that accord with the experience of enlightenment, as taught by the historical Buddha and as lived by later followers.

This dynamic quality gives the Buddhist canon great diversity. The Pali canon of Theravada (South and Southeast Asian) Buddhism was composed and written down by the 1st century AD, but it remained in manuscript form until the 19th century. It consists of 31 texts, of varying antiquity, grouped into three "baskets" (Tripitaka): rules for monastic practice, sayings of the Buddha, and scholastic analysis.

The rise of Mahayana Buddhism, and its spread to East Asia, produced a Chinese canon, whose first block printing was completed in 983. It includes some 1,076 items, and is approximately 70 times the length of the Christian Bible. However, sectarian and individual practice has tended to emphasize one particular text, and such scriptures as the Lotus Sutra have been enormously popular.

Tibetan Buddhism also has a massive canon of over 300 volumes, dating from the 14th century, much of it consisting of translations of Indian sources now lost. Here too, the daily life of both monks and laity focuses on a few, selected texts for meditational, ritual, or philosophical elaboration.

To inquire into "Bibles" elsewhere in the world thus reveals a stunning variety of content, of attitudes toward texts, and of what it means to be religious. This discovery should caution us against a simplistic cross-cultural comparison of scriptures.

At the same time, it should invite us to think more deeply about the distinctive features of the Bible, and of Christian attitudes toward it, while pondering other traditions, and other expressions, of religious faith.

CONFUCIUS

Confucianism, once thought to be a dead doctrine,

has made an astonishing comeback during the past 20 years.

Cited as a major force behind East Asia's economic

"miracles," it is now finding a renewed following among

mainland Chinese grown disillusioned with communism.

Yet what exactly Confucianism means is hard to say.

All the more reason, Jonathan Spence urges,

to return to the man himself—

and to the little we know about his life and words.

JONATHAN D. SPENCE

Jonathan D. Spence is George B. Adams Professor of History at Yale University. His many books include The Death of Woman Wang *(1978),* The Gate of Heavenly Peace *(1981),* The Search for Modern China *(1990), and, most recently,* Chinese Roundabout *(1992).*

Across the centuries that have elapsed since he lived in northern China and lectured to a small group of followers on ethics and ritual, the ideas of Confucius have had a powerful resonance. Soon after his death in 476 B.C., a small number of these followers dedicated themselves to recording what they could remember of his teachings and to preserving the texts of history and poetry that he was alleged to have edited. In the fourth and third centuries B.C., several distinguished philosophers expanded and systematized ideas that they ascribed to him, thus deepening his reputation as a complex and serious thinker. During the centralizing and tyrannical Ch'in dynasty that ruled China between 221 and 209 B.C., the works of Confucius were slated for destruction, on the grounds that they contained material antithetical to the obedience of people to

their rulers, and many of those who prized or taught his works were brutally killed on the emperor's orders.

Despite this apparently lethal setback, Confucius's reputation was only enhanced, and during the Han dynasty (206 B.C.–A.D. 220) his ideas were further edited and expanded, this time to be used as a focused source for ideas on good government and correct social organization. Despite the pedantry and internal bickering of these self-styled followers of Confucius, his ideas slowly came to be seen as the crystallization of an inherent Chinese wisdom. Surviving the importation of Buddhist metaphysics and meditative practices from India in the third to sixth centuries A.D., and a renewed interest in both esoteric Taoist theories of the cosmos and the hard-headed political realism of rival schools of legalistically oriented thinkers, a body of texts reorganized as "Confucian," with their accumulated commentaries, became the basic source for competitive examinations for entrance into the Chinese civil service and for the analysis of a wide spectrum of political and familial relationships: those between ruler and subject, between parents and children, and between husband and wife. In the 12th century A.D., a loose group of powerful philosophers, though differing over the details, reformulated various so-called Confucian principles to incorporate some of the more deeply held premises of Buddhism, giving in particular a dualistic structure to the Confucian belief system by separating idealist or universalist components—the inherent principles or premises, known as the *li*—from the grosser matter, or manifestations of life-in-action (the *ch'i*).

A final series of shifts took place in the last centuries of imperial China. During the 16th century elements of Confucian doctrine were deepened and altered once again by philosophers who emphasized the inherent morality of the individual and tried to overcome the dualism that they felt Confucians had erected between nature and the human emotions. In the 17th century Confucian scholars confronted the promise and challenge of newly imported scientific ideas from the West, brought by Jesuits and other Catholic missionaries. During the following century Confucian scholars embarked on a newly formulated intellectual quest for the evidential basis of historical and moral phenomena, one that led them cumulatively to peaks of remarkable scholarship. In the 19th century these scholars began to cope with Western technology and constitutional ideas and with the development of new modes of education. But in the 20th century Confucian ideas were attacked from within and without China as contributing to China's economic backwardness, myopic approach to social change, denial of the idea of progress, resistance to science, and a generally stultified educational system.

These attacks were so devastating that as recently as 20 years ago, one would have thought that the chances of Confucius ever again becoming a major figure of study or emulation were slight indeed, in any part of the world. In Communist China, where he had been held up to ridicule or vilification since the Communist victory of 1949, his name was invoked only when mass campaigns needed a symbol of the old order to castigate, as in the "Anti-Confucius and anti-Lin Biao Campaign" of 1973–74. But in that case the real focus of the campaign was Chairman Mao's former "closest comrade-in-arms," General Lin Biao, not the discredited sage of Lu. In Taiwan, though constant lip service was paid to the enduring values of Confucianism, the doctrine that lived on under that name was slanted in content

and attracted few of the brightest young minds. It was a version of Confucian belief that followed along lines first laid down by Nationalist Party ideologues during the 1930s in an attempt to boost their own prestige and give a deeper historical legitimacy to party leader Chiang Kai-Shek. Although in Taiwan as in other parts of Asia there were great scholars who continued to explore the sage's inner meaning, in many Asian schools Confucius was also invoked in support of authoritarian and hierarchical value systems. In Europe and the United States, though Confucian texts were studied in East Asian and Oriental studies centers, they did not arouse much excitement, and the young—if they were interested in earlier Asian studies at all—were likely to be far more interested in Taoism or Buddhism.

Now, however, the revival is in full swing. Confucian study societies have sprung up inside the People's Republic of China, with government approval. In Taiwan, Confucianism is studied as a central aspect of philosophical inquiry, and so-called New Confucians are linking his ideas on conduct and the self to certain preoccupations in modern ethics. In the United States especially, many colleges now teach sophisticated and popular courses in "Confucian belief," and a distinguished stream of "Confucian" academics jet around the world as conference participants and even as consultants to foreign governments on the sage. Translations of Confucius's work, and that of his major followers, are in print with popular presses, often in variant editions. And "Confucian principles" are cited approvingly as being one of the underpinnings of the disciplined work habits and remarkable international economic success of a number of Asian states.

The renewed interest in Confucius is not the result of any rush of new information about him. There has been no newly discovered cache of intimate details about him or his family that could engage the public interest, no fresh sources that can be ascribed to him and thus deepen our sense of his achievement, or that could serve as the basis for new controversies. The scraps of information about Confucius are so slight that they barely give us an outline, let alone a profile, of the man. (The modern name Confucius is an early Western rendering of the sage's Chinese honorific name, "K'ung-fu-tsu.") We are almost certain that he was born in 551 B.C. We have a definite year of death, 479 B.C. He was born in the kingdom of Lu, one of the many small states into which China was then divided and which corresponds roughly to the area of modern Shandong province. His parents might have had aristocratic roots, but they were neither prominent nor wealthy, and though Confucius received a good education in historical and ritual matters, his parents died when he was young, and the youth had to fend for himself. He acquired a number of skills: in clerical work, music, accounting, perhaps in charioteering and archery, and in certain "menial activities" on which we have no other details. Sometime between 507 and 497 B.C. he served in the state of Lu in an office that can be translated as "police commissioner" and that involved hearing cases and meting out punishments. Before and after that stint of service he traveled to various neighboring states, seeking posts as a diplomatic or bureaucratic adviser but meeting with little success. Because of some feud he was, for a time, in mortal danger, but he handled himself with calmness and courage. He married and had one son and two daughters. His son predeceased him, but not before producing an heir. One of his daughters married a student of Confucius who had served time in jail. Confucius approved the match because he believed that the young man had in fact done no wrong. During his later years Confucius was a teacher of what we might now call ethics, ritual, and philosophy; the names of 35 of his students have come down to us.

To compound the problems caused by this paucity of biographical information, we have nothing that we can be completely sure was written by Confucius himself. What we do have is a record of what some of his disciples and students—or their students—said that he said. Usually translated as *The Analects of Confucius*, this collection is brief, aphoristic, and enigmatic. But the *Analects*, despite the problem of indirect transmission, remain our crucial source on Confucius's beliefs, actions, and personality. Not surprisingly, scholars disagree on how to interpret many passages and how much to believe in the authenticity of the different parts of this text. The best and perhaps the only gauges of authenticity are internal consistency, tone, and coherence. One can also look at the construction of each book— there are 20 in all, each running about five pages in English translation—and search for

obvious distortions and later additions. The last five of the books, for example, have lengthy sections that present Confucius either as a butt to the Taoists or as an uncritical transmitter of doctrines with which he can be shown in earlier chapters to have disagreed. It is a fairly safe assumption that these were added to the original text by persons with a special cause to plead. Other books give disproportionate space to Confucius's praise of a particular student whom we know from other passages that he rather disliked. Perhaps in such cases we are witnessing attempts to correct the record by later followers of the student concerned. There does not seem to be any political censorship; indeed, one of the mysteries of the later uses of Confucianism concerns the way that the original text as we now have it has been preserved for two millennia even though it seems quite obviously to contradict the ideological uses to which it was being put. Interpretation and commentary, that is to say, carried more weight with readers than did the original words.

Given the bewildering array of philosophical and political arguments that Confucianism has been called on to support, and given, in particular, the generally held belief that Confucius was a strict believer in hierarchy and the values of absolute obedience to superiors, and that he lacked flexibility and imagination, it is an intriguing task to read the *Analects* with open eyes and without any presuppositions drawn from later interpretative attempts. What was, in fact, the central message of the man Confucius himself?

Personally, almost two and a half millennia after his death, I find that Confucius is still especially valuable to us because of the strength of his humanity, his general decency, and the fervor of his belief in the importance of culture and the act of learning. He emphatically did not feel that he had any monopoly on truth. Rather, he was convinced that learning is a perpetual process that demands flexibility, imagination, and tenacity. He scolded students who would not get up in the morning, just as he scolded those who were unctuous or complacent. He said that he had no interest in trying to teach those who did not have the curiosity to follow up on a philosophical argument or a logical sequence of ideas after he had given them an initial prod in the right direction. He let his students argue among themselves—or with him—and praised those who were able to make moral decisions that might benefit humankind in general. But at the same time he adamantly refused to talk about the forces of heaven or to speculate on the nature of the afterlife, since there was so much that he did not know about life on this Earth that he was convinced such speculations would be idle.

It is clear that Confucius derived great pleasure from life. Once, one of his students could not think what to say to an influential official who had asked what sort of a person Confucius really was. Hearing of the incident, Confucius gently chided his student with these words: "Why did you not simply say something to this effect: He is the sort of man who forgets to eat when he tries to solve a problem that has been driving him to distraction, who is so full of joy that he forgets his worries and who does not notice the onset of old age?"

This brief exchange comes from *The Analects of Confucius*, book VII, section 19, and it is typical of words that Confucius left us, words through which we can in turn analyze his character.* Another example could be taken from Confucius's views concerning loyalty to the state and the value of capital punishment. In later periods of Chinese history, it was commonplace to assert that "Confucian" bureaucrats and scholars should always put their duty to the state and the dynasty they served ahead of personal and family loyalties. Chinese history is also replete with grim details of executions carried out in the name of "Confucian" ideology against those who violated the state's laws. But in the most clearly authenticated books of the *Analects* that we have, we find completely unambiguous views on these central matters of human practice and belief. What could be clearer than this?

The Governor of She said to Confucius, "In our village there is a man nicknamed 'Straight Body.' When his father stole a sheep, he gave evidence against him." Confucius answered, "In our village those who are straight are quite different. Fathers cover up for their sons, and sons cover up for their fathers. Straightness is to be found in such behavior." (XIII/18)

*All citations of the *Analects* are from D. C. Lau's Penguin Books translation, *Confucius, The Analects*. In some cases I have made minor modifications to his translations.

On executions, Confucius was equally unambiguous:

Chi K'ang Tzu asked Confucius about government, saying, "What would you think if, in order to move closer to those who possess the Way, I were to kill those who do not follow the Way?" Confucius answered, "In administering your government, what need is there for you to kill? Just desire the good yourself and the common people will be good. The virtue of the gentleman is like wind; the virtue of the small man is like grass. Let the wind blow over the grass and it is sure to bend." (XII/19)

If it were humanly possible, Confucius added, he would avoid the law altogether: "In hearing litigation, I am no different from any other man. But if you insist on a difference, it is, perhaps, that I try to get the parties not to resort to litigation in the first place." (XII/13) In the long run, the fully virtuous state would be forever free of violent death: "The Master said, 'How true is the saying that after a state has been ruled for a hundred years by good men it is possible to get the better of cruelty and to do away with killing.' " (XIII/11)

Since the words of Confucius have been preserved for us mainly in the form of aphorisms or snatches of dialogue—or the combination of the two—one way to find a coherent structure in his thought is to track the remarks he made to specific individuals, even if these are widely scattered throughout the *Analects*. Sometimes, of course, there is only one remark, especially in the case of those whose behavior Confucius considered beyond the pale. My favorite example here is his dismissal of Yuan Jang, allegedly once his friend: "Yuan Jang sat waiting with his legs spread wide. The Master said, 'To be neither modest nor deferential when young, to have passed on nothing worthwhile when grown up, and to refuse to die when old, that is what I call being a pest.' So saying, the Master tapped him on the shin with his stick." (XIV/43) That tapping on the shin, perhaps playful, perhaps in irritation, shows an unusual side of Confucius. Was he trying to add physical sting to his sharp words? More commonly with him, it was a laugh or a shrug that ended a potentially confrontational exchange.

With several of his students, Confucius clearly felt a deep rapport, even when they did not see eye to eye. One such student was Tzu-lu, who was more a man of action than a scholar. Confucius loved to tease Tzu-lu for his impetuosity. Thus, after telling his students that if he were on a raft that drifted out to sea, Tzu-lu would be the one to follow him, Confucius added wryly that that would be because Tzu-lu had at once more courage and less judgment than his teacher. On another occasion, when Tzu-lu asked if Confucius thought he, Tzu-lu, would make a good general, Confucius replied that he would rather not have as a general someone who would try to walk across a river or strangle a tiger with his bare hands. (V/7 and VII/11)

Different in character, but still very much his own man, was the merchant and diplomat Tzu-kung. Confucius acknowledged that Tzu-kung was shrewd and capable, and made a great profit from his business deals. He even agreed that Tzu-kung's type of intelligence was especially useful in the world of literature and thought: "Only with a man like you can one discuss the Odes. Tell such a man something and he can see its relevance to what he has not been told." (I/16) But Confucius did not like Tzu-kung's insistence on always trying to put people in a ranked order of priorities, as if they were so many objects—"For my part I have no time for such things," Confucius observed—and he was equally upset if he felt that Tzu-kung was skimping things that really mattered because of his private feelings: "Tzu-kung wanted to dispense with the practice of ritually killing a sacrificial sheep at the announcement of the new moon. The Master said, 'You love the sheep, but I love the Rites.' " (XIV/29 and III/17)

Most readers of the *Analects* feel that the student called Yen Yuan was clearly Confucius's favorite, and the one closest to the Master by behavior and inclination. Yen Yuan was poor but lived his life without complaining. He did not allow poverty to sour or interrupt his search for the Way, and his intelligence was truly piercing. As Tzu-kung, not a modest man, put it, "When he [Yen Yuan] is told one thing he understands 10. When I am told one thing I understand only two." To which Confucius sighed in agreement, "Neither of us is as good as he is." (V/9) In a similar vein, Confucius praised Yen Yuan's prudence, contrasting it with Tzu-lu's bravado. As Confucius phrased it, Yen Yuan was the kind of man who "when faced with a task, was fearful of failure," and who knew how "to stay out of sight when set aside;" furthermore, Yen Yuan was not above making mistakes, but more important, "he did not make the same mistake twice." (VII/11 and VI/3) When Yen Yuan died young, before being able to achieve his full promise, Confucius gave way to a conspicuous display of immoderate grief. When some of his students remonstrated with him for showing such "undue sorrow," Confucius's answer was brief but powerful: "If not for him for whom should I show undue sorrow?" (IX/10)

Confucius lived to a fine old age, and not even regret over the loss of his favorite student and his own son could blunt the pleasures he felt at his own mounting experience and the attainment of something that might be approaching wisdom. He did not boast about the knowledge he had acquired—indeed he thought he was lucky to have got as far as he had. As he put it once to Tzu-lu: "Shall I tell you what it is to know? To say you know when you know, and to say you do not know when you do not, that is knowledge." (II/17) His own greatest ambition, as he once told Yen Yuan and Tzu-lu jointly, was "to bring peace to the old, to have trust in my friends, and to cherish the young." (V/26) On another occasion he went even further, telling his followers, "It is fitting that we hold the young in awe. How do we know that the generations to come will not be the equal of the present?" (IX/23) In the passage that is perhaps the most famous of his sayings, Confucius gave his own version of the stages of life, and it is as different as anything could be from Shakespeare's "Seven Ages of Man," with its heart-rending account of man's descent into the weakness and imbecility of old age after a brief phase of youthful vigor. Whereas according to the *Analects*, the Master said, "At 15 I set my heart on learning; at 30 I took my stand; at 40 I came to be free from doubts; at 50 I understood the Decree of Heaven; at 60 my ear was attuned; at 70 I followed my heart's desire without overstepping the line." (II/4)

Certainly we should not read Confucius as though he were always right. And as we read through the *Analects* we can find Confucius revealing a fussy and sometimes impatient side. Some of his vaunted arguments seem like quibbles, and he could be punctilious to the point of prudishness. His political motivations are often obscure, and he seems to appreciate various struggling rulers' foibles less than his own. But cleared of the accumulation of unsubstantiated details and textual over-interpretations that have weighed him down across the centuries, we find to our surprise an alert, intelligent, and often very amusing man.

How then did he get the reputation that he did, one at once more austere, more pompous, harsh even, and as a reinforcer of the status quo? Strangely enough, part of the reappraisal resulted from the efforts of the man who is undeniably China's greatest historian, Ssu-ma Ch'ien, who lived from around 145 to 89 B.C., during the Han dynasty. In his life's work, a composite history of China entitled simply *Historical Records*, which was completed between 100 and 95 B.C., Ssu-ma Ch'ien aimed to integrate the histories of all China's earlier states and rulers with the steady and inexorable rise to power of the centralizing Ch'in dynasty (221–209 B.C.), and he determined to give Confucius an important role in this process. Thus Ssu-ma Ch'ien paid Confucius the ultimate accolade by placing his story in the section devoted to the ruling houses of early China, as opposed to placing him with other individual thinkers and statesmen in the 70 chapters of biographies that conclude the *Historical Records*. In the summation of Confucius's worth with which he ended his account, Ssu-ma Ch'ien gave concise and poignant expression to his homage:

> In this world there have been many people—from kings to wise men—who had a glory while they lived that ended after their death. But Confucius, though a simple commoner, has had his name transmitted for more than 10 generations; all those who study his works consider him their master. From the Son of Heaven, the princes, and the lords on down, anyone in the Central Kingdom who is dedicated to a life of learning, follows the precepts and the rules of the Master. Thus it is that we call him a true Sage.

To give substance to this judgment, Ssu-ma Ch'ien took all known accounts written over the intervening three centuries that purported to describe Confucius, following the principle that if there was no clear reason for discarding an item of biographical information, then he should include it, leaving for later generations the task of winnowing the true from the false. Thus was Confucius given cou-

rageous ancestors, his birth described in semi-miraculous terms, his own physical distinction elaborated upon. In one curious addition, Confucius's father was described as being of far greater age than the sage's mother: By one interpretation of the phrase used by Ssu-ma Ch'ien, that the marriage was "lacking in proportion," Confucius's father would have been over 64, while his mother had only recently entered puberty. Confucius's precocious interest in ritual and propriety, his great height and imposing cranial structure, the fecundity of the flocks of cattle and sheep that he supervised in one of his first official posts, his preternatural shrewdness in debate, his instinctive brilliance at interpreting unusual auguries—all of these were given documentary precision in Ssu-ma Ch'ien's account. The result is that Confucius not only emerges as a key counselor to the rulers of his native state of Lu, but the meticulousness of his scholarship and his flair for editing early texts of poetry, history, and music are presented as having attracted an ever-widening circle of hundreds or even thousands of students from his own and neighboring states.

Having constructed this formidable image of a successful Confucius, Ssu-ma Ch'ien was confronted by the need to explain the reasons for Confucius's fall from grace in Lu and for his subsequent wanderings in search of rulers worthy of his service. Being one of China's most gifted storytellers, Ssu-ma Ch'ien was up to this task, presenting a convincing scenario of the way the sagacity of Confucius's advice to the ruler of Lu made him both respected and feared by rival rulers in northern China. One of them was finally able to dislodge Confucius by sending to the ruler of Lu a gift of 24 ravishing female dancers and musicians, along with 30 magnificent teams of chariot horses. This gift so effectively distracted the ruler of Lu from his official duties—most important, it led him to forget certain key ritual sacrifices—that Confucius had no choice but to leave his court.

In various ways, some subtle, some direct, the portrait of Confucius that Ssu-ma Ch'ien wove incorporated diverse levels of narrative dealing with the unpredictability of violence. This was surely not coincidental, for the central tragedy of Ssu-ma Ch'ien's own life had been his court-ordered castration, a savage punishment inflicted on him by the Han dynasty emperor Wu-ti (r. 141–87 B.C.). Ssu-ma Ch'ien's "crime" had been to write a friend a letter in which he incautiously spoke in defense of a man unjustly punished by the same emperor. Despite this agonizing humiliation, which placed the historian in the same physical category as the venal court eunuchs he so deeply despised, Ssu-ma Ch'ien refused to commit suicide; he maintained his dignity by making his history as grand and comprehensive as possible—his presentation of Confucius being a stunning example of his dedication to craft and content. Thus he describes Confucius as a man who had the bureaucratic power to make major judicial decisions but who did so only with care and consideration of all the evidence. When Confucius acted harshly, according to Ssu-ma Ch'ien, it was only when the long-term threat to his kingdom was so strong that leniency would have been folly. This explains one shattering moment in Ssu-ma Ch'ien's biography. One rival leader was planning to overthrow the ruler of Lu, but each of his ruses was seen through and foiled by Confucius. At last, in desperation, the rival ruler ordered his acrobats and dwarfs to perform wild and obscene dances at a ritual occasion that the ruler of Lu was attending. Confucius, according to Ssu-ma Ch'ien, ordered the dwarfs killed.

In another dissimilar but equally powerful comment on violence, Ssu-ma Ch'ien showed that even the descendants of a man of Confucius's integrity could not escape Emperor Wu-ti's willful power. Thus at the very end of his long biography, before the final summation, Ssu-ma Ch'ien lists all of Confucius's direct descendants in the male line. When he comes to the 11th in line, An-kuo, the historian mentions tersely that An-kuo had died "prematurely" under the "ruling emperor." Ssu-ma Ch'ien knew—and knew that his readers knew—that An-kuo had been executed on Wu-ti's orders for involvement in an alleged court coup. The line had not, however, been stamped out, because An-kuo's wife had borne a son before her husband was killed.

Ssu-ma Ch'ien's attempt to reconstruct a convincing psychological and contextual universe for Confucius was a brilliant one, and his version was elaborated upon and glossed by scores of subsequent scholars, even as suitable pieces of the Confucian legacy were seized upon by later rulers and bureaucrats to justify some current policy decision or to prove some philosophical premise. But after more than two millennia of such accretions, it seems time to go back to the earlier and simpler version of the record and try to see for ourselves what kind of a man Confucius was. The results, I feel, in our overly ideological age, are encouraging to those who value the central premises of humane intellectual inquiry.

The World of the Middle Ages, 500–1500

World historians have a bit of a problem with this period of time. In the history of Western civilization, the medieval period, or the Middle Ages, is the time of retreat after the fall of the Roman Empire. The thousand-year span also covers feudalism, the growth of the nation-state, the Black Death, reestablishment of long-distance trade, and the domination of the Roman Catholic Church. For a generation of scholars schooled in Western civilization, this time means the origin and development of the civilization. Yet, for world historians, it is obvious that the events in the West, although important for the future, fade in significance before the advances of China and Islam. The "Middle Ages" were "golden ages" for those civilizations. The end result is that the thousand-year span is still important for world history, but the period is significant for reasons beyond the development in the West.

Arab scholarship expanded with the spread of Islam, and in the eighth century, scholars discovered in Sanskrit math texts in India the concepts of zero and decimals. This they later transferred to the Western world where it became a part of mathematical knowledge. According to Abdesselam Cheddadi, Arab historian Ibn Khaldun was one of the greatest historians of his age, a person who emphasized factual accuracy. He followed in the tradition of Herodotus, but he is only one example of Arab success in this period.

This is also the time of the expansion of the Mongol Empire under the leadership of Genghis Khan. The Mongols used a new warfare technology—effective light cavalry—with a fierceness that brought them control of Asia. Morris Rossabi writes about this horse technology and its importance to the Mongol warriors. Marco Polo benefitted from the peace brought by the Mongols to travel safely from Venice through Asia and back. Polo's adventure became an inspiration for the later explorations of European navigators.

For Western civilization in Europe, this was a time of formation. The Roman Catholic Church dominated the continent and systematically forced women into subordinate roles. In England, in contrast, the beginnings of Parliamentary rule and personal liberties came when the barons forced the harried King John to sign the Magna Carta, which is considered the foundation document of the current government of Great Britain. During the same thirteenth century, the first mechanical clock, invented by an unknown genius, appeared in Europe. This key invention changed attitudes toward time and inspired further improvements such as miniaturization of parts and mass production. It led into the Industrial Revolution. By the fifteenth century, Europeans were ready to reach out into the world as no other civilization had done. The stage had been set for an age of discovery.

Looking Ahead: Challenge Questions

Compare the life of Church women with those of Athens and Egypt in the ancient period of time. Had life improved for women?

What was the role of warfare in the struggle for power and the Magna Carta?

What is the significance of Arab scholarship in world history?

What was the effect of the mechanical clock in history?

In what ways did the Middle Ages prepare Europe for an age of discovery? What was the particular role of technology?

altam pfunditatem expositionis libror
ut pdixi sentiens. uiribusq; receptis.de
egritudine me erigens uix opus istud
decem annis consummans. ad finem
pduxi. In diebus autem HEIDRICI
moguntini archiepi 7 Conradi roma
norum regis 7 Cunonis abbatis in
monte beati DYSIBODI pontificis.
sub papa Eygenio hę uisiones 7 uerba
facta sunt. Et dixi 7 scpsi hec ñ secundu
adinuentionē cordis mei aut ullius ho
minis. sed ut ea in celestib' uidi. audiui
7 pcepi. p secreta misteria di Et iterum
audiui uocem de celo michi dicentem.
Clama g̃ 7 scribe sic.

Incipiunt capitula libri SCIVIAS
SIMPLICIS HOMINIS.

Capitula pime uisionis pime partis.

I. De fortitudine 7 stabilitate cĩuitati
regni dei.

II. De timore domini.

III. de his qui pauperes spũ sunt.

IIII. Quod uirtutes a dõ nementes timtes dm
7 pauperes spũ custodiunt.

V. Quod agnitiom di abscondi ñ possunt
studia actuum hominum.

VI. Salemon de eadem re.

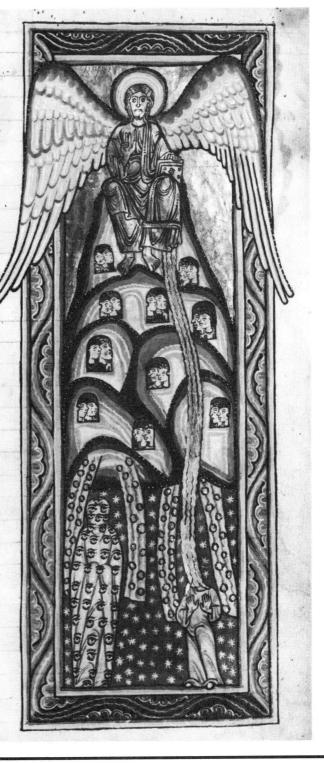

Lilavati, gracious lady of arithmetic

FRANCIS ZIMMERMANN

Francis Zimmermann, French philosopher and eth-nologist, is director of research at the National Centre for Scientific Research (CNRS).

DURING the eighth century AD, Arab scholars working in India on Sanskrit mathematical texts made two major discoveries which they developed and later transmitted to the Western world: the place-value notation of figures using the decimal system coupled with the "zero" concept, and a trigonometry which incorporated the use of sines.

It was not merely by chance that these major advances in the fields of writing, calculation and triangulation were made by Indian mathematicians; they all touched on matters of traditional interest in India, whose scholars had always shown a particular taste and talent for grammatical forms.

Mathematics, like all the other scientific disciplines in ancient India, was subject to the constraints and stylistic forms of the Sanskrit language as well as to the demands of verse since most scientific texts were written in verse form.

The great mathematical treatises, written in Sanskrit, usually by a Brahman (a member of the highest, priestly caste), consisted of a basic, often cryptic, text made up of *sutras* or aphorisms, or else of verses that were learned by heart. A stream of prose commentaries explain the full meaning of these ancient texts, confirming that they were aphoristic in nature and deliberately conceived as summaries of a master's teachings, expressed

---

A simple problem taken from the twelfth-century Indian mathematician Bhaskara's *Lilavati* ('Arithmetic')

अथ बिश्लेषजात्युदाहरणम्—
पञ्चाशोऽडि्डकुलात्कदम्बगमगमदृयंशः त्रिछीःध्रं त्रयो.
बि्श्लेषत्रिगुणो मृगासि कुटजं दोलाद्यमानोऽपरः ।
कान्ते केतकमाळतीपरिमछगाम्रेक्काळमिया-
दूनाहूत इवस्ततो भ्रमति खे भृङ्गोऽछिसंख्यां वद ॥

Example of the reduction of fractions to a common denominator:

One-fifth of a swarm of bees flew towards a lotus flower, one-third towards a banana tree. (A number equal to) three times the difference between the two (preceding figures), O my beauty with the eyes of a gazelle, flew towards a Codaga tree (whose bitter bark provides a substitute for quinine). Finally, one other bee, undecided, flew hither and thither equally attracted by the delicious perfume of the jasmine and the pandanus. Tell me, O charming one, how many bees were there?

Let x = the number of bees

$$x = \frac{x}{5} + \frac{x}{3} + 3 \times \left(\frac{1}{3} - \frac{1}{5}\right) + 1$$

Reducing the fractions to a common denominator, we get:

$$x = \frac{3x}{15} + \frac{5x}{15} + 3 \times \frac{(5-3)}{15} + 1$$

$$x = 15$$

Reprinted with permission from *The UNESCO Courier*, November 1989, pp. 18-21.

in such a way as to stick in the memory of his pupils.

Evidence of the early use of numbers, in the sense of graphic symbols, is to be found in inscriptions on stone or copper that have been studied by archaeologists—such as the numbers 4 and 6, for example, found in the Asoka inscriptions which date back to the third century BC. They are very rarely to be found, however, in proper mathematical texts. Arabic numerals, so called because they were made known to the rest of the world by Arab authors, are, in fact, of Indian origin. In general, however, they were rarely used in Sanskrit texts, in which numbers are written out in full or symbolized by alphabetical codes. To be more precise, we must distinguish clearly between the basic texts, generally written in verse, and the prose commentaries which alone provide us with information about the way in which numbers were written down during the actual process of calculation.

Numbers were set out vertically over several lines, or at least this is what emerges from a commentary written by Bhaskara the Elder in 629 AD on the *Aryabhatiya*. Unfortunately, the life-span of Indian manuscripts was short, averaging only about three centuries. Written on paper or on palm leaves, they were a prey to mildew and insects. The manuscripts of Bhaskara's commentary that have come down to us are modern copies and cannot be taken as evidence of the manner of writing of more ancient times. The twelfth-century Bakhsali manuscript, which is probably the oldest document in this sense, shows calculations in Arabic numerals spread over several lines and contained in cartouches, or boxes, within the body of a mathematical text written in Sanskrit.

The absence of graphic symbols and numbers in the aphorisms and verses of the classic mathematical texts does not mean that symbolism is totally excluded, but that the symbolism employed is grammatical or rhetorical in nature. Thanks to the virtually limitless synonymical possibilities of the Sanskrit language, numbers are represented by literary phrases and metaphors. Thus, *nayana* (eye) or *bahu* (arm) are the names of the number 2. *Agni* (fire) means 3 (by allusion to the three Vedic forms of ritual fire) and *adri* (mountain) means 7 (a reference to the seven mountains of India of Hindu religious geography). The Sanskrit words for "sky" or "space" stand for zero. The order of the figures making up a number is the reverse of modern numerical systems—for example, the number 23 would be written as *agninayana*.

This symbolism is useful for writing in verse form series of figures which today would be laid out in tabular form. In India, as elsewhere, the astronomical data in almanacs have for centuries been presented in columns of numbers. But this mode was an Arab invention and in the ancient Sanskrit texts numbers were presented in the form of a line or a verse of poetry.

Another form of numerical symbolism fre-

The ratio of the circumference of a circle to its diameter (π)

चतुरधिकं शतमष्टगुणां द्वाषष्टिस्तथा सहस्राणाम् ।
अयुतद्वयविष्कम्भस्यासन्नो वृत्तपरिणाहः ॥

caturadhikam satam astagunam dvasastis tatha sahasranam
ayutadvayaviskambhasyasanno vrttaparinahah

"Add four to one hundred, multiply by eight, add 62,000. This will give you the approximate value (*asanna*) of the circumference of a circle with a diameter of two myriads."

This verse, written by the sixth-century Indian mathematician Aryabhata, gives the oldest known formulation of the approximate value of the ratio that later became known as π:

$$\frac{\text{circumference}}{\text{diameter}} = \frac{62832}{20000} = 3.1416$$

---

quently used in astronomical and mathematical texts is based on the Sanskrit alphabet. Several such systems exist. The *katapayadi* system, which is widely used in southern India, makes it possible for very large numbers and trigonometric tables to be expressed in the form of mnemonic words, aphorisms or verses. The system is flexible enough to enable such numbers to be expressed in phrases which also have another meaning. For example, the priestly injunction *acaryavag abhedya*, which means literally "The word of the Master must not be betrayed", is coded writing of the number 1434160, a chronogram for the 1,434,160th day of the era of Kali, the day on which the philosopher Sankaracarya introduced certain reforms.

Did this poetic form of expression have an influence on mathematical reasoning? Was there some specific characteristic, something special in the way of thinking or the social status of Indian mathematicians which led them to shape their teachings in a literary mould?

There has never been a caste or even a real school of mathematicians in India. Mathematicians, if we class as such those who wrote or used Sanskrit texts dealing with geometry, arithmetic or algebra, worked in fairly close collaboration with experts in Vedic and Brahmanic ritual. Brahmans or members of a high caste and steeped in Sanskrit culture, they were classed among scientists as *jyotirvid*, or "experts on stars". Mathematical texts were usually inserted in treatises on astronomy, and trigonometry only really came into its own in the study of the angular distances between stars.

Like all the Brahman sciences (the *sastra*), mathematics had been developed primarily for religious purposes, as an aid to the proper performance of ritual. We know nothing of the life of the great Indian mathematicians, but we can picture fairly accurately the ritualistic and scholastic setting within which they worked, so heavily coloured by it is the style of Sanskrit texts. After the pupils had memorized a text by repeating it word for word, time and again until it was "clasped to their bosoms" (until they had learned it by heart), the teacher would provide them, orally, with the illustrations, demonstrations and calculations that the text concealed. This was the key that opened up the paths of knowledge and an instrument of spiritual fulfilment.

The *Lilavati*, a text by the twelfth-century mathematician Bhaskara the Learned, was traditionally used for this purpose for arithmetic and this explains why it terminates with a verse with a double meaning in which Bhaskara compares his *Lilavati*, his "gracious one" (it also means arithmetic), to a woman endowed with all the graces of the *jati* (a word which means both of noble lineage and, in a technical sense, the reduction of fractions to a common denominator). "Joy and happiness in this world shall continually increase for those who hold her *kanthasakta*, close in their arms or clasped to their bosoms (learned by heart by repetition)."

From ritual geometry to Bhaskara's treatise

The oldest of these texts that have come down to us are the *sulbasutras*, "maxims concerning measuring cords", which are believed to have been written between the fifth and the first century BC. They are treatises which lay down the rules for building altars used for Vedic ritual sacrifices and made of bricks laid in accordance with symbolic forms. The geometric constructions which are taught in these treatises are based on knowledge of several special cases of right-angled triangles (for example, with sides measuring 3-4-5, or 5-12-13, 7-24-25, etc.) and on the general rule according to which "the diagonal of a rectangle produces (by the construction on it of a square) the equivalent of the product of both the rectangle's length and breadth; and the diagonal of a square produces (by the construction on it of a square) twice its own area." Here, however, the rule is not expressed as a theorem, but as a maxim, as a formula to ensure the proper functioning of ritual and as a building guideline. The word *sutra* itself, which at first meant "aphoristic in style", came, in the later treatises, to mean a "rule" in the technical sense of a rule for building.

There are no theorems in Indian mathematics, only rules based on reasoning which starts from an intuitive point of departure. The rules, aphorisms and the mnemonic verses of the basic texts are not the outcome of a demonstration but rather guidelines for a geometric construction to be carried out by the reader or the commentator. Even in algebra, the typical line of reasoning links areas to the products of factors and implies the construction of a geometric figure.

It has often been said that the Indians were algebraists rather than geometers yet, in fact, throughout all the commentaries on the teachings of Aryabhata (sixth century), Brahmagupta (seventh century) and Bhaskara (twelfth century), geometry was the source of the practical applications of the rules of arithmetic and algebra. A geometric space and a numerical ensemble were taken together as two facets of the same reality. The algebraic solution was grafted on to the geometric construction. To demonstrate was to display the solution, to render it intuitively manifest. As one commentator said: "A demonstration by quantities should be made for the benefit of those who do not understand the demonstration by areas." Thus, in Indian mathematics, to reason is to explain an intuition.

The master-chronologers of Islam

ABDESSELAM CHEDDADI

Abdesselam Cheddadi is a Moroccan historian who teaches at the faculty of education sciences at Rabat. An authority on Ibn Khaldun, he has translated into French the great Arab historian's autobiography (Sindbad publishers, Paris, 1984) and extracts from his history (Sindbad, Paris, 1987).

THE most striking feature of Islamic historical writing or *tarikh* is its sheer volume. Only a small part of it has so far been published and new texts are continually being discovered. From the second half of the first century of the Hegira (late seventh century AD) to the thirteenth century (nineteenth century AD) the writing of Islamic history continued almost without a break wherever the Islamic faith was professed. The language used was primarily Arabic, but there were also writings in Persian, Turkish and Malay. Although essentially written by Muslims, it also attracted Christian authors, especially in Egypt and Syria.

A second important feature of Islamic historiography is its very great diversity. It comprises forms and genres ranging from vast universal or general histories and monographs to annals, dynastic and genealogical tables or lists divided into *tabaqat* (classes), as well as biographical dictionaries and local histories. It also covers many fields: religious, political, administrative and social life; scientific, literary and artistic activities; schools of thought and ideological trends; travel, the topography of cities, monuments; natural disasters, famines, epidemics....

The historians who worked in this tradition were also curious about non-Islamic civilizations, western and northern Europe, India, China, the Far East and Africa. They were interested in any information relating to man, his relations with his social and cultural environment and his relations with God. Ibn Khaldun (see box) noted that they wrote just as much for the "crowds" and for "simple folk" as for "kings" and "the great". This view of history as universal in scope and the attempt to reach a wide audience prefigured modern approaches to the subject.

A grasp of time

A further point of similarity with modern historiography lay in the importance attached very early on to time and to chronology. From the first to the fourth century of the Hegira (seventh-tenth century AD) a vast amount of knowledge about time was amassed in Islamic culture. Drawing on earlier Arab tradition, it incorporated Persian, Indian, Greek and Egyptian material and also leaned on the work of astronomers and geographers. The masterly conspectus achieved by al-Biruni in the first half of the fifth/eleventh century is impressive for its tone of objectivity. It represents the most extensive and most rigorous survey of knowledge about time that we possess up to the modern era.

Muslim historians benefited greatly from this knowledge. From the second/eighth century onwards it gradually became common practice to give dates, to follow a chronological order and to provide tables. For most of the facts reported by historians it became a virtually absolute rule

Reprinted with permission from *The UNESCO Courier,* March 1990, pp. 35-39.

175

Above, illustration from a Turkish manuscript recording a journey (1605-1606).

Originality and limitations

The originality, but also the limitations of Islamic historiography lie in its conception of historical information (*khabar*). *Khabar* means the fact, the event, as incorporated into discourse, related in a "story". The historian does not deal in raw facts. He starts from a given which is the story as reported by written or oral tradition, or by a living witness (who may be the historian himself). His most important task is therefore to authenticate or validate stories by subjecting accounts and channels of transmission to critical scrutiny. The historian does not seek to discover or establish facts but to gather, classify and organize information while making sure of its validity. The intrinsic truth of stories was a relatively minor concern until Ibn Khaldun, who based historical criticism on knowledge of the laws of *'umran* (the human order, society).

Bound to accept traditional sources, often down to the finest detail, the historian could incorporate them into a wide variety of genres or organize them at will within more or less voluminous compilations, but he could not formulate them in his own way, reconstruct them or recast them according to his own perspective.

In Islamic historiography then, the past is not reconstructed as it was by some Greek historians, nor is there any theological history as there was in the Christian Middle Ages. This accounts for its widely acknowledged impartiality and also for its stationary conception of time, which contains in itself no potential for change or progress but simply gives external order to a sequence of events. It was Ibn Khaldun again who, in considering the emergence, evolution and decline of vast human groups such as the Arabs, Berbers, Persians and the *Rum* (Greeks, Romans and Byzantines) added a new dimension to this vision.

Three major periods

The first major period of Islamic historiography, which extends up to the third century of the Hegira, is crowned by at-Tabari's chronicle *Tarikh ar-Rusul wa al-Muluk (History of Prophets and Kings)* (see box). A calendar based on the Hegira soon came to be adopted generally. The *isnad* method, whereby the names of those who transmitted information from generation to generation are cited, was first developed for the purposes of the religious sciences and then applied

to note the year, month and day when they occurred. This contrasts with medieval historiography in the West where it was not until the eleventh century AD that a unified chronological system began to be widely accepted and where, as late as the fourteenth century, the chronology of the main historical events was still uncertain.

At-Tabari

AT-TABARI (839-923) did not invent Islamic historiography but he is its most illustrious figure. His *Tarikh ar-Rusul wa al-Muluk (History of Prophets and Kings)* long served as a model. This chronicle, which relates the history of the Islamic world year by year in the first three centuries of the Hegira, was continued by later authors, and many abridged versions and adaptations were made of its account of the pre-Islamic period. It was incorporated in other general surveys such as Ibn al-Athir's *al-Kamil (The Complete History)* in the thirteenth century AD and Ibn Kathir's *al Bidayah wa an-nihayah (The Beginning and the End)* in the following century.

At-Tabari was trained as a jurist, traditionalist and historian. For close on thirty years he journeyed through the cities and countries of the Middle East in a quest for knowledge which took him to the greatest scholars of his time. He was interested not only in history, Qur'anic exegesis and the traditions of the Prophet, but also in grammar, ethics, mathematics and medicine. His fame also rests on his monumental *Tafsir*, or commentary on the Qur'an.

His *History*, which is the culmination of a process which can be traced back to the first century of the Hegira, is guided by a constant concern to show how each item of information has been passed down through an unbroken line, which is subjected to critical scrutiny. He applied a strict chronological order to the raw material of history, and gave a more ample and finished form to the universal history sketched out by ad-Dinawari in his *Akhbar at-Tiwal (The Long Stories)* and by al-Ya 'qubi in his *Tarikh*.

At-Tabari's *Tarikh ar-Rusul wa al-Muluk* is described as a history of the world from the Creation up to the author's own time. In fact, as he explains in his preface, it is first and foremost a history of the relations between God and His creatures, whether of obedience and gratitude or of rebelliousness and revolt. Its main protagonists, after Iblis/Satan and Adam and his sons, are the prophets and kings. Biblical history is included, and neither Graeco-Roman and Byzantine history nor Persian history is neglected.

It is an irreplaceable mine of information. The author cites his sources for each fact reported and in many cases reproduces the accounts in which they are mentioned, thereby giving us access to early materials that are now lost. In the words of the historian Franz Rosenthal, at-Tabari in his *History* demonstrates "the scrupulousness and untiring inspiration of the theologian, the precision and love of order of the jurist and the perspicacity of the politician versed in law".

ABDESSELAM CHEDDADI

Ibn Khaldun

IBN KHALDUN was one of the greatest historians and thinkers of all time. He wrote a long autobiography thanks to which we are familiar with the details of his life. Born in Tunis in 1332, he came from a line of senior government officials and scholars of Andalusian origin, descended from ancient Yemeni Arab stock. He received a thorough religious, literary and scientific education at the hands of the most eminent scholars in the Maghrib. During his adolescence Ifriqiya was conquered by the Marinid king Abu al-Hasan, who entered Tunis in 1348. The following year his father and mother were carried away by the Black Death. In 1352 he went to Fez where he stayed for some ten years and served as private secretary to the sultan Abu Salim. But neither there nor in Granada, to which he travelled in 1362, nor later in Bejaia or Tlemcen, did he manage to lead a stable life or to achieve his political ideal. He did however acquire detailed knowledge of court life and the workings of the state and observed the world of the Arab and Berber tribes.

In 1375, at the age of forty-three, he withdrew from public life in order to devote himself to science. In the castle of Ibn Salamah, near Frenda in Algeria, he wrote the first version of the *Muqaddimah (Introduction to History)*. The need for more extensive documentation forced him to leave his refuge. He returned to Tunis where he taught and completed the first version of the *Kitab al-'Ibar*, his monumental history of the world. But, fearing the intrigues of his enemies, he left the Maghrib for good in 1384 and settled in Egypt. In Cairo he was given an introduction to the Mamluk ruler as-Zahir Barquq and took on teaching and judicial duties, while continuing to work on his voluminous opus. Five years before his death in 1406, during the siege of Damascus, he met the Mongol Timur, of whom he left a striking portrait.

Ibn Khaldun's concerns were primarily those of a historian. Wishing to give a comprehensive account of his age which might serve as a model for future historians, dissatisfied with traditional methods of authenticating and verifying facts, he formulated a theory of society on which all his historiography was to be based. In the *Muqaddimah* he laid the foundations of what would today be called anthropology. Here we can give no more than a glimpse of the rich fund of concepts he brought into play.

Central to his theory of society is the concept of *'um-*

(continued)

ran. For lack of a more adequate term, this can be translated as "civilization", but only if this word is stripped of any connotation of an opposition between "advanced" societies and "primitive" societies. A more radical concept, based on the religious idea of the Creation, *'umran* designates the fact of human life, the human order in general. Fundamentally equal and free, human beings are God's creatures, and as such are the rulers of the Earth, but they differ from one another by virtue of their living conditions, which are themselves determined by geographic and climatic conditions. The term also denotes the forms of social life or, in a more restrictive sense, urban life with its dense concentration of humanity, contrasting with life in mountain or desert regions.

In *'umran* Ibn Khaldun distinguishes two states, which are at the same time the two main stages in human evolution. *Badawah*, the original agro-pastoral phase, close to nature, satisfying only the barest needs, yields to *hadarah*, the complex urban stage which gives rise to surpluses, in which society fulfils itself and achieves its purpose. It is the fate of *'umran* to oscillate in accordance with an implacable law between these two poles.

For Ibn Khaldun, *mulk* (power) was the basic factor responsible for social and historical dynamics. As a source of the highest prestige, it is the goal of all human aspiration and desire, spurring·men to action. Precarious by nature, it passes from one group to another, from one nation to another. As a means of distributing economic surpluses and structuring society, it has a pivotal role in the transition from *badawah* to *hadarah*. Around this central principle of social life Ibn Khaldun structured his history. In studying the Arabs and Berbers he concerned himself with those nations that successively held power. His narrative traces the rise of political groups from their Bedouin status to the heights of power, and their subsequent downfall.

These concepts tie in with many others, which include, in the social sphere, cohesion (*'asabiyah*), kinship (*nasab*), protection (*walah, istinah*), honour (*nu 'ra*); in the political sphere, constraint (*ikrah*), coercion (*Qahr*), domination (*ghalab* or *taghallub*), prestige (*jah*); and in the economic sphere, means of subsistence (*ma 'ash*), gain or profit (*kasb*), value (*qimah*) and work (*a 'mal*).

The concepts he employs, the laws governing the functioning of Arab-Berber society which he identifies, and the bird's-eye view that he provides of many aspects of Islamic history, are still indispensable tools of anthropological and historical research into Islamic society. Far from being superseded, this rigorous, coherent set of theories continues to be a mine of scientific knowledge for modern researchers.

ABDESSELAM CHEDDADI

to the biography of the Prophet, to stories of the Muslim conquests and gradually to all kinds of stories.

The earliest historical writing appeared and sometimes crystallized in a number of genres, including *maghazi* and *sira* (the biography and deeds of the Prophet), *futuh* (Muslim conquests), *ahdath* (major political events), *akhbar al-awa 'il* (stories of pre-Islamic kings and nations), *ayyam al- 'arab* (stories of the Arab past), *ansab, ma'athir* and *mathalib* (genealogies, exploits and failures); biographies of scholars, lists of teachers, political and administrative chronicles, history of the Umayyad and 'Abassid dynasties, and collections of secretaries' letters. It gradually became the usual practice to date facts and events precisely and to follow a chronological order.

Numerous compendiums were published, such as al-Waqidi's *Maghazi*, Ibn Ishaq's *Sira*, Ibn Sa 'd's *Tabaqat*, ad-Dinawari's *Akhbar at-tiwal*, al-Baladhuri's *Ansab al-ashrai* and al-Ya 'qubi's *Tarikh*. Together this constituted a vast historical literature, relatively little of which has survived but whose existence is attested by the titles listed in subsequent bibliographies, like Ibn an-Nadim's *Fihrist*, completed in 377 of the Hegira (998 AD).

The second period, known as the classical period, is marked both by the accentuation of these various tendencies with, however, some slackening of the *isnad* method, and by the emergence of new genres. After at-Tabari, but less influential than he, al-Masudi composed the *Golden Meadows*, another universalist history.

From the fourth century of the Hegira onwards the writing of history became a more or less official activity involving greater use of national or provincial archives. This period was notable for the work of a line of historians starting with Hassan Ibn Thabit Ibn Sinan as-Sabi and, later, Miskawayh's *Tajarib al-umam (History of the Buyid Dynasty)*, continued in the following century by Abu Shuja'.

The history of cities developed into a major genre. Many works were produced, the best known of which is al-Khatib al-Baghdadi's *History of Baghdad*. Biographical dictionaries relating to religious and intellectual life became more sophisticated and more numerous. They included lists of poets and other specialists, directories of scholars belonging to different juridico-religious schools, catalogues of writers and lives of saints. In the various regions of the Islamic empire a thriving historiographical tradition thus took root.

In the mid-fifth century of the Hegira political upheavals in the Islamic world were not without an effect on historiography. A third period began, marked by an ebb in production until the mid-sixth century. Syria then came to the fore for a while with historians like Ibn at-Tayyi, Ibn Abi ad-Dam and Ibn an-Nazif, who wrote universal histories, followed soon after by Ibn al-Athir, the author of *al-Kamil (The Complete History)*. Then it was the turn of Egypt to produce major historians such as Ibn Hajar, al-Maqrizi, al-'Ayni, Ibn Tighribirdi, as-Sakhawi and as-Suyuti. The same period saw the birth in the Maghrib of Ibn Khaldun whose pioneering work was admired in his time but who had no successors.

Above, manuscript page from a collection of prose and verse biographies of Sufi saints, written by Hosayn Bayqarah (1469-1506), the last of the Timurid sovereigns of Persia.

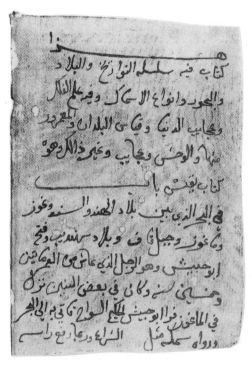

Right, page from a 12th-century Arabic manuscript describing the customs of China and India.

All the Khan's Horses

With fresh mounts in reserve, Genghis Khan's warriors could outlast any enemy

Morris Rossabi

Formerly at Case Western Reserve University's China Institute, Rossabi is now a professor of Chinese and Inner Asian history at City University of New York (Queens College) and a visiting professor at Columbia University. The author of Khubilai Kahn *and* Voyager from Xanadu, *he is [working on] a multivolume history of the Mongols and a study of Roy Chapman Andrews's Mongolian expeditions.*

In August 1227, a somber funeral procession—escorting the body of perhaps the most renowned conqueror in world history—made its way toward the Burkhan Khaldun (Buddha Cliff) in northeastern Mongolia. Commanding a military force that never amounted to more than 200,000 troops, this Mongol ruler had united the disparate, nomadic Mongol tribes and initiated the conquest of territory stretching from Korea to Hungary and from Russia to modern Vietnam and Syria. His title was Genghis Khan, "Khan of All Between the Oceans."

Genghis Khan and his descendants could not have conquered and ruled the largest land empire in world history without their diminutive but extremely hardy steeds. In some respects, these Mongolian ponies resembled what is now known as Przewalski's horse (see box). Mongols held these horses in highest regard and accorded them great spiritual significance. Before setting forth on military expeditions, for example, commanders would scatter mare's milk on the earth to insure victory. In shamanic rituals, horses were sacrificed to provide "transport" to heaven.

The Mongols prized their horses primarily for the advantages they offered in warfare. In combat, the horses were fast and flexible, and Genghis Khan was the first leader to capitalize fully on these strengths. After hit-and-run raids, for example, his horsemen could race back and quickly disappear into their native steppes. Enemy armies from the sedentary agricultural societies to the south frequently had to abandon their pursuit because they were not accustomed to long rides on horseback and thus could not move as quickly. Nor could these farmer-soldiers leave their fields for extended periods to chase after the Mongols.

The Mongols had developed a composite bow made out of sinew and horn and were skilled at shooting it while riding, which gave them the upper hand against ordinary foot soldiers. With a range of more than 350 yards, the bow was superior to the contemporaneous English longbow, whose range was only 250 yards. A wood-and-leather saddle, which was rubbed with sheep's fat to prevent cracking and shrinkage, allowed the horses to bear the weight of their riders for long periods and also permitted the riders to retain a firm seat. Their saddlebags contained cooking pots, dried meat, yogurt, water bottles, and other essentials for lengthy expeditions. Finally, a sturdy stirrup enabled horsemen to be steadier and thus more accurate in shooting when mounted. A Chinese chronicler recognized the horse's value to the

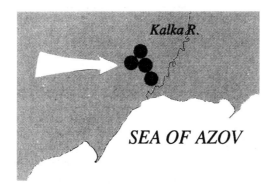

For almost ten days before the Kalka River battle on May 31, 1223, more than 20,000 invading Mongols (dots) feigned retreat before a Russian force (white arrow) of 80,000 men. At the Kalka River, the Mongols finally re-formed their ranks.

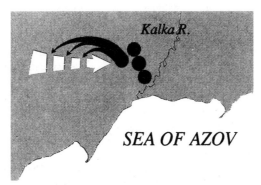

After pursuing the Mongols for days, the exhausted Russian troops were spread out along a twenty-mile line. The Mongols charged, with 5,000 mounted archers (black arrows) in the lead.

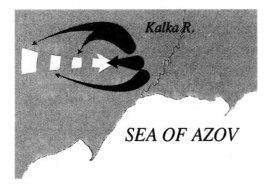

Once the leading Russian detachments were separated from their support columns and thrown into disarray, 5,000 Mongol heavy cavalry troops (black arrow) engaged them in close combat. Ten thousand light cavalry troops (gray) followed the retreating Russians, capturing or slaughtering most of them.

Mongols, observing that "by nature they [the Mongols] are good at riding and shooting. Therefore they took possession of the world through this advantage of bow and horse."

Genghis Khan understood the importance of horses and insisted that his troops be solicitous of their steeds. A cavalryman normally had three or four, so that each was, at one time or another, given a respite from bearing the weight of the rider during a lengthy journey. Before combat, leather coverings were placed on the head of each horse and its body was covered with armor. After combat, Mongol horses could traverse the most rugged terrain and survive on little fodder.

According to Marco Polo, the horse also provided sustenance to its rider on long trips during which all the food had been consumed. On such occasions, the rider would cut the horse's veins and drink the blood that spurted forth. Marco Polo reported, perhaps with some exaggeration, that a horseman could, by

nourishing himself on his horse's blood, "ride quite ten days' marches without eating any cooked food and without lighting a fire." And because its milk offered additional sustenance during extended military campaigns, a cavalryman usually preferred a mare as a mount. The milk was often fermented to produce kumiss, or *araq,* a potent alcoholic drink liberally consumed by the Mongols. In short, as one commander stated, "If the horse dies, I die; if it lives, I survive."

Mobility and surprise characterized the military expeditions led by Genghis Khan and his commanders, and the horse was crucial for such tactics and strategy. Horses could, without exaggeration, be referred to as the intercontinental ballistic missiles of the thirteenth century. The battle of the Kalka River, now renamed the Kalmyus River, in southern Russia is a good example of the kind of campaign Genghis Khan waged to gain territory and of the key role of horses.

After his relatively easy conquest of Central Asia from 1219 to 1220, Genghis Khan had dispatched about 30,000 troops led by Jebe and Sübedei, two of his ablest commanders, to conduct an exploratory foray to the west. After several skirmishes in Persia, the advance forces reached southern Russia. In an initial engagement, the Mongols, appearing to retreat, lured a much larger detachment of Georgian cavalry on a chase. When the Mongols sensed that the Georgian horses were exhausted, they headed to where they kept reserve horses, quickly switched to them, and charged at the bedraggled, spread-out Georgians. Archers, who had been hiding with the reserve horses, backed up the cavalry—with a barrage of arrows as they routed the Georgians.

Continuing their exploration, the Mongol detachment crossed the Caucasus Mountains, a daunting expedition during which many men and horses perished. They wound up just north of the Black Sea on the southern Russian steppes, which offered rich pasturelands for their horses. After a brief respite, they first attacked Astrakhan to the east and then raided sites along the Dniester and Dnieper Rivers, inciting Russian retaliation in May of 1223 under Mstislav the Daring, who had a force of 80,000 men. Jebe and Sübedei commanded no more than 20,000 troops and were outnumbered by a ratio of four to one.

Knowing that an immediate, direct clash could be disastrous, the Mongols again used their tactic of feigned withdrawal. They retreated for more than a week, because they wanted to be certain that the opposing army continued to pursue them but was spaced out

A Horse of a Different Chromosome?

by Oliver A. Ryder

Although Genghi[s] Khan's armies probably never numbered more than 200,000 troops, they may have had as many as 800,000 horses. Thirteenth-century sources, including *The Secret History of the Mongols,* give a tantalizing account of the training of Mongol horses. Captured in the wild and broken-in during the first two years of their lives, the young horses were then allowed to graze for three years. At the age of five they were once again ridden and prepared for combat. The Mongols depended on their horses so much, and gathered so many of them, that John of Plano Carpini, a papal emissary to the Mongol court from 1246 to 1247, noted with amazement that "they have such a number of horses and mares that I do not believe there are so many in all the rest of the world." What kind of horses were they?

A number of Mongol scholars, including historians James Chambers and Charles R. Bawden, have noted that the horses used by Genghis Khan and his descendants resembled Przewalski's horse, the species of wild horse that formerly inhabited the Gobi Desert and the steppes of Mongolia.

Przewalski's horse is named for Russian explorer and naturalist N. M. Przhevalsky, who first saw herds of the yellowish brown species in the central Asian steppes in about 1876. Both Przewalski's and the domestic horse are descended from the same lineage in the family Equidae, but Przewalski's horses differ from domestic horses morphologically, behaviorally, and genetically. All domestic breeds have 64 chromosomes, whereas Przewalski's have 66. (First-generation hybrids have 65 chromosomes and may interbreed with either domestic or Przewalski's horses.) Przewalski's horses have an erect, dark brown mane, no forelock, and white noses. Their coat has a distinctive dun color with a yellowish tinge on the back that becomes lighter toward the flanks and almost white under the belly. Their appearance is accentuated by bulky heads and, especially in stallions, stocky, well-muscled necks. Although their behavior has never been observed in wild populations, studies of herds kept in large enclosures and reserves suggest that, like feral domestic horses, stallions defend harems of mares from male competitors.

Przewalski's horses became extinct in the wild when the last survivors disappeared from the Dzungarian gobi of Mongolia in 1970, but were saved from total extinction by the existence of captive populations bred in zoos. Plans are now under way to return the only true wild horse to its ancient homelands in Mongolia, China, and adjacent regions of Russia. Experimental studies of herds of zoo-raised Przewalski's horses placed in new prairie and semidesert steppe environments suggest that adaptation to the wild environment can be rapidly accomplished. Perhaps one day they will repopulate their homelands and again roam freely in the wild.

Oliver A. Ryder holds the Kelberg Genetics Chair at the Zoological Society of San Diego's Center for Reproduction of Endangered Species. He has published extensively on the genetics of Przewalski's horses and other endangered species, and is particularly interested in the conservation of Asian arid steppe ecosystems and their wildlife.

over a considerable distance. At the Kalka River, the Mongols finally took a stand, swerving around and positioning themselves in battle formation, with archers mounted on horses in the front.

The Mongols' retreat seems to have lulled the Russians into believing that the invaders from the East were in disarray. Without waiting for the remainder of his army to catch up and without devising a unified attack, Mstislav the Daring ordered the advance troops to charge immediately. This decision proved to be calamitous. Mongol archers on their well-trained steeds crisscrossed the Russian route of attack, shooting their arrows with great precision. The Russian line of troops was disrupted, and the soldiers scattered.

After their attack, the archers turned the battlefield over to the Mongol heavy cavalry, which pummeled the already battered, disunited, and scattered Russians. Wearing an iron helmet, a shirt of raw silk, a coat of mail, and a cuirass, each Mongol in the heavy cavalry carried with him two bows, a dagger, a battle-ax, a twelve-foot lance, and a lasso as his principal weapons. Using lances, the detachment of heavy cavalry rapidly attacked and overwhelmed the Russian vanguard, which had been cut off from the rest of their forces in the very beginning of the battle.

Rejoined by the mounted archers, the combined Mongol force mowed down the straggling remnants of the Russian forces. Without an escape route, most were killed, and the rest, including Mstislav the Daring, were captured. Rather than shed the blood of rival princes—one of Genghis Khan's commands— Jebe and Sübedei ordered the unfortunate commander and two other princes stretched out under boards and slowly suffocated as Mongols stood or sat upon the boards during the victory banquet.

The battle at the Kalka River resembled, with some slight deviations, the general plan of most of Genghis Khan's campaigns. In less than two decades, Genghis Khan had, with the support of powerful cavalry, laid the foundations for an empire that was to control and govern much of Asia in the thirteenth and fourteenth centuries. He died on a campaign in Central Asia, and his underlings decided to return his corpse to his native land. Any unfortunate individual who happened to encounter the funeral cortege was immediately killed because the Mongols wished to conceal the precise location of the burial site. At least forty horses were reputedly sacrificed at Genghis Khan's tomb; his trusted steeds would be as important to him in the afterlife as they had been during his lifetime.

WOMEN AND THE EARLY CHURCH

Brent Shaw offers
a forceful
reassessment of
the women
martyrs and
heroines whose
activities on behalf
of the faith
provoked unsettled
admiration from
the church fathers.

Brent Shaw is Professor of History at the University of Lethbridge, Alberta, and is author of the article 'The Passion of Perpetua' in Past and Present, *vol. 139 (1993).*

Consider a tombstone from late fifth-century southern Italy: 'Leta, the priest (*presbytera*), lived 40 years, 8 months, 9 days. Her husband set this up for her'. Or a Latin inscription from Salona in Dalmatia, dated earlier in the same century: 'I Theodosius purchased this grave plot from the holy priest (*presbytera sancta*) Flavia Vitalia for three gold pieces'. Two notices that would seem to attest the existence of female

priests – not unusual in the world of Graeco-Roman antiquity, except that these women were Christians. As late as the fifth and sixth centuries AD women like these were found exercising priestly authority in Christian churches in locales as diverse as the cities of Asia Minor, Greece, Gaul, Sicily and southern Italy. It is also known how very unusual most of these cases were.

The women in Sicily and southern Italy who assumed the power and duties of priests did so in circumstances of considerable local social upheaval where, apparently, few qualified men were available. Their usurpation of male authority was harshly condemned by Pope Gelasius in a letter to the churches of the region (AD 492-96). However significant their mere existence might be for staking out current theological claims, or as ammunition in contemporary ecclesiastical conflict, they are exceptions that prove the rule – that women were gradually, inexorably, and deliberately excluded from formal positions of authority within the organisation of the Christian Church. A whole series of church councils, between those at Nicaea (325) and at Orange (441), repeatedly issued 'canons' or formal decrees that prohibited women from the ranks of the priesthood and from any involvement

in priestly liturgical duties, such as baptism and the eucharist.

Yet the changes in the societies that made up the Roman Empire which were provoked by the new religion of Christianity – ones that transformed the face of what we now somewhat hesitatingly call 'Western Civilization' – must have involved the half of the population who were women. Modern students of that process, however, have advanced much stronger claims than those of mere involvement. They have asserted that women, especially in the ranks of the aristocratic élite, were in the vanguard of the process of conversion and of the evangelisation of the new faith. It has been argued that women were far more influential in the forging of actual early church communities than has been generally recognised in the past. Scholars claim that women once widely performed liturgical roles, including those of baptism and giving the eucharist, later denied to them – a history of early empowerment deliberately obscured, in part, by the later re-editing of church documents. Finally, there are claims concerning the liberating effects of a Christianity that opened both new avenues of action and formal powers to women from which they had previously been barred. Any attempt to test these claims, and to understand the actual historical experience of women in early Christianity, however, is unendingly blocked by the nature (indeed, the sheer lack) of the surviving historical evidence. There is no doubt that some of the relevant records still exist. More assiduous searching in the last decade or so has brought many previously known but obscure and marginalised documents to the centre of the historian's agenda. But these records are almost entirely written by men. Although they do mention women, debate their roles and behaviour, provide interesting details about their lives, and sometimes even place them at the centre of their accounts, almost none of them were actually written by women themselves – a critical caveat that must constantly be borne in mind in all that follows.

After all, what historians *can* know depends on available records. The production of such records depends on an active literacy that specialises in the writing and the canonisation – the systematic organisation and preservation – of textual materials. What evidence there is clearly suggests a very limited literacy of this type amongst the women of the Roman Empire in which Christianity emerged. Literacy itself was probably restricted to a sizeable, though proportionately small, part of the whole population. Within the sector that might be deemed literate, women's literacy had a rather special character that matched the dominant moral codes of the time. It tended to be passive and consuming rather than active and producing. Women of the aristocratic élite, of whom we know the most, were literate in the sense that they were taught to read – usually, it seems, by their mothers. 'Saint' Jerome, who was especially close to these women, and parasitic on their wealth and social rank, writes at length in one of his letters to a mother how she should cut out little shapes of letters and with them teach her daughter, by this conventional method, to feel and thus to learn her letters. And of reading itself, there are good indications that they did a lot. The fourth-century Roman aristocratic woman Paula knew her scriptures, and certainly her Hebrew, better than her spiritual guru Jerome. Her contemporary Melania (the Elder) had read 'seven or eight times' the 'three million lines' of the Greek theologian Origen; and, similarly, 250,000 lines of the writings of other Greek 'Fathers' of the church.

When it came to the production of literary texts, however, a whole series of empowerments, conventions, and active restrictions meant that this remained, from the beginning to the end of the antique world in which Christianity evolved, a sphere of activity almost wholly controlled and dominated by men. When women who were literate did advance beyond the passive skills of reading to writing, with certain striking exceptions it was to the private sphere activities of composing letters and of keeping diaries (adjudged by men to be a morally inferior activity). Where active expression was involved, the evidence that we have indicates that it took place in a vast and amorphous world of oral communication labelled talk, conversation, innuendo, and gossip – but not formal public rhetoric. This was a powerful, potentially dangerous, and largely uncontrollable, realm of communication where reputations could be made or destroyed by persons as low as household slaves. But this world is largely, and one fears, permanently, lost to modern-day historians.

The developmental path traversed by Christianity, from the domain of personal to institutionalised power, itself provoked problems of integration. This is true despite the great diversity of structure and belief found in early Christian communities, since the various divergent movements within it, including those labelled schismatic or heretical, developed their own formal organisations or 'churches', and were just as committed to their institutions as any orthodoxy. Donatism – a separate regional variety of Christianity in North Africa from the early fourth century AD – was viewed as dissenting, heretical, schismatic, and dangerous by its orthodox critics, but was every bit as committed to its own texts, hierarchies, church buildings and edifices, readers, deacons, priests, bishops, and elaborate defences of their authority and prerogatives, as were any 'orthodox' Catholics in Italy or elsewhere. The problem is that Christianity, which ended by developing powerful and complex ecclesiastical institutions, had begun life as a quasi-millenarian prophetic 'Jesus move-

ment' in the region of Palestine. It had spread westward by the dual agencies of individual effort, will and charisma, and the social unit of the household or family. In both eastern and western Mediterranean worlds, therefore, the model or image of the family, so crucial to the spread of early Christianity, became subject to intense ideological scrutiny and regulation. But eventually the family basis of a nascent Christianity soon had to be integrated with, and made subordinate to, formal organisations that embodied values quite different from those of the rebellious expectations of a new personal faith that offered its converts the hope of a substantially changed future.

In Pauline writings, those millennial expectations of the repressed are clearly signalled. Slaves who converted, especially those who were slaves of Christian masters, quickly assumed that the end of time was now at hand and a whole new order was dawning. Since they were just as much the 'brothers' and 'sisters' of their masters and mistresses, and since all were equally the 'sons' and 'daughters' or 'the slaves' of the one God, they reasonably expected that they would be freed from the conventional ties that both bound and ranked them. This misapprehension had to be corrected – as Paul himself made clear in his reply to one Philemon about his escaped slave Onesimus. The case was not an isolated one. The parallel message, and opportunities, broadcast to women of free status no doubt evoked similar expectations and responses. The problem was: how were *they* to be contained? This was not as easily solvable a problem as that of the slaves, many of whom, it must not be forgotten, were women. Slave women who had millennial expectations of more freedom were, no doubt, like slave men, simply ordered (as Paul himself specifically ordained) to get back to their proper place. The larger problem was with free women.

Mediterranean male protocols of both Greek and Roman societies had rather blunt and severe prescriptions on the proper place of women of free status, especially that of wives. What actually happened in the circumstances of daily life was, no doubt, something rather different. The existence of a strong conflict between prescription and reality is indicated by need constantly to restate the protocols themselves in every conceivable form of communication, oral and written, from the high literature of the city-state, in its poetry and drama, to the more mundane extra-canonical technical treatises of doctors and architects. Another indication is that even a male ideologue like Aristotle was forced to concede that although a father and husband's authority over the children and slaves of his own household was 'like that of a king' (the absolute power to command obedience), his relationship to his wife was 'political'. That is to say, the latter relationship was a process of constant negotiation, debate, and arbitration typical of the distribution of power in a democratic polity. The man was always supposed 'to win' this contest, and a specific order within the household, with the man as 'head', was to be maintained.

But any strong millenarian or ecstatic religion, and not just Christianity, that attracted adherents from the 'inferior' elements in the family, by its very nature constituted a threat to family order. In most cases, household heads that faced such systematic threats could be expected to be backed by strong action from their state that would both reaffirm existing norms of the family and the traditional position of women. The so-called Bacchanalian conspiracy in Rome in 186 BC was just such a case. It was a hysterical reaction against the perceived threat of cult cells in Rome and Italy supposedly dedicated to vile secret rituals dedicated to the Greek god Bacchus, groups including free women and slaves that were corrupting young men, and were forming a dangerous and subversive 'state within a state'. Revelations and betrayals led to a systematic repression throughout Italy by the consuls and the Roman senate that prohibited women from such worship and ordered that guilty daughters and wives be handed over to their families for punishment in household courts headed by their fathers and husbands. But early Christian communities did not have this advantage. They had to stabilise the order of the family and household, probably the principal formal container of the new religion down to the end of the first century, while simultaneously facing increasingly hostile local communities that actively courted the violent

intervention of officials of the Roman state.

Christian communities responded by restating, with categorical fervour, traditional family relationships in a series of formal regulations. These are exemplified in the so-called 'Household Tables' found in several of the New Testament books (Ephesians 5.21-6.9; Colossians, 3.18-4.1; 1 Timothy, 2.9-6.2; 1 Peter 2.18-3.12 are the main texts) – tables whose prescriptions were ceaselessly re-iterated in the West by the church 'Fathers' from Tertullian to Augustine, and beyond. The imperatives of these texts insisted that all persons – father-husband, mother-wife, children, and, finally, slaves – were to be maintained in a fixed, hierarchical social order, all subordinated to each other and, finally, all were to be subject in fear to God the Father and Lord (*dominus* meaning 'slave owner') as his children and slaves. This much desired 'proper order' was threatened in numerous structural ways. One of these was that of differential conversion – the main problem here (not necessarily an overwhelming statistical regularity, but rather a perceived problem) being those cases where wives converted to Christianity while their husbands did not. The problem was a long-standing one that characterised the many religious movements into local societies where the new beliefs were not neatly contained as state or civic cults under the supervision and control of the male heads of household who constituted the fully recognised citizens who controlled the levers of government.

As an extension of the rule of order within the household, out of which a good part of the early and formative existence of the church was derived, rules of bodily space and of voice were gradually, but surely, imposed on the architecture of the church itself. Women and girls were seated separately from men and boys – women were ranked: matrons were separated from virgins, widows from those groups, and young girls from all of them. There was also a gradual but finally decisive move to impose head coverings on women (somewhat misrepresented in many modern discussion as 'veils') as a symbol of submission to the 'head' of household and God the Father. These measures had different tempos and regional variations in the Christian

communities of the ancient Mediterranean. A recently published sermon of Augustine, for example, attests the new provision of separate entrance doorways for men and women in the main basilica at Carthage – an innovation imposed only in the early 400s AD. The general tendency of all these measures, however, was in one direction: a purposefully imposed inconspicuousness and silence.

A current meliorist strain in historical interpretation finds it difficult to face the near obvious. Repression can be successful. The vast written records of the early church preserve not one female theologian, even though there is consistent evidence of women's involvement in theological debates and in teaching. Although there might have been some lower order officials, the priesthood and other high offices became closed to women as the church gradually constituted its own 'public sphere' parallel to that of the state. Of course, the process involved constant struggle, and a repression that was never completely closed or finally achieved. Although the church in the west was finally to draw the line at the level of the priesthood, as late as the fifth and sixth centuries women deacons were both ordained and recognised as a formal clerical part of the ecclesiastical hierarchy. In the ritual by which new Christians were created, that of baptism, the 'born again' had to have evil demons driven from their body – a critical function performed by exorcists. Exorcists were just as much a part of the formal hierarchy of church offices as were priests. And women regularly held the office of exorcist – women who were therefore seen to wield considerable spiritual, and secular, power. Moreover, the constant emergence of forms of Christianity that challenged orthodoxy, or of esoteric brands of Christian or 'near-Christian' beliefs and thought, such as those called 'gnostic', produced milieux in which orthodox norms were constantly challenged and questioned. But those who would find 'feminine' emphases in the alternative theodicies of 'gnosticism', must face the unpleasant fact that the feminine principle in this theodicy, however important, was roughly the equivalent of the Devil in 'mainstream' Christian ideology, and that even the 'gnostics' held that the perfected being was going to be male, and that each woman would have to be transformed into a man before achieving that final perfection.

While the church could define and close off specific times and physical spaces that defined its offices and formal powers, it would always have to face challenges that would well up out of the non-ecclesiastically controlled personal behaviours. There were several distinct spheres where the simple actions, experiences or given social positions of individuals bestowed power on them that could not be immediately or directly controlled by the church. These included: transcendent personal experiences such as dreams, prophesies, and ecstatic performance; extraordinary demonstrations of personal bravery and fortitude that even élite Roman men would value as a species of manliness (*virtus*); and the possession of independent status in the secular world outside the direct control of the church – high social rank and wealth. Finally, there were new opportunities offered by the emergence of 'heretical' movements which were, by definition, not under the control of the authorities. In any one of these areas (or better, in combinations of them) women effectively circumvented, and therefore challenged, the continuing efforts of men to monopolise the institutional powers of Christian churches.

A typical phenomenon that exemplifies some of these opportunities, much studied because well-documented cases are so rare, is the movement labelled 'Montanism' (after Montanus, its supposed male head). Emerging from the remote heartlands of Asia Minor in the mid-second century, Montanist adherents exhibited ecstatic experience – dreams, prophetic utterances – with tendencies to separate themselves from the formal churches of the region. Whatever roles and powers 'Montanist' women like the Quintilla, Maximilla, and Priscilla were able to assume, they seem to have had no substantial known impact on the powers of women in the 'orthodox' church. These women may well have been able to denounce their husbands, abandon their marriages, and assume priestly roles (all of this, however, reported in a later hostile rhetoric), but by the time 'Montanism' can be identified in a western Mediterranean context – at Carthage in North Africa

at the end of the second century and beginning of the third, it was being effectively tamed to orthodox ends. Women could and, indeed, did prophesy – but, as Tertullian reported of his congregation in Carthage, only at the appropriate time, in church, and the publication of the message was permitted only after the woman had been debriefed by the male presbyters in seclusion after the service. The views of Tertullian (himself labelled a Montanist) on these 'heretical women who dared to teach, exorcise, heal, and baptise' was blunt:

> Women are not permitted to speak in church, to teach, to baptise, to offer eucharist, to undertake any other male duty, or to arrogate to themselves any priestly task whatsoever.

The combined elements of independence from direct male control in the household, personal wealth, and the breakdown of the controls of a single central church could produce opportune circumstances in which a woman could become unusually effective. In AD 312 at Carthage, Lucilla, a wealthy woman of high social standing, refused to apologise for her practice of bestowing a kiss on a holy relic. Caecilian, the priest who dared to reprimand her, suddenly found himself opposed for election to the vacant position of Bishop of Carthage by a male slave from Lucilla's own household. This servant, named Majorinus, was trained, funded and supported by Lucilla and defeated Caecilian in the election. The ensuing battles within the church at Carthage led directly to one of the greatest of the 'schisms' in the history of the church in the West – the emergence of a separate North African or 'Donatist' church. Lucilla, however, was not alone. A century later, Augustine could refer to at least two parallel cases of independent wealthy women who stood at the head of the creation of more schismatic or breakaway movements within the church in North Africa.

The ideology of a church that placed such a high value on virginity was naturally hostile to remarriage and exalted the status of the widow. Because of this, and its prohibitions against divorce, Christianity created a new social group, that of widows, in numbers and with a definition never before seen in the pre-Christian world. But the very existence of a new order of independent women

with their own wealth posed a constant threat to the church's desired order. Jerome could condemn a very wealthy woman, a widow, whom he saw ostentatiously distributing alms as a quintessential hypocrisy – but then she had found her place, as much of any of Jerome's highly touted virgins. Reality, however, often confounded the rhetoric. After much sweating and effort, and in hand-wringing despair, Jerome's contemporary, Ambrose, the Bishop of Milan, confessed that there were only twenty known virgins in the large Italian city of Bononia (Bologna). It was not for want of numerous lengthy exhortations to virginity, amongst them Jerome's letter to the noble-woman, Eustochium, that preached the new ascetic ideals. But even Jerome had to admit that his treatise was stoned by the people of Rome.

Indeed, it was the wealthy élite women whom Jerome himself so castigated and fawned upon, 'small women weighed down by sins', who were, in his view, the cause of 'heresies'. But in his own letters we can trace his changed attitudes to a wealthy woman as she shifted status from dependent wife to independent widow. While her husband was still alive, the Spanish noblewoman Theodora merited only perfunctory reference. After her husband's death, she became the object of special attention. She was now one of those widows upon whom Christian ideology bestowed so much prestige. That standing, and her wealth, meant power – and hence the need of incessant instruction from men like Jerome on proper behaviour.

In the critical period of its growth and institutionalisation, and of attacks on it from those who detested and feared Christians, the church could not control the fact that the very process of persecution drew women as well as men into the public arenas of the empire where these matters were finally settled. In their public demonstration of courage, or bodily resistance, of iron-willed and open confrontation with supreme figures of authority – from their own fathers to the Roman governors who put them on trial – women martyrs were perhaps the most difficult case with which the church had to cope. They became central actors in public venues, and active front-line defenders of the faith in a conflict that pitted them against the diabolical forces of the state. Given the prevalent moral codes of that world, the actions of these women meant that great power and glory accrued to their names. So, for example, the pogrom against Christians in the city of Lugdunum (Lyons) in AD 177, highlighted the achievements of a Christian woman who would otherwise have been regarded as 'contemptible' and 'cheap' by the prevalent male values of her world: the slave woman Blandina. But in the words of the man who reported her death, by enduring the almost unspeakable tortures vented on her body, Blandina acquired a fame and renown like that of a 'noble athlete'. She had proven to the population of a major Roman city that she had greater endurance and fortitude than many men. Reports of such achievements by women that confuted the normative values placed on them were subsequently most difficult to explain away.

Much of the same could be said of Perpetua, a woman who was executed in the arena at Carthage in AD 203 on the charge of being Christian. The difference in her case is that she was not only a freeborn, wealthy woman of high social standing, but she was also a woman who wrote. It is from her hand that there survives one of the very few, if not only, extensive pieces of narrative prose written by a woman during the whole period of the high Roman Empire. The challenge presented by women like Blandina and Perpetua was to be found in the ideological backwash following their deaths. Their behaviour and achievements in huge public arenas, before crowds of spectators who witnessed their trials, and before tens of thousands who watched their deaths in amphitheatres of the empire, was systematically to refute both assumptions and claims about 'feminine fragility' and 'unworthiness' that underwrote the subordination and silence so insisted upon by Paul and his successors.

The general response to this was to control the very accounts by which persons through time would come to know of the achievement of women martyrs. In most cases, this was easily done because the male ideologues who were the only recorders of the acts of the martyrs, could directly rewrite these women's experiences in a theological form that left only divine interpretations (and explanations) open for their actions. For the most part, this reduced to the truism that they were able to act like men because of the infusion of the spirit of the Christian deity into their bodies. Perpetua's case, however, was more problematic, since she had left a detailed record of her own experiences in her own words. This account then had to be rewritten, reshaped, parodied, mimicked, and preached about till the end of the Roman Empire in the West. Like her bodily martyrdom, her words were an implicit threat to the assumed norms that underwrote the institutional power of the church.

Though signs are notably few in the records that have survived – what else would one expect? – there is nonetheless a myriad of little clues, micro-points of evidence, that point to recurrent resistance to the edifices of male power in ecclesiastical institutions. Such were women in Tertullian's Carthage in the late second and early third century who prophesied, who taught, who told him that he had no business imposing dress codes on them, and still others who insisted on following their modes of worship and actively proselytised for their own beliefs – whose 'silliness', 'madness' and 'unspeakable arrogance' were sufficient to provoke from Tertullian a terrible anger, and a litany of regulatory prose. Despite his efforts, women like these were still present in the Christian congregation of the North African metropolis as late as the fourth and fifth centuries – women who refused to take direction from male priests in the matter of proper behaviour. And in fourth- and fifth-century Rome there were those who, like the noble Marcella, assumed that they could teach the Christian message, and who could hold their own in acrimonious theological debate.

The examples need not be multiplied. They are sufficient to show that, with each generation, there was a continual struggle, a conflict of Aristotle's 'political type', between the men and women who contested the new resource of the church, the new family of Christ. That is why church councils had to keep reiterating those laws that systematically excluded women from its ranks. And that is precisely why the heavy overlay of male ideology (of which the vast bulk of surviving ecclesiastical and theological writings were an important part) had to be restated with every new generation. And why, although those records are indeed 'our history', we must rewrite them.

FOR FURTHER READING:
For original sources see the collections by Ross S. Kraemer, *Maenads, Martyrs, Matrons, Monastics: A Sourcebook on Women's Religions in the Greco-Roman World*, (Fortress, 1988) and by Elizabeth A. Clark, *Women in the Early Church*, (Glazier, 1983); the formative modern critical analysis is that of Elisabeth Schüssler Fiorenza, *In Memory of Her: A Feminist Theological Reconstruction of Christian Origins*, (Crossroad, 1983); on women and 'gnosticism', Elaine Pagels, *The Gnostic Gospels*, (Random House, 1979); replies by Suzanne Heine, *Women and Early Christianity: A Reappraisal*, (Augsburg, 1988); Karen L. King (ed), *Images of the Feminine in Gnosticism*, (Fortress, 1988); on ecclesiastical office, Roger Gryson, *The Ministry of Women in the Early Church*, (Liturgical Press, 1976); Aimé G. Martimort, *Deaconesses: An Historical Study* (Ignatius, 1985); on sexuality, Peter Brown, *The Body and Society: Men, Women, and Sexual Renunciation in Early Christianity*, (Columbia University Press, 1988); on widows, Bonnie B. Thurston, *The Widows: A Women's Ministry in the Early Church*, (Augsburg, 1989); on virgins, Joyce E. Salisbury, *Church Fathers, Independent Virgins*, (Verso, 1991).

HAZARDS ON THE WAY TO THE MIDDLE AGES

Barbara Tuchman

Barbara Tuchman holds two Pulitzer Prizes for history. This essay is drawn from a lecture before the Massachusetts Historical Society.

A historian sets out in search of a "verray parfit gentil knight," and encounters many surprises along the road.

 he problem of writing a book laid in the Middle Ages—specifically in France in the second half of the fourteenth century—is that one can never be certain of achieving a likeness that is valid. At 600 years' distance the Middle Ages gleam like a fairy-tale castle on a glass hill, and at the foot is an abyss. The gap in received ideas between then and now—in habits of thought, conduct, politics, beliefs—is so wide as to make it virtually impossible to leap across, impossible for the historian to be sure of understanding what motivated people of that time, impossible to be sure of describing it as it really was.

My object is to try to portray fifty years of a tormented and disintegrating society in which I see reflections of our own. A particular person's life is used for purposes of narrative and focus. The fifty years are those that followed the Black Death of 1348–1350, the most lethal disaster of recorded history, so far. The person in question is not a king or queen or sovereign or royalty of any kind, because they are too special and too often used; nor a commoner, because commoners' lives in most cases were not wide-ranging enough, nor individually sufficiently documented; nor a cleric or saint, such as Catherine of Siena, for instance, because they are outside my comprehension. So I am left with a noble: his name is Enguerrand de Coucy

VII, and he is ideal for the purpose. Except for a single article published in 1939, nothing has ever been written about him in English, and there is no formal biography in French either, except for a doctoral thesis of 1890 that exists only in longhand manuscript, and French script at that.

I read this in Paris, under the eaves on the top floor of the Ecole de Chartes, somewhat hampered by parsimony with electric light. Actually, while it filled out certain episodes, it did not contain very much that I had not already found, and the one thing I really wanted, the author's list of sources, was missing. It might not have helped in any case, because one of the afflictions of French history is that certain sources available to earlier historians have since disappeared, many destroyed in the French Revolution and others in World War I. Some Coucy documents originating with the Crown exist in the national collections, and key documents such as his will and his religious foundations exist in print. But no local Coucy archive survives, partly because Mazarin destroyed most of the castle during the Fronde, and the Germans in 1917 blew up what was left.

Nevertheless, Enguerrand VII is a perfect subject, because from the time his mother died in the Black Death to his own marvelously appropriate death in the culminating fiasco of knighthood that closed the century, his life was as if designed for the historian. He suppressed the peasant revolt called the Jacquerie. He married the eldest daughter of King Edward III of England, thereby acquiring double allegiance of great historical interest. He freed his serfs in return for due payment. He campaigned three times in Italy, conveniently at Milan, Florence, and Genoa, and became the Crown's Italian expert. He commanded an army of brigand mercenaries, the worst scourge of the age, in an effort to lead them out of the country like the Pied Piper. He picked the right year to revisit England, 1376, the year of Wycliffe's struggle, the Good Parliament, and the death of the Black Prince, at whose deathbed he was present. He was escort for Emperor Charles IV at all the stage plays, pageantry, and festivities during the imperial visit to Paris. He was chosen for his eloquence and

From *The Atlantic Monthly*, December 1975. © 1975 by Barbara W. Tuchman. Reprinted by permission of Russell & Volkening, Inc., as agents for the author.

tact to negotiate with the urban rebels of Paris in 1382, and at a truce parley with the English at which a member of the opposite team just happened to be Geoffrey Chaucer. He was agent or envoy to the Pope, the Duke of Brittany, and other difficult characters in delicate situations. He was a patron and friend of Froissart, and owned the oldest surviving copy of the *Chronicle*. His castle was celebrated in a poem by Deschamps. He assisted at the literary competition for the *Cent Ballades*, of which his cousin, the Bastard of Coucy, was one of the authors: On the death of his father-in-law, King Edward, he returned his wife *and* the Order of the Garter to England. His daughter was "divorced at Rome by means of false witnesses" by her dissolute husband. He commanded an overseas expedition to Tunisia. He founded a monastery at Soissons. He testified at the canonization process of Pierre de Luxembourg. At age fifty he was challenged to a joust by the Earl of Nottingham, Earl Marshal of England, aged twenty-three, as the person most fitting to confer "honor, valor, chivalry, and great renown" on a young knight (though from what I can gather, Coucy was too busy to bother with him). He was of course in the King's company at the sensational mad scene when Charles VI went out of his mind, and at the macabre Dance of the Savages afterward. It was his physician who attended the King and who later ordered his own tomb effigy as a skeleton, the first of its kind in the cult of death. Finally, as "the most experienced and skillful of all the knights of France," he was a leader of the last Crusade, and on the way to death met the only medieval experience so far missing from his record, an attested miracle. In short, he supplies leads to every subject—marriage and divorce, religion, insurrection, literature, Italy, England, besides, of course, war and politics. For more about my remarkable friend, you will have to wait for my book, which is a long time off.

am not happy with history in categories—intellectual, military, economic, or other. C. V. Langlois' book *Connaissance de la Nature au Moyen Age* contains a statement of purpose which I should like to adopt: he wanted to find and reveal "what were the aspects of contemporary life; the ordinary and general manner of living, of thinking, acting, feeling? The customs, habits, beliefs, prejudices? In short, what was the material, moral, and in-

tellectual atmosphere in which men of that time were plunged?"

The difficulty is that the mental and moral furniture of the period is so different from ours as to create what seems like a different civilization.

The main barrier, I believe, is the Christian religion as it then was: the air, the law, the matrix of medieval life, pervasive, ubiquitous, inescapable, in fact, compulsory. Chivalry—meaning the set of ideas comprising loyalty, honor, prowess, courtesy, largesse, and so-called courtly love—is another barrier, for chivalry was really the politics and, at least for the noble estate, the manners of the time. Both these sets of ideas were taken for granted—though not without dissent—and, at the same time, were normally and regularly violated every day by everyone to whom they applied. To do otherwise was impossible, because the Church set itself, at least in theory, against the natural instincts of sensual man and of economic man, and chivalry was a glorious ideal that honored man's self-image more than it suited his daily habits. The persistent medieval gap between ideas and practice makes a difficult passage for the historian, not unlike a passage through one of those tunnels of distorting mirrors and sliding floors in an amusement park.

hat is the overall problem, but I should like to mention some lesser hazards: to begin with, what might be called "swimming data," that is to say, dates, money, numbers, nomenclature, and other such factors, which ought to be definite, but in the Middle Ages are anything but. People sigh when one mentions dates, but they are basic; if one does not know what precedes and what follows, one cannot know cause and effect, and one cannot tell a story. Medieval records do not make it easy.

The year began at Easter, which means that the time between January 1 and Easter, whenever that was, is not what we think it was; but whether it was the year before or the year after is a running enigma. You have to know when Easter fell, which might have been at any time between March 22 and April 22; but in the case of official English documents, it doesn't matter, because they used the regnal year dating from the first year of the current king's reign (ah, but what *month* did it begin? There's a trap). On the continent, some chanceries, but not all, used the papal year. If a chronicler placed an event, let us say, on March 30, 1356 (which, by the way, he never does, for reasons to be explained), and if Easter came before March 30, the year *is* 1356; but if not, it is 1357. Depending upon what month Edward III began his reign, 1356 is either 29 Edward or 30 Edward, or, put the other way around, if a document is dated 30 Edward, does it refer to 1356 or 1357? God alone knows what year it is in Avignon.

However, a chronicler never does mention March 30 or any date by number, but speaks rather of the day before St. John the Baptist's Day, or two days after the Nativity of the Virgin, or the Monday after Epiphany, or the third Sunday in Lent. This requires a list of saints' days at hand as well as a list of the days when Easter fell; the one I used, called the *Trésor de Chronologie*, unaccountably had blanks for 1347, 1356, 1364, and 1369. How come? Did Easter just wander off and get lost?

The result of all this is to confuse not only historians but the inhabitants of the fourteenth century themselves, who rarely if ever agree on the same date for any event.

Let me tell you about money; it is worse. The fourteenth century used the florin, the ducat, the livre, the pound, the ecu, and the franc, all of which apparently were based on the Roman pound, shilling, and pence system, with the pound supposedly containing 3.5 grams of gold. But wait, there is money in coin and money of account, which expresses value, not weight, and they no longer match. What's more, the various gold coins, florins, etcetera, which presumably once equaled each other, no longer match because one or another gets debased in gold content. They now seem to hover at about one fifth of a pound sterling (but why sterling, when we thought the standard was gold? I can't answer that), except for the livre tournois, of which six equal one florin. What's *tournois*? Well, the French used both a livre parisis and a livre tournois, four of one equaling five of the other, and even occasionally a livre bordelais, meaning, I suppose, from Bordeaux, although Bordeaux was of course held by the English. Compared to French money, as was once said of a particularly slippery statesman, an eel is a leech.

Philip VI and Jean II devalued the currency so often that they wore out the livre and took to coining the ecu, which was worth about two or three sous (or shillings), except that another authority, according to my notes, says it was worth 22.5 sous. No sooner has one become adapted, if not resigned, to the ecu, when out of nowhere appears a new character called the mouton d'or. In the case of a bishop's ransom in 1358, the sum was fixed at 9000 ecus d'or, plus fifty silver marks, plus one good warhorse valued at 100 moutons d'or. Why, in God's name, *three* currencies? Why *marks*, all of a sudden?

For a while I thought the mouton d'or might be something like today's—or yesterday's—English guinea: a pound and a little bit more to confuse the tourist, except that this could not be right, because when the word "gold" is attached, it implies an actual coin. Like the question whether the insides of cathedrals were painted, which I pursued for a long time, the mouton d'or was one of those problems about which no one seemed certain.

Medievalists on the whole are kind, helpful, friendly people, except for a regrettable tendency to reply to any question, "That's not my period." I am deeply indebted to many of them for answers that genuinely illuminate a problem, but they are tremendous specialists who do not like to peek over the walls of their specialty. They study life in sharply sliced sections—monasticism, land tenure, banking and credit, pilgrimages, or whatever—and in the process they learn a vast amount that is invaluable to those of us who come after. But a hazard of the process, I think, is losing curiosity about life as a whole.

ne of my questions was about the chastity belt: to what extent was it really a device in normal use, or was it, despite the one or two alleged examples in museums, more of a literary fancy? I asked the author of a scholarly and indispensable work nominally on contraception but actually covering many aspects of sexual theory and customs. He said he knew nothing about the chastity belt; when pressed, he said that that was not his subject; he was concerned with people who *wanted* sex, not those who wanted to *avoid* it. Now there is specialization for you.

In the case of Picardy, where the Coucy dynasty lived for 400 years, what was my distress to discover, in a book by a modern scholar entirely devoted to medieval Picardy, that the domain of Coucy and its region were not once mentioned, not even in the index. On meeting the author later at the Sorbonne, I asked him why he had left Coucy out. Because, he said, it belonged to a region of different soil formation, which did not grow wheat like the rest of Picardy, and so he had not included it. However, when I went to Laon, capital of the diocese, the local archivist indignantly denied that the area had not grown wheat in the fourteenth century. This disagreement is par for any medieval condition, which brings me to the problem of discrepancies and conflicting evidence.

6. THE WORLD OF THE MIDDLE AGES, 500–1500

You can take it as an axiom that any statement of fact will be met by a statement of the opposite. Women outnumbered men because men were killed off in the wars; men outnumbered women because women died in childbirth. Common people were familiar with the Bible; common people were unfamiliar with the Bible. Nobles were tax exempt; no they were not tax exempt. French peasants were filthy and foul-smelling and lived on bread and onions; French peasants ate pork, fowl, and game, and enjoyed frequent baths in the village bathhouses. I could extend the list indefinitely. The contraries range over everything from small specifics to the total view of the period, which most people see as decline but which one brave historian calls "Dawn of a New Era." Take a tiny matter like the Black Prince's voyage to Bordeaux in 1355. "With a brisk wind in his sails he scudded over in three days," says one historian, while another states flatly that he was at sea for two weeks. The time in this case is of no importance one way or another, but a ground strewn with these discrepancies makes hard going.

Even the most learned scholar trips. Even Delachenal, the great reliable, whose five volumes on Charles V are an ocean of erudition. Along comes Perroy, dean of the Hundred Years' War, with the shattering discovery that the alleged peace conference at Bruges of January–March 1374, which Delachenal had treated at length and the existence of which Perroy himself had never doubted, never in fact took place! It seems Delachenal was misled by letters of authority issued to the English and French and ecclesiastical envoys who, however, according to Perroy, never met in person. Where Homer nods, lesser folk are bound to stumble. Faced with all these discrepancies, one simply has to make a choice, based on the degree of confidence in the source and on inherent probability.

umbers are the obvious stumbling block but not the most dangerous, because it is clear from the outset that medieval statistics cannot be taken seriously. Chroniclers are forever numbering armies or plague deaths or city crowds in tens or scores of thousands which financial and other records show to have been enlarged by several hundred percent. The English invaders of 1359, said to number 20,000 by Froissart and 10,000 by Chandos Herald, turn out, under examination of pay records, to have numbered 1750 knights and

about 3500 foot soldiers, or about one quarter of Froissart's figure. The plague toll for Avignon in 1348, put by one observer at 120,000, is a figure more than double what has since been estimated as the city's entire population.

G. G. Coulton, the historian who must have known more about the Middle Ages than anyone who ever lived, offers a guidepost when he speaks of the "chronic and intentional vagueness" of medieval figures. Numbers were intended not as data, but as a device of literary art to astonish and amaze the reader. The reason they so often appear in multiples of six—6000 and 60,000—is that, according to Coulton, the figure 600 was commonly used in Roman speech as the equivalent of "limitless" or "countless." Lack of precision and an affinity for round numbers were, of course, the natural consequence of using Roman numerals. Here you bump into another discrepancy: Arabic numerals are said to have come into use by the twelfth century. Well, if they did, they must have been confined to merchants and bankers, because they certainly did not reach the chroniclers.

Like dates, numbers are basic because they tell you what proportion of the population is involved in a given situation, and a false idea of this will give a false historical picture. Medieval exaggeration of armies, for instance, led to a misunderstanding of medieval war as analogous to modern war, which it was not, in means, methods, or purpose. In 1381, England's basis for calculating the poll tax was so far off that returns proved to be only two thirds of expectations, with the result that the government had to impose a second tax, which precipitated the Peasants' Revolt, the greatest crisis of the English Middle Ages. Such are the perils of careless numbers.

Immediate post-medieval historians repeated without question the chroniclers' figures, which went on being repeated thereafter. Only late in the nineteenth century, and much more in our own time, did historians begin to re-examine the records. One result has been to change entirely our estimate of the population. Boissonade, in the nineteenth century, gave Paris a population of 300,000 before the Black Death, which J. C. Russell, the pope of modern demography, has now cut down to 100,000. Levasseur, in the nineteenth century, gave France before the Black Death a population of 60 million, which today is thought to be the figure for all of Europe at that time. Agreement stops here. Russell now puts the pre-plague population of France at 21 million, Ferdinand Lot at 15 to 16 million, and Perroy at a lowly 10 to 11 million, exactly half of Russell's figure. Here's a clear case of what I mean by hazards. Size of population affects studies of everything else—taxes, life expectancy, commerce and agriculture, famine and plenty—and here we have figures by modern authorities which differ by 100 percent.

Names, by comparison, are a minor confusion. The trouble derives from the spelling, which was more or less phonetic. Judging by the different spelling of names on either side of the Channel, pronunciation of French, which was the common language of the English and French upper class, must have been close to mutually unintelligible. For some eccentric reason, Enguerrand becomes Ingelram in English. My nearest mishap came in the case of Arnaut de Cervole, a notorious brigand captain of mercenaries. On coming across frequent mention of such a captain named, or spelled, Canolles, I took this to be a variant of Cervole and put him in Cervole's place, until after a while the circumstances just did not fit. It turned out that Canolles was actually a French version of Knowles or Knolles, an equally notorious *English* brigand. This sort of thing, though not major, tends to make one nervous.

he empty spaces in medieval history are pitfalls too. The chroniclers were not interested in, or at any rate paid little or no attention (except in the case of ruling figures) to, personality and appearance or individual circumstance. They ignored the psyche. Biographies, autobiographies, and letters exist in a few cases, mostly for clerics and saints, but rarely for nonroyal, nonliterary laymen, with the bright exception of the Merchant of Prato, marvelously reconstructed as a character from his letters by Iris Origo. Again, except for royalty, portraiture too was nonexistent in the fourteenth century. One is left to piece together a character only from his or her acts, which is possible but chancy.

With Enguerrand a personality is gradually taking shape, like a message emerging from secret ink, of a man of immense *savoir-faire,* cooler, more level-headed, more realistic than most of his contemporaries, less given to their "furious follies," more acquainted with common sense. I think this will appear from his conduct and relationships; nevertheless, much is missing. Why, for example, did Coucy twice refuse the offer of the constableship, the most powerful and lucrative lay post in France? His given reason does not seem to me to be adequate, but so far I know no more. I can only hope that when I come to writing that chapter, the process of arranging the material in a logical narrative will produce, as it so often does in my experience, a possible answer.

hanging fashions in history can be a hazard for any period and especially for the Middle Ages, because an interval of 600 years can nourish quite a few sets of revisionists. With a loud crack, the most violent revision came in the nineteenth century, when historians discovered the common man. "Formerly," to quote Simeon Luce, whose history of the Jacquerie was a sign of the change, "the common ground of historians was the cult of nobility, as it is now the adoration of the people." That was written in 1862; worship of the masses was not invented by Chairman Mao.

During the three centuries following the fourteenth, history was virtually a genealogy of nobility, devoted to tracing dynastic lines and connections, and infused by the idea of the noble as a superior person. These works of enormous antiquarian research teem with information, including the item found in Anselm about the Gascon lord who bequeathed a hundred livres "for the dowries of poor girls, especially those whom I deflowered, if they can be found." I do not think that Père Anselm included that with a sly wink indicating the frailty of nobles, but rather as evidence of noble charity to be expected of a *grand seigneur.*

Then, with sunburst and thunder, comes the French Revolution and the great reversal . . . the common man is hero, the poor are *ipso facto* virtuous, kings and nobles are monsters of iniquity, like Chinese landlords in communist history, though perhaps not quite achieving that totality of villainy. In the era of the Great War, nationalism becomes pre-eminent; then, in the ensuing era of disillusion, history becomes sober—no more flags, glory, virtue, or villainy. Ideology yielded to the data. We enter the intense fact-finding of the *Annales,* when every historian marks out his square yard of territory and turns over every particle of dust, every document, every name—and sometimes finds gold. One investigator of religious observance found a town with surviving church records of the number of communion wafers sold over a space of two years, and by comparing these with tax records of the number of hearths, came up with an estimate of the frequency of attending Mass—about once or twice a year. I am entranced by that kind of work, even if this result merely confirmed an existing estimate without proving anything new. The only trouble is that when these historians write books, they manage to conceal whatever gold they may have found in a lamentable failure of synthesis. I admire them all, but I *wish* they would condense.

Today, while the industrious diggers are still at work, ideology rules over the data again in the revisionism of the New Left. Fortunately, so far, they have not greatly disturbed the Middle Ages, absorbed as they are in the history of last week, not to mention of the day after tomorrow, where I earnestly hope they will remain.

Through all these changing angles of vision, the Middle Ages glimmer like a castle in a fairy tale, never really to be entered, never really known. The gap in assumptions is too wide. Fear of hell, for instance, fear of a real afterlife of the soul, which for the majority of mankind was to be eternal damnation; and, on the other hand, belief that absolution for sin, or what we would call freedom from guilt, could be bought for money like a pound of cheese, that wickedness could be spiritually wiped out by a fee—these are only two of the foundations of conduct that created a life we cannot enter into.

Or take the idea that financial profit beyond a minimum necessary for livelihood was immoral; that buying goods wholesale and selling them without added work at a higher retail price was sinful; that money was in fact evil; that, in short, St. Jerome's dictum was final: "A man who is a merchant can seldom if ever please God." That did not, of course, stop the medieval businessman from doing business, though it is said that he never opened his strongbox without seeing the Devil on the lid, which is a very different state of mind from the conviction that what is good for General Motors is good for the country.

Can the historian transport himself inside minds that held these attitudes? Never completely, I think, but their circumstances can tell us something about our own situation. Here I would add a word of warning. Expect contradictions; do not look for uniformity. No aspect of society, no habit, custom, movement, development, is without crosscurrents. Starving peasants in hovels live alongside comfortable peasants in feather beds. Children are neglected and children are loved. Knights talk of honor and turn brigand. Amid depopulation and disaster, ostentation and extravagance were never more extreme. Irreconcilables clutter the scene. No age is tidy or ever made of whole cloth, and none is a more checkered fabric than the Middle Ages.

Finally, one must be wary of a trap built into all recorded history—the disproportionate survival of the negative. It is a cliché to say that protest and dissent speak louder than conformity, that happy are the people whose annals are blank; or, put another way, that the normal does not make history. What makes a cliché is a general truth, and the ef-

fect of this one is to leave an impression of violence, corruption, and decadence blanketing the second half of the fourteenth century without air holes, so to speak.

Unquestionably, the period was, as Sismondi wrote, "a bad time for humanity," a time which has been variously called out of joint, in moral disarray, of sinking values, of perpetual strife, of general helplessness; of bad government, oppressive taxes, chronic brigandage, scarcity, misery, plague, and menace of revolution; a time with a damaged soul, a time of Satan triumphant. That's why I chose it. But havoc in a given period does not cover all of the people all of the time. Somewhere someone is enjoying pleasure, beauty, and fun, music and games, love and work. While smoke by day and the glow of flames by night mark burning towns, the sky over the neighboring vicinity is clear; where screams of tortured prisoners are heard in one place, bankers count their coins and peasants plough behind placid oxen somewhere else.

In the midst of the Black Death, with its foul sores and smell, piles of bodies, terror of contagion, parents' and children's desertion of each other, abandoned fields and rotting harvests, brilliant tournaments were held with feasting and dancing. In Florence in 1378, after the violent upheaval called the Revolt of the Ciompi, Coluccio Salutati, chief executive officer of the city, wrote, "I am aware that among outsiders there are reports of great disorders, that some are saying that this city is ravaged by fire, sacked for plunder, and disgraced by murder. Rumor is a wordy liar . . . but I, having been an eyewitness of these things, know that some houses were fired but very few; that robbery was committed but on a small scale; that there have been murders but only a few, in fact hardly any. Florence is not in ashes, is not reeking with blood, is not suffering from plunder."

History is a police blotter recording the murders and robberies, fires and rapes. It is made by the documents that survive, and these lean heavily on crisis and disaster, crime and misbehavior, because such things are the subject matter of the documentary process—of treaties, judicial trials, moralists' denunciations, literary satire, papal bulls. No pope ever issued a bull to approve of something. Likewise bishops on episcopal visits reported at length on evils and abuses, while the well-behaved, orderly parish merited only a *bene stat*.

The Church was especially subject to a negative overload, on the principle established in 1401 by Nicholas de Clamange, who, in denouncing unfit and worldly prelates, said that in his anxiety for reform he would not discuss the good clerics, because *"they do not count alongside the perverse men"* (my italics). What with the Papal Schism and other evils, the fourteenth-century Church was undoubtedly at a low point in prestige, credibility, and (what people minded most) spirituality; hence heresy and ultimately the Reformation. That event blocks our view of the medieval Church, partly owing, I think, to the preponderance, in English anyway, of Protestant historians. H. C. Lea, for example, in his classic *History of the Inquisition,* unfolds an astonishing record of crimes, frailties, and corruption, all of it true, I feel sure, including the bishop who kept his own daughter as a concubine for twenty years. But Lea was not looking for the positive, as he himself recognized. Even contemporary satire was exceedingly harsh; yet the Church must have had *something* to retain the hold it did. I came to the point of making a special entry in my card file for "positive side of the Church," but I have to say that it never grew very fat. Resorting to the *Catholic Encyclopedia* as a balance was not very helpful either, because in difficult matters it operates by judicious omission.

One must conclude that the fourteenth-century Church deserved a bad press. Yet I try to keep in mind, for the whole of that sad century—and for our own—Salutati's words: "Florence is not in ashes."

THE MAKING OF MAGNA CARTA

Ruth I Mills

On 15th June, 1215, at Runnymede, between Windsor and Staines by the river Thames, King John of England sealed a document called 'The Articles of the Barons'. The charter between the King and his subjects had a life of only about ten weeks and it was a later version that bore the name—Magna Carta—by which they both became known to history.

John was the youngest of the four surviving sons of King Henry II of England and his Queen, Eleanor of Aquitaine, and as such he had not been expected to rule. One by one, however, his brothers died—Henry, Geoffrey, and, finally in 1199, King Richard perished while fighting on the Continent.

Richard had been an exceptional warrior and had joined the 3rd Crusade to the Holy Land but while there he quarrelled with his French and German allies and made a treaty with his enemy, Saladin. On his way back to England he had been captured by the Archduke of Austria and held for ransom by the Emperor of Germany.

During Richard's absence, from 1190 until 1194, John had tried to persuade the barons to support him in an effort to seize the throne. The rebellion failed when Richard returned from captivity to quell the uprising, but when the King died, John gained by lawful succession the crown he had been unable to wrest from his brother. Those barons who had resisted John's rule now feared retribution. They fortified their castles in anticipation of John's wrath, but the influential Earl of Pembroke, William Marshal, persuaded them to pledge fealty to the new King.

Under John's command, the barons defended their Norman and Angevin castles against the

King John ratifying Magna Carta at Runnymede (The Mansell Collection)

From *British Heritage*, October/November 1990, pp. 41-44. © 1990 by Cowles Magazines, Inc. Reprinted by permission of *British Heritage*, P.O. Box 8200, Harrisburg, PA 17105-8200.

Above: Pope Innocent III, who reigned from 1198 to 1216 (The Mansell Collection). Opposite: King John, Innocent's nemesis and later his vassal (The Mansell Collection)

French. According to the French, John had forfeited the right to his French lands by supposedly murdering the son of the Duke of Brittany (who had been a contender for the British throne) and marrying the already-engaged Isabelle of Angoulême. Unfortunately, the barons met with little success and by 1204 the last of the castles had fallen to the enemy. The frustrated barons claimed that John was a poor leader, disinclined toward fighting and inept at it. John accused them of acting irresponsibly after many of them had turned their castles over to the French without a fight.

The cost of John's campaigns in France and his exhorbitant lifestyle, in addition to unpaid bills stemming from Richard's crusade and ransom, swelled England's debts. When John demanded that his barons pay higher taxes, many refused, saying that they had no more to give. The King grew ever more insistent. He imposed fees for the preservation of the 'King's peace', exacted huge fines for trivial offences, increased inheritance and dowry charges and demanded that castles be turned over to him. He took barons' sons as hostage and murdered them whenever his demands were not met. Widows were deprived of rightful inheritances.

On 12th July, 1205, Hubert Walter, the Archbishop of Canterbury, died, bringing the King into conflict with the Church as well. John, as every English King before him, named a successor. Simultaneously, the Canterbury monks, by Canon Law, nominated their own successor. John's envoy and the monks went to Rome to present their choices to Pope Innocent III, but he rejected them both. During December, 1206, he prevailed upon the Canterbury monks to elect Cardinal Stephen Langton, an Englishman born at Langton-by-Wragby, Lincolnshire.

John refused to accept Langton and forced him into exile in France. Pope Innocent retaliated by laying an interdict on England on 23rd March, 1208. English churches were closed and all clerical services were suspended except for baptisms and confession for the dying. Many bishops and monks, fearing John's wrath, fled to France.

In 1209 Innocent realized that John was not repentant and, determined to employ harsher measures, he ordered King John's excommunication. The edict was not announced in England until 30th August, 1211, because most of the clerics remaining in England were either sympathetic towards the King or afraid of incurring his anger.

During the excommunicate years John's actions became even more extreme. Rumours of his cruelty were rampant. The barons kept silent, not knowing who among them were John's spies. Secretly, though, they took heart in the prophesy announced by a hermit, Peter of

Wakefield, in the spring of 1212: 'Within the year King John will lose his crown to one pleasant in God's sight.'

At first John laughed, but when he discovered that his subjects believed the prophecy he became enraged. John imprisoned the hermit and his son and awaited the outcome of the prediction. Frightened that this might presage a French invasion or a baronial uprising, and seeking now to reconcile himself with the Pope and thereby win his support, John sent an envoy to Rome to say that Stephen Langton was welcome in England.

Innocent no longer trusted John, however, and he sent an envoy to France commanding King Phillip to invade England in a 'holy war'. Unknown to Phillip, Innocent's envoy then continued to England, where, in January 1213, he told John that his choices were to irrevocably accept Langton or suffer invasion.

King John was now afraid he would lose all and not only repeated his willingness to accept Langton but also gifted the Kingdoms of England and Ireland to Pope Innocent who, with his successors, would serve as Lord of these lands in perpetuity. The Pope accepted the offer and on Ascension Day, 1212, John was still the ruler of England, even though he was technically now only a vassal of the Pope. The hermit's prophecy had not come true. Tied to horses' tails, Peter and his son were dragged to the gallows and hanged.

At Winchester on 20th July, 1213, Archbishop Stephen Langton removed the excommunication from King John, who swore that he'd act justly toward his subjects. Many barons scoffed. The King's promises, they said, were worthless. Within days John ordered military service for another continental campaign, but many barons refused to go.

Langton realized that a serious break between the King and his subjects was impending and, serving in the Archbishop of Canterbury's traditional rôle as church primate and first adviser to the King, he sought for a surer way of reaching agreement than through another verbal promise. At a meeting with several barons at St Paul's on 25th August, 1213, Langton promised them his support provided they acted legally—by means of a charter. He showed them the King Henry I Coronation Charter, considered 'ancient custom that is just', which promised that the excesses of King William Rufus's reign would not be repeated. That charter, Langton explained, could serve as the precedent for a new charter, one fair to baron, merchant, peasant and King, according to the 'laws of nature's God'—justice.

In May 1214 John was defeated in his attempts to recover the lands he had lost to the French, and, blaming his failures on the barons' lethargy, he again requested that they pay the expenses of his campaigns. He closeted himself with his advisers, whom the barons called 'evil counselors'. The barons met together as well, to sharpen their fighting skills and demand to be heard.

Aware that the malcontents' numbers were growing, John agreed to a meeting in London on the day of the Feast of the Epiphany, 6th January, 1215. There the barons, dressed in battle gear, exacted a promise from John that he would hear their proposal for redress of grievances during Easter week.

During that spring Marshal and Langton acted as intermediaries. At the Easter meeting, John refused to consider draft after draft of the barons' statement of redress whilst complaining to England's Lord, Pope Innocent, about the barons' intransigence. On Ash Wednesday, 1215, John declared himself a holy crusader, thus ensuring by Canon Law that no one could take or destroy his property.

The longer King John delayed, the less the barons trusted Langton's sincerity. At last they decided that force was the only avenue open to them. Assisted by peasants, barons began assaulting Royal castles at the end of April. On 17th May the residents of London opened the city gates to the insurgents and by 6th June, John asked for a truce. He ordered the barons to compose another statement of redress of grievances and granted many of the demands he had previously refused.

Finally, both sides to the argument met at Runnymede on 15th June, 1215. The recalcitrants promised they'd pledge fealty to John were he to seal 'The Articles of the Barons'. After minor details of the charter were worked out, John affixed his seal and 'The Articles of the Barons' became the law of the land. Sixteen years of turmoil seemed over.

Instead, horrendous events took place that rocked the Nation. First the barons refused to pledge fealty to King John and retained their private armies. Threatened with excommunication, they finally disbanded, but once back home, they fortified their castles and prepared for war. On 16th August, word reached England that Pope Innocent, in defence of his crusader-vassal, had issued an order on 18th June for Langton to excommunicate each dissenting baron. Then, on 24th August, the supreme blow came: Pope Innocent, Lord of England, had annulled the charter of liberties.

Langton, however, defied the Pope and refused to excommunicate the barons. He had urged them to seek a charter and knew the Pope had been misinformed. Planning to attend the Lateran Council in Rome, he decided to arrive early and explain the barons' position to Pope Innocent. As Langton embarked, the Pope's envoy suspended him from his see.

The barons now realized that Langton had worked on their behalf and had sacrificed his own position for them. He had failed to establish a charter, but every baron knew St Augustine's dictum: 'When all else fails, war is justified.' They were determined to succeed where Langton had not by defeating John in battle and dividing up the Kingdom amongst themselves. But, not having been actively engaged in warfare for a decade, the rebels were no match for John's supporting barons and mercenaries. From the autumn of 1215 until the spring of 1216, John's forces prevailed. By May the insurgents controlled only London and a few castles.

Meanwhile, in Rome, Pope Innocent refused to heed Langton's pleas. If not for the intervention of his fellow cardinals, the Archbishop would have been expelled from his post. Forbidden by the Pope to return to England, Langton went again into exile in France in January 1216.

In May 1216, the war in England took on a new dimension. Prince Louis of France invaded John's domain at the barons' invitation, in return for a promise of the British throne should he succeed. At the same time, several barons who had been loyal to John deserted him. Louis and his troops easily restored castle after castle to the rebellious barons, while John raced frantically about the Kingdom, doing whatever he could to preserve his lands. His last trip, on 9th October, took him to the Lincolnshire tidal flats where, supposedly, his treasure was lost in quicksand. Ten days later the King died of dysentery. His 10-year-old son became King Henry III.

John's death marked a drastic reversal of the political climate. Many barons who'd opposed John deserted Louis and pledged fealty to King Henry. William Marshal became Regent to the young King and took command of the Royal Army. Within the year Louis was expelled from England. By then Pope Innocent had died and been replaced by Pope Honorious III, who had respected Langton's position.

One of the Marshal's first acts as Regent was to revise the barons' charter, deleting certain offensive clauses and those pertaining to Royal forests. The remaining clauses, those ensuring personal liberties, became the Great Charter, Magna Carta, sealed 12th November, 1216, by the Regent.

During the ensuing years of Henry's reign and that of his son, King Edward I, Magna Carta was further revised and reconfirmed many times and in 1297 it became a part of the Revised Statutes. Almost a century in the making, Magna Carta now stands as a beacon, for under its medieval concerns are found timeless ethical principles that Stephen Langton called the 'laws of nature's God'.

CLOCKS
REVOLUTION
IN TIME

Ancient Clepsydra

David Landes

The question to ask is: Why clocks? Who needs them? After all, nature is the great time-giver, and all of us without exception, live by nature's clock. Night follows day; day, night; and each year brings its succession of seasons. These cycles are imprinted on just about every living being in what are called circadian ('about a day') and circannual biological rhythms. They are stamped in our flesh and blood; they persist even when we are cut off from time cues; they mark us as earthlings.

These biological rhythms are matched by societal work patterns: day is for labour, night for repose, and the round of seasons is a sequence of warmth and cold, planting and harvest, life and death.

Into this natural cycle, which all people have experienced as a divine providence, the artificial clock enters as an intruder.

WHEN IN THE LATE SIXTEENTH century Portuguese traders and Christian missionaries sought entry into China, they were thwarted by a kind of permanent quarantine. Chinese officials correctly perceived these foreigners as potential subversives, bringing with them the threat of political interference, material seduction, and spiritual corruption. The ban was not lifted for decades, and then only because Matteo Ricci and his Jesuit mission brought with them knowledge and instruments that the Celestial Court coveted. In particular, they brought chiming clocks, which the Chinese received as a wondrous device. By the time Ricci, after numerous advances and retreats, finally secured permission from the court eunuchs and other officials to proceed to Peking and present himself to the throne, the emperor could hardly wait. 'Where', he called, 'are the self-ringing bells?' And later, when the dowager empress showed an interest in her son's favourite clock, the emperor had the bell disconnected so that she would be disappointed. He could not have refused to give it to her, had she asked for it; but neither would he give it up, so he found this devious way to reconcile filial piety with personal gratification.

The use of these clocks as a ticket of entry is evidence of the great advance

European timekeeping had made over Chinese horology. It had not always been thus. The Chinese had always been much concerned to track the stars for astrological and horoscopic purposes. For the emperor, the conjunctions of the heavenly bodies were an indispensable guide to action, public and private – to making war and peace, to sowing and reaping, to conceiving an heir with the empress or coupling with a concubine. To facilitate the calculations required, court mechanicians of the Sung dynasty (tenth and eleventh centuries) built a series of remarkable clock-driven astraria, designed to track and display the apparent movements of the stars. The clock mechanism that drove the display was hydraulic – a water clock (clepsydra) linked to a bucket wheel. As each bucket filled, it activated a release mechanism that allowed the big drive wheel to turn and bring the next bucket into position. The water clock in itself was no more accurate than such devices can be; but in combination with the wheel, it could be adjusted to keep time within a minute or two a day. By way of comparison, the ordinary drip or flow water clocks then in use in Europe probably varied by a half-hour or more.

These astronomical clocks marked a culmination. The greatest of them, that built by Su Sung at the end of the eleventh century, was also the last of the series. When invasion and war forced the court to flee, the clock was lost and its secret as well. From this high point of achievement, Chinese timekeeping retrogressed to simpler, less accurate instruments, so that when the Jesuits arrived some five hundred years later with their mechanical clocks, they found only objects that confirmed their comfortable sense of technological, and by implication moral, superiority.

Meanwhile European timekeeping made a quantum leap by moving from hydraulic to mechanical devices. The new clocks, which took the form of weight-driven automated bells, made their appearance around 1280. We don't know where – England possibly, or Italy – and we don't know who invented them. What we do know is that the gain was immense and that the new clocks very rapidly swept the older clepsydras aside. Since these first mechanical clocks were notori-

ously inaccurate, varying an hour or more a day, and unreliable, breaking down frequently and needing major overhauls every few years, one can only infer that water clocks left even more to be desired. The great advantage of the mechanical clock lay in its relative immunity to temperature change, whereas the drip or flow of the water clock varied with the seasons while frost would halt it altogether (the temperature did not have to go down to freezing to increase viscosity and slow the rate). In the poorly heated buildings of northern Europe, especially at night, this was a near-fatal impairment. Dirt was another enemy. No water is pure, and deposits would gradually choke the narrow opening. The instructions for use of a thirteenth-century water clock installed in the Abbey of Villers (near Brussels) make it clear that no one expected much of these devices: the sacristan was to adjust it daily by the sun, as it fell on the abbey windows; and if the day was cloudy, why then it was automatically ten o'clock at the end of the morning mass.

Why Europe should have succeeded in effecting this transition to a superior technology and China not is an important historical question. Anyone who looked at the horological world of the eleventh or twelfth century would have surely predicted the opposite result. (He would have also expected Islam to surpass Europe in this domain.) The Chinese failure – if failure is the right word – cannot be sought in material circumstances. The Chinese were as troubled and inconvenienced by the limitations of the water clock as were the Europeans; it can get very cold in Peking. (The Chinese tried substituting mercury or sand for water, but mercury kills and neither behaves very well over time.) Instead the explanation must be sought in the character and purposes of Chinese timekeeping. It was, in its higher forms, a monopoly of the imperial court, as much an attribute of sovereignty as the right to coin money. In this instance, dominion over time and calendar was a major aspect of power, for it laid the cognitive foundation for imperial decisions in every area of political and economic life. So much was this the case that each emperor began by proclaiming his own calendar, often different from that of his predecessor; by so doing,

he affirmed his legitimacy and identity.

Timekeeping instruments were therefore reserved to the court and certain of its officials; there was no civilian clock trade. Such great astronomical clocks as were built for the throne were undertaken as special projects, the work of a team assembled for the occasion. Each of these machines was a *tour de force*, and each built on earlier models, researched in the archives by way of preparation. There was, then, no continuous process of construction and emendation; no multiplicity of private initiatives; no dynamic of continuing improvement. Instead we have these occasional peak moments of achievement, highly fragile, vulnerable to political hostility and adventitious violence, easily buried and forgotten once the team of builders had dissolved or died.

Outside these rarefied circles, the Chinese people had little interest in time measurement for its own sake. Most of them were peasants, and peasants have no need of clocks. They wake with the animals in the morning, watch the shadows shorten and lengthen as the sun crosses the sky, and go to bed once night falls – because they are tired, illumination is costly and they must get up very early. They are not unaware of the passage of time, but they do not have to measure it. Time measurement is an urban concern, and in medieval China the authorities provided time signals (drums, trumpets) in the cities to mark the passage of the hours and warn the residents of such things as the closing of the gates to the separate quarters or neighbourhoods. But such noises could not easily be used to order the daily round of activities, for the Chinese did not number the hours sequentially; rather they named them, so that auditory signals transmitted limited information. Such as they were, they sufficed, for the organisation of work created no need for closer or continuous timing. The typical work unit was the household shop, comprising master, assistants, and apprentices. The day started at dawn, when the youngest or newest apprentice woke to make the fire and wake the rest; and work continued until night imposed its interruption. This mode of production set no artificial *clocktime* limited to labour; nature fixed the bounds.

In contrast, medieval Europe did have a constituency concerned to track and use time. This was the Christian church, especially those monastic orders that followed the rule of Benedict. This rule, which was defined in the sixth century, became over time the standard of monachal discipline in western Europe. The aim of the rule was to ensure that the entire day be ordered and devoted to the service of God – to pray above all, but also to work, which was defined as another kind of prayer. The daily prayer offices numbered seven (later eight), six (later seven) in the daytime and one at night. The institution of a nocturnal office was peculiar to Christianity and sharply differentiated it from the other monotheistic religions. It went back to the prayer vigils conducted by the earliest Christians in imminent expectation of the *parousia*, or second coming. It was these vigils that were later merged with the morning prayer to constitute the canonical hour known as matins.

The obligation to rise to prayer in the dark imposed a special condition on Christian worship. Whereas Jews (and later Muslims) set their times of prayer by natural events (morning, afternoon, and evening) that do not require the use of an artificial timekeeper, Christians needed some kind of alarm to wake to matins. In the cities of the Roman empire, the night watch could give the signal. In medieval Europe such municipal services had long disappeared, and most abbeys were located in rural areas. Each house, then, had to find its own way to satisfy the requirement, usually by means of an alarm device linked to a water clock. This would rouse the waker, usually the sacristan, who would then ring the bells that called the others to prayer. Most house rules – for although the principle was general, there was little uniformity in the details of practice – enjoined the sacristan to be scrupulous in his performance of this duty, for his negelct imperilled the salvation of his brethren (and the larger church) as well as his own. 'Nothing, therefore, shall be put before the Divine Office', says the Rule.

To the ordinary monk, getting up in the dark of the night was perhaps the hardest aspect of monastic discipline. Indeed the practical meaning of

'reforming' a house meant first and foremost the imposition (reimposition) of this duty. The sleepyheads were prodded out of bed and urged to the offices; they were also prodded during service lest they fail in their obligations. Where the flesh was weak, temptation lurked. Raoul Glaber (early eleventh century) tells the tale of a demon who successfully seduced a monk by holding the lure of sweet sleep:

> As for you, I wonder why you so scrupulously jump out of bed as soon as you hear the bell, when you could stay resting even unto the third bell... but know that every year Christ empties hell of sinners and brings them to heaven, so without worry you can give yourself to all the voluptuousness of the flesh...

The same Glaber confesses to two occasions when he himself woke late and saw a demon, 'come to do business with the laggards'. And Peter the Venerable, Abbot of Cluny in the twelfth century, tells the story of Brother Alger, who woke thinking he

had heard the bell ring for nocturns. Looking around, he thought he saw the other beds empty, so he drew on his sandals, threw on his cloak, and hastened to the chapel. There he was puzzled not to hear the sound of voices lifted in prayer. Now he hurried back to the dormitory, where he found all the other monks fast asleep. And then he understood: this was all a temptation of the devil, who had awakened him at the wrong time, so that when the bell for nocturns really rang, he would sleep through it.

These, I suggest, are what we now know as anxiety dreams. They clearly reflect the degree to which time-consciousness and discipline had become internalised. Missing matins was a serious matter, so serious that it has been immortalised for us by perhaps the best known of children's songs:

Frère Jacques, Frère Jacques,
Dormez-vous? dormez-vous?
Sonnez les matines, sonnez les matines,
Ding, dang, dong; ding, dang, dong.

We know far less than we should

A monastic water-driven wheel clock of thirteenth-century Europe. The mechanism is hard to make out, but the picture suggests that water-driven wheel clocks of the Chinese type were used (or at least known) in Europe before the advent of the weight-driven wheel-clock.

Manuscript illustrations from the fifteenth century show the metaphorical importance clocks had in a medieval application of the concept of time. The goddess Attemprance, half-figure in a cloud, grasps a clock with hanging bells in both hands; large bell above. A French manuscript illustration of the late fifteenth century.

(Left) Manuscript illustration of 1450 showing a huge, intricate clock, standing on earth, but with its open and visible wheel-work and dial and bell in heaven. The four traditional symbols of the evangelists are shown on the four corners of the dial. The goddess Attemprance, resting on the clouds, is winding the clock.

the monastic time service. The enhanced temporal consciousness may be related to the revival of monastic life after the millennium and in particular to the needs of the Cistercian order – that economic empire with its agricultural, mining, and industrial enterprises, its ever-turning water wheels, its large labour force of lay brethren, its place in the forefront of European technology.

One of the innovations of this period seems to have been the combination clepsydra/mechanical alarm. This worked as follows: when the water in the recipient vessel reached an appropriate height, it tripped a weight-driven escape wheel, so called because it meshed with pallets that alternately blocked and released it (allowed it to escape). This stop-go motion in turn imparted a to-and-fro oscillation to the rod or *verge* holding the pallets; hence the name *verge escapement*. Attach a small hammer to the end of the verge, and it could ring a bell. Put an oscillating cross bar on the end, and you had a controller for a clock.

The first clocks were probably alarms converted in this manner. The very name *clock* meant bell, and these were essentially machines to sound the passing hours. Their use entailed a drastic change in the character of European timekeeping. Because the mechanical clock beat at a more or less uniform rate, it sounded equal-length

like about monastic horology in the Middle Ages, and such information as we have is confused by the use of the general term *(h)orologium* for any and all kinds of timekeeper. It seems clear, however, that the century or two preceding the appearance of the mechanical clock saw important improvements in technique and a growing emphasis on the details of hours – what later came to be known as mean (average) time. But the standard of medieval Europe was the sun, and the hours were natural, equal fractions of the day and night. Thus as days got longer, daylight hours lengthened and night hours shrank; and vice versa. These seasonally variable hours (often called temporal hours) were easily measured by the water clock; all one had to do was change the scale with the seasons. But an automated bell was another story: changing the times of ringing to take account of changing hours would have been a difficult and time-consuming task. So Europeans learned a new time standard in which the sun rose and set at different hours as the days passed. This seems natural enough to us, but it must have come as a shock at first. (Some places chose to start their day at sunrise, which took care of one end of the problem, though not the other).

In effect the new clock offered a rival time standard in competition with the older church time. It was not only the hours that differed; it was the signals also. The old water clocks did not sound public, tower bells. They told the time for the bell ringer, who usually rang, not the unequal, temporal hours, but the hours of prayer, the so-called canonical hours. These were not equally spaced and did not lend themselves to the kind of calculation we take for granted: how long since? how long until? It was equal hours that made this possible and thereby contributed significantly to the growing numeracy of the urban population. Insofar as the medieval church resisted the new time standard, it gave over an important symbol of authority to the secular power. Where once people punctuated their day by such marks as sext, none, and vespers, now they thought in terms of hours and, very soon, minutes.

The transition from church time to lay time was at once sign and consequence of the rise of a new, urban social order. The new machines appealed from the start to the rich and powerful, who made them the preferred object of conspicuous consumption. No court, no prince could be without one. But far more important in the long run was the rapid acceptance of the new instrument in cities and towns, which had long learned to regulate many aspects of civil life by bells – bells to signal the opening and closing of markets, waking bells and work bells, drinking and curfew bells, bells for opening and closing of gates, assembly and alarms. In this regard, the medieval city was a secular version of the cloister, prepared by habit and need to use the clock as a superior instrument of time discipline and management.

The pressure for time signals was especially strong in those cities that were engaged in textile manufacture – the first and greatest of medieval industries. There the definition of working time was crucial to the profitability of enterprise and the prosperity of the commune. The textile industry was the first to go over to large-scale production for export, hence the first to overflow the traditional workshop and engage a dispersed work force. Some of these workers – the *ciompi* in Florence, the 'blue nails' (stained by dye) in Flanders – were true proletarians, owning none of the instruments of production, selling only their labour power. They streamed early every morning into the dye shops and fulling mills, where the high consumption of energy for heating the vats and driving the hammers encouraged concentration in large units. Other branches of the manufacture could be conducted in the rooms and cottages of the workers: employers liked this so-called putting-out because it shifted much of the burden of overhead costs to the employee, who was paid by the piece rather than by time; and the workers preferred it to the time discipline and supervision of the large shops. They could in principle start and stop work at will, for who was to tell them what to do in their own home?

The bells would tell them. Where there was textile manufacture, there were work bells, which inevitably gave rise to conflict. Part of the problem was implicit in the effort to impose time discipline on home workers. In principle, payment by the piece should have taken care of the matter, with workers responding to wage incentives. In fact, the home workers were content to earn what they felt they needed, and in time of keen demand, employers found it impossible to get them to do more, for higher pay only reduced the amount

(Left) A sketch of a clock tower by Villard de Honnecourt, circa 1225-1250. An early example of a chiming clock tower which kept equal hours and provided regular signals — a constraint for worker and employer alike.

of work required to satisfy these needs. The effort to bring the constraints of the manufactory into the rooms and cottages of spinners and weavers made the very use of bells a focus of resentment.

Meanwhile in the fulling mills and dyeshops the bells posed a different kind of problem, especially when they were controlled by the employer. Consider the nature of the wage contract: the worker was paid by the day, and the day was bounded by these time signals. The employer had an interest in getting a full day's work for the wages he paid; and the worker in giving no more time than he was paid for. The question inevitably arose how the worker could know whether bell time was honest time. How could he trust even the municipal bells when the town council was dominated by representatives of the employers?

Under the circumstances, workers in some places sought to silence the *werkclocke*: at Therouanne in 1367 the dean and chapter promised 'workers, fullers, and other mechanics' to silence 'forever the workers' bell in order that no scandal or conflict be born in city and church as a result of the ringing of a bell of this type'. Such efforts to eliminate time signals never achieved success: as soon suppress the system of wage labour. Besides, once the work day was defined in temporal rather than natural terms, workers as well as employers had an interest in defining and somehow signalling the boundaries. Time measurement here was a two-edged sword: it gave the employer bounds to fill, and to the worker bounds to work. The alternative was the open-ended working day, as Chrétien de Troyes observed of the silk weavers of Lyons in the twelfth century:

> ... nous sommes en grand'misère,
> Mais s'enrichit de nos salaires
> Celui pour qui nous travaillons.
> Des nuits grand partie nous veillons
> Et tout le jour pour y gagner

> ... we are in great misery,
> The man who gets rich on our wages
> Is the man we worked for.
> We're up a good part of the night
> And work all day to make our way ..

It was not the work bells as such, then, that were resented and mistrusted, but the people who controlled them; and it is here that the chiming tower clock made its greatest contribution. It kept equal hours and provided regular signals, at first on the hour, later on at the halves or quarters, and these necessarily limited the opportunities for abuse. With the appearance of the dial (from the word for day), of course, it was possible for all interested parties to verify the time on a continuous basis.

The early turret clocks were very expensive, even when simple. Wrought iron and brass needed repeated hammering, hence much labour and much fuel. The casting of the bells was a precarious operation. The placement of the mechanism usually entailed major structural alterations. The construction and installation of a tower clock might take months if not years. Teams of craftsmen and labourers had to be assembled on the site and there lodged and boarded. Subsequent maintenance required the attendance of a resident technician, repeated visits by specialised artists, and an endless flow of replacement parts.

These costs increased substantially as soon as one went beyond simple timekeepers to astronomical clocks and/or automata. The medieval accounts show this process clearly: the sums paid to painters and woodcarvers bear witness to the growing importance of the clock as spectacle as well as time signal. The hourly parade of saints and patriarchs; the ponderous strokes of the hammer-wielding *jaquemarts*; the angel turning with the sun; the rooster crowing at sunrise; the lunar disc waxing and waning with the moon – and all these movements and sounds offered lessons in theology and astronomy to the up-gazing multitude that gathered to watch and wonder at what man had wrought. The hourly pageant was an imitation of divine creation; the mechanism, a miniaturisation of heaven and earth. As a result, the show clock was to the new secular, urbanising world of the later Middle Ages what the cathedrals had been to the still worshipful world of the high Middle Ages: a combination of a sacrifice and affirmation, the embodiment of the highest skills and artistry, a symbol of prowess and source of pride. It was also a source of income – the lay analogue to the religious relics that were so potent an attraction to medieval travellers. When Philip the

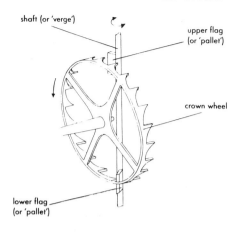

Diagram illustrating the 'verge' escapement. An escapement is the mechanism which could control and slow down the speed at which the weights of a clock dropped. The 'verge' escapement is the earliest surviving form.

Bold of Burgundy defeated the Flemish burghers at Rosebecke in 1382 and wanted to punish those proud and troublesome clothiers, he could do no worse (or better) than seize the belfry clock at Courtrai and take it off to his capital at Dijon.

These public clocks, moreover, were only the top of the market. They are the ones that history knows best, but we know only a fraction of what was made. In this regard, the records are misleading: they have preserved the memory of a spotty, biased selection and largely omitted the smaller domestic clocks made to private order. As a result, it was long thought that the first mechanical clocks were turret clocks, and that the smaller domestic models were the much later product of advances in miniaturisation. Yet there was no technical impediment to making chamber clocks once the verge escapement had been invented. Indeed, since the mechanical clock is a development of the timer alarm, itself made to chamber size, small may well have preceded big.

Whichever came first, the one logically implied the other, so that we may fairly assume that both types of clock were known and made from the start. In the event, the first literary allusion to a mechanical clock refers to domestic timepieces. This goes back to the late thirteenth century, in Jean de Meung's additional verse to *Le roman de la rose*. Jean, a romantic poet of curiously worldy interest, attributes to his Pygmalion a fair array of chamber clocks:

Et puis faire sonner ses orloges
Par ses salles et par ses loges
A roues trop subtillement
De pardurable mouvement.

And then through halls and chambers,
Made his clock chime
By wheels of such cunning
Ever turning through time.

By the end of the fourteenth century, hundreds of clocks were turning in western Europe. A new profession of horologers had emerged, competing for custom and seeking severally to improve their product. There could be no surer guarantee of cumulative technical advance. Few inventions in history have ever made their way with such ease. Everyone seems to have welcomed the clock, even those workers who toiled to its rules, for they much preferred it to arbitrary bells. *Summe necessarium pro omni statu hominum* was the way Galvano Fiamma, chronicler of Milan, put it when he proudly marked the erection in 1333 (?) of a clock that not only struck the hours but signalled each one by the number of peals. And this in turn recalls an earlier inscription on a clock installed in 1314 on the bridge at Caen:

Je ferai les heures ouïr
Pour le commun peuple rejouir.

I shall give the hours voice
To make the common folk rejoice.

Even the poets liked the new clocks. That is the most astonishing aspect of these early years of mechanical horology, for no group is by instinct and sensibility so suspicious of technical innovation. Here, moreover, was an invention that carried with it the seeds of control, order, self-restraint – all virtues (or vices) inimical to the free, spontaneous imagination and comtemplation so prized by creative artists. Yet it would be anachronistic to impute these ideals to the thirteenth and fourteenth centuries; they came much later. The medieval ideal was one of sobriety and control, along with due respect for worthy models. Besides, it was surely too soon to understand the potential of the new device for forming the persona as well as dictating the terms of life and work. Instead, the availability of this new knowledge gave all a sense of power, of enhanced efficiency and potential, of ownership of a new a valuable asset, whereas we, living by

(Right The clockmaker at work, from a sixteenth-century wood engraving.

the clock, see ignorance of or indifference to time as a release from constraint and a gain in freedom. Everything depends, I suppose, on where one is coming from. In any event, the early celebrators of the clock were no mere poetasters: thus Dante Alighieri, who sang in his *Paradise* (Canto X) the praises of the 'glorious wheel' moving and returning 'voice to voice in timbre and sweetness' – *tin tin sonando con si dolce nota* (almost surely a reference to a chamber clock, unless Dante had a tin ear), therein echoing the pleasure that Jean de Meung's Pygmalion took in his chiming clocks a generation earlier. And a half-century later we have Jean Froissart, poet but more famous as historian, composer of 'love ditties', among them *L'horloge amoureuse* (1369):

... The clock is, when you think about it,
A very beautiful and remarkable instrument,
And it's also pleasant and useful,
Because night and day it tells us the hours
By the subtlety of its mechanism

Even when there is no sun.
Hence all the more reason to prize one's machine,
Because other instruments can't do this
However artfully and precisely they may be made
Hence do we hold him for valiant and wise
Who first invented this device
And with his knowledge undertook and made
A thing so noble and of such great pride.

The invention and diffusion of the mechanical clock had momentous consequences for European technology, culture, and society – comparable in their significance to the effects of the later invention of movable type and printing. For one thing, the clock could be miniaturised and, once small enough, moved about. For this, a new power source was needed, which took the form of a coiled spring, releasing energy as it unwound. This came in during the fifteenth century and gave rise to a new generation of small domestic clocks and, by the early sixteenth, to the watch, that is, a clock small enough to be worn on the person. Domestic clocks and, even more, the watch were the basis of the private, internalised time discipline that characterises modern personality and civilisation – for better or worse. Without this discipline, we could not operate the numerous and complex activities required to make our society go. (We could, no doubt, have recourse to public signals, as in the army. But that would mean a very different kind of collectivity).

For another thing, the mechanical clock was susceptible of great improvement in accuracy, even in its smaller form. This potential lay in its revolutionary principle of time measurement. Whereas earlier instruments had relied on some continuous movement – of shadow (the sundial) or fluid (the clepsydra) – to track the passage of time, the mechanical clock marked time by means of an oscillating controller. This took the form of a bar or wheel swinging to and fro. The swings (pulses or beats) could then be counted and converted to time units – hours, minutes, and eventually sub-minutes. To the ancients who invented the sundial and water clock, a continuous controller on what we would not call the analogue principle seemed only logical, for it was an imitation of time itself, always passing. But in the long run, its possibilities for improvement were limited not only by the inherent flaws of sunlight (no use at night or in cloudy weather) and flowing liquids, but by the difficulty of sustaining an even, continuously moving display. Time measurement by beats or pulses, on the other hand – the digital principle – had no bounds of accuracy. All that was needed was an even, countable frequency. The oscillating controller of the first medieval clocks usually beat double-seconds. Frequency was decidedly uneven, hence the large variation in rate. It took almost four hundred years to invent a vastly superior controller in the form of the pendulum, which in its seconds-beating form could keep time within less than a minute a day. Today, of course, new controllers have been invented in the form of vibrating quartz crystals (hundreds of thousands or even millions of beats per second), which vary less than a minute a year; and atomic resonators (billions of vibrations per second), which take thousands of years to gain or lose a second. These gains in precision have been an important impetus to scientific inquiry; indeed, almost all of them came about because scientists needed better timekeeping instruments. How else to study process and rates of changes?

Finally, the clock with its regularity came to stand as the model for all other machines – the machine of machines, the essence of man's best work in the image of God; and clockmaking became the school for all other mechanical arts. No one has said it better than Lewis Mumford in *Technics and Civilization*:

The clock, not the steam engine, is the key-machine of the modern industrial age... In its relationship to determinable quantities of energy, to standardization, to automatic action, and finally to its own special product, accurate timing, the clock has been the foremost machine in modern technics; and at each period it has remained in the lead: it marks a perfection toward which other machines aspire.

All of this was there in germ in the oscillating controllers of the first mechanical clocks. The builders of those clocks did not know what they had wrought. That the clock was invented in Europe and remained a European monopoly for some five hundred years, and that Europe then built a civilisation organised around the measurement of time; – these were critical factors in the differentiation of West from Rest and the definition of modernity.

FOR FURTHER READING:
David S. Landes, *Revolution in Time: Clocks and the Making of the Modern World* is published by Harvard University Press; on January, 16th at £17. Ernest von Bassermann-Jordan, *The Book of Old Clocks and Watches* (4th ed., revised by Hans von Bertele; New York: Crown, 1964); Eric Bruton, *The History of Clocks and Watches* (New York: Rizzoli, 1979); Carlo Cipolla, *Clocks and Culture, 1300-1700* (New York: Walker, 1967); Jacques Le Goff, *Time, Work, and Culture in the Middle Ages* (University of Chicago Press, 1980); Lewis Mumford, *Technics and Civilization* (New York: Harcourt, Brace, 1934); Joseph Needham, Wang Ling, and Derek J. de Solla Price, *Heavenly Clockwork: The Great Astronomical Clocks of Medieval China* (Cambridge University Press, 1960); also articles in *Antiquarian Horology*, the journal of the Antiquarian Horological Society of Great Britain.

1500: The Era of Discovery

If the most important events in world history are the agricultural and industrial revolutions, then perhaps the division point in world history should be 1800, rather than 1500. This would roughly include the start of the Industrial Revolution and the liberal political revolts in France and the United States. Still, 1500 marks the Reformation, Renaissance, and the great global explorations of the West. This is the start of Western domination of the world that continues to the present. Therefore, most world historians accept 1500 as a breaking point for teaching purposes. So it is with the two volumes of *Annual Editions: World History*.

In this unit, the European thrust into the unknown world is discussed. It is this exploration that pushes Western civilization ahead in the world.

If it had not been for indifference, internal economic problems, and perhaps arrogance, the Chinese would have been competitors in the exploration of Africa. Zheng He, a court eunuch and Muslim, led a powerful fleet westward in the early fifteenth century, but his efforts were left unexploited by the Chinese government, and he was commanded to stay at home. This is explained by Samuel Wilson in his report "The Emperor's Giraffe."

It was a fortuitous turn of history for the Europeans. The Portuguese were pushing down the western coast of Africa to find a water passage to India when Columbus, a poor student of geography, sailed westward across the unchartered ocean to find a new land. David Gelman outlines the impact of these voyages that changed the course of history. Then, in the next article, Peter Copeland gives insight into the life of the common sailors that accompanied Columbus on this fateful adventure.

Poor Columbus! During the quincentenary of his voyage he was vilified by Native Americans, environmentalists, humanists, and others. At the anniversary in 1892, there was a great fair organized in his honor in Chicago and Columbus was regarded as a hero. Now, over a hundred years later, he is condemned as a villain who commited genocide. These events prove the truth that every generation rewrites history to suit itself. But, like it or not, the voyages did take place and the world was transformed. Robert Hay summarizes the arguments about Columbus and concludes that it was the start of the Europeanization of the world.

Further explorations came closely after Columbus's encounter with the New World. Within a generation, Juan Sebastian d'Elcano completed Magellan's circumnavigation of the globe. Simon Winchester captures the difficulty of the feat in his essay "After Dire Straits, an Agonizing Haul across the Pacific." At the moment, however, as Charles Tilly concludes, the impact of Columbus and the other intrepid explorers who were reaching out into the world had no immediate impact. China still dominated the Far East and Islam the Middle East. Through their spirit and technology, however, Europeans were able to outflank the Muslims' world to open up an era of trade and exploitation that later gave them command of the globe.

Looking Ahead: Challenge Questions

Compare Zheng He and Columbus. Why did Zheng He fail and Columbus succeed in interesting their civilizations in exploration?

Was Columbus a representative of his world, or was he unique?

Does knowledge about Columbus and exploration have any current relevance? Explain.

Considering what you have read about historiography, how should historians treat Columbus?

How did exploration affect native populations?

What technology helped Columbus succeed?

The Emperor's Giraffe

Not every powerful country chooses world domination

Samuel M. Wilson

Samuel M. Wilson teaches anthropology at the University of Texas at Austin.

A huge fleet left port in 1414 and sailed westward on a voyage of trade and exploration. The undertaking far surpassed anything Columbus, Isabella, and Ferdinand could have envisioned. The fleet included at least sixty-two massive trading galleons, any of which could have held Columbus's three small ships on its decks. The largest galleons were more than 400 feet long and 150 feet wide (the *Santa Maria,* Columbus's largest vessel, was about 90 by 30 feet), and each could carry about 1,500 tons (Columbus's ships combined could carry about 400 tons). More than one hundred smaller vessels accompanied the galleons. All told, 30,000 people went on the voyage, compared with Columbus's crew of 90-some.

The commander's name was Zheng He (Cheng Ho), the Grand Eunuch of the Three Treasures and the most acclaimed admiral of the Ming dynasty. He was sailing from the South China Sea across the Indian Ocean, heading for the Persian Gulf and Africa. As the historian Philip Snow notes in his wonderful book *The Star Raft* (1988), "Zheng He was the Chinese Columbus. He has become for China, as Columbus has for the West, the personification of maritime endeavour." The flotilla was called the star raft after the luminous presence of the emperor's ambassadors on board.

Zheng He did not really set out to explore unknown lands—neither did Columbus, for that matter—for the Chinese were aware of most of the countries surrounding the Indian Ocean. For centuries, China had been a principal producer and consumer of goods moving east and west from Mediterranean, African, and Middle Eastern trading centers. With this trade came cultural and ideological exchange. Zheng He, like many Chinese of his time, was a Muslim, and his father and his father before him had made the pilgrimage to Mecca. But in Zheng He's day, the trade routes were controlled by Arabian, Persian, and Indian merchants.

Private Chinese traders had been barred from traveling to the West for several centuries. China had been conquered by Genghis Khan and his descendants in the 1200s, and the Mongol emperors of the subsequent Yüan dynasty were the first to impose these constraints. In 1368 the Chinese expelled the Mongol rulers and established the Ming dynasty, which was destined to rule for the next 300 years. (Thus, in 1492 Columbus was searching for a "Gran Khan" who had been put out of business 124 years earlier.) After the period of Mongol rule, China became strongly isolationist, placing even more severe restrictions on Chinese traders.

In 1402 an outward-looking emperor named Yong'le (Yung-lo) came to power. Seeking to reassert a Chinese presence on the western seas and to enhance the prestige of his rule and dynasty, he began funding spectacular voyages by Zheng He. As sociologist Janet Abu-Lughod notes in *Before European Hegemony* (1989), "The impressive show of force that paraded around the Indian Ocean during the first three decades of the fifteenth century was intended to signal the 'barbarian nations' that China had reassumed her rightful place in the firmament of nations—had once again become the 'Middle Kingdom' of the world."

As Zheng He pressed westward in 1414, he sent part of the fleet north to Bengal, and there the Chinese travelers saw a wondrous creature. None like it had ever been seen in China, although it was not completely unheard of. In 1225 Zhao Rugua, a customs inspector at the city of Quanzhou, had recorded a secondhand description of such a beast in his strange and wonderful *Gazetteer of Foreigners.* He said it had a leopard's hide, a cow's hoofs, a ten-foot-tall body, and a nine-foot neck towering above that. He called it a *zula,* possibly a corruption of *zurafa,* the Arabic word for giraffe.

The giraffe the travelers saw in Bengal was already more than 5,000 miles from home. It had been brought there as a gift from the ruler of the prosperous African city-state of Malindi, one of several trading centers lining the east coast of Africa (Malindi is midway along modern Kenya's coast, three degrees south of the equator). Zheng He's diplomats persuaded the Bengal king to offer the animal as a gift to the Chinese emperor. They also persuaded the Malindi ambassadors to send home for another giraffe. When Zheng He returned to Beijing, he was able to present the emperor with two of the exotic beasts.

A pair of giraffes in Beijing in 1415 was well worth the cost of the expedition. In China they thought the giraffe (despite its having one horn too many) was a unicorn (*ch'i-lin*), whose arrival, according to Confucian tradition, meant that a sage of the utmost wisdom and benevolence was in their presence. It was a great gift, therefore, to bring to the ambitious ruler of a young dynasty. The giraffes were presented to the emperor Yong'le by exotic envoys from the kingdom of Malindi, whom the Chinese treated royally. They and their marvelous gift so excited China's curiosity about Africa that Zheng He sent word to the kingdom of Mogadishu (then one of the most powerful trading states in East Africa and now the capital of modern Somalia) and to other African states, inviting them to send ambassadors to the Ming emperor.

The response of the African rulers was overwhelmingly generous, for China and Africa had been distant trading partners from the time of the Han dynasty (206 B.C. to A.D. 220). In the *Universal Christian Topography,* written about A.D. 525 by Kosmas, a Byzantine monk known as the Indian Traveler, Sri Lanka is described as a trading center frequented by both Chinese and Africans. Envoys from a place called Zengdan—the name translates as "Land of Blacks"—visited China several times in the eleventh century. And a Chinese map compiled in the early fourteenth century shows Madagascar and the southern tip of Africa in remarkable detail, nearly two centuries before the Portuguese "discovered" the Cape of Good Hope. Archeologists find china (why the English word came to be synonymous with glazed pottery and porcelain, instead of silk or spices, is unclear) from the Han and later dynasties all along the east coast of Africa.

The African emissaries to the Ming throne came with fabulous gifts, including objects for which entrepreneurs had long before managed to create a market in the Far East—tortoise shell, elephant ivory, and rhinoceros-horn medicine. On their many visits they also brought zebras, ostriches, and other exotica. In return, the Ming court sent gold, spices, silk, and other presents. Zheng He was sent with his fleet of great ships on yet another voyage across the Indian Ocean to accompany some of the foreign emissaries home. This escort was the first of several imperially supported trips to Africa. According to official records, they went to Mogadishu, Brava, and perhaps Malindi; Snow (in *The Star Raft*) suggests that these Chinese expeditions may have gone still farther—to Zanzibar, Madagascar, and southern Africa.

Meanwhile, as the Chinese were pushing down the east coast of Africa, Portuguese mariners were tentatively exploring the west coast. They had started the process in the early fifteenth century and were steadily working their way south. Bartolomeu Dias reached the Cape of Good Hope in 1488 and was the first of these mariners to see the Indian Ocean. Surely the Europeans and Chinese were poised to meet somewhere in southern Africa, where perhaps they would have set up trading depots for their mutual benefit.

This did not happen, however. Emperor Yong'le died in 1424, and by 1433 the Ming dynasty discontinued its efforts to secure tributary states and trading partners around the Indian Ocean. In Beijing, those favoring an isolationist foreign policy won out, and the massive funding needed to support Zheng He's fleet—difficult to sustain during what was a period of economic decline in China—was canceled. As Edwin Reischauer and John Fairbank note in *East Asia: The Great Tradition* (1960):

The voyages must be regarded as a spectacular demonstration of the capacity of early Ming China for maritime expansion, made all the more dramatic by the fact that Chinese ideas of government and official policies were fundamentally indifferent, if not actually opposed, to such an expansion. This contrast between capacity and performance, as viewed in retrospect from the vantage point of our modern world of trade and overseas expansion, is truly striking.

The contrast also refutes the argument that as soon as a country possesses the technology of overseas trade and conquest it will use it. Zheng He's fleet was 250 times the size of Columbus's, and the Ming navy was many times larger and more powerful than the combined maritime strength of all of Europe. Yet China perceived her greatest challenges and opportunities to be internal ones, and Yong'le's overseas agenda was forgotten. Restrictions on private trade were reimposed, and commercial and military ventures in the Indian Ocean and South China Sea in subsequent centuries were dominated by the Portuguese, Arabs, Indians, Spaniards, Japanese, Dutch, British, and Americans. Zheng He's magnificent ships finally rotted at their moorings.

Columbus and His Four Fateful Voyages

David Gelman

Marooned on Jamaica, ailing and out of favor, with perhaps two embittered years of life remaining to him, Christopher Columbus dispatched to his monarchs a rambling, semicoherent letter invoking at one point a tribute to himself, written as if it were meant to be sung by angels:

"When He saw thee of an age with which He was content, He caused thy name to sound marvellously in the land. The Indies, which are so rich a part of the world, He gave thee for thine own . . . Of the barriers of the Ocean Sea, which were closed with such mighty chains, He gave thee the keys . . ."

It was an encomium he could no longer expect from the world. Returning from his epic first voyage, Columbus had been welcomed with honors, a triumphal march, a summons to dine with the king and queen. By the time he died 13 years later, many of his rights and titles had been stripped away, and the crown barely acknowledged his existence. He had become an embarrassment, blamed for instigating a ruthless slave trade in the New World and making a botch of the settlements he established there. To a large extent, this extraordinary reversal of fortune was brought on by his own blundering greed. Yet the fault was not entirely his. Above all, perhaps, he was guilty of having been too faithful to his mission, an endeavor launched "in the name of Jesus," but more palpably driven by the quest for gold. Columbus was first and foremost a man of his time, the product of an ethos shaped as much by commerce as by Christianity, in which it seemed

equally the work of the Lord to find the gold and propagate the faith.

It's easy enough to be cynical about him nowadays. Over the centuries, his reputation has tended to expand and deflate like some unruly Thanksgiving Day parade balloon. Yet in the broad sweep of history, most scholars agree, Columbus is a figure of unique importance. If his landing on American soil was not the first by a European (that distinction probably belongs to the Norseman, Leif Eriksson, who is believed to have touched somewhere on the Newfoundland coast around 1000), it was the most decisive. It marked the beginning of sustained contact between the Old World and the New—the beginning, really, of the world we know. "The likelihood of transatlantic voyages before Columbus was so great, you can probably say it did happen, but there was no impact, no consequence," says historian William McNeill. "What makes Columbus's voyage important was the response of Europe to the news of the discovery. Europe was poised to follow up."

Europe had been seeking some such expansion of its horizons for centuries. By the Middle Ages, Europeans were already beguiled by the opulent East, which remained, however, veiled in mystery. The elite could purchase precious silks, carpets and spices from Genoese, Venetian or Pisan merchants, who got them from Turkish traders at Alexandria, Aleppo or Damascus. But, for the most part, they were blocked from venturing any farther eastward. "This was the Iron Curtain of the late Middle Ages," writes Daniel Boorstin, author of "The Discoverers." Then,

observes Boorstin, "for a single century, from about 1250 to about 1350, that curtain was lifted, and there was direct human contact between Europe and China."

The brief opening arose courtesy of Genghis Khan, who led his Mongol armies down to Beijing in 1214 and spent the next 50 years expanding his empire across much of Eastern Asia and Eastern Europe. The khan may have been looked on as a barbarian, but he and his heirs encouraged free commercial trade by offering the Europeans well-policed roads with low customs fees. One taker was the adventurous 17-year-old Venetian named Marco Polo, who made the overland trek to China with his father and uncle and returned 24 years later with tales of unbounded wealth and luxury. Observes Boorstin: "Without Marco Polo, who stirred the European imagination with impatience to reach Cathay [the khans' capital city], would there have been a Columbus?"

The Chinese conquest of the Mongols in 1368 rang down the curtain on land travel to the East again, shifting momentum to the search for a sea route. No one pushed this quest more zealously than the Portuguese. Historians believe the Portuguese launched several forays westward on the Atlantic in the decades before 1492, but their main thrust was toward the southern tip of Africa. Portuguese ships kept inching down the west coast of the continent until a skipper named Bartolomeu Dias rounded the Cape of Good Hope and confirmed the existence of a water connection to the Indian Ocean. Forced to turn back by his men in the face of threatening seas, Dias returned to Lisbon with the news just in time to squelch the patiently nurtured ambitions of a Genoese named Columbus.

Picture the Discoverer at this moment in his life: an obscure navigator nearing 40, deeply in debt, sustained only by a daring notion of sailing west to reach the East and a cockeyed idea of how much ocean he must cross to get there. When Dias's storm-battered caravels limped into the harbor of Lisbon in December 1488, Columbus is thought to have been in Portugal trying for the second time to wangle King João II's backing for a westward expedition. With the eastward passage around Africa now feasible, Columbus's project was judged superfluous.

But the navigator was used to rejection. Since 1484, Columbus had devoted himself to promoting his "Enterprise of the Indies," first in Portugal and then in Spain. Now, like some wild-eyed adventurer in a Robert Louis Stevenson novel, Columbus petitioned Ferdinand and Isabella, flourishing a map that he had modified with the dubious geographical calculations of Ptolemy and Marco Polo. In 1491, a special commission, headed by Isabella's confessor, rendered an unfavorable opinion of the plan; in the spring of 1492, a second commission dismissed it anew. But after 10 years of war, Spain succeeded that spring in liberating Granada from the Moors, freeing the monarchs to turn to other matters. A last-ditch effort by Columbus's supporter Luis de Santángel, the king's financial adviser, convinced them that they might gain huge influence from Columbus's venture at relatively small cost. After eight desperate years, the plan was at last approved.

On the whole, Columbus is probably given less credit than he deserves for his almost fanatical persistence. Given that he was an impecunious foreigner with an uncertain grasp of geography, he "had to have been a very convincing public-relations man," says McNeill. "That a foreigner would be able to sell that bill of goods to the Spanish crown is really quite amazing."

After all the struggle and rejection, Columbus at last had a contract in his pocket, signed by the Spanish monarchs. In the Capitulations of Santa Fe, as the document was called, the crown agreed to grant him noble status, together with the offices of admiral, viceroy and governor in all the islands and mainlands that he might claim for Castile in the Atlantic. As for profits from the venture, one tenth, plus some investment options, would go to Columbus and the rest to the crown. "Here he was, an outsider from Genoa who was promised one tenth of all the riches and who managed to get himself classified as a noble in Spanish society," notes McNeill. "Columbus did extremely well for himself."

Finally, the great voyage of discovery got underway. The day before Columbus set sail was also the deadline for all Jews to leave the country. The same tide that bore him seaward carried the last of Spain's estimated 100,000 Jews into centuries-long exile. Samuel Eliot Morison, the patrician yachtsman-historian who wrote what has become the standard reference work on Columbus, imagined the embarkation scene as it might have been painted by El Greco: "One of those gray, calm days" under motionless cloud masses, "when the sea is like a mirror of burnished steel." The three square-rigged sailing vessels—the largest, the Santa María, was no bigger than a tennis court—begin moving down the Saltés River at about 5:15 a.m. It is Friday, Aug. 3, 1492. Not a leaf stirs as the men pull the oars. Morison even hears the friars chanting their morning prayer in the monastery of La Rábida on a cliff overlooking the harbor: "The Captain General, who often had joined in that hymn during his stay at La Rábida removes his hat; seamen who are not working follow his example . . ." It's a scene of hushed, poetic piety, one we almost want to believe—because history, in fact, is about to take one of its great leaps.

But between the embarkation and the sighting of land in the Americas, there was almost no drama. There were no storms or prolonged calms; the winds were brisk and steady. Compared with what later befell explorers Vasco da Gama and Ferdinand Magellan, or some of Columbus's own subsequent crossings, it was practically a luxury cruise. The days were balmy, the men went swimming at times in the glassy sea; at night they slept on deck.

Not all was serene, even so. Columbus kept a detailed journal of the voyage, which comes down to us in the form of an abstract by a Dominican monk, Bartolomé de Las Casas, sometimes in Columbus's words, more often in his own. From the journal and other sources it emerges that, experienced though they were, the crew were scarcely eager to sail off into a limitless sea. It was a measure of their uneasiness that little more than a week after they left the Canary Islands the voyagers began seeing signs of land on every side. "Friday, September 14th: The crew of the Niña stated that they had seen a tern and a tropic bird; and these birds never go more than twenty-five leagues from land."

"Monday, September 17th: They saw much vegetation and it was very delicate and was weed from rocks . . . They concluded that they were near land."

By Oct. 8, they did seem to be nearing something. "Thanks be to God," wrote Columbus, "the breezes were softer than in April at Seville . . . they are so laden with scent." And still there was no land. "Here the men could now bear no more; they complained of the long voyage." By some accounts, the crew wanted to turn back, but Columbus pleaded, if they didn't reach land in two or three days, "cut off my head and you shall return."

It was not until two hours past midnight on Oct. 12 that a lookout on the Pinta actually saw what looked like a line of white cliffs to the west. Ten weeks after he embarked from Palos de la Frontera, Columbus landed on an island he christened San Salvadora. Scholars still debate whether this was Samana Cay, San Salvador (Watlings Island) or any of a number of small islands in the Bahamas. What we do know is that after Columbus landed, his explorations took him to several other islands, including Cuba and Hispaniola (today, the Dominican Republic and Haiti). On Christmas Eve, 1492, the Santa María ran aground on shoals off Haiti's coast and had to be abandoned. Columbus had to leave 39 men behind in a colony he named La Navidad (for Christmas). Not to waste an opportunity, he ordered them to trade goods with the natives in exchange for gold.

The hope of finding some putative

mother lode of gold drove Columbus relentlessly through the islands. Gold danced before his eyes, in the necklaces, bracelets and nose rings the natives wore: "On October 13th: . . . So I resolved to go to the south-west to seek the gold and precious stones." "October 23rd: I did not delay longer here [on Cabo del Isleo] since I see that here there is no gold mine." In "The Conquest of Paradise," author Kirkpatrick Sale, a dedicated Columbus revisionist, counts no fewer than 140 uses of the word *oro* (gold) in Columbus's journal of the first voyage. He apparently could not admire the lush beauty of the islands without also estimating their potential value. "Here was a true son of Renaissance materialism," Sale snorts. Historian Carla Phillips demurs. Columbus, she argues, was desperate to justify the costs of the enterprise. "It's important for him to find vast harbors and rich mines in order to confirm his theories about what is out there."

Toward the natives, Columbus behaved with a kind of schizoid duplicity. From the moment he beheld them he saw an attractive, peaceable and friendly people who would make good Christians and "good servants." He rewarded their generosity with hawk bells, glass beads and other "trifles of small value," and periodically took them captive. And sometimes he dropped all pretense of good will: " . . . these people are very unskilled in arms . . . when Your Highnesses so command, they can all be carried off to Castile or held captive in the island itself, since with fifty men they would be all kept in subjection and forced to do whatever may be wished." Given the attitude of their visitors, it's not surprising the natives grew hostile—so that before he left for home, Columbus felt obliged to fortify La Navidad settlement, which was nevertheless wiped out to the last man by the islanders.

Meanwhile, Columbus grew increasingly anxious about finding the mainland. He still seemed to believe Cipango (Japan) or Cathay (China) was just around the next cove. But there were only more islands. (On his second voyage, still thwarted in the search, he would take depositions from his crew declaring Cuba to be part of the Asia mainland.) He sailed home, finally, aboard the Niña, picking up the westerlies he needed by heading north

from Hispaniola, and arriving on March 15, 1493, 32 weeks after he left, without having lost a man at sea. "He was a very competent seaman," says McNeill.

When Leif Eriksson reached the North American continent the news fell like a tree in the forest; almost no one heard it. When Columbus announced his discovery, in a letter to Luis de Santángel written during his return voyage, the word spread quickly, thanks to an already vigorous printing industry. Though some challenged Columbus's assertion that he had reached the Indies, the impact on the European imagination was profound, providing a forward thrust to the whole enterprise of New World exploration.

In response to his famous missive, Columbus received a letter from Ferdinand and Isabella, commanding him to court and addressing him as "Don Cristóbal Colón, their Admiral of the Ocean Sea, Viceroy and Governor of the Islands that he hath discovered in the Indies." He would never again experience anything like the grand reception he was accorded, first at Córdoba, then at Barcelona, where he created a sensation by presenting to the monarchs seven natives of "the Indies," along with gold artifacts and samples of allegedly rare spices. "It would have been well for him had he then taken his profits and retired with honor, leaving to others the responsibility of colonization," observes Morison. Instead, he embarked westward again, this time in the panoply of 17 ships, with 1,500 crewmen, soldiers and colonists and the requisite plants, domestic animals and tools for a permanent settlement. But the cresting hopes that rode with him were doomed to failure. From the moment of his return, the arc of the admiral's career sweeps downward. His relations with the natives rapidly descended into a kind of Kurtzian darkness.

With La Navidad destroyed, Columbus founded a new colony at La Isabela, closer to the rumored source of gold. But it was plagued by illness and rebellion. The admiral had no gift for administration; he could not control hundreds of Spaniards avid for conquest. There were repeated episodes of rape, pillage and murder by marauding bands of Spaniards. Returning from a trip to find a mutiny brewing, Col-

umbus placed all munitions on board his flagship under command of his younger brother Diego. But when Columbus was away, the violence erupted again. Later, several of the troublemakers seized some caravels that Columbus's other brother Bartolomé had brought from Spain and sailed home, where they circulated slanders against the Columbus brothers.

Historians say Columbus may have made a fatal mistake at this point when he ignored a summons from Ferdinand and Isabella to come home. Instead of appeasing the monarchs and silencing the slanders, he decided to deal with the turbulent situation at La Isabela and try to begin regular exports to Spain. As a first step, he rounded up about 1,600 Tainos who had been resisting the Spaniards and crammed 550 of them aboard four ships, to be transported home as slaves. Then he and his brothers set about subjugating all of Hispaniola to reap its gold, with the use of slave labor.

They did, finally, find a rich vein of gold in the southern part of the island; eventually, the gold strike made Columbus rich and repaid the crown some of its initial investment. He nevertheless returned home under a cloud, still having failed to establish a stable colony. What's more, he had angered the monarchs by enslaving people now regarded as Spanish subjects. It was more than a year before the crown would outfit another voyage. On this third crossing, he managed at last to reach mainland America—Venezuela, as it happened. Ill at the time and slipping into what some historians think was a half-mad mysticism, he speculated that he had found the Garden of Eden itself. Phillips insists he was sane. "He had a very firm belief that he was chosen by God," she argues. "His whole mental map was Biblical."

Meanwhile, conditions on Hispaniola had grown worse under Diego, who had been left in charge. Because of the negative reports filtering back, Ferdinand and Isabella ordered an investigation, which ended with all three Columbus brothers shipped home in chains. The monarchs appointed a new governor of the islands, Nicolás de Ovando, who set sail with a fleet twice the size of Columbus's largest. When Columbus embarked on his fourth and final voyage in 1502, still hoping to find a direct passage from

Cuba to Asia, he was reduced to four small ships and a kind of renegade status, barred from the colony at Santo Domingo. His worm-eaten boats, barely afloat, had to be grounded on a Jamaican reef. A caravel rescued the expedition a year later, but after his return to Spain in November 1504, the admiral never sailed again.

Columbus spent the rest of his life lobbying to have his grants and titles restored. On May 20, 1506, he died at 55, feeling betrayed by the monarchs he thought he had served with the steadfastness of a Job. The glory passed to those who came after him. After Amerigo Vespucci reached the mainland of the New World, the German cartographer Martin Waldseemüller named it America on his famous map of 1507, in Vespucci's honor. Europe, at any rate, remained

less interested in settling the Americas than finding ways around them. Just before the end of the 15th century, a Portuguese named Vasco da Gama completed the trip that Bartolomeu Dias had begun, sailing around the tip of Africa to Calicut, on the southwest coast of India. By 1515, the treasures of India, China and Japan were coming to Europe around the Cape of Good Hope on Portuguese ships.

In 1513, another explorer searching for gold in the Americas, Vasco Núñez de Balboa, climbed a peak on the Panamanian isthmus and beheld the mighty Pacific, the first European to do so. And in 1519, Ferdinand Magellan, a Portuguese of aristocratic birth, sailing for the Spanish crown, undertook the most extraordinary voyage of all. Setting out with five barely seaworthy ships, racked by violent storms, near

starvation and a mutiny, he managed to find a passage from the east coast of South America to the Pacific through the straits that now bear his name. His ships, or what was left of them, then completed a three-year circumnavigation of the globe that Magellan himself did not survive.

Yet it is the comparatively idyllic first voyage of Columbus that has come down to us, in almost folkloric colors, as the great voyage of discovery. We know little of what the Vikings felt as they sailed to Vinland in the icy dawn of modern history. But it is Columbus, pressing confidently into uncharted seas, leaning forward to catch the first spice-laden scent of a continent he never doubted he would find, who speaks to the voyager in all of us.

With Susan Miller

The Sailors of Palos

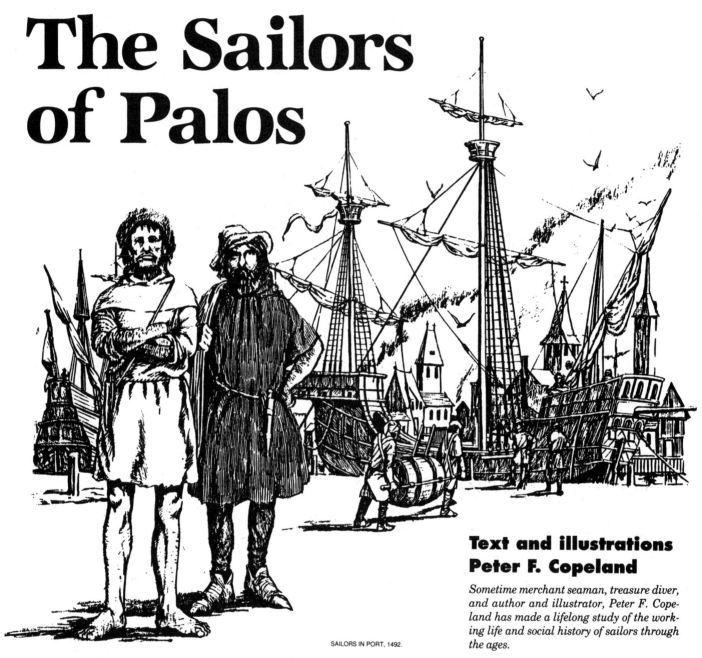

SAILORS IN PORT, 1492.

**Text and illustrations
Peter F. Copeland**

Sometime merchant seaman, treasure diver, and author and illustrator, Peter F. Copeland has made a lifelong study of the working life and social history of sailors through the ages.

When Christopher Columbus's two surviving ships arrived back in Europe from the New World in March 1493, the Admiral of the Ocean Sea returned to lasting but troubled fame. But the mariners who had accompanied him across unknown seas and through storm and shipwreck remained virtually forgotten to history. Here an artist-historian tells us who some of these sailors were and what their seafaring lives were like.

From *American History Illustrated*, March/April 1993, pp. 58-68. © 1993 by Cowles Magazines, Inc. Reprinted by permission.

It was early March 1493, and the great voyage was nearly over. En route back to Spain from the far-off Indies, the storm-beaten *Niña*, flagship of Christopher Columbus, had put into Lisbon. Her consort, the original flagship *Santa María*—or what was left of her—lay shattered on a reef off the island of Hispaniola.*

The *Niña's* sailors were at work, repairing and renewing their weathered ship, and anticipating a speedy return to Spain and their home port of Palos. They had little time to speculate on the fate of the *Pinta*, the sister caravel last seen one stormy night a month before in mid-ocean.** There was much to be done. A new set of sails must be laid out, cut, and sewn. Running rigging must be renewed; standing rigging needed repair. Already shoreside carpenters were measuring and sawing aloft and on deck, while caulkers worked at sealing the leaky hull. Other sailors turned-to to clean and wash down the hold. Soon they would load sacks and barrels of stones from the banks of the River Tagus, to be packed as ballast in the now lightly laden vessel.

Within a few days, news of Columbus's epochal seven-month voyage and discovery of a sea route across the Western Ocean to the Indies and far Cathay would begin to reverberate across Portugal and Spain, and indeed be trumpeted throughout Europe. Greeted as a hero by all who heard of his enterprise, the admiral already basked in his celebrity. It was, at least for the moment, everything for which the determined explorer could hope.

Columbus returned to Europe in 1493 to lasting but troubled fame for achievements that still cast an imposing shadow today, five hundred years later. But what of the nearly ninety officers and sailors who accompanied him across unknown seas, enduring storm and shipwreck? Unlike Columbus, his mariners have passed the succeeding centuries in virtual obscurity. Who were these sailors and what were their lives like—both in port and during their odyssey of discovery?

A HARBOR SCENE.

Most of the men and boys who signed on for the Voyage of Discovery during the summer of 1492 came from Palos and the other seaside towns and villages of Andalusia in southern Spain. A few, however, were Basques and Gallicians from the northern part of the country, and five—a Portuguese, a Venetian, a Calabrian, and two Genoese—were foreigners.

The crewmen ranged in age and experience from seasoned veterans of the sea accustomed to the rigors of shipboard life to youths no older than twelve years of age. They included skilled specialists such as boatswains, carpenters, caulkers, coopers, gunners, pilots, stewards, and surgeons, as well as untrained boys.

Legend suggests that Columbus's sailors were criminals and convicts,

*On Christmas Eve 1492, as the flagship sailed along the coast of Hispaniola, Columbus, who had been on deck for several days, went below for a few hours of sleep. The night being fine and the sea calm, the officer of the watch also went below, and the watch on deck settled down to sleep—with the helmsman (disobeying the admiral's standing orders) leaving the tiller in the hands of one of the ship's boys. During the night, with the youth at the helm, the *Santa María* went aground on a coral bank, wedging in so firmly that all efforts to kedge her off proved fruitless. Her seams eventually opened and she had to be abandoned.

**The two ships and their crews were unexpectedly reunited on March 15, when both entered the harbor of Palos on the same tide.

WORKING ALOFT.

and hides. Windlasses cracked and groaned as gangs of chantey-singing sailors, clad only in wide-bottomed underdrawers, strained at the capstan bars.

Some of the vessels anchored in the harbor or tied alongside the wharves might have hailed from such far-off places as Denmark and Egypt. Most were lateen-rigged caravels built in western Andalusia—familiar sights along the shores of Spain, Portugal, and throughout the Mediterranean.

A large three-masted deep-sea ship loading horses through a side-port opening also might be seen on the waterfront, tied up alongside tiny coastal trading vessels manned by crews of two men each, or near a fishing boat newly arrived from Iceland and deeply laden with a cargo of dried codfish. Here also might be a ship-of-war, with banners fluttering from her fore and aft castles, taking aboard chests of arms and casks of salt-meat and wine.

Columbus's flagship *Santa María* was a Gallician-built *nao*—a round-bellied, three-masted, square-rigged former merchantman of the type commonly seen in the Mediterranean. Heavy and unwieldy, she measured about eighty-five feet long, had a beam of thirty feet, and displaced more than one hundred tons. Columbus called her "a dull sailor, and unfit for discovery." During the voyage of discovery the *Santa María* shipped a crew of forty men and boys.

The *Niña* and *Pinta* both were caravels, small, lightly-built, broad-bowed vessels that had begun life as lateen-rigged ships with no square sails—a typical Mediterranean rig. Both ultimately were re-rigged as *caravela redondas*, with square sails on the fore and mainmasts, and lateen sails on their mizzens. The *Niña* had a fourth mast aft of the mizzen, called a *bonaventura* mast, upon which was shipped a smaller lateen sail; it is possible that the *Pinta* did also. The *Niña* was about sixty-seven feet long, with a beam of twenty-one feet; tradition tells us that the *Pinta* was somewhat larger. The *Niña* carried a crew of twenty-four men and boys, and the *Pinta* shipped twenty-six crewmen.

A typical merchant ship of the era was described as a "grim and dark city, full of bad odors, filth, and uncomfortable living

dragooned for a desperate enterprise, but in fact only one man among them was a convicted murderer. He and two cohorts were pardoned on condition of volunteering to serve. The vast majority of the sailors joined the expedition—after initial hesitation—for the adventure of the voyage and the hope of gaining riches in the far-off Indies.

Strange and picturesque to the shorefolk he encountered, the seaman of Columbus's time lived apart in his own world of ships and seaports. He had been to distant lands and seen fascinating sights. He wore odd clothes and spoke a language that sounded peculiar and sometimes even incomprehensible.

To landsmen unfamiliar with the fifteenth-century sailor's world, the bustling seaports he frequented must have seemed exciting and exotic places. In many harbors the waterfront itself was

called the "lowere city" and sometimes was separated by a tall wooden palisade from the rest of the town—the "upper city"—where dwelt the merchants and well-to-do tradesmen.

This lower city—with its population of fisherfolk, chandlers, peddlers, shipwrights, rogues, slatterns, and drunks—was a place of noise and smells and mud. Packs of half-wild dogs roamed through the narrow, filthy alleys that led down to the ships. The air was filled with the raw stench of hides, fish, and sewage and the sounds of wine vendors, soap sellers, and other street peddlers crying their wares. Here, too, one might hear the chanted prayers of a black-robed priest—his pious petitions for the mariners laboring on the seas occasionally interrupted by songs and shouts emanating from nearby taverns.

The waterfront itself was crowded with merchants, beggars, sailors, and itinerant laborers looking for odd jobs. Ships at the quayside loaded and discharged such cargoes as fish, salt, oil, grain, wine, conditions." At sea the vessel's masts and hull creaked and groaned continually as, with her short keel and round bilges, she pitched and rolled heavily even in a moderate sea. Built with timber from the high Pyrenees, Columbus's ships were fastened with wooden pegs and hand-wrought iron spikes, and they leaked like weathered wash-tubs.

The captain of a Spanish ship of the fifteenth century was commander of the vessel and crew, but not necessarily a seaman. He might be a military officer of the crown, a member of a noble family, or, like Columbus, the holder of a Royal Commission that in Columbus's case declared him "Captain General" of the fleet as well as captain of the *Santa María*.

Second to the captain in line of command stood the master—the man who actually supervised the operation of the ship. He was an experienced seaman in overall charge of each day's sailing, getting the vessel underway, stowing cargo, and anchoring. Sometimes the master also was the ship's captain; occasionally he was its owner as well.

Below the master was the first mate or pilot (*piloto* in Spanish), the navigation officer responsible to the master for the operation of the ship and the work of the seamen. He was, ideally, an experienced ship handler, wise in the ways of the weather, the tides, and the sea. The pilot brought aboard with him such navigational materials as charts, compass, sandglasses, astrolabe or quadrant, and sounding leads. Both master and pilot received a rate of pay about twice that of the sailors.

The *Santa María*, as flagship of Columbus's expedition, carried several additional officials to fulfill special assignments. There was an interpreter to converse with the Asians the explorer expected to meet; a secretary of the fleet to record the discovery of new lands that might be found and claimed; and two royal agents to note expenses and take charge of the Crown's portion of any treasure recovered. There were also a comptroller of the fleet and a silversmith.

Also serving aboard the *Santa María* was the *alguazil de la armada*, or marshal of the fleet. Each of the two other vessels had a marshal of the ship. These men were responsible for maintaining

discipline and administering punishment as required.

A surgeon aboard each vessel served the medical needs of the crew, and a steward was responsible for the food stores, firewood, water, and wine. The steward saw to trimming and maintaining lamps and tending the fires over which hot meals were prepared.

Equal in rank with the steward was the boatswain, who led the seamen in their daily tasks and who reported to the mate. The boatswain carried out the orders of the master and mate in the stowing of cargo; he continually inspected masts, spars, rigging, and sails for wear and repair; and he had charge of all the ship's cable and lines. He also was responsible for keeping the deck clean and shipshape; for maintaining the good condition of the ship's boat; and for making sure that the galley fire was put out each night.

Next below the steward and boat-

swain were the ship's petty officers, or *oficiales*—sailors who practiced special trades such as carpentry, caulking, or cooperage. The caulker, responsible for keeping the deck and hull watertight, had a store of rope yarn, oakum, tallow, oil, pitch, scupper nails, and lead sheets for stopping leaks. He also was in charge of the ship's pumps. The cooper had the important job of making up, caulking, and repairing the ship's casks and barrels, buckets, tubs, hogsheads, and other such wooden containers—all vital for the storage of water, wine, and oil.

Next in this shipboard hierarchy were the experienced seamen or *marineros*, and finally, at the bottom, the apprentices and boys or *grumetes*. There were twenty-six watch-standing sailors aboard the *Santa María*, fourteen aboard the *Niña*, and fifteen aboard the *Pinta*.

Columbus was captain of the *Santa*

RAISING THE MAIN YARD.

María as well as admiral of the fleet. The ship's owner, Juan de la Cosa, sailed as master, with Peralonso Niño as his mate. Juan Sánchez was surgeon, and Pedro de Terreros was Columbus's personal steward. Diego de Arana was marshal of the fleet, and Rodrigo de Escobedo was secretary or *escrivano* of the armada. Luis de Torres, a converted Jew, was the official interpreter. He spoke Hebrew, Aramaic, and some Arabic.

Thirty-year-old Vicente Yáñez Pinzón was captain of the *Niña*, and Juan Niño was master. Sancho Ruiz de Gama served as pilot; Bartolomé García was the boatswain; and Alonso de Moguer was surgeon.

Martín Alonzo Pinzón—brother of Vicente—was captain of the *Pinta*, and his other brother Francisco Martín Pinzón sailed as master. Cristóbal García Sarmiento was pilot, and Juan Quintero was boatswain. García Fernández was steward, and a man named Diego was surgeon.

Most of the ordinary seamen and apprentices whose names appeared on the rosters of Columbus's ships were listed only by their first name and place of origin. Among those assigned to the *Santa María*, for example, was a boy known to us only as Juan, who was listed as a servant. Juan could have been a ship's boy,

an apprentice seaman, or the personal servant of one of the officials aboard the ship. Probably coming from a village in Andalusia, he may have been recommended by a brother or cousin among the members of the crew. His parents could have been peasants who worked the stony coastal land, or possibly fisherfolk. In any case, the social standing of Juan's family would have been very near the bottom of medieval society.

The average seafarer of Columbus's time was illiterate, as were the great majority of people ashore. His life expectancy was short due to his exposure to the perils of the sea, warfare, and waterfront life. Accustomed to coping with primitive conditions, he was tough and

cynical, with not much respect for the law but a realistic fear of the strong arm of authority.

Sailors are mentioned briefly here and there in the reminiscences of travelers of the medieval world—ship's passengers, pilgrims, merchants, and clerics. They also appear in some of the works of authors and playwrights of the day. In his *Canterbury Tales*, fourteenth-century writer Geoffrey Chaucer described a "shipman" who was traveling to the shrine to make a votive offering, perhaps in obedience to a vow made in time of peril on the sea. The sailor's rough and homely attire, his awkwardness on horseback, his weather-beaten complexion, and his seafaring speech made him a subject of jest to his fellow pilgrims. He nevertheless was a jovial and welcome companion for the travelers and "certainly he was a good felawe."

Medieval seamen also appeared in a morality play given by the Guild of Shipwrights for the pageant of Corpus Christi in London in the year 1415. Portrayed as being distinctly different from shore folk, the sailors were distinguished by the "quaint expressions of

THE "SANTA MARIA."

their profession," their rough and boisterous humor, and their contempt for the soft and sheltered life of their shoreside cousins.

Superstitious, as so many seafarers through the ages have been, the typical sailor of Columbus's time deeply believed in omens and portents of doom. He accepted the existence of gigantic sea monsters that lived far out in the depths of the unknown ocean. He looked with a child's eyes upon odd things seen in far places and had a great faith in the miraculous. Anything that frightened him or seemed unexplainable, he believed to be of supernatural origin. If a strange bird alighted upon his ship, he took it as an unfavorable omen; and he feared the presence on board of a priest or woman as a sure way to raise up the devil. One medieval ocean traveler recalled that "during the night hours when the wind was high, the sailors would think they could hear sirens singing, wailing and jeering, like insolent men in their cups."

Columbus's sailors were as superstitious as any. They had been skeptical and uneasy about this voyage of exploration to the far Indies. There were old-timers among them who had sailed down the African coast to Guinea and out into the Western Ocean to the Canary Islands and the Azores. They knew that the Portuguese had sailed far reaches of the Atlantic in quest of the mythical islands of Brazil, Antilla of the Seven Cities, and the fabled isles of St. Brendan, but without success.

The same circumstances that made the sailor prone to superstition tended to make him more religious than his kinfolk ashore. His religious convictions conformed to a deeply devout though violent and authoritarian period. The cruelty and amorality of his time did not shake his belief in the existence of an avenging deity or in the strict authority of the Holy Church.

Although lacking in formal education, the able-bodied sailor of the fifteenth century was proficient at the peculiar skills of his trade through years of apprenticeship. He had to be able to steer at the tiller, splice line, caulk seams, make and mend sails, take accurate soundings, and be adept at small-boat handling. He was required, among his other duties, to work at loading and discharging the ship's cargo and to make and take in sail in all weather. He had to be familiar with the process of weighing and letting go the anchors and of securing them when brought aboard. He also had to be fairly skilled at rough carpentry and to be practiced in the use of weapons and in gunnery, for he would be called upon to defend his ship in time of need. Hardy and strong, he was as agile as a monkey; when going aloft he often climbed hand-over-hand up the lines of the standing rigging.

The sailors of Columbus proved as talented as any in the skills of the *marinero*. Before the expedition departed from the Canary Islands on its outbound voyage, Columbus decided to convert the *Niña* from a lateen to a square rig. With no shipyards or skilled artisans available, Captain Pinzón chose a gang from among the ship's own crew to do the job, which included cutting and sewing new sails for the fore and main yards. The work began on August 26, and the *Niña* was ready to sail just three days later. It is a tribute to Columbus's sailors that the only complaint voiced by the admiral about poor workmanship concerned the shipwrights of Palos, whose faulty caulking caused the *Niña* and *Pinta* to leak badly.

The clothing of Columbus's sailors was simple and their possessions few. Typical garb consisted of wide-bottomed knee-length breeches; a loose-fitting hooded blouse of coarse linen or old sail cloth; and, perhaps, a sleeveless vest-like overgarment slit at the sides and tied with laces. Although the sailor sometimes wore stockings and shoes, in milder climes he usually went barefoot. Most seamen wore red woolen stocking caps of the type made in Toledo. Columbus gave several of these caps as gifts to the natives he encountered in the New World.

The Spanish seaman's foul-weather garment has been described as a brown

THE "PINTA."

cloth robe or overcoat called *papahigo* or "storm sail" in sailors' slang, that resembled the habit of the Franciscan friars. This, the sea gown worn by mariners all over western Europe, was the distinctive garment that identified them as seafarers. Chaucer's shipman of the *Canterbury Tales,* for example, wore "a gown of falding (a coarse cloth) to the knee." This, plus the pilgrim's habit of wearing his sailors' knife hung from a thong slung over his shoulder, marked him as a seaman in the eyes of his fellow travelers.

The sailor tightened his sea gown at the waist with a belt or perhaps a bit of ships' hempen line; when working on deck he often knotted the front or tucked it through his waist belt to keep it out of the way.

Ships' officers wore cloaks, jackets, or doublets of cloth or dressed leather that laced down the front; hose and a variety of styles of hats or caps, all in brighter colors than the rough simple clothing of the sailors. At his belt, the ship's officer wore a dagger rather than a sailor's

sheath knife. At sea the officers sometimes reverted, in part at least, to more common sailors' garb. Columbus is reported habitually to have worn a brown sea gown, which was mistaken by some observers as being the hooded brown habit of a Franciscan monk. It is interesting that a man so vain of his rank and titles would choose to wear a garment so rough and uncouth in medieval eyes.

Sleeping and sanitary accommodations aboard Columbus's ships were primitive. The captain and sailing master probably had small cabins, each barely large enough to contain a narrow wooden bunk. Other officers slept on mattresses under the quarterdeck, forward of the helmsman. When not in use, the mattresses were rolled up in grass sacks and lashed along the bulwarks.

The ordinary sailors generally had to

MANNING THE PUMP.

sleep in the open on the cambered deck, where hatch covers offered the only flat surfaces and coils of line served as pillows—or if more fortunate, to huddle under the shelter of the forecastle. On many vessels of that time the sailors were forbidden to sleep in the protection of the ship's hold, even during stormy weather, as it would take too long to roust them out in an emergency. In the *Santa María,* with her large crew, this rule may not have been enforced.

To relieve a call of nature the sailor had to swing up over the bulwarks and hang in the rigging over the ship's lee side, "making reverence to the sun," as the saying was, and hope that he would not be swept away by a visiting wave. The lower rigging had to be washed down each day as a consequence of this necessity.

When the ship was becalmed, the men might bathe themselves on deck, scooping up sea water in buckets; the more adventurous might, in calm weather, even go over the side if there were no sharks about. Most sailors wore whiskers or a full beard, because the average man of that day shaved only once a week if he shaved at all.

The staples of the Spanish sailor's diet were hard biscuit; bacon; salt meat and fish; chick peas and beans; garlic and olive oil; rice and raisins. No cook was carried to prepare the sailors' meals; this duty probably fell to one of the ships' boys. The officers ate aft, their food prepared by the captain's servant.

Hot meals, when they were available, always were soups or stews prepared with salt meat or fish, broken ship's biscuit, rice, and whatever spices were available, with rare additions of onions or potatoes. One such stew, called *lobscouse,* was eaten by seafaring men until the end of the age of sail. On Fridays, if the weather held, the sailors' hot meal was bean soup seasoned with garlic and peppers.

Columbus described his idea of the stores to be carried on a voyage of discovery thus: good biscuit seasoned and not old, flour salted at the time of milling, wine, salt meat, oil, vinegar, cheese, chick peas, lentils, beans, salt fish, honey, rice, almonds, and raisins. The salted flour could be mixed with water or wine, made into cakes of unleavened bread, and baked in the ashes at the bottom of the open iron firebox in which the hot meals were prepared. This primitive stove, called a *fogón*, was brought up from below in fair weather and set on deck near the lee rail. The fire was kindled upon a bed of earth or sand that covered the bottom of the firebox. Supplies of firewood were stowed in every available corner of the ship.

When conditions permitted, a hot meal was prepared before noon so that the watch below could eat before turning to and the watch on deck could dine after being relieved. Gathering around the smoking firebox, the hungry sailors extended their bowls for stew or soup and then found a place on the crowded, cluttered deck or on the hatch. Sprawling or kneeling or sitting as conditions allowed, and with a knife their only utensil, they ate "from their lap" in the fashion of the poor folk in the Middle Ages. As one observer noted, they "pull out their knives of different shapes made to kill hogs or skin lambs or for cutting bags, and then grab in their hands the poor bones and peel them clean of their sinews and meat as if all their lives they had practiced anatomy in Guadelupe or Valencia. In a prayer, they leave them clean as ivory."

It did not take many days at sea for the food supplies to become wormy and rancid in the damp shipboard environment. And the casks of fresh water soon became foul and stinking—though when laced with wine the brackish liquid became at least barely palatable. Sometimes sailors carried their ration below decks to eat in the dark—to avoid seeing the maggots that infested it.

To supplement their diets, the sailors caught fish as often as possible. On Columbus's outward voyage, when supplies were still relatively plentiful and fresh, such catches were a luxury. During the return, however, they became a dire necessity. The admiral recorded in his *Diario* on January 25—more than three weeks before reaching the Azores—that the crew of the *Niña* had "killed a porpoise and a tremendous shark . . . [they] had quite some need of it because they were carrying nothing to eat except bread and wine and yams from the Indies."

Mariners marked the passage of time at sea with the turning of a sandglass, which was done by an apprentice sea-

A MEAL ON DECK IN FAIR WEATHER.

man. As the sand ran out at the end of each half-hour, the helmsman rang a bell to remind the apprentice to turn the glass. This was the origin of the ship's-bell time used to this day.

With each turning of the glass during the night watch, the *grumete* called out to the lookout in the masthead "*Ah! de proa! Alerta, buena guardia!*" to which the lookout called back "*Buena guardia!*" to prove he was awake—a procedure still followed aboard some merchant ships in recent times.

Ceremony and formality accompanied the passage of each watch at sea. Just before sundown and before the first night watch, the crew was called to evening

prayers. An apprentice carried the binnacle lamp aft along the deck, singing "Amen and God give us a good night and a good sailing. May the ship make a good passage, captain and master and good company." Then the apprentices led the sailors in prayer, chanting the *Pater Noster*, the *Ave Maria*, and the *Credo*, after which all hands sang the *Salve Regina*. For the sailors these chanted rituals of the church were comforting and expected, their only link to their distant homeland.

The night watches also had their moments of formal spoken reverence, as described by Felix Fabri, a traveler of 1480: "When the wind is quite fair and not too strong all is still save only he who watches the compass and he who holds the handle on the tiller, for these, by way of returning thanks for a voyage and good luck, continually greet the breeze, praise God, the Blessed Virgin and the Saints, on answering the other, and they are never silent so long as the wind is fair. Anyone on board who hears this chant of theirs would fall asleep."

At daybreak the youngest boy of the watch sang or chanted a prayer that invoked a blessing of the True Cross, the Holy Trinity, and the true God, keeper of the immortal soul, concluding:

Blessed be the light of day
And he who sends the night away.

Then the boy recited the *Pater Noster* and the *Ave Maria* and added a plea to God for a good voyage and the hope that he would grant good days to the officers of the after guard and to the sailors forward.

The sailors and apprentices were divided into two watches, each group alternating at watch-standing duties of four hours each. If he was not already on watch, the sailor's day began at seven in the morning when the deck boy sang out *"Al quarto!"* (on deck) and the men of the morning watch crawled out from whatever sheltering spot they had found to sleep away their few hours of rest. No one needed time to dress, for all hands slept in their clothes. One sailor went aft to relieve the helmsman, who steered from his position under the quarterdeck in an enclosed, gloomy little space cut off from the rest of the ship. He handled the heavy tiller below decks, without any view of the sea or the sails; his orders were shouted down to him through a small hatch by the mate standing on the quarterdeck above. Before him, secured to the mizzenmast, was the binnacle, a box containing the compass and its lantern.

In maintaining his assigned compass course the helmsman was aided by the feel of the ship under his feet and the orders of the mate from above. Steering was a rough job. When a heavy sea slammed against the rudder, the swinging tiller might knock the helmsman off his feet. To minimize this, a relieving tackle, which could be adjusted to allow for the set of the sea, was rigged to the tiller. Not every sailor was a skilled helmsman. Columbus noted in his journal that his sailors sometimes steered

badly, carelessly allowing the *Santa María* to run as much as several points off the ordered course.

The first duty of the men of the morning watch was to man the wooden pumps that stood just forward of midships on the main deck, to remove the water that had accumulated in the bilges during the night. The bilge water came up "foaming like hell and stinking like the devil." Seamen believed, however, that if the bilges stank they would enjoy a lucky voyage; the stale water sloshing about in the bottom of the hold ensured that the beams and planks would remain swollen tight and that the crew would not be laboring forever at the pumps.

The men then scrubbed the deck with buckets of sea water and stiff-bristled brooms. In hot, dry climates this scrubbing and sloshing of water over the decks was repeated several times a day to keep the planking from drying out and shrinking in the hot sun. With their buckets, the men then washed down the lower rigging, deadeyes, and main shrouds where they had been soiled by men relieving themselves over the side during the night.

Those on the morning watch were responsible for taking up the slack in the running gear so that all the lines were taut. The sailors also regularly tarred all of the standing rigging, stays, and shrouds. The deck boys were put to making up spun yarn and chafing gear out of old lines and making oakum from old rope yarns for the caulker's use.

When sail was to be taken in, the main yard was quickly lowered to the deck and the sailors gathered the canvas and secured it to the yard with lashings, after which all hands manned the topping lifts and hauled the yard and its furled sail back up to the masthead. In good weather there was no need to raise and lower the heavy yard because sailors could climb the rigging and straddle the yard while gathering up the sail.

When rain was expected and the wind permitted, the sailors manned the mainsail clew lines and raised a corner of the sail to form a belly in the canvas with which to catch some of the precious rainwater, which then would be drained into buckets and casks.

During a storm at sea, life was a nightmarish struggle, with the sailors fighting to take in sails and all hands laboring constantly at the crude hand pumps or (when as often happened, the pumps broke down) forming bucket brigades to bail the ship out by hand. Steering with the heavy wooden tiller in bad weather was a brutal wrestling match that left the helmsman exhausted and covered with bumps and bruises.

In storm and howling winds many among the crew were both sick and terrified, and the sailors were not reluctant to pray to God and call upon the saints for mercy. During Columbus's homeward voyage, when the *Niña* fought to survive a February storm off the Azores, the admiral himself "ordered that lots should be drawn for a pilgrimage to Santa María de Guadalupe and to take a five-pound wax candle [and] for another pilgrim to go to spend a night at vigil in Santa Clara de Moguer and to have a Mass said. . . . After this the admiral and all the men made a vow that, as soon as they reached the first land, all would go in their shirtsleeves in procession to pray in a church dedicated to Our Lady."

During such miserable times there were no hot meals and little sleep. At the end of his watch the sailor, soaked to the skin, rolled himself in his rough gown and napped, perhaps curled up in a sodden coil of mooring line among the rats and roaches under the forecastle, until the boatswain's whistle rousted him out for another emergency. After the storm passed, the mariners often discovered to their further dismay that the sea stores had suffered storm damage or that wine or water casks had been stove in, requiring that both food and drink thereafter be severely rationed.

During most of his time at sea, the sailor had precious little leisure time that was not spent in trying to sleep or tending to necessary personal chores. When in port or at anchor, however, or in gentler hemispheres where emergencies were infrequent, the seamen found time for entertainment. Storytelling was a universal pastime among mariners and included tall tales of adventures past and hardships endured, of feats of gluttony and drinking bouts ashore, and of romances in different ports. The board game of checkers (*damas* in Spanish) was widely played, and men off watch squandered many a

1401: "Among all the occupations of sea-farers there is one which, though loathsome, is yet very common, daily and necessary. I mean the hunting and catching of lice and vermin. Unless a man spends several hours in this work when he is on pilgrimage, he will have but unquiet slumbers."

Although there always have been men who loved the sea in spite of all of its hardships and dangers, there was one feature of the fifteenth-century sailor's calling that probably attracted him more than anything else—the lure of money. The peasant farmer seldom saw hard cash in his life. What his family could not grow, weave, or craft itself must be obtained through barter. To a youth growing up in such a world the idea of regular wages was most attractive. The sailor was paid in cash for his time and labor.

A sailor's monthly wage of eight hundred *maravedis*—enough to buy two fat pigs—was about the same as that earned by the manservant to a nobleman. A ship's master earned more than double that amount—the price of a cow. For those who sailed with Columbus, the enterprise held both the distant promise of a fortune to be discovered in the Indies and also a stipulated monthly salary to be earned in hard money paid from the Royal treasury.

Despite all they had experienced and endured, the crews of the *Niña* and *Pinta* who returned to Palos in March 1493 were in remarkably good shape. None had been lost due to disease or accidents at sea.* Before setting out in August 1492 they had received four months' pay in advance. Now, as they prepared to drop anchor, the seamen could look forward to collecting the balance owed them and to telling all who would listen of the strange sights they had seen. Although history would focus its gaze on the man who commanded the expedition, the seamen whose labors brought the two surviving ships back to their home port could bask, at least for a time, in his reflected glory.

SAILORS IN PORT.

hard-earned coin gambling with dice under the forecastle head.

Singing was another popular recreation for sailors far from home. We are told that after sighting the islands of the New World, the crew of the *Pinta* sang and danced around the mainmast to the accompaniment of pipes and a tambourine. Shipmates also passed their free hours at sea fishing with hand line and harpoon; gathering flying fish that landed on deck; and spotting and identifying types of birds that approached the ships.

Yet another leisure-hour activity was described by a seafaring pilgrim in

*Sadly, more than a third of Columbus's sailors did not survive to enjoy their hard-won rewards. When the *Santa María* ran aground and was wrecked off Hispaniola, the admiral, having insufficient room aboard the remaining ships for all of his crewmen, built a fort—named La Villa de Navidad in honor of the Christmas feast day—and left thirty-nine men behind. When his second expedition returned to Villa de Navidad in November 1493, Columbus found the fort in ashes and the men dead at the hands of local Taino tribesmen—the Navidad garrison having allowed greed and lust to destroy the good relations that Columbus had established with the natives.

Five Hundred Years Later:
RECONSIDERING COLUMBUS

"[The] acrimonious debate about the moral questions involved in the European conquest of New World peoples will continue to form one of the many contexts in which we remember Columbus—and judge him."

Sebastiano del Piomo, *Portrait of Columbus*, oil (1519).

N.Y. Public Library Picture Collection

Robert P. Hay

Dr. Hay, Associate History Editor of USA Today, *is associate professor of history, Marquette University, Milwaukee, Wis.*

WE ARE ENTERING the period of the Quincentenary of the voyages of Christopher Columbus, with all the hoopla that will be appertaining to it. There will be the usual parades and fireworks. Busts of the man will be recast, and some will be newly created. Commemorative stamps, coins, and medals will appear in bedazzling array. Conferences, replete with learned scholars from all over the world, are being planned. New books and papers are being published, and for many older works about to be republished there will be new and lucrative markets. Schoolchildren by the millions will be shown likenesses of the intrepid Genoan, told of his daring exploits, and required to write appreciative essays about him.

At one level, it all seems entirely fitting and proper, for Columbus long has been regarded by many as America's first great hero. Indeed, at the level of its popular culture during the late 18th century and throughout the 19th, he was one of the very few non-Americans to be cast in truly heroic terms. In the patriotic oratory of the age, there often was a juxtaposition of

the supposedly decadent Old World and the New World of innocence and virtue. Just when a decaying, declining Old World needed it the most, a New World had been presented to a desperate humanity—or so many a Fourth of July orator assured his listeners.

For those millions whose theory of historical causation was a rather blatant, unapologetic providentialism, it seemed nothing less than the very breath of God that had blown those vessels westward. Throughout history, whenever God had some great work to accomplish on Earth, he called forth a human instrumentality to do his bidding. Thus had it been with Moses; thus it would be with Washington; and thus it was with Columbus. Behind the latter, then, was the Almighty, revealing an America that was to be a haven for the oppressed, a beacon for the world, the hope for universal humanity for all time to come. In such a dramatic and psychologically reassuring scenario, Christopher Columbus was playing on center stage, a European metamorphosed into both an American hero *and* agent of God.

Even if patriotic tradition and the folklore of our culture long ago transformed Columbus and 1492 into something very special and eminently worthy of celebration, we must remind ourselves

of the elemental fact that Americans seemingly have been in a rather celebratory mood for more than one-third of a century. For 10 years or so during the 1950s and 1960s, we either were anticipating or actually participating in the Civil War Centennial. Then we looked ahead to the Bicentennial of the Revolutionary Era. In 1974, there was the great ceremony in the U.S. Capitol on the occasion of the Bicentennial of the First Continental Congress. Noted U.S. historians Merrill Jensen and Cecelia Kenyon, together with that immensely popular Briton-become-American Alistair Cooke, addressed a joint session of Congress and, via television, the American people. Soon, it was time to lift our glasses and our hearts in honor of the Bicentennial of the Declaration of Independence.

During the 1980s, one celebration quickly followed another: the Bicentennial of the Treaty of Paris in 1983, the Bicentennial of the Constitution in 1987, and, in 1989, the Bicentennial of the inauguration of George Washington, the First Congress, and the Supreme Court. This list does not even include 1985's 40th anniversary of the end of World War II, 1989's Bicentennial of the beginning of the French Revolution, or 1990's Year of Benjamin Franklin, which was commemorated by a host of events in Philadelphia and elsewhere. Now that we are in the decade of the 1990s, clearly it is Columbus' turn.

What is all this celebrating—running almost nonstop from the late 1950s to the present—really about? What does it mean? In one way, the late 20th century seems rather a curious time for so much glee. To be sure, as Americans imbued since the Enlightenment with the idea of human progress, we prefer to look on the bright side of things, to point out the strides we have made in health care, longevity, and quality of life. Even so, in our more balanced moments, we are forced to admit that this century also has been one of death and devastation.

We understandably prefer that face of the 20th century we see in the visages of people like Woodrow Wilson, Winston Churchill, Mohandas K. Ghandi, Eleanor Roosevelt, and the Anwar Sadat of his last few years. Yet, we know deep down that our century has other faces, other sides, as well. In nightmarish dreams that simply will not go away, we behold anew the countenances of Adolf Hitler, Joseph Stalin, Idi Amin, and Pol Pot. We recollect the amount of time, energy, and resources we have invested in the creation of the technology of mass destruction. This has been a century of progress and a century of death.

It well may be that we have been doing so much celebrating lately not *despite* this troubling ambivalence we have about the kind of century we have made, but, rather, *because of* it. We need to rejoice, and never more so than when we are confined in a debilitating bleakness of spirit. Beyond this, there is another important reason why we Americans have been so eager to find things in the past to celebrate in the present. In this commemorative activity, frivolous though it be at times, we also may detect something of the deep cultural craving of our age for a sense of connectedness with the past. As we return—historically, vicariously, and through deeds of commemoration—to that point where, as we often say, American history per se had its very beginnings, we are looking not just for Columbus, but for ourselves.

Conflicting biographies

Much of our attention during this Columbian Quincentenary naturally will focus on the Genoan himself. That also was true a half-century ago, as Samuel Eliot Morison of Harvard University commemorated an earlier anniversary of the voyages by publishing his pioneering *Admiral of the Ocean Sea: A Life of Christopher Columbus.* To many, it remains perhaps the best single work on

Columbus ever published. In part, the book's fame rests upon Admiral Morison's meticulously having retraced Admiral Columbus' course to the New World. Most previous biographers, as Morison pointed out, had gotten Columbus only to the water's edge. They had not concentrated on the man actually at sea, "on his chosen element." Because Morison had experienced the watery world of Columbus firsthand and had placed the adventurer in his proper seafaring context, there is a sense of high drama in *Admiral of the Ocean Sea.*

Even so, there are questions regarding this biography. Was the author simply too adoring of his subject? Discussing the sorrows of Columbus' final years, Morison says: "Waste no pity on the Admiral of the Ocean Sea! He enjoyed long stretches of pure delight such as only a seaman may know, and moments of high, proud exultation that only a discoverer can experience." Has Morison interpreted the Columbian legacy much too positively? Has he overgeneralized in the last few lines, when he writes: "The whole history of the Americas stems from the Four Voyages of Columbus; and as the Greek city-states looked back to the deathless gods as their founders, so today a score of independent nations and dominions unite in homage to Christopher the stout-hearted son of Genoa, who carried Christian civilization across the Ocean Sea."

Readers desiring a more balanced treatment, or even a decidedly unbalanced one in the other direction, may wish to consult Kirkpatrick Sale's *The Conquest of Paradise: Christopher Columbus and the Columbian Legacy.* Here, Columbus is no hero. Sale's Columbus is greedy and cruel—and even an incompetent sailor. He is no bearer of the truth to faraway lands, but the perverse plunderer of what had been a New World paradise—before he and his European kind arrived. In a critique of Sale's work entitled "Debunking Columbus" (*The New York Times Book Review,* Oct. 7, 1990), William H. McNeill, professor of global history at the University of Chicago and a member of the Christopher Columbus Quincentenary Jubilee Committee, blasted *The Conquest of Paradise,* calling various parts of it "ridiculous," "absurd," "silly," and "callow."

One need not accept either Morison's glorification of Columbus as quite literally a Christopher—the bearer of Christ and Christian civilization—or Sale's denunciation of him as a kind of serpent in a new Eden. However, what is clear in both these renditions, and many other scenarios besides, is that it is virtually impossible to keep focused on the person himself. Inevitably, it seems, we go from the flesh-and-blood man to questions of just what he—

and 1492—really symbolize. Culturally, environmentally, globally—what does the Columbian Age mean? The debate, almost as old as the age itself, rages on, intensified by this time of commemoration.

To begin with, there is the issue about the rise of modern technology and what it has done for (and to) humankind. The four Columbian voyages and all the traversing of the oceans that was to follow would not have been feasible without the changes in naval architecture and improvements in navigational instrumentation at the dawn of the modern age. A heavier and heavier reliance on technological innovation has been one of the most important phenomena defining our age as "modern."

It is a long way from Columbus' astrolabes and compasses to our atomic bombs and genetic engineering. Nevertheless, we have traveled that road during the last five centuries, and many now are wondering out loud about the wisdom of our having done so. In *The Declaration of a Heretic,* Jeremy Rifkin has painted a terrifying picture in which our faith—a blind one as he sees it—in science and its technological applications has brought us to the brink of annihilation. Technologies are made to be used, and these atomic and genetic technologies *will* be, perhaps to destroy the globe, perhaps to manipulate life forms (including our own) until they have been altered beyond all recognition.

What Rifkin leaves out, his critics contend, are all the positive consequences of technological change, the wonders wrought by the Commercial and Industrial Revolutions, even the military hardware that made possible the winning of World War II and perhaps with it the saving of Western civilization. This debate goes on and on, often acrimonious, with no end in sight. Was Columbus the bearer of Christ or of technology?

Columbus also has been made out to be the symbol of the emergence of the nation-state. It was the marital union between Ferdinand of Aragon and Isabella of Castile, and the consequent political union that created something approximating modern Spain, that formed the necessary political and economic context for Columbus' voyages. One by one, the emerging nation-states of Europe mimicked the Portugese and Spaniards, seeking their own shares of the treasures of these other worlds. By the 17th century, the English and French were in on the act, and there even were places called the New Netherlands and New Sweden. Unified belatedly in the second half of the 19th century, the Italians and Germans predictably had the same dream of empire. In the 20th century, especially in the aftermath of World War II and the breakup of most of these once mighty European empires, the concept of the nation-state has led to a great proliferation

We Can No Longer, In Good Faith, Celebrate Columbus

"[He] set into motion a sequence of greed, cruelty, slavery, and genocide that, even in the bloody history of mankind, has few parallels."

Hans Koning
Mr. Koning is the author of Columbus, His Enterprise *(Monthly Review Press).*

n the center of Santa Fe, N.M., stands a monument with the inscription: "TO THE HEROES who have fallen in the various battles with Savage Indians in the Territory of New Mexico." I came upon it while walking with my daughter, who went to college there, and a friend of hers, who is a Tewa Indian. Looking at the bloodthirsty statue with those two girls, one in part descended from the Heroes, the other from the Savage Indians, I wondered when we ever will start to undo the brainwashing inflicted on our children when they are taught history.

American youngsters have to raise their heads above a sea of blood, with an entire civilization of teachers and TV and film producers telling them how the extermination of the Pequots and Apaches equaled pride, virility, and love of country. In my home state of Connecticut, where the Pequots were slaughtered in battles of muskets against bows and arrows and where the surviving women and children were sold in the Caribbean as slaves, there is a Pequot Inn and a Pequot Library; it is as if the Germans had opened a "Jewish Inn" in Buchenwald. What is truly amazing is that so many young people manage to immunize themselves against all this.

James Baldwin, the black writer, once told me how his little joke that, in his family, Columbus Day was not celebrated rarely created any reaction at all with his audiences. They simply didn't know what he was talking about. Ever since I published my biography of Columbus in 1976, I have found how many people are impervious to the simple facts about this man, how they refuse to hear them—as if a stranger were attacking the reputation of their mother or sister. It lies within our comfortable liberal tradition that we do not like events to be depicted in harsh colors. We don't like people to be written about as all bad; only fanatics and extremists do that. Yes, Columbus was a man of his time, and it was a cruel and crude time, but he also was our first immigrant, the first true Yankee go-getter, getting the better of superstition and stick-in-the-mud aristocrats.

Nevertheless, extreme as it may seem, it is impossible to think of any shadings or nuances in a character portrait of Christopher Columbus. Grant him the fierce ambition to be the first reaching Asia by sailing west. It was a blind ambition, because he thought the world was a third smaller than it is. Were there no America, his ships never could have made it to China or Japan. That was the reason the Spanish academicians rejected his plan—not that they were superstitious, or didn't know the world was round, or were prejudiced against a man from Genoa. Grant him his "first," and a juicy one it was, but what else is there to say?

Columbus set into motion a sequence of greed, cruelty, slavery, and genocide that, even in the long, bloody history of mankind, has few parallels. He was a man greedy in both small and large ways—as when he took for himself the reward for first sighting land away from the *Pinta* lookout by claiming that he, Columbus, had seen a light in the night and thus was the first. He also was cruel in petty ways, as when he set a dying monkey with two paws cut off to fight a wild pig, and wrote about it with glee in a letter to the King of Spain. He was cruel on a continental scale when he set into motion what Friar Bartolomé de las Casas called "the beginning of the bloody trail of conquest across the Americas."

Columbus had promised his backers mountains of gold. When these did not materialize, he organized a system for squeezing a comparable amount of loot from the simple societies he found in the Caribbean. Before he went back home in chains to Spain, those same Indians who had welcomed him and his men as gods had begun to commit mass suicide by eating poisoned roots. Within two genera-

tions, the Carib Indians were gone from the face of the Earth, and this "Catholic" enterprise had not converted one single soul among them

In Columbus' Hispaniola (now Haiti and the Dominican Republic), a scheme was put into practice of forcing the Indians to collect the little alluvial gold the streams carried. Any Indian, man or woman, had to do so, and those who failed to bring in their proper quota had both hands cut off. To squelch any resistance, their chiefs were hanged, in rows of 13, their feet just touching burning wood—green wood, to make them suffer and scream longer—as an example for the others. Indians who fled into the mountains were chased with dogs that had been fed on Indian flesh by way of training for this task. Why were the chiefs hanged in rows of 13? "In honor of the Redeemer and his Twelve Apostles," the documents of the time inform us. When the woman chief Anacoana and her followers tried to surrender to the Spaniards, Columbus invited them to a feast. When they were assembled in a large wooden hut, the Spaniards set fire to it at all four corners.

What more is there to be said? South of our border, Oct. 12 now is commemorated as "the day of the race"—the race, that is, as it now exists of Spanish, Indian, and African blood. You can not find fault with that. Those children of conquerors and slaves are the only achievement of the conquest, the only wealth it has produced. The slaves Columbus shipped back to Spain all died. The gold and silver that the later conquistadores discovered in South America resulted in a deadly inflation in Spain and a ruined peasant class. It paid for the mercenaries the Spanish monarchy hired to fight its religious wars against the Protestant Dutch, but Spain lost those wars anyway.

Now we are facing the Quincentennial, 1992, 500 years later. In Uruguay, the native population will celebrate Oct. 11, 1492, as "the last day of freedom." In Mexico, there will be sober seminars and discussions and the publication of a new study of Mexican history. Here in the U.S., we will have an orgy of flag-waving, of plastic and facsimile *Santa Marias*, of speeches about the noble son of the humble Genoa weaver, with a traveling "First Encounters" exhibition to pour a semineutral academic sauce over it all.

Are we committed then to continue this bloody track? Shouldn't we try to have our thoughts on the anniversary of the day it all began run in a new direction? Our false heroes have burdened American's history and character for too long. Isn't it time we wind up that enterprise of Columbus and start thinking of a true New World?

of countries so that today our very divided world has a so-called United Nations, with a current membership of some 150 polities.

Nationalism is the ideology that justifies, rationalizes, and even makes holy this division of the world's people into so many contentious and quite often warring realms. Especially since the French Revolution, the fires of nationalism often have burned out of control in the souls of men. Scholars have seen a direct link between nation-state rivalries on the one hand and the devastating wars characterizing the modern era of human history on the other.

Why has modern man allowed himself to get so caught up in nation-state rivalries? Why has this costly, bloody, seemingly endless form of King-of-the-Mountain been our favorite international game? It hardly seems fair to suggest that a Genoan in the employ of Spain a half-millenium ago bears culpability for the horrible devastation visited upon the modern world by misguided forms of nationalism. Nevertheless, it is true that the man Morison would have us see as a bearer of Christ also was a bearer of the ambitions of the nation-state. It was his patron, and he did its bidding.

Columbus stands as symbol, too, for the Europeanization of the world. He and those who followed him in the colonizing centuries to come carried European languages, religion, values, and cultural norms to the Americas, the Middle East, Asia, and Africa. What they carried most of all was a sense of European superiority, a sort of cultural yardstick that could be—and was—used to measure non-European peoples everywhere and adjudge them to be somehow gravely deficient. So strong was the grip of ethnocentrism that few challenged it in any serious or sustained way until the birth of cultural anthropology in the late 19th century.

With the sort of cultural anthropology pursued by Franz Boas, Margaret Mead, and Ruth Benedict came the idea of cultural relativism—the refusal to make any prior assumptions regarding the superiority or inferiority of any given culture vis-à-vis another. Even so, Eurocentric theories of value continued to be applied by many, and apologists for empire continued to be popular even after most of the Old European empires had been broken up in the post-World War II period.

Few articulated the European position that Europeanization, whatever its failings, had been a net plus for the world more forcefully than Winston Churchill. In his History of the English-Speaking Peoples, he celebrated the diffusion of English language, law, government, and culture throughout the globe. Yet, what was the balance sheet on Anglicization? What had all this exploration, colonization, commercialization, industrialization, and development accomplished? The title of the final book of his four-volume work answers the question succinctly: out of it all had come the emergence of The Great Democracies.

Many in the Third World, however, have interpreted the coming of Columbus and his fellow explorers very differently. To them, Europeanization more often is synonymous with exploitation both of indigenous peoples and of resources. There is hardly any rejoinder to the contention that Europeanization of the New World has resulted in a net loss in the number of distinct human cultures. This trend began early, when whole tribes sometimes disappeared from Caribbean islands as a result of the Spanish conquest, and continues today. Upwards of 100 distinct human cultures already have been obliterated in Brazil alone because of attempts to destroy the rain forests and impose European patterns of agriculture, cattle-raising, and economic development.

Where indigenous peoples have not been destroyed outright, they generally have seen their cultures profoundly altered by contacts with the Europeans, resulting in an anthropological tragedy of enormous proportions. By the time of the conceptual and theoretical breakthroughs of the 20th-century anthropologists, many cultures no longer were around to be studied. Often, those that were had been so altered by Europeanization that it no longer could be certain just what was being studied. If it is true that one learns to be more fully human by studying human cultures in their vast array of forms, then some portion of our very humanity already has been lost in this process of Europeanization.

Moreover, culture worldwide is being more and more Europeanized, Americanized, and thus homogenized with every passing day. Will we really be better off, happier, more fulfilled, more fully human when we finally have achieved what could be called "the Kentucky-fried-chickenization of the world"? Or will it be just a world of dull-gray sameness?

There is a tragedy here, even if one were to assume the stance of a perfectly objective cultural anthropologist. It is the moral dimension of cultural contact, conflict, conquest, and liquidation that has excited so many over time. Columbus himself set a precedent for enslaving and killing the Native Americans. Even Morison was forced to admit that a "cruel policy" initiated by Columbus and continued by other Europeans was nothing less than genocide. The debate about European intentions and moral culpability has been intense and unending, going all the way back to the time when the atrocities first began to occur.

One of the chief sources remains the work of Bartolomé de las Casas. As a young priest, he had participated in the conquest of Cuba, but then became a vociferous critic of Spanish treatment of the Indians. Las Casas tells us of the systematic depopulations, as men and women literally were worked to death and their children died from a lack of milk or even were drowned by their mothers in acts of sheer desperation. He relates many horrible stories. For example, "Two of these so-called Christians met two Indian boys one day, each carrying a parrot; they took the parrots and for fun beheaded the boys." Even though he had been an eyewitness to such deeds, after the fact, Las Casas hardly could believe what he had seen. "My eyes have seen these acts so foreign to human nature, and now I tremble as I write." Millions had perished, he reports, from war, slavery, and the work in the mines.

As Howard Zinn reminds us in A People's History of the United States, what Columbus and his men did to people in the Caribbean, "Cortes did to the Aztecs of Mexico and Pizarro to the Incas of Peru." Even if the European brutality was less in English America than in New Spain, the English settlers could be cruel enough in their own right and were so from the earliest days. When Richard Greenville landed his seven ships in Virginia in 1585, the Indians who greeted him were hospitable. However, when one of them stole a small silver cup, the entire Indian village was sacked and burned. Why, Zinn has asked, should this American history be told only from a European point of view and in a way that justifies the brutal deeds of the conquerors? What about the conquered? Who tells their story? What about the victims?

The controversy about whether the Indians may be seen best as innocent victims is certain to be a part of any commemoration of 1492 and what flowed from it. Historian Forrest McDonald believes it is the Europeans, not the Native Americans, who are more likely to be treated unfairly in our history books nowadays. "It is fashionable to accuse the white man of every manner of crime against the American Indians." The latter "are generally depicted as simple, peaceful, happy, and free people who were perfectly attuned to nature and had wondrous things to teach the whites. The invaders burst into this paradise of the 'noble savage,' plundering, slaughtering, and stealing land. Of all the burdens of guilt that white Americans must bear, we are frequently told, injustice committed against the Indians is among the heaviest."

Having recapitulated the case against the conquerors, McDonald quickly pronounces his judgment on it: "It is a bum rap." Their lack of immunity to a wide variety of diseases was what really sealed the Indians' doom. During the first half-century after the whites arrived, McDonald points out, more than 90% of the approximately 6,000,000 people who made up the Aztec and Inca empires had succumbed to smallpox. Eventually, measles, malaria, yellow fever, and other infectious diseases killed off even more Native Americans. In McDonald's scenario, it is all a matter of disease, not morality. "No question of morality is involved: nothing the newcomers did, apart from simply being there, had anything to do with the demise of the red man."

This contention is a sweeping one, and it hardly is shared by the bulk of today's historians. Eugene Genovese, for instance, does agree with McDonald on one point, but then stridently rebuts him on several others: "I have some sympathy for Professor McDonald's outburst against the silly moralizing that tries to make Americans out to be premature Nazis." History is replete with conquest and slaughter, and certainly not all of it is the work of Europeans. Some considerable portion has been of Mongol, Muslim, Hindu, Zulu, and Aztec origin, just to mention a few of the other perpetrators of history's most untoward deeds.

What Genovese strongly objects to in the McDonald position is that the Indians were somehow, "by European standards, dirty, treacherous, ignorant, and superstitious." Were the Indians as a whole really treacherous? "Toward whom?," Genovese asks. "About what? Did the United States government ever make a treaty with the Indians that it did not break? Were the Indians more treacherous than the princes of Renaissance Italy, those much admired benefactors of the early modern world? More treacherous than the Borgia Pope Alexander VI or his famous daughter Lucrezia?"

Europeans' legacy

This acrimonious debate about the moral questions involved in the European con-

quest of New World peoples will continue to form one of the many contexts in which we remember Columbus—and judge him. So, too, will all the questions having to do with the long-range environmental impact of the Europeanization of the world. Even if we object to "silly moralizing," we must admit that the Indians of North America lived here for perhaps 20-30,000 years with very little by way of environmental impact. By contrast, those of European descent have changed the environment tremendously in the five centuries of the Columbian period, especially the last two. It may well be that it is the bulldozer, not the cross, that now is our truest symbol. If, in an earlier time, we would not think of letting New World "savages" stand in our way, neither, later on, would we let nature herself. Again and again, nature has given way as we have bulldozed out what we thought would be our better future. Now, however, we have reached a point where we wonder out loud whether the environment can continue to absorb these devastating onslaughts from modern man. We wonder about our very vision of the world. Could it conceivably be bogus?

There is no going back. Those of European descent have created a history since 1492 and, like all histories, once made can not be unmade. In a real sense, for better or for worse, it is the story of that intrepid Genoan—and all *he* stood for then, all *he* stands for still, and all that *we* have made of what Europe long ago discovered. In these five centuries of the Columbian Age, we suspect that we have increasingly worshipped at shrines having little connection with the Christianity that Columbus dreamed of being the bearer.

At one shrine, we dutifully bow the knee to technology. We say a prayer, hoping against hope that we, even at this late date, are just one little technological innovation away from that very best world of our own

imagining. At another shrine, we bow before the nation-state. Billions of worshippers of every race and clime bow with us, ardently believing this god to be the answer. We can not bring ourselves to believe that these wars of the modern age, so devastating both in human and material terms, have much to do with our nation-state or even with nationalism. After all, we can not really be expected to believe that we worship a god who has failed.

Yet, important as they are, these are really just some of many side altars. The altar that we approach now is for the worship of Europeanization itself. It has brought to us and to the world all the wonders of progress—commercialization, industrialization, and vast improvements in the quality of life. This is the god who is multilingual, who has spoken to us at one time or another in Spanish, Portugese, English, French, Dutch, German, Italian, and many other tongues. On bended knee, we offer up our thanks for Shakespeare, Bacon, Locke, and Newton. With Churchill there beside us, we thank this god of ours for spreading the truths of democratic politics around the globe. This worship is good for us, makes us feel all right again, holds our little worlds together.

In due course, though, our worship ends, and our minds turn again to remembering Christopher Columbus after 500 years. What are we to do? What are we to think? At least we know the answer to the first part of our query. We *will* celebrate. Of that we may be sure, even if we are a little more uncertain now as to just what it is that we will be celebrating—progress, genocide, democracy, plunder, what? The second question is even more troubling. We can not begin to answer it in one word, or a few, or even many. Before we take our leave of him, we look one last time into the eyes of the Genoan adventurer. Columbus, we ask, just what have you wrought?

After dire straits, an agonizing haul across the Pacific

*It was only a generation after Columbus
that Magellan's tiny fleet sailed west,
via his strait, then on around the world*

Simon Winchester

*Simon Winchester is the author of eight books that
combine history and travel, including* The Pacific
(Hutchinson), from which this article was adapted.

Balboa found the ocean. Then, in their droves, explorers emerged to circle and probe and colonize it, but first, in that most daring of all endeavors, to cross it.

No one could be sure how wide it was. No one could be sure where lay the Terra Australis Incognita, which Ptolemy had postulated and which Mercator would argue was a necessary balance for a spherical world—without it the whole planet might simply topple over, to be lost among the stars. No one knew the weather or the currents or the winds. But one small certainty spurred the would-be circumnavigators onward. It was that the Spice Islands, the Moluccas, lay at the farthest side of whatever might lie beyond the waters, pacific or unpacific, that Balboa had discovered.

Traders buying nutmegs and cloves from Arabian merchants had known about the Spice Islands for centuries; in the 1200s Marco Polo knew roughly where they were, for he saw junk traffic in the ports of North China loaded with spices and manned by crews who had come from the south. In 1511 a Portuguese expedition led by Antonio d'Abreu actually discovered them by moving eastward, after passing the tip of Africa, to Malacca, thence down the strait and past the immense island of Borneo to the confused archipelago where nearly all known spices grew in wild profusion.

To reach their goal, d'Abreu's men had gone halfway round the world from Europe to the Orient.

The geographical fact they established was of great political and imperial importance. Since 1494, when the Treaty of Tordesillas was signed, all of the unknown world to the east of an imaginary line that had been drawn 370 leagues west of the Cape Verde Islands would belong to Portugal. Everything to the west of that line would belong to Spain. So far as the Atlantic and the Indian oceans were concerned, there was no problem; but what about the other side of the world? Conquest, squatter's rights, annexation, force majeure—these cruder tools of geopolitics might well dictate its eventual position. Thus the Moluccas, if discovered by going eastward around the globe, would belong to Portugal—at least by the logic of some explorers. But the Moluccas claimed by a party going westward might belong to Spain. So while d'Abreu and his colleagues went off eastward, even braver or more foolhardy men, carrying the banner of Castile, were determined to discover—heroically and, as it turned out for many of them, fatally—the way to reach this same Orient by traveling westward across the vast unknown.

There is thus a nice irony in the fact that the man who undertook the seminal voyage, and did so in the name of Spain, was in fact Portuguese. He was born Fernao de Magalhaes, and the Portuguese—"He is ours," they insist—rarely care to acknowledge that he renounced his citizenship after a row, pledged his allegiance to King Charles I (later to become Emperor Charles V) and was given a new name: Hernando de

Magallanes. The English-speaking world, which reveres him quite as much as does Iberia, knows him as Ferdinand Magellan.

He set off on September 20, 1519, with a royal mandate to search for a passage to El Mar del Sur, and thus to determine for certain that the Spice Islands were within the Spanish domains. He had not the foggiest notion of how far he might have to travel. For all Magellan's 237 men in their five little ships knew, Balboa's Panama and the northern coast of South America, which Columbus had sighted in 1498 on his third voyage, might be the equatorial portions of a continent extending without a break to the Antarctic pole, making the southern sea they sought quite unreachable from the west. Johann Schöner's globe of the world, then the best known, placed Japan a few hundred miles off Mexico. The historian López de Gómara asserts that Magellan always insisted that the Moluccas were "no great distance from Panama and the Gulf of San Miguel, which Vasco Núñez de Balboa discovered." Magellan would rapidly discover precisely what "no great distance" was to mean.

The five vessels that would soon make history—the *Victoria*, the *Trinidada* (the *Trinidad*), the *San Antonio*, the *Concepción* and the *Santiago*—were small, the largest being 120 tons, and hopelessly unseaworthy. ("I would not care to sail to the Canaries in such crates," wrote the Portuguese consul in Seville, with obvious pleasure. "Their ribs are soft as butter.")

They set sail from the Guadalquivir River under the proud corporate title of the Armada de Molucca, amply armed but hopelessly provisioned, with crews composed of men of nine different nationalities including a lone Englishman. There was one Moluccan slave, Enrique, who would act as an interpreter if the crossing was accomplished. There was a journalist, too, Antonio Francesca Pigafetta, who may also have been a Venetian spy. In any case, Pigafetta's diaries remained the source for all future accounts of the voyage; he had joined the ships, he said, because he was "desirous of sailing with the expedition so that I might see the wonders of the world."

The sorry tales of sodomy and mutiny, of yardarm justice and abrupt changes of command, and of all the other trials that attended the armada on its path south and west across the Atlantic do not belong here. The truly important phase of the journey starts on February 3, 1520, when the vessels left their anchorage near today's Montevideo and headed south. No charts or sailing directions existed then. The sailors were passing unknown coasts, and confronting increasingly terrifying seas and temperatures that dropped steadily, day by day.

They began to see penguins—"ducks without wings," they called them, *patos sin alas*—and "sea-wolves," or seals. Seeking a way to the Pacific, they explored every indentation in the coast off which they sailed, and with depressing regularity each indentation—even though some were extremely capacious and tempted the navigators to believe that they might be the longed-for straits—proved to be a cul-de-sac. They spent much of the winter, from Palm Sunday until late August, in the center of a chilly and miserable bay at what is now Puerto San Julian (see map on page 88). The winter was made doubly wretched by an appalling mutiny and the consequent executions and maroonings that Captain-General Magellan ordered; by the wrecking of the *Santiago*, which he had sent on a depth-sounding expedition; and by the realization of the dreadful damage done to the remaining ships by the chomping of those plank-gourmets of the seas, teredo worms.

But one important discovery was made at Puerto San Julian: these southern plains were inhabited by enormous nomadic shepherds who herded not sheep, but little wild llamas known as guanacos, and who dressed in their skins. Magellan captured a number of these immense people—one pair by the cruel trick of showing them leg-irons and insisting that the proper way to carry the shackles was to allow them to be locked around their ankles. Magellan's men also liked the giants' tricks: one, who stayed aboard only a week but allowed himself to be called Juan and learned some biblical phrases, caught and ate all the rats and mice on board, to the pleasure of the cook and the entertainment of the men. Magellan called these men *"patagones"*—"big feet"; the land in which he found them has been known ever since as Patagonia.

By late August the fleet set sail again. Two men had been left behind, marooned for mutiny by Magellan's orders. They had a supply of wine and hardtack, guns and shot, but when other, later expeditions entered the bay, no trace of them was found. They may have been killed by the giants; they may have starved to death. All that the men of the armada remembered were their pitiful wails echoing over the still waters as the ships sailed out of the bay into the open sea, and then south.

By the time the flotilla had reached 50 degrees south latitude (not far from the Falkland Islands), the men were restive. Their artless plea now was: If the expedition wanted to reach the Spice Islands, why not turn east toward them and pass below the Cape of Good Hope, as others had? Magellan, sensible enough to know this would make a nonsense of the whole plan to render the Spice Islands Spanish, refused. But he promised that if no strait was found by the time they had eaten up another 25 degrees of latitude, he would turn east as they wished. The murmurs stilled. The Captain-General clearly had no idea of the utter impossibility of navigating at 75 degrees south latitude, for on that longitudinal track his ships would get stuck fast in the thick ice of what is now the Weddell Sea, hemmed in by the yet unimagined continent and the unendurable cold of the Antarctic.

The Captain-General sights a virgin cape

On October 21, 1520, Magellan sighted a headland to starboard. Cabo Virjenes, which today is equipped with a lighthouse that flashes a powerful beam and a radio direction beacon, is an important navigation point on the South American coast. It marks, as Magellan was soon to discover, the eastern end of the strait that bears his name—the tortuous entrance, at long last, to the Pacific.

Ranges of immense, snow-covered mountains crowded into view; there could be, Magellan must have thought, no possible exit. Still, he ordered the *San Antonio* and the *Concepción* into the headwaters of the bay—only to be horrified when he saw them being swept into a huge maelstrom of surf and spindrift by unsuspected currents and winds. But he had no time to dwell on such miseries, for an immense storm broke over his own ship, the *Trinidad*, as well as the *Victoria*, alongside. Men were hurled overboard. One vessel was dismasted; the other nearly turned turtle several times. The storm went on and on and on. When relief finally came to the exhausted crews, the only recourse, it seemed, was to turn tail and head for home. The expedition was over, an abject failure.

Yet just at that moment (one occasionally suspects that the mythmakers have been at work on the story) the lookout sighted sails on the western horizon. They were indeed what they could only have been: the two scouting vessels had returned. Not shattered and aground, they were safe and sound. The joy Magellan must have felt at realizing his men were still alive was, however, as nothing when, as the *San Antonio* and the *Concepción* drew closer, he saw their yardarms hung with bunting, music being played, and the crews dancing and singing.

As an account of the long voyage puts it, "Suddenly, they saw a narrow passage, like the mouth of a river, ahead of them in the surf, and they managed to steer into it. Driven on by wind and tide they raced through this passage and into a wide lake. Still driven by the storm they were carried west for some hours into another narrow passage, though now the current had reversed, so what appeared to be a great ebb tide came rushing towards them. They debouched from this second strait into a broad body of water which stretched as far as the eye could see toward the setting sun. . . ."

By tasting the water and finding it salty, and then making sure that both the ebb tides and flood tides were of equal strength (tests that argued against this body of water being a river), the captains of the scout ships realized they had, indeed, discovered the way through. Magellan, believing that his ultimate goal was within his grasp, brushed aside the persistent doubter's view that he should, despite the discovery, turn back *eastward* for the Moluccas. "Though we have nothing

to eat but the leather wrapping from our masts," he declared, "we shall go on!"

The Strait of Magellan is as darkly beautiful as it is useful. Before I first visited the strait I supposed, wrongly, that since its latitude to the south is more or less the same distance from the Equator as Maine's latitude is to the north, the coastline would also be vaguely similar. But it is much starker, more hostile, more grand. Heading west, as Magellan did, the land begins flat, and wind reduces such trees as there are to stunted survivors. Even today the strait is not an easy place for sailing vessels: ". . . both difficult and dangerous, because of incomplete surveys, the lack of aids to navigation, the great distance between anchorages, the strong current, and the narrow limits for the maneuvering of vessels," says the pilot manual.

"A cargo of falsehood against Magellan"

For Magellan and his men it was a nightmare. The currents were treacherous. Unexpected winds, now known as williwaws, flashed down steep cliffs, threatening to drive the little fleet onto the rocks. He lost another ship; though he did not know it at the time, the *San Antonio* had turned tail and was heading back to Spain, "bearing a cargo of falsehood against Magellan." She also took away supplies vital for all of the fleet—one-third of the armada's biscuits, one-third of its meat and two-thirds of its currants, chickpeas and figs. The men began begging to turn back.

Days passed. Finally, on November 28, 1520, *Trinidad*, *Victoria* and *Concepción* passed beyond the horrors of the strait, and sailed westward into an evening that became, suddenly, magically serene. We are told that "the iron-willed Admiral" broke down and cried. Then he assembled his men on deck. Pedro de Valderrama, the *Trinidad*'s priest, stood on the poop deck and called down on the crew of all three remaining vessels the blessing of Our Lady of Victory. The men sang hymns. The gunners fired broadsides. And Magellan proudly unfurled the flag of Castile.

"We are about to stand into an ocean where no ship has ever sailed before," Magellan is said to have cried (though it has to be emphasized that there is no hard evidence that he did so). "May the ocean be always as calm and benevolent as it is today. In this hope I name it the Mar Pacifico." And just in case it was not Magellan who first uttered the name, then perhaps it was Pigafetta: "We debouched from that strait," he later wrote, "engulfing ourselves in the Pacific Sea."

The European dawn breaks on the Pacific

The concept of the Pacific Ocean, the greatest physical unit on Earth, had been born. Balboa had seen it. D'Abreu had ventured onto its western edges. Magellan had reached its eastern periphery. Now it was up to the explorers to try to comprehend the enormity of their discovery. But before they could do that, Magellan had to sail across it. This was his determined aim, and the aim of those who sponsored his venture.

So the Captain-General ordered the sails set to carry the shrunken, but now at long last triumphant, armada northward. He thought it might take three or four days to reach the Spice Islands. It was a savage underestimate—a tragically optimistic forecast, based quite probably on the terrible inability of long-distance navigators to calculate longitude (an inability that insured that not a single estimate then available to Magellan was even 80 percent of the true size of the ocean).

Not that anyone suspected tragedy as they breezed to the north of Cape Desado. Far from it. Once the armada had reached the lower southern latitudes, the winds began to blow balmily and unceasingly from the southeast. They were trade winds, just like those well known in the southern Atlantic and Indian oceans, and they were pleasantly warm. Their effect produced nothing but splendid sailing: no undue swells, no angry squalls, no cyclonic outbursts. Just endless days and nights of leisured running before a steady, powerful breeze. "Well was it named Pacific," wrote Pigafetta later, confirming his master's choice of name, "for during this period we met with no storms."

And for weeks and weeks, simply by wafting before the winds with sails unchanged, the fleet managed to miss every single one of the islands with which the Pacific Ocean is littered. Magellan's course, sedulously recorded by his pilot, Francisco Albo, shows him—almost uncannily—leading his vessels past the Juan Fernández Islands, past Sala y Gómez and Easter islands, past Pitcairn, Ducie, Oeno and Henderson and, indeed, past everything else. His astrolabe, his crude speed recorder, his hourglass (a watchkeeper would be flogged for holding it against his chest, since to warm it made the sand flow faster, the hour pass more quickly, the watch be more rapidly over) served Magellan admirably: he plotted the likely course to the Spice Islands, and his ships took him there, more or less.

Any deviation could have caused disaster. Had he strayed just 3 degrees north of Albo's recorded track, he would have hit the Marquesas; 3 degrees south, he would have come to Tahiti. He was a hundred miles off Bikini Atoll. He passed within half a day's sailing of razor-sharp coral reefs—thundering surfs, huge spikes and lances that would have ruined his ships forever. At this distance in time, it seems as if some guardian angel had Magellan's tiny fleet under benevolent invigilation for days and nights too numerous to count. Yet this providence had a less kindly face. Six weeks out of the strait, Magellan's men began to die. In the monotony of a long, landless passage, what proved unbearable was the lack of food aboard the sea-locked ships.

Much of the stores had already gone, carried off on the treacherous *San Antonio*. **Such food as the three ships carried began to rot under the soggy tropical airs. The penguins and seals they had killed and salted in Patagonia started to turn putrid;** maggots raged through the ships, eating clothes and supplies and rigging; water supplies turned scummy and rank. Men began to develop the classic symptoms of scurvy—their teeth loosened in their gums, their breath began to smell horribly sour, huge boils erupted from their shrunken frames, they sank into inconsolable melancholia.

In January men began to die. One of the Patagonian behemoths whom Magellan had persuaded aboard was, despite his immense physique and power, the first to go; he begged to be made a Christian, was baptized "Paul" and then died. By mid-January a third of the sailors were too sick to stagger along the decks. Their food was limited to scoops of flour stained yellow by the urine of rats, and biscuits riddled with weevils.

The depression and deep anxiety afflicted Magellan too. At one point he flung his charts overboard in a fit of rage. "With the pardon of the cartographers, the Moluccas are not to be found in their appointed place!" he cried. The fleet did, in fact, strike land in late January—a tiny island they called St. Paul's, and which seems to be the minute atoll now known as Pukapuka, in the French Tuamotu group. (Four centuries later, Pukapuka was the first island to be spotted by Thor Heyerdahl aboard the balsa raft *Kon-Tiki* after his long drift westward from Callao in Peru.) They stayed a week, replenishing their water butts and feasting on turtle eggs. They left in an optimistic mood; surely, they surmised, this island must be the first of a vast skein of atolls and lagoons stretching to the now close Moluccas. But it was not to be; the ships had barely traversed a third of their ocean. Soon the hunger pains, the racking thirst and the sense of unshakable misery began anew, and the dying began once more.

After meals of leather—land!

More and more terrible the voyage steadily became. By March 4 the flagship had run out of food completely. Men were eating the oxhides and llama skins used to prevent the rigging from chafing (not too bad a diet—so long as the crew's scurvy-ridden teeth hung in). The smell of death, the knowledge that it was both inevitable and impending, gripped Magellan's sailors. And then dawned March 6, when a seaman called Navarro, the only man still fit enough to clamber up the ratlines, spied what everyone was waiting for—land.

A great cheer went up. Cannon were fired. Men fell to their knees in prayer. A squadron of tiny dugouts sped from shore to meet the Spaniards. Magellan had reached the islands he first called Las Islas de las Velas Latinas and later, after much of his cargo had been filched, Las Islas de Ladrones, the Islands of Thieves. He had made his landfall at what we now call Guam. It was March 6, 1521. Magellan had crossed the Pacific. A voyage the Captain-General had supposed might take three or four days had, in fact, occupied three and a half months.

The fleet stayed in Guam for only three days—to rest, make minor repairs and take on food (such as the "figs, more than a palm long," which must have been bananas) and fresh water. Then Magellan set off, still toward the Moluccas, standing down for the southwest and to the Philippines, islands of which all travellers to these parts had often heard, but which no European had ever seen. Though the Spice Islands, it must be recalled, were the armada's prescribed goal, the official mandate and ambition of Magellan was to discover, name and seize in the name of Spain the immense archipelago that lay north of them.

The only Briton on the expedition, Master Andrew of Bristol, died on this last, short passage. He was never to see the islands that, a novelist was later to write, were "as fair as Eden, with gold beaches, graceful palms, exotic fruits and soil so rich that if one snapped off a twig and stuck it into the ground it would start straightway to grow."

Magellan made his landfall on March 16 on an island at the southern end of the large Philippine island of Samar. Two days later, the first contact was made with Filipinos, though the name "Philippines" was not to be given to the place until 1543, when explorer Ruy López de Villalobos named one after the Infante, later to become King Philip II, the Spanish monarch whose reign made the words "Spanish Armada" infamous. (The name "Philippines" caught on later to mean the entire island group.) The significant moment came two days later still, when the ships sailed down the Gulf of Leyte and the Surigao Strait, where, more than four centuries later in World War II, one of the world's last great naval battles was fought, and Adm. William F. Halsey reduced the Japanese Imperial Navy to vestigial strength.

Once through the strait, Magellan landed at the island that guarded its entrance, Limasawa. Eight inhabitants sailed out to the *Trinidad* in a small boat. On orders from the Captain-General, his Moluccan slave, Enrique, hailed them. In a moment that must have seemed frozen in time, it became clear that the men in the approaching boat understood the words of the Moluccan perfectly.

Their language was being spoken to them by a man on a huge ship that had come to them from the east. The linguistic globe—even if not necessarily the physical globe—had been circumnavigated. A man who had originated in these parts had traveled across Asia and around Africa to Europe as a slave, and had now returned home by the Americas and the Pacific. Enrique de Molucca may well have been, strictly speaking, the first of humankind to circumnavigate the world; he was never to be honored for so doing.

Nor, by the unhappy coincidence of ill-temper and wretched misfortune, was Ferdinand Magellan ever to be able to savor his own triumph. Just six weeks after landing he was dead, cut down on a Philippine island in a skirmish that is as unremembered as the place in which it happened is unsung—a flat and muddy little island called Mactan, where an airport has now been built to serve the city of Cebu.

The circumstances of the Captain-General's end, however, are riven into every Iberian schoolchild's learning, even today. Despite his crew's objections, Magellan insisted on exploring. He was pleased at the relative ease with which the people took to Christianity. (It is perhaps worth remembering that the Catholic faith, which Magellan and his priests brought to Samar and Cebu and northern Mindanao, flourishes there still today. The Philippines, in fact, is the only predominantly Christian country in Asia, and the influence of the church contributed significantly to the recent overthrow of President Ferdinand Marcos.)

But the successful sewing of the seeds of Christianity were to be Magellan's undoing. His horribly inglorious end came in late April. The precise circumstances were chronicled. Magellan had demonstrated what he felt was his superior status to the local raja of Cebu, and had made Christians of him and all his followers. But significantly, the rest of the Philippine nobility did not go along. Many local junior rajas objected, especially the minor raja of Mactan, a man named Cilapulapu and now known to all Filipinos simply as Lapu Lapu. He declared that he was not going to pay fealty to this Christian interloper, come what may. He cared little enough for the raja of Cebu, let alone the Cebuano's newfound foreign friends.

The Spaniards soon got wind of this rebellious mood, and on April 27 Magellan and 60 of his men paddled across the narrow strait to Mactan, in an attempt to bring Lapu Lapu to heel. "You will feel the iron of our lances," Lapu Lapu was told by Magellan's interlocutor. "But we have fire-hardened spears and stakes of bamboo," replied a defiant chieftain. "Come across whenever you like."

The last stand at Mactan Island

The waters at the northern end of Mactan are very shallow and degenerate into warm swamps. A selected 48 of the Spaniards, dressed in full armor, had to wade the last few hundred yards to do battle with the Mactan warriors. They fought for an hour, thigh-deep in the water. Then Magellan plunged his lance into the body of an attacker and was unable to withdraw it quickly enough. It was a fatal delay. Another islander slashed Magellan's leg with a scimitar. He staggered. Scores of others crowded around him as he fell, and as Pigafetta was to write, "thus they killed our mirror, our light, our comfort and our true guide."

7. 1500: THE ERA OF DISCOVERY

It is worth remembering that Fernao de Magalhaes was a native Portuguese—of whom it used to be said, because they were such energetic explorers, "they have a small country to live in, but all the world to die in." There is a monument near the spot where he fell, a tall white obelisk, guarded solicitously for the past 15 years by a man with the splendid name of Jesus Baring. There are two accounts of the event, one engraved on either side of the cross. Señor Baring derives much amusement from showing his occasional visitors—and there are very few, considering how globally important this spot should be—how markedly they differ.

The one on the monument's eastern side—the side that pedant geographers will recognize as marginally nearer to the Spanish Main—records the event as a European tragedy. "Here on 27th April 1521 the great Portuguese navigator Hernando de Magallanes, in the service of the King of Spain, was slain by native Filipinos. . . ." On the other side, by contrast, it is seen as an Oriental triumph—a heroic blow struck for Philippine nationalism. "Here on this spot the great chieftain Lapu Lapu repelled an attack by Ferdinand Magellan, killing him and sending his forces away. . . ." Baring points to the latter and roars with laughter. "This is the real story. This is the one we Filipinos like to hear!"

Lapu Lapu is thus the first, and to many Filipinos the greatest, of Filipino heroes. These days his memory is being revived, his exploits retold, his adventures made the stuff of comic strips, films and popular songs. Each April there is a full-scale reenactment of the Battle of Mactan on the beach, with an improbably handsome Cebuano film star playing the part of the seminaked hero and, when I was last there, the Philippine Air Force officer Mercurion Fernandez playing the role of the armor-clad Magellan. The two sides struggle gamely in the rising surf until that epic moment when Officer Fernandez contrives to collapse into the shallow sea and grunts his last. The assembled thousands then cheer. Such is Filipino pride in the raja of Mactan that there are firebrands—in Manila as well as in Cebu—who believe their country should shed its present name, a reminder that it is a colonial conquest, and be reborn as LapuLapuLand.

Little more needs to be said of the tiny armada now, save to note what most popular historians choose to forget. The *Concepción* was scuttled; the flagship *Trinidad*, which tried to make for home via the Pacific once more, was blown north as far as Hakodate in Japan, captured by a Portuguese battle group and became a total loss in the Spice Islands, which had been its original goal. But one of the ships, the doughty little *Victoria*—at 85 tons she was the second smallest of the original five—did make it back to Spain.

The *Victoria* scudded home under the charge of Juan Sebastian d'Elcano, previously the executive officer of the *Concepción*. She made Java. She made it round the top of Africa, through waters where freak waves sometimes cause modern oil tankers to founder. She made the Cape Verde Islands, where the crew realized that despite meticulous log-keeping, they had lost an entire day from their calendar: the concept of crossing the international date line was unknown—and profoundly unimaginable—to them.

On September 6, 1523, the *Victoria* made the harbor of Sanlucar de Barrameda, from where she had set off almost exactly three years before. Juan Sebastian d'Elcano had brought just 17 men back with him: 237 had started out. Circumnavigation, it happened, was a most costly business.

But well rewarded. D'Elcano was given an annual pension and a coat of arms as handsome as it was aromatic: a castle, three nutmegs, 12 cloves, two crossed cinnamon sticks, a pair of Malay kings bearing spice sticks, and above all, a globe circled by a ribbon emblazoned with the motto *Primus Circumdedisti me*. "Thou first circumnavigated me."

The Europe of Columbus and Bayazid

Charles Tilly

Charles Tilly *directs the Center for Studies of Social Change at the New School for Social Research in New York City, and is the author of* Coercion, Capital and European States, AD 990-1990 *(Cambridge: Blackwell, 1990).*

From the perspective of Sultan Bayazid II, the Ottoman ruler in Istanbul, Columbus' expeditions may have been a distant diversion. In fact, they belonged to a set of profound changes in relations between Islamic and Christian territories on a world scale. For the 500 years before 1492, the fortunes of Europe depended heavily on Muslims—Arabs, Turks and others—who in various guises linked Europeans to the rest of the Eurasian system of trade and empire.

Long past 1492, the massive Muslim presence to Europe's southeast constituted a major factor in European trade, war and foreign relations. After 1492, however, Europeans outflanked their Muslim rivals in the Atlantic and Pacific, while meeting them on almost equal terms in the Indian Ocean. Such eastward powers as Venice and Russia continued grudgingly to bargain with their Muslim neighbors well past 1492, but Iberians led an aggressive European effort to obliterate Muslims through expulsion, massacre or forced conversion, to contain their empires, and to invade their commercial space.

As Aragonese, Castilian and Portuguese adventurers succeeded on some fronts and worked out accommoda-

tions on others, seafarers and conquerors from Holland, France and Great Britain followed them. Except in East Asia, Europeans of one stripe or another became the dominant powers in most of the world's mainland temperate regions. Outside of South America, however, north Europeans displaced Iberians from much of the territory the latter had first opened up to European exploitation. The great moves began during the 14th and 15th centuries, as the Ottomans expanded while Mongol and North African Muslim powers splintered. Columbus' voyages to the Caribbean therefore mark the midpoint of an enormous shift in the relations between Asia and Europe, between Muslims and Christians, between ancient circuits of trade and newly fashioned seaways.

Until the 14th century, Europe had lived as the northwestern periphery of a vast economic system extending into the Pacific and pivoting on the Mongol-dominated territories of Central Asia. Before then, empires rose and fell in Europe, notably around the Mediterranean and the Black Sea, but only the Roman Empire occupied as much as half of the European space and incorporated it firmly into the Eurasian system of trade, politics and culture. Neither the thin, wavering strands of commerce nor the scattered pockets of productive agriculture could sustain enough extraction to support large armies, priestly hierarchies, elaborate bureaucracies, or sumptuous royal courts.

In northwestern Europe, not even daring, rapacious Norsemen could assemble a substantial empire. Norse raiders conquered and settled in the British Isles, Normandy, North America and what later became Rus-

From *Middle East Report,* September/October 1992, pp. 2-5. © 1992 by the Middle East Research and Information Project (MERIP), Inc. Reprinted by permission of MERIP/*Middle East Report,* 1500 Massachusetts Avenue, NW, Suite 119, Washington, DC 20005.

sia, but only in Iceland did they establish a substantial colony that remained subordinate to their Scandinavian base. Viking virtuosi of seaborne warfare resembled the Mongols on their steppe. They lacked, however, both a major trade route to protect (for a price) and adjacent grain-growing kingdoms from which to extract tribute (on threat of sacking and killing). It was the Vikings' successors who solved the problem of basing empires on seapower. They did so at first by preying on maritime trade routes along which Muslims had long worked as active intermediaries.

Europe Subordinate

As Byzantine, Persian, Arab and then Ottoman empires displaced the Romans and once again subordinated Europe's southeastern half to the silk-trading Baghdad-Hanchow axis, the rest of Europe fragmented and became peripheralized. Nevertheless, from the 10th to the 13th centuries, the whole Eurasian system ran so energetically that much of Europe prospered: commerce flourished, population expanded and cities grew, especially in those sections of the continent most strongly connected to the great belts of Eurasian trade. In the year 1000, the world's largest cities were probably Constantinople, Córdoba, Kaifeng, Sian, Kyoto, Cairo and Hasa; in that ranking, Europe's Seville, Palermo and Kiev lagged far behind. At the millennium, then, the world's largest cities lay largely outside of Europe, while Europe's largest cities spun in the orbit of Islam.

The explorations of Columbus began the definitive integration of the Americas into the orbit of Europe as the Spaniards extended plantation cultivation of tropical crops into the Caribbean.

By 1300, the list began with Hangchow, Peking, Cairo and Canton, with Paris, Granada, Constantinople, Venice, Milan and Genoa among the top 20. Around 1500, the world's largest cities were very likely Peking, Vijayanagar, Cairo and Hangchow—two in China, one in India, one in Muslim Africa—with Paris, Istanbul, Adrianople and Naples leading the European hierarchy but still much smaller than their Asian counterparts. Although in 1700 Japan's Edo probably led the globe, for the first time three of the world's 10 largest cities were European:

Istanbul, London and Paris. A clear shift of the hierarchy toward northern Europe occurred between AD 1000 and 1700, especially after 1500.

Over the two centuries following 1300, the Black Death intermittently severed the connection between Europe and Asia while fragmentation of the Mongol empire placed formidable barriers on overland trade routes. China with-

---

The European map of 1492 divided up into some 200 statelike units, many of them overlapping into territory and many of them comprising patchworks of semi-autonomous governments.

---

drew from its previously expansive maritime trade, and sailing vessels of Atlantic powers began to press the galleys that had previously dominated the Mediterranean. Europeans started to use the gunpowder that had come from Asia. The Ottoman capture of Constantinople in 1453 (the first and exemplary major deployment of siege artillery in Europe) defined the confrontation of Christendom with Islam while cementing a love-hate relationship between Muslim Turkey and Orthodox Russia.

All these changes made Europe more of a connected, autonomous unit than it had ever been before. Europe and adjacent sections of that vast complex took a century or more to recover from the demographic devastation wrought by the Black Death. After having maintained a fast pace between the 10th and 13th centuries, then collapsing halfway through the 14th, population growth only accelerated again during the 16th century. Soon the whole Eurasian system began to grow again. Henceforth, Europe occupied a far more prominent position in relation to the rest of the world than ever before, more prominent than during the Roman Empire.

The end of the 15th century therefore brought a watershed in European economies and politics. Columbus' explorations of 1492 began the definitive integration of the Americas into the orbit of Europe. Soon Spaniards were extending to the Caribbean experiments in plantation cultivation of such tropical crops as sugar that they and their Portuguese neighbors had been conducting on closer Atlantic islands such as the Canaries, and were buying African slaves to do the heavy labor. In counterpart to the European flora and fauna (e.g., dandelions, horses and measles) that spread across the Americas, mainland American products soon became mainstays of European life. To its 15th-century American adventure

Europe owes not only Coca-Cola, tango and jazz, but also maize, potatoes, tobacco and syphilis.

Not that Europe passed through the golden gate into today's world in or around 1492. The political texture of 1492 differed wonderfully from our own. At that point, the kingdom of Aragon, buoyed by Catalan seafaring, extended from the Iberian mainland to Sardinia and Sicily. The Catholic Pope ruled one of Italy's major states. An enormous kingdom of Poland exercised superficial sovereignty over much of Eastern Europe, while the territory we now call Russia fragmented into zones controlled by the prince of Moscow, the republic of Pskov, the Golden Horde, the Krim Tatars and many another conqueror from the Eurasian steppe. Much of "Germany" lay nominally under Habsburg suzerainty, but actually consisted of nearly independent bishoprics, free cities, duchies and other tiny jurisdictions.

On the map of 1492, we might claim to recognize England, Ireland, Scotland and France in something approaching their contemporary boundaries, but that would require us to ignore large subsequent eastward conquests by France, not to mention the troubled formation of what we now call, with some exaggeration, the United Kingdom. Altogether, some 200 statelike units, many of them overlapping in territory and many of them comprising patchworks of semi-autonomous governments, divided up the European map of 1492.

The wars of the latter part of the 15th century built the European state system and constructed the platform for European conquests outside the continent.

Nor did Europe dominate the world. In 1492, China wielded formidable weight in the East. The lands and seas of Islam lay astride the world's central commercial and cultural connections, and Islamic influence was still expanding between Southeast Asia and Africa. On the Indian Ocean and the overland routes to Asia, Europeans long followed or compacted with Muslim merchants before they started to displace them. Columbus' search for a westerly route to "the Indies" was no idle fancy, but an enterprise with visibly substantial payoff if it worked. By 1492, European ships were fending off the expansive Ottoman Empire while breaking into the Muslim commercial space of the Indian Ocean. By 1492, Vasco da Gama had reached India from Portugal. Portuguese, then Spanish, then Dutch traders and sailors started to dominate non-European seas. In 1500-1501, Pedrálvarez Cabral's fleet sighted Brazil before circling east to India and then returning to Portugal. Between 1519 and 1522, one ship of

Ferdinand Magellan's fleet circumnavigated the globe, though Magellan himself lay dead in the Philippines.

Europe's War States

From the world's perspective, Europe was becoming a major pole of economic and political activity. From a narrowly European viewpoint, the late 15th century initiated a shift in the commercial center of gravity from the southeast to the northwest, from the Mediterranean and Black seas to the Atlantic. Although Iberian states led that reorientation, it soon involved French ports, the Low Countries, the Baltic, and then the British Isles. In 1496, for example, Flanders and England signed the *Intercursus Magnus*, a commercial treaty according mutual privileges and recognizing the importance of the wool-and-textile trade that already linked them. The Atlantic, long a far edge of peripheries, was coming into its own.

In 1492 the dual monarchy of Castile and Aragon—the linked but not merged inheritances of Ferdinand and Isabella—completed the conquest of Granada. The conquest eliminated the last substantial vestige of once-great Muslim empires from Iberia. Under threat of death, those Spanish Jews who did not convert, at least nominally, to Catholicism began their diaspora across Europe and around the Mediterranean. Jews gathered in what had been outposts of their vast communication system: Poland, Lithuania, the Netherlands, the Indian Ocean, the Ottoman empire. Some gathered across the Strait of Gibraltar in what is now Morocco, Algeria and Tunisia. Unconverted and unmassacred Muslims also fled there and to nearby Muslim territory.

Responding in part to the threat of a united Spain, France began a fateful military invasion of Italy only two years later. Spain sent competing forces into Italy almost immediately, and the previously contentious but relatively autonomous Italian city-states found themselves pawns of great power politics. That French bid for Italian hegemony initiated the era of wars on a European scale.

The French Valois and Spanish Hapsburgs alone waged war with each other 11 distinct times between 1494 and the 1559 Treaty of Cateau-Cambrésis. As of 1492, the character of warfare and the international system were changing rapidly. During the wars of Burgundy in the 1470s, Swiss infantry massed into pike-squares and demonstrated its ability to defeat skilled cavalry. That strategic shift, plus the widening use of extensive fortifications in defense against siege artillery, greatly increased the financial and manpower requirements of armies, not to mention the demand for military architects and Swiss mercenaries. Those wars in turn built the European state system, constructed the platform for European conquests outside the continent, and helped form the centralized, differentiated, autonomous and bureaucratic states that eventually came to predominate in Europe and then in the world as a whole.

At the same time, the expansion of European trade along the sealanes of the Atlantic, Pacific and Indian

7. 1500: THE ERA OF DISCOVERY

Oceans offered a powerful stimulus to capital accumulation, which in turn gave warmaking states growing wealth on which to build their armed forces. What Immanuel Wallerstein calls the capitalist world-system, centered on Europe, began to take shape. Events of the great year 1492 did not, of course, cause all those momentous processes. Yet the rapid change in Iberia's position and the breakthrough across the Atlantic, for which 1492 was critical, pushed them vigorously.

The world of Islam continued to play an important part in European history, not only as a source of ideas, as a target of trade and as a continual object of warfare, but also as a presence in southeastern Europe. The Ottomans had taken Constantinople in 1453, Bosnia in 1462, Albania in 1467, the Crimea in 1474, and were threatening Hungary; by 1526, they were to occupy Buda. They were battling Venice for control of Dalmatia, Albania and the Morea. At their peak, in the mid-16th century, the Ottomans ruled almost all of the Balkan peninsula, including significant parts of what is now Hungary. In fact, Ottoman expansion and contraction set the major rhythms of Balkan revolutions after 1492. Only since World War I have the region's inhabitants ceased to live in strong connection with the power based in Istanbul.

In our own time, as Western-allied Israel struggles with Arab neighbors, as North African states deal with the European Community, as Turkey again becomes a major diplomatic player in the former Soviet Union, the relationships of enmity, alliance and interpenetration between Europe and the Islamic world that have prevailed through most of the last millennium again take center stage. In that regard, 1492's voyages to America were no more than distant diversions.

Credits/ Acknowledgments

Cover design by Charles Vitelli

1. Natural History
Facing overview—Photo courtesy of NASA. 10-11—*Scientific American* graphics by David Starwood. 12-13—*Scientific American* graphics by Patricia J. Wynne.

2. The Beginnings of Culture, Agriculture, and Urbanization
Facing overview—WHO photo. 41—© by G. Dagli Orti, Paris. Bibliothèque Nationale, Lisbon.

3. The Early Civilizations to 500 B.C.E.
Facing overview—United Nations photo. 47, 49-51 (top), 52—*Scientific American* illustrations by Roberto Osti. 48-51 (bottom) Photos by Dr. Theya Molleson, Department of Paleontology, The Natural History Museum, London. 72-73—Photos by Joyce Tyldesley, Liverpool University, England.

4. The Later Civilizations to 500 C.E.
Facing overview—United Nations photo. 98—*History Today* Archives photo. 102—Map by Bowring Cartographic. 108—Mansell-Graudon Collection photo. 110—Photo and illustration by Michael Holford. 111—Photos courtesy of the Trustees of the British Museum. 112, 113 (bottom),

114—Mansell-Alinari Collection photos. 113 (top)—National Museum of Naples photo.

5. The Great Religions
Facing overview—Photo by Brian Spykerman. 124, 127, 128 (bottom), 130—Photos by Dr. Caroline Maline and Dr. Simon Stoddart, University of Bristol, England. 125 (top)—*Scientific American* map by Johnny Johnson. 125 (bottom)—Photo courtesy of the National Museum of Archaeology, Malta. 128-129—Illustrations by Patricia J. Wynne after drawings by Steven Ashley and Dr. Caroline Malone.

6. The World of the Middle Ages, 500–1500
Facing overview—Photo by Rheinisches Bildarchiv, Germany. 176, 179—Illustrations courtesy of Bibliothèque Nationale, Lisbon. 200—Illustration from *The Cyclopaedia of Arts, Sciences, and Literature* by Abraham Rees, London, 1920. 202-203—Illustrations courtesy of Bodleian Library Film Strip Service, Oxford. 204—Illustrations courtesy of Bibliothèque Nationale, Lisbon. 206—Mansell Collection illustration.

7. 1500: The Era of Discovery
Facing overview—Library of Congress Collection photo. 216-223, 225—Illustrations by Peter F. Copeland.

ANNUAL EDITIONS ARTICLE REVIEW FORM

NAME: _____ DATE: _____

TITLE AND NUMBER OF ARTICLE: _____

BRIEFLY STATE THE MAIN IDEA OF THIS ARTICLE: _____
_____

LIST THREE IMPORTANT FACTS THAT THE AUTHOR USES TO SUPPORT THE MAIN IDEA:
_____
_____
_____
_____
_____
_____

WHAT INFORMATION OR IDEAS DISCUSSED IN THIS ARTICLE ARE ALSO DISCUSSED IN YOUR
TEXTBOOK OR OTHER READING YOU HAVE DONE? LIST THE TEXTBOOK CHAPTERS AND PAGE
NUMBERS:
_____
_____
_____
_____
_____
_____

LIST ANY EXAMPLES OF BIAS OR FAULTY REASONING THAT YOU FOUND IN THE ARTICLE:
_____
_____
_____
_____

LIST ANY NEW TERMS/CONCEPTS THAT WERE DISCUSSED IN THE ARTICLE AND WRITE A SHORT
DEFINITION:
_____
_____
_____
_____
_____